SPEECH
COMMUNICATION

PRENTICE-HALL SERIES IN SPEECH COMMUNICATION

Larry L. Barker and Robert J. Kibler
Consulting Editors

THIRD EDITION

SPEECH COMMUNICATION
Fundamentals and Practice

RAYMOND S. ROSS, Ph.D.
Professor of Speech Communication
Wayne State University

PRENTICE-HALL, INC., ENGLEWOOD CLIFFS, NEW JERSEY

Library of Congress Cataloging in Publication Data

Ross, Raymond Samuel
  Speech communication: fundamentals and practice.

  Includes bibliographical references.
  1. Oral communication. 2. Public speaking.
I. Title.
PN4121.R689 1974   808.5   73-20132
ISBN   0-13-827410-X

PRINTED IN THE UNITED STATES OF AMERICA

10 9 8 7 6 5 4 3

PRENTICE-HALL INTERNATIONAL, INC., *London*
PRENTICE-HALL OF AUSTRALIA, PTY. LTD., *Sydney*
PRENTICE-HALL OF CANADA, LTD., *Toronto*
PRENTICE-HALL OF INDIA PRIVATE LIMITED, *New Delhi*
PRENTICE-HALL OF JAPAN, INC., *Tokyo*

Contents

Preface, ix

PART ONE
THE NATURE OF HUMAN COMMUNICATION   1

Chapter 1   THE COMMUNICATION PROCESS   7

Definitions, 7
Perception and Human Understanding, 19
Listening, 29
Summary, 34

Chapter 2   AUDIENCE PSYCHOLOGY   42

Collective Phenomena, 42
Summary, 56

Chapter 3   LANGUAGE HABITS AND SEMANTICS   61

Language as Code and Symbol, 61
Abstraction, 74
Specificity, 76
Language and Personality, 77
Improving Your Language Habits and Semantics, 78
Semantics and General Semantics, 79
Summary, 85

v

Chapter 4   EMOTION AND CONFIDENCE   91
The Nature of Emotion, 96
Controlling Emotion, 100
Summary, 105

PART TWO
NONVERBAL COMMUNICATION   111

Chapter 5   BODY ACTION LANGUAGE   115
The Role of Bodily Expression, 115
The Elements of Bodily Action, 119
Standards of Good Bodily Action, 123
Summary, 125

Chapter 6   VOICE AND ARTICULATION   130
Voice and Personality, 130
The Vocal Process, 132
Variable Characteristics of Voice, 135
The Articulatory Process, 140
Pronunciation, 141
Summary, 145

PART THREE
MESSAGE PREPARATION   155

Chapter 7   PURPOSE AND DELIVERY IN SPEECH COMMUNICATION   157
General Purposes for Speaking, 157
Types of Delivery, 160
Characteristics of Good Delivery, 164
Characteristics of Bad Delivery, 165
Summary, 166

Chapter 8   PREPARING AND ORGANIZING THE MESSAGE   171
Preparing the Speech, 171
Organizing the Speech, 178
Summary, 199

Chapter 9   PRESENTING INFORMATION   204
How We Learn, 204
Primary Objectives, 208
Audio-Visual Aids, 222
Summary, 232

PART FOUR

THE PSYCHOLOGY OF PERSUASION 239

Chapter 10   DIMENSIONS OF HUMAN MOTIVATION   243

Springboards of Motivation, 243
Theories of Persuasion, 259
Source and the Psychological Order, 264
Summary, 277

Chapter 11   THE LOGICAL SUPPORTS OF PERSUASION   286

Pathos vs. Logos, 286
Evidence, 286
Authority, 287
Examples, 288
Statistics, 288
Inductive and Deductive Proof, 289
Fallacies, 296
Summary, 301

PART FIVE

SMALL-GROUP AND SPECIAL OCCASION COMMUNICATION 309

Chapter 12   DISCUSSION: COOPERATIVE COMMUNICATION   312
The Nature of Discussion, 312
Agendas, 318
Discussion Leadership, 330
Observing and Evaluating Discussion, 334
Summary, 337

Chapter 13   AUDIENCE PARTICIPATION SITUATIONS   348
Questions and Interruptions, 348
General Principles, 350
Rules for Answering Questions, 351
Generating Participation, 353
Summary, 355

Chapter 14   SPECIAL OCCASION SPEAKING   359
Scope of This Chapter, 359
Speeches of Introduction, 359
Speeches of Presentation and Acceptance, 362
Tribute and Commemorative Speeches, 363
After-Dinner Speeches, 367
Adapting Material to Radio and Television, 372
Summary, 374

Appendix A COMMUNICATION AND THE SURVIVAL
OF DEMOCRACY 379

Appendix B COMMUNICATION MODELS 388

Appendix C OUTLINES 393

Index, 405

Preface

The goal of this book is to enable its readers to better appreciate the crucial importance of the arts and skills of speech communication as agents of social control in our complicated pluralistic society.

Responsible speech communication, whether as rhetoric, art, or behavioral science, seeks to generate agreement among people and cultures. To communicate is usually the beginning of understanding.

This book, now in its third edition, attempts as before to reflect the realities of the time in which we are living, the state of the art of rhetorical communication, that which is pedagogically possible, and probable, and most importantly, the realistic needs of a still changing legion of young citizens.

Its approach is an eclectic one, borrowing the best of the old from our rich speech heritage and wedding to it the vital behavioral and interpersonal research of today. If the first edition of this book in 1965 was as influential as some have said in bringing the Speech Association into the twentieth-century Speech *Communication* Association era, then perhaps the third edition can continue the process without pushing us into the twenty-first century before we get there!

This is a basic speech communication text for the mid- and late 1970s. In it you will find the long-standing emphasis on behavior and practice as related to language, thought, voice, and action. The book still focuses primarily on the speaker and his audience. However, you will find that its basic communication model is still dyadic, indicating the importance of one-to-one transactional communication. The model is extended in this edition, however, to better accommodate small-group encounters and one-to-many audience situations.

Those of you familiar with the earlier editions will note that the third edition has been reorganized and divided into five parts:

  I. The Nature of Human Communication
  II. Nonverbal Communication
  III. Message Preparation
  IV. The Psychology of Persuasion
  V. Small-Group and Special Occasion Communication

Each part begins with an introduction in which I attempt to amalgamate the latest theorizing with proven practical experience. Except for critical updating many of the standard chapters remain the same. However, this is not true of all. A new, additional chapter on *audience psychology* borrows heavily from social psychology and collective behavior taxonomies; the popular chapter on the *communication process* has been extended and changed considerably; the *nonverbal dimension* is covered in greater detail; and the chapter on *persuasion* has been completely rewritten and extended to better reflect the exciting work being done both in and out of the speech communication field. In making these changes I have attempted to relate the most important modern persuasion theories in an uncomplicated way to the needs and assignments of students.

Even in the face of these modern contributions, the soundness of the traditional speech communication curriculum is *not* deemphasized. Purpose, delivery, preparation, outlining, arrangement, logic, and anxiety are all discussed fully.

Speech training has always infused itself with fresh energy from other fields, a practice that has encouraged the continual growth of speech communication and has also rescued it from countless fads and overemphases. The new "theory" courses are usually good communication courses, but they are not typically practice or speaking courses. It is the view of this book that communication theory should also be taught in the performance course so the student can readily apply it to an actual speech.

In reflecting modern educational psychology, each of the five parts attempts to preset a student's receptors by indicating in its introduction the general objectives sought. In addition to a thorough summary for purposes of reinforcement, each chapter now concludes with a list of (1) speech communication principles, (2) general learning outcomes,

(3) specific learning outcomes, (4) communication competencies (written as behavioral objectives), and (5) projects and tasks. The projects and tasks, along with the other end-of-chapter materials, represent a major change in the third edition. They are realistic materials and assignments that were culled from years of experience and the forthright suggestions of many veteran teachers.

This latest edition has three functional and useful appendices. The first is an excellent model speech[1] with its lines numbered to facilitate assignments; the second is a collection of communication models to accommodate those students and teachers who prefer more of such an emphasis or for purposes of class discussion; the third appendix includes additional model speech outlines as requested by numerous users. A more extensive treatment of message preparation is also included in appropriate chapters.

I am indebted to my colleagues and students at Wayne State University for their encouragement, training, and support. I am also indebted to the corporations, labor unions, and people of Detroit, who have taught me so much of the practical side of speech communication and interpersonal relations. Professor William A. Boyce deserves thanks for his careful reading and criticism of the voice and articulation material. And how could one even begin to write about human communication without the touch of a charmer like Ricky upon each and every page?

RSR

[1]"Communication and the Survival of Democracy," delivered by Dr. Theodore Clevenger, Jr., President of the Speech Communication Association at the annual SCA convention, Chicago, Illinois, December 30, 1972.

SPEECH
COMMUNICATION

PART ONE

THE NATURE
OF
HUMAN
COMMUNICATION

Suppose you call in two of your friends and communicate a rumor; then suppose that each relays the rumor to two of his friends. Allowing fifteen minutes for each communication and assuming a hypothetical chain of contacts that is neither duplicated nor broken, this rumor theoretically would reach every person in the world in only eight hours and thirty minutes. Talk about a grapevine! If you have ever played the game of passing along a message orally to see how much distortion takes place by the time it reaches the last person at your party, you can guess what probably would happen in our hypothetical worldwide grapevine. One wonders how we achieve any understanding at all.

To understand the nature of human communication is an eternal quest. If we are to survive in the world as we find it, we must have some introduction to the vital dimensions of the process of communication, collective behavior or audience psychology, language habits and semantics, and emotion and confidence. These will be discussed in Part I. Nonverbal communication, especially the specific dimensions of body language and voice, will be given special attention in Part II.

We need first to know something about the human communication process, which more than anything else gives man his special nature among all living things. Man's overwhelming need to communicate and express himself constitutes as intimate a part of his nature as his physiology. Man is unique among all other forms of animals because of his rationality and

super-sophisticated system of communication. They have permitted him to
time-bind by recording the discoveries of yesteryear so that others yet un-
born may profit from the past. This ability, in conjunction with man's
creativeness, has led to an information explosion.

The amount of material to be stored and communicated in this period
of man's history is truly enormous. It is probably true, as one scholar has
estimated, that man has discovered more knowledge within the last fifty
years than through all the centuries before, that human knowledge has
more than doubled within the last century! Our present specialization of
knowledge adds to our problems. Communication must somehow bridge
these isolated islands of specialization.

In this day of often harsh, outspoken confrontations, just *trying* to understand a differing point of view may become threatening. There is a transactional nature to interpersonal communication. It is a process involving a
commonality of experience and a mutuality of influence.

The sheer amount of communication that goes on is fantastic. Surveys indicate that we spend 75 percent of our waking time in communication activity,
that is, in listening, speaking, reading, and writing. When one considers the
telephone system and the mass media, the volume of emitted signals becomes
astronomical. It is estimated that the American public makes some 133
billion telephone calls a year.

Communication is of vital importance to business and industry. Research
tells us that business managers may spend 75 to 90 percent of their time
doing nothing but communicating, and about three-quarters of that time is
spent in oral face-to-face situations.[1]

One top executive pointed up the importance of communication when
he said,

> Poor communications cost companies billions a year in ill-conceived actions
> based on misunderstandings and baseless rumors. If our corporations are to grow
> in size and complexity, then our managers will have to become articulate.[2]

The importance is further reflected in

> the establishment of communications departments in many companies and in
> requests for special training courses and increased numbers of professional con-
> sultants. Management is estimated to spend over $112,000,000 a year on publica-
> tions.[3]

One division of a major automobile producer is estimated to spend over
$75 million a year on advertising alone.

[1] C. S. Goetzinger and M. A. Valentine, "Communication Channels, Media, Directional
Flow and Attitudes in an Academic Community," *Journal of Communication*, 11, No. 1
(March 1961), 23–26; also idem, "Communication Patterns, Interactions and Attitudes of
Top-Level Personnel in the Air Defense Command," *Journal of Communication*, 13, No. 1
(March 1963), 54–57.

[2] *Steel: The Metalworking Weekly* (Cleveland, Ohio: Penton Publishing Company, June
28, 1965), p. 29.

[3] M. Joseph Dooher and Vivienne Marquis, eds., *Effective Communication on the Job*
(New York: American Management Association, 1956), p. 16.

Colleges and universities have responded to the needs of society by offering numerous courses in speech and general communication. Doctoral degrees in speech communication are being granted in ever increasing numbers and in more specialized aspects of the field. Strong graduate programs are being developed in all parts of the United States. A considerable literature is growing that is both behaviorally and rhetorically oriented. Many speech communication teachers and majors have become adept in numerous fields because of the growing awareness of the interdisciplinary nature of communication and speech training.

The importance of speech communication training to you, the student, is indicated by the requirement of the subject by many schools. Moreover, the testimonials of successful men have affirmed the value of speech training, and research has indicated its usefulness to you in better understanding your other university courses. Dr. Charles Hurst studied 157 college sophomores, 70 with speech training and 87 without such training. He sought to describe the educational implications arising from the relationships between formal instruction in a basic speech course and increased readiness to undertake work at the next academic level. He discovered that a significant and positive relationship between these two factors definitely does exist. More specifically, the speech group showed a statistically significant gain in ability to demonstrate learning and reasoning on a standardized test of academic aptitude; the gain experienced by the nonspeech group was not found to be statistically significant. Further, the speech group was found to be significantly superior on a measure of study skills and practices. A finding of interest to all grade-conscious students was that improvement of the speech group in ability to achieve in classroom work, as measured by comparison of mean honor-point averages, was found to be superior to the improvement of the nonspeech group. In fact, the speech group showed a net gain as compared with a net loss for the nonspeech group. Hurst concluded:

> The data of this study clearly suggest that the basic speech course is an agent of synthesis, providing students with a schematic basis for orderly thinking and improved control of the multivariate phenomena constituting the total personality.[4]

One scholar defines speech as "a tool of social adjustment, which reflects the efficient personality."[5] Wiseman and Barker suggest that "physical, social, and mental existence depend upon communication. Each affects the other until it would be foolish to try to distinguish where one begins and the other leaves off. Communication shapes personality and personality determines the pattern of communication."[6]

---

[4]Charles Hurst, "Speech and Functional Intelligence: An Experimental Study of Educational Implications of a Basic Speech Course" (unpublished doctoral dissertation, Wayne State University, 1961).

[5]Elwood Murray, *The Speech Personality* (Philadelphia: J. P. Lippincott Company, 1944), p. 10.

[6]Gordon Wiseman and Larry Barker, *Speech—Interpersonal Communication* (San Francisco: Chandler Publishing Company, 1967), p. 5; see also Lee Thayer, *Communication and Communication Systems* (Homewood, Ill.: Richard D. Irwin, Inc., 1968), p. 17.

Perhaps for our purposes we can say that speech training may have as much impact on personality as personality may have on speech.

In addition to insight into the process nature of human communication, we need to know something of how man perceives, how he attends to stimuli. This is the purpose of Chapter 1.

Crowds, mobs, protest groups, and other agents of modern hyperinter-stimulation call for a modern audience classification system or taxonomy. Such a taxonomy, involving contagion, regression, anonymity, suggestibility, and other active dimensions, is provided in Chapter 2, "Audience Psychology." The life laboratory all around us offers real opportunities for study if we have a model to which we can relate. The more well known passive audience and the complicated, often ambivalent small group are also vital to students of speech communication. Behavior in these groups, too, is surveyed for insights and recommendations related to public speaking and interpersonal communication.

How many times have you been turned off or put down by a poorly chosen word, a gross generalization, or other language behavior inappropriate to the situation? If you think a *stable* in ghetto talk is for horses, you're in for a surprise! Chapter 3 addresses itself to "Language Habits and Semantics."

Man is an emotional animal. As such, he often has his communication apparatus impeded or stimulated by the mere presence of an audience. When one considers the modern social climate, complete with its unyielding complexity, dogmatic language, emerging cultures, and all-too-frequent substitution of violence for persuasion, perhaps he has good reason. The analysis of emotion in Chapter 4 is meant to be a practical answer to at least some of the problems of speech fright that may interfere with effective human communication.

A general review of the hoped-for *learning outcomes* that should result from a close reading of Part I, particularly when related to class projects and performances, follows. A more specific set of learning outcomes or lesson objectives and communication competencies, along with creative, relevant projects and tasks, is appended to each chapter.

We should so develop an awareness of the speech communication attributes of man that our behavior will increasingly reflect an openness, tolerance for ambiguity, concern for context, caution with language, and greater respect for feedback, mutual influence, and man's dependence upon man.

We should better understand the enormous complexity of the process of human communication.

We should gain a working understanding of the process nature of human communication and its transactional nature.

We should learn the factors and attributes of effective listening behavior.

We should understand and be able to extend creatively our own thinking about an audience behavior taxonomy and/or model.

We should be able to distinguish between crowds, mobs, and audiences and demonstrate insight into the roles such collectivities play in speech communication.

We should become aware of the importance of audience analysis in speech communication.

We should learn the cardinal importance of good language habits and semantics as they relate to meaning and our total communication effectiveness.

We should learn about the sensitive nature of words and language segments and their impact upon human behavior and understanding.

We should learn of the basic nature of human emotion and its relation to confidence.

We should learn the basic principles for alleviating and controlling speech fright.

We should learn the importance of speech communication training for successful growth and development.

Chapter One

The Communication Process

DEFINITIONS

Before we can consider the skills involved in speech communication training and practice, we must understand how the communication process works.

When asked to define communication, many people reply that it is the transmission or transfer of meaning from one mind to another. To most speech teachers today, this definition not only is technically in error, but may actually impede the learning of more specific skills that must be acquired.

In dealing with definitions of speech and communication we range from "speech is the great medium through which human cooperation is brought about"[1] to the more specific definition of the American College Dictionary, "the imparting or interchange of thoughts, opinions, or information by speech, writing, or signs." Let us examine some others that are useful.

[1]Grace A. de Laguna, *Speech: Its Function and Development* (New Haven, Conn.: Yale University Press, 1927), p. 19.

Communication is the eliciting of response and successful human speech communication is the eliciting of the desired response through verbal symbolization.[2]

Human communication is a subtle set of processes through which people interact, control one another, and gain understanding.[3]

Communication is social interaction through symbols and message systems.[4]

Communication has as its central interest those behavioral situations in which a source transmits a message to a receiver(s) with conscious intent to affect the latter's behaviors.[5]

Speech is ongoing multisymbolic behavior in social situations carried on to achieve communication. We define communication as a social achievement in symbolic behavior.[6]

The sequence of events which must occur to produce a communication event may be viewed as involving a minimum of five sequential ingredients: (1) a generator of a (2) stimulus which is (3) projected to a (4) perceiver which (5) responds discriminatively (assigns meaning).[7]

Communication is a social function . . . , a *sharing* of elements of behavior, or modes of life, by the existence of sets of rules. . . . Communication is not the response itself but is essentially the *relationship* set up by the transmission of stimuli [signs] and the evocation of responses.[8]

Communication is an ongoing process. Ideas originate in an individual's cognitive framework; they are coded and sent through some channel or channels; the messages are received and decoded by another person who responds according to his own cognitive framework.[9]

[2]From *Business and Professional Speech Communication* by Harold P. Zelko and Frank E. X. Dance. Copyright © 1965 by Holt, Rinehart and Winston, Inc. Reprinted by permission of Holt, Rinehart and Winston, Inc., p. 5.

[3]Alfred G. Smith, ed., *Communication and Culture: Readings in the Codes of Human Interaction* (New York: Holt, Rinehart and Winston, Inc., 1966).

[4]George Gerbner, "On Defining Communication: Still Another View," *Journal of Communication*, Vol. 16, No. 2 (June 1966), 99.

[5]Gerald R. Miller, "On Defining Communication: Another Stab," *Journal of Communication*, Vol. 16, No. 2 (June 1966), 92.

[6]A. Craig Baird and Franklin H. Knower, *Essentials of General Speech* (New York: McGraw-Hill Book Company, 1968).

[7]Robert S. Goyer, "Communication, Communicative Process, Meaning: Toward a Unified Theory," *Journal of Communication*, Vol. 20, No. 1, (March 1970), 8. The position taken by Goyer on signs and symbols is that operationally they are both observable as substitute, or surrogate, representatives of some other event.

[8]Related statements from Colin Cherry, *On Human Communication* (Cambridge, Mass., and London, Eng.: The M.I.T. Press, 1966), pp. 6–7. Arrangement and selection and brackets are this author's. Cherry uses the word *sign* for any physical event used in communication–human, animal, or machine—and avoids the term *symbol.*

[9]Remo P. Fausti and Edward L. McGlone, *Understanding Oral Communication* (Menlo Park, Calif.: Cummings Publishing Company, 1972), p. 22.

ship communication in terms of the perceptions, constructs, and notions two people might have regarding the personalities involved.[14] He labeled the personalities John and Thomas, and suggested that there are *three* Johns: (1) the real John, known only to his maker; (2) John's ideal John, never the real one, and often very unlike him; and (3) Thomas's ideal John, never the real John, nor John's John, but often very unlike either. There are, of course, three equivalent Toms. To Holmes's three categories we can add a *fourth*, "John's Tom's John," that is, John's notion of what Tom's notion is of him. We can diagram this interaction, as shown in Figure 1–1.

The whole transaction involves mutual influence, as depicted by the

[14]Oliver Wendell Homes, *The Autocrat of the Breakfast-Table* (Boston: Phillips, Simpson and Co., 1858), p. 59.

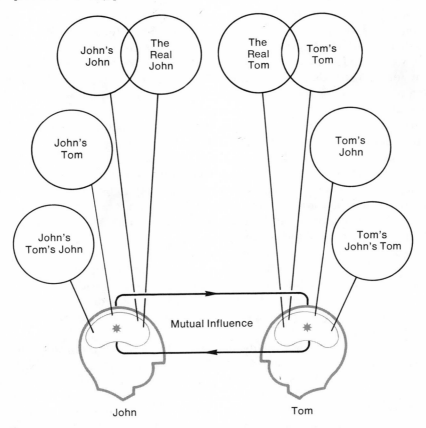

FIGURE 1–1.   Interaction as Transactional Communication.

transactional process loop. If a third or fourth person is added to the interaction, the complexity of transactional human communication is increased geometrically.

Although it is technically impossible to separate the parts of so integrated a process, for our purposes it may be helpful to divide it arbitrarily into sequential events. Let us assume we have a message (which might be referred to as an idea or concept or meaning) that we wish to convey to another person. Our brain or thinking apparatus now sorts through our storehouse of knowledge, experience, feelings, and previous training to refine and select the precise meaning we are seeking. Before it is transmitted, it goes through a phase that we may think of as a language-attaching or coding event; that is, the refined idea is now encoded or put into signs and symbols that we commonly think of as language. Gesture, facial expression, and tone of voice may also be considered as signs, symbols, or codes. Our meaning could, for example, be put into a sign language, a foreign language, or even international Morse code. This code is then transmitted, and it has meaning to you, the sender. The way in which it is coded, the medium or channel chosen for its transmission, and the finesse with which it is transmitted have much to do with the meaning it will have for the receiver. Assuming that the medium for this illustration is simply the air between you and the listener, we now have the encoded message, the transmission, and the signal being received by the other person. The receiver next proceeds to decode the signal or at least attempts to decode it. If the signal is in a code with which he is not familiar, such as a foreign language, not much communication will take place. The listener proceeds to sort out, select, and elicit meanings from *his* storehouse of knowledge, experience, and training until there has been created in his own mind a near replica of the images and ideas contained in the mind of the sender.

To the extent that this replication is similar to the sender's, we have achieved communication. The idea, concept, or meaning in the mind of the listener is therefore heavily dependent upon, if not restricted to, the knowledge and experience he can bring to bear on the code. The value of knowing your listener and the value of audience analysis now become evident.

We shall thus operationally define intentional communication as a *transactional process involving a cognitive sorting, selecting, and sending of symbols in such a way as to help a listener elicit from his own mind a meaning or response similar to that intended by the communicator.* We now see why seemingly obvious meanings (in *our* minds) are often distorted or misunderstood by others. Perhaps this is what is meant when we hear the saying "One cannot teach a man what he does not already know"; and perhaps this better explains the old teaching rule of "Go from the known to the unknown."

The word *model* typically refers to the representation of a thing or a process. When producing a model of a physical object we have relatively little trouble. We can make model trains, boats, and airplanes and learn much about their physical behavior. However, when we attempt to make models of more abstract things, where physical measurement is difficult, we have the very real problem of oversimplifying to the point of poor or dangerous representation or of simply being unable to agree on our observations. The interaction between John and Tom shown in Figure 1–1 is a model.

We may use words, numbers, symbols, and pictures to illustrate our models of things, theories, or processes. In geometry we accept the theorem stating that the "square of the hypotenuse of a right triangle is equal to the sum of the squares of the legs." This statement is a form of verbal model. If we draw a picture of this theorem as well, we have a verbal-pictorial model.[15] The advantages of using a model are quickly evident. The model gives you another, different, closer look. It provides a frame of reference, suggests informational gaps, points up the problem of abstraction, and helps get a problem expressed in symbolic language where there is some advantage in using figures or symbols.

Of course some drawbacks, such as oversimplification and other dangers inherent in gross abstraction, exist in the use of models. Campbell and Hepler warn us of yet another danger in their use:

> After a scientist plays for a long time with a given model he may become attached to it, just as a child may become, in the course of time, very attached to a doll (which is also a model). A child may become so devoted to the doll that she insists that her doll is a real baby, and some scientists become so devoted to their model (especially if it is a brain child) that they will insist that this model *is* the real world.[16]

Communication experts have used primarily verbal-pictorial models in trying to give us a closer and more scientific look at the process. The working definition of communication suggested earlier for this text is really a verbal model, which will shortly be illustrated pictorially. First, let us look at several models that appear to be in essential agreement.

15See especially Ronald L. Smith, *General Models of Communication*, Purdue Communication Research Center, Special Report No. 5 (Lafayette, Ind.: Dept. of Speech, Purdue University, August 1962); see also Larry L. Barker and Robert J. Kibler, *Speech Communication Behavior: Perspectives and Principles* (Englewood Cliffs, N.J.: Prentice-Hall, Inc., 1971).

16James H. Campbell and Hal W. Hepler, eds., *Dimensions in Communication* (Belmont, Calif.: Wadsworth Publishing Co., Inc., 1970), p. 19.

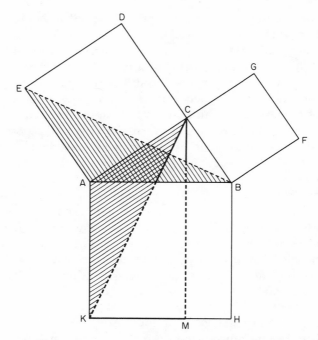

FIGURE 1–2.　The Square of the Hypotenuse of a Right Triangle is Equal to the Sum of the Squares of the Legs, or AKHB = ACDE + BFGC.

WHO

SAYS WHAT

IN WHAT CHANNEL

TO WHOM

WITH WHAT EFFECT

FIGURE 1–3.　Lasswell Model.[17]

| Intentive behavior of → speaker | Encoding behavior → of speaker | Message → | Decoding behavior of → hearer | Interpretive behavior of hearer |

FIGURE 1–4.　Carroll Model.[18]

[17]H. D. Lasswell, "The Structure and Function of Communication in Society," in *The Communication of Ideas,* ed. Lyman Bryson (New York: Harper & Row, Publishers, 1948), p. 37.

[18]John B. Carroll, *The Study of Language* (Cambridge, Mass.: Harvard University Press, 1955), p. 88.

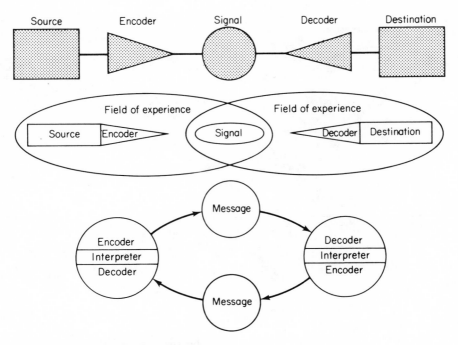

FIGURE 1–5.   Three Schramm Models.[19]

Key:
1. Encoding—Making the information or feeling into a form which can be transmitted.
2. Sending—Transmitting the encoded message.
3. Decoding—The relating of the message to the "picture in the mind" of the receiver.

Each one gives you just a little different perspective. The second is a simple verbal model posed as five questions. The last one shown (Figure 1–7) is the specific model for the writer's theories and is explained in more detail. Additional models which you may wish to study and discuss are shown in Appendix B.

The encoder and decoder can perform their functions only in terms of their respective fields of experience. In this sense, then, the decoder and encoder are each limited by their experience. There must be an overlap of information or some experience common to both decoder and en-

[19]Wilbur Schramm, "How Communication Works," in *The Process and Effects of Mass Communication*, ed. Wilbur Schramm (Urbana, Illinois: University of Illinois Press, 1955), pp. 4–8.

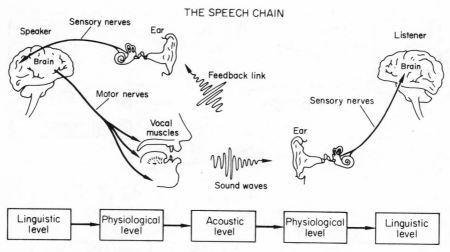

FIGURE 1–6. Denes-Pinson Model.[20]

coder for the communication to be meaningful and thus convey the intended message.

Finally, the decoding of a message by the receiver results in encoding. Whether this encoding results in an overt communication or not depends upon the barriers in the way. However, the process is constant and continual. One individual communication is merely part of a greater network of communication.

The roles of encoder and decoder are interchangeable, and each person involved in the process is both encoder and decoder as well as interpreter.

Since no model of anything, much less a complicated process, can ever be 100 percent accurate or complete, you are not expected to be in perfect agreement with the previous models or the one that follows. However, with the previous material as a background or frame of reference, perhaps more insights are now available to you as you elicit meanings from your storehouse of knowledge to decode the Ross model (see Figure 1–7).

Let us return to our initial explanation of the communication process. You will recall the verbal model in the form of a definition:

> Communication is a transactional process involving a cognitive sorting, selecting, and sending of symbols in such a way as to help a listener elicit from his own mind a meaning or response similar to that intended by the communicator.

[20]Figure 1–6 from *The Speech Chain* by Peter B. Denes and Elliot N. Pinson, © 1963 Bell Telephone Laboratories, Inc. Reprinted by permission of Doubleday & Company, Inc.

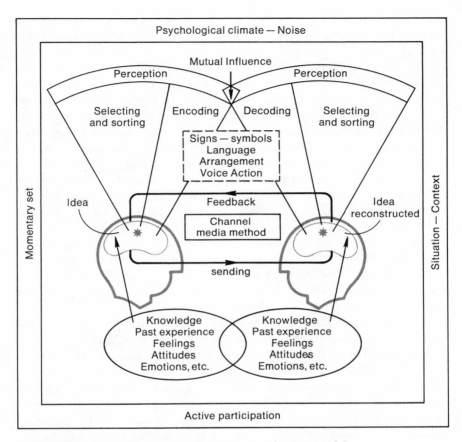

FIGURE 1–7. Ross Transactional Communication Model.

In interpreting the Ross model, remember that its focus is primarily directed at that process that involves the *human* organism and particularly his sign-symbol behavior.[21] He is capable of being both sender and receiver at the same time; he is, as Zelko and Dance[22] would say, a transceiver!

Let us now assume that our person on the left side of the model

[21]Some writers are primarily interested in mathematical theories and models applied to electrical engineering, others to animal communication, and so on. See especially: C. E. Shannon and W. Weaver, *The Mathematical Theory of Communication* (Urbana, Ill.: University of Illinois Press, 1949), p. 98; and Jon J. Eisenon, J. Jeffery Auer, and John V. Irwin. *The Psychology of Communication* (New York: Appleton-Century-Crofts, 1963), Ch. 10, William Etkin, "Communication Among Animals."

[22]From *Business and Professional Speech Communication* by Harold P. Zelko and Frank E. X. Dance. Copyright © 1965 by Holt, Rinehart and Winston, Inc. Reprinted by permission of Holt, Rinehart and Winston, Inc., pp. 6–7.

wishes to communicate a message (a concept or idea) to the other person. The idea is represented by the star on the model (inside his brain). Let us suppose the concept is an abstract one like *love*. The fan projecting from each brain represents, let us assume, man's 13½ billion brain cells. In this brain are stored his knowledge and past experience, his feelings, attitudes, emotions, and many more things that make him the person he is. Our sender now proceeds, figuratively, to sort through and select from his storehouse of knowledge and past experience, choosing items that help him refine and define what he is trying to say. He has to have a basis or set of criteria for this operation, a program if you will. We can think of the brain in some ways as a computer. The forebrain, for example, becomes a kind of servo-mechanism or input regulator where we feed in the program. His program had better include at least three instructions or he's already in trouble! They are: (1) What do I have stored under *love*? (2) What do I know about the other person? and (3) What do I have filed for this particular situation and context? One can visualize the program assessing the storehouse, accepting, rejecting, cross-referencing, synthesizing—in short, selecting and sorting the appropriate knowledge, past experience, and so on.

While there is some confusion among scholars as to exactly how, and particularly *when*, the encoding, or sign/symbol attaching event, takes place, it is useful, if only for instructional purposes, to think of it sequentially. Our sender must now proceed to choose his codes and should apply minimally the same program or questions discussed previously. More will be said of this critical process in Chapter 3. The sender now emits the stimuli, which, let us assume, are primarily oral. He might, of course, have chosen to write a memo or use a blackboard.[23] Let us further assume that there is no unusual distraction or noise in the situation, and further that the sensory apparatus of both parties is adequate. Since our message concerned *love*, the situation and context factors may be fairly critical, not to mention the specific facts about the other person.

Finally (and this whole operation could involve but seconds), the stimuli strike the receiver's sensory end organs. This is the first part of human perception—*sensation*; the second part is the *interpretation* of what those sensations mean, again in this highly specific situation. More will be said of the process of perception in this section immediately following.

The model now suggests that our receiver proceeds to *decode* the signs,

---

[23]There are many interesting researches on media or channel selection. See especially T. L. Dahle, "Transmitting Information to Employees: A Study of Five Methods," *Personnel*, 31 (1954), 243–46.

symbols, language, and so on, ultimately drawing upon and eliciting from his storehouse of knowledge and experience those meanings that will allow him to create a message concerning *love*. To the extent that this re-creation is similar to the sender's intended message, we have communication. This reconstructed idea, then, is heavily dependent upon what a person already knows.

The term *feedback* in the model calls for a moment of important consideration. In engineering, feedback refers to some of the transmitted energy being returned to the source. The automatic pilot used in airplanes is an example of self-correcting machinery that uses feedback. The analogy to human communication breaks down a bit when one considers the kind of electronic feedback all of us have observed with public-address systems or tape recorders (in which a reentry of some of the sound from the speaker to the microphone causes a howl or loud noise). For speech purposes we may think of feedback as useful in a self-correcting, or perhaps we should say audience-adapting, sense. As our transmitted signal is bounced off our receiver, it feeds back information that allows us to correct and refine our signal. A quizzical look, a frown, a yawn, the sound of our own voice—any of these may cause us to reevaluate and recode our emitted signals. On the other hand, speech fright to the point of emotional disintegration (such as forgetting) can be compared to intense feedback of the howl or public-address system type, which momentarily—but completely—shorts out the sending device. The complicated phenomenon of speech fright will be covered in a later chapter. For now, let us think of feedback as something that we should make work for us.

Cartoonist David John McKee catches the problem of near-zero feedback in the clever sketches that follow (see Figure 1–8).[24] Comic-strip character Funky Winkerbean illustrates yet another form of feedback[25] (see Figure 1–9).

The models just described are essentially two-person or dyadic. However, the same kind of general communication principles should apply with modifications to audiences and even interpersonally complex, co-acting small groups. Modified models of the transactional communication process will be discussed in Chapter 3.

Models previously described suggest the importance of a person's self-image as it relates to speech communication, human relations, and behavior modification. We may use words like *self-percept, self-concept,*

[24]Drawings by David John McKee, by permission of *The Times Educational Supplement* (London), March 27, 1964. Published in the United States by *Saturday Review* (New York), Sept. 19, 1964, p. 68.
[25]"Funky Winkerbean" by Tom Batiuk, courtesy of Publishers Hall Syndicate.

Making a Point . . .

—Drawings by David John McI
—Times Educational Supplement, London, March 27, 1...

SR/September 19, 196...

FIGURE 1–8.

FUNKY WINKERBEAN   By Tom Batiuk

FIGURE 1–9.

and *self-identity* to talk essentially about a man's notion of himself.[26] As our models and previous discussions of the social-psychological nature of man indicate, a large portion of our self-concept is shaped by interactions with people whom we consider significant to us. We develop concepts of our physical, emotional, and social selves. We tend to perceive, respond, act, and communicate to a considerable extent in terms of this complex self-image. For the most part we try to be consistent with our self-image. When grossly frustrated, perhaps by too positive or too negative a self-image, we may resort to various forms of compensatory behavior. A realistic self-image can be a critical part of communication and perception as well as motivation generally. Every person is the center of his own phenomenal field; the way he experiences and perceives it is his own reality. We all live by a perceptual map that is never the *real* territory.

PERCEPTION AND HUMAN UNDERSTANDING

The other half of sending is receiving. An understanding of the way people receive, decode, and assign meaning is critical. Listening is much more than hearing acuity. All of our sensory apparatus may be involved in helping us interpret even a primarily oral signal. The perception process is for our purposes identical to the communication process except that the emphasis is on receiving instead of sending. The receiver or perceiver is thought to posit hypotheses, which he accepts or rejects. Postman[27] calls this a cycle of hypothesis involving information, trial

---

[26]John J. Sherwood, "Self Identity and Referent Others," *Sociometry*, 28 (1965), 66–81.

[27]L. Postman, "Toward a General Theory of Cognition," in *Social Psychology at the Crossroads*, eds. J. H. Rohrer and M. Sherif (New York: Harper & Row, Publishers, 1951), p. 251; see also J. S. Bruner, "Personality Dynamics and the Process of Per-

and check, confirmation or nonconfirmation. The meaning then is supplied primarily by learning and by past experience.

Sensation and Interpretation

Have you ever been on a train that was stopped next to other trains in a railroad terminal? Have you then felt, seen, and heard all the signs indicating movement, only to find that it is the other trains that were moving? Perhaps you discovered this when another train or trains were actually gone, or perhaps you fixed your gaze on something you *knew* was not moving, such as the ceiling of the station, a roof support, or the ground itself.

The point is that perception involves essentially two acts: (1) the *sensation* caused by the stimulation of a sensory organ and (2) the *interpretation* of the sensation. In our study of speech we are primarily concerned with the interpretation; as has been discussed earlier, it is primarily through our knowledge and experience that we interpret or attach meaning to a symbol.

The complexity of human communication is further indicated by the various levels of perception now thought to exist. We talk of subliminal or subthreshold perception, that is, a receiving of impressions below the level of conscious awareness. This is not to be confused with so-called extrasensory perception. Many experiments have been conducted in this field, most of them involving visual projections at speeds above our physiological level of perception but below our awareness level or, in some cases, at our awareness level but below our recognition level. They are complicated by the fact that people vary in their perceptual abilities not only one from another but also in their own individual range of acuity. The best-known of all subthreshold experiments[28] involved the projection of nonsense syllables. Meaningless combinations of letters were associated with electric shock. When these stimuli were later presented at subthreshold levels (at speeds too rapid to permit their conscious identification), the subjects' emotional reactions were more intense than their reactions to other nonsense syllables not previously associated with

---

ceiving," in *Perception: An Approach to Personality*, eds. R. R. Blake and G. V. Ramsey (New York: The Ronald Press Company, 1951). For a detailed discussion of perception see S. Howard Bartley, *Principles of Perception*, 2d ed. (New York: Harper & Row, Publishers, 1969).

[28]R. S. Lazarus and R. A. McCleary, "Autonomic Discrimination Without Awareness: A Study in Subception," *Psychological Review*, 58 (1951), 113–22.

shock. The subjects had been able to identify the stimuli unconsciously before they could do so consciously.

During a six-week experiment in a New Jersey theater in 1957, sales of popcorn and a soft drink allegedly were increased by the use of subthreshold messages superimposed over the regular film. No adequate account of procedures is available for verification.[29] A more recent study by Gibb involving subthreshold prestige suggestion superimposed over video tape did indicate some attitude change.[30]

A person's set, expectancy, or preparation to perceive[31] has much to do with his level of perception as well as his individual acceptance of a stimulus. The consciousness defends itself through an apparent refusal to accept certain messages. On the other hand, we may wish or desire so very much to hear something that, regardless of the actual code or words emitted, we attend, interpret, and attach meaning in terms of what we wish to hear. One of the great barriers to good communication is the tendency to hear what we wish to hear, see what we wish to see, and believe what we wish to believe. This kind of behavior is called *autistic thinking*. Piaget defines autism as "thought in which truth is confused with desire."[32] In its extreme form, this kind of perception and thinking grows out of an abnormal emotional need for ego-satisfaction, and we actually have a mental disorder known as *paranoia*. The foregoing indicates that perception is a function of *internal* as well as external sources of stimulation. Signals that originate within us also enter into the problem and can function to either stabilize or distort perception.[33]

Another closely related perceptual and communication problem arises because of a normal tendency to completeness. In communications that appear to be only partially complete, we often read in the unsaid part or complete the pattern. If we do not arrive at a sense of completeness or closure, we often feel upset, ill at ease, confused, and unhappy. This tendency can be an important factor in motivation. Perhaps you have had a teacher who communicates just enough knowledge in a stimulating way, motivating you to do further reading and research so that you can complete or close the pattern. The problem arises when we close incomplete communication patterns in ways not intended by the speaker. This tendency is illustrated by an incomplete triangle. We find it more

[29]H. Brean, "Hidden Sell Techniques Are Almost Here," *Life*, 44 (1958), 102–4.

[30]J. Douglas Gibb, "An Experimental Study of the Effects of a Subthreshold Prestige Symbol in Informative and Persuasive Communication" (unpublished doctoral dissertation, Wayne State University, 1966).

[31]Charles M. Solley and Gardner Murphy, *Development of the Perceptual World* (New York: Basic Books, Inc., Publishers, 1960), p. 239.

[32]J. Piaget, *The Child's Conception of Physical Causality* (London: Routledge & Kegan Paul Ltd., 1930), p. 302.

[33]Solley and Murphy, *Development of the Perceptual World*, pp. 259–60.

reasonable, more comfortable to see Figure 1–10 as a complete triangle.

Sometimes our habits and previous experiences cause us to leave things out. Read the three messages in Figure 1–11 quickly.

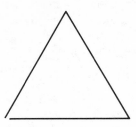

FIGURE 1–10.   Pattern Closing Tendencies.

FIGURE 1–11.

Many people see nothing unusual about these messages even after two or three readings. The good, rapid readers seem to have the most trouble. Why should this be so? A group of second and third graders had no trouble finding the double words in each message. We perceive to a certain extent what our habits, our emotions, and our knowledge and past experiences let us perceive. A good reader has learned to skim and to ignore nonessential words. The beginning reader sees literally one word at a time.

Test your perceptual ability on the next stimulus (Figure 1–12). Do you see anything familiar or identifiable? Do you see a message?

You should see a word in white on a partial black field. Your experience is typically just the opposite—the area *between* the letters is in

FIGURE 1–12.

black instead of the letters themselves.[34] Even after you see the message, it may escape you momentarily as your long-standing habits and previous experience patterns assert their influence.

Try reading the simple word and its mirror image in Figure 1–13. It's easier if you examine just the bottom half of the stimulus.[35]

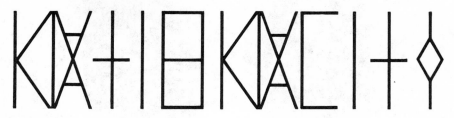

FIGURE 1–13.

Experience should help you the next time, shouldn't it? Let's see. Can you decode or elicit meanings for the next stimulus (Figure 1–14)? You've had practice!

FIGURE 1–14.

The next problem (Figure 1–15) should be easy for you if you stretch your experience a little.[36]

FIGURE 1–15.

Your mental set or disposition to interpret has a lot to do with what you "see." Look for a *vase* in the next figure (Figure 1–16)! You should find it very quickly because that is, after all, what you were looking for.

---

[34]This is referred to as a figure-ground transformation. The word is *LEFT*.
[35]The word is *nationality*.
[36]David Krech and Richard S. Crutchfield, *Elements of Psychology* (New York: Alfred A. Knopf, Inc., 1958), p. 93.

FIGURE 1–16.

Now look at the *vase* again, only this time it's not a *vase*, it's two *faces!* One face on the left, the other on the right looking directly at each other. Do you get the message?

Some patterns seem to make no sense at all in terms of *what* we "know." Would you believe the two curved segments in Figure 1–17 are identical?

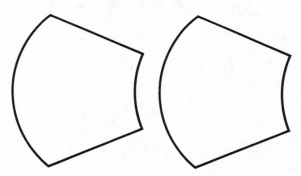

FIGURE 1–17.

A group of professional photographers had an almost impossible time trying to "see" the following photograph (Figure 1–18). What do you see?

Don't proceed until you see a cow looking right at you! If you haven't seen it by now, you may actually regress, particularly if you've asked for help and your friends see it immediately. Communication is like that. We don't do our best when we begin to feel awkward, stupid, or left out. How are you doing with LEFT and THE? Can you lose them? When things or experiences are new or novel to us, we may

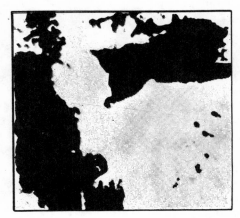

FIGURE 1–18.

literally understand or "see" one moment and "not see" the next. This would be a good time to review the communication models again, wouldn't it?

Perception tends to be selective for many reasons, and we are well advised to remember it. The three photographs in Figure 1–19 are all reproduced from the same negative; they are shown as they might appear to three different people.

Sometimes our prior set can be manipulated in such a way as to affect what we see. Let's try it. Can you all see the "young woman" in Figure 1–20A?

Now study Figure 1–20B. You should find the "young woman" quickly because you've been pre-set, as it were; but do you also see the "old hag"? Your prior set didn't include her and she should prove more difficult to find.

You should find her easily in Figure 1–20C. Now perhaps it's easier to find her in the composite picture (Figure 1–20B). This is what E. G. Boring originally referred to as an ambiguous stimulus (Figure 1–20B). R. W. Leeper performed the experiment above with groups of subjects and confirmed the effect of *prior set*.[37] Previous exposure to either version predicted that it would be "first" found in the composite picture. Many replications in the Wayne State University Speech Communication Laboratory support Leeper's pioneering work.

Our friend Charlie Brown (see Figure 1–21) illustrates humorously how others' perceptions and subsequent communications affect our output, if not *what* we see.

[37]R. W. Leeper, "A Study of a Neglected Portion of the Field of Learning: The Development of Sensory Organization," *Journal of Genetic Psychology*, 46 (1935), 41–75, see also Julian E. Hochberg, *Perception* (Englewood Cliffs, N.J.: Prentice-Hall, Inc., 1964), p. 70.

A young man "on the town"

A person needing to cash a check

Someone who is late for an appointment

FIGURE 1–19   Selective Perception.[38]

[38]Reprinted with permission of Macmillan Publishing Co., Inc. from *Communications: The Transfer of Meaning* by Don Fabun. Copyright © 1968, Kaiser Aluminum & Chemical Corporation.

FIGURE 1–20A.

FIGURE 1–20B.

FIGURE 1–20C.

FIGURE 1–21.[39]

For Carl Rogers, "Every individual exists in a continually changing world of experience of which he is the center."[40] Whether one calls it the phenomenal field or the experiential field, man exists in a sea of experiences, both conscious and unconscious. For Rogers this is a private world that can really be known only to the individual. The way each person perceives his private world is reality for him. We do not react

[39] © 1960 United Feature Syndicate, Inc.
[40] Carl R. Rogers, *Client-Centered Therapy* (Boston: Houghton Mifflin Co., 1951), p. 483.

to absolute reality but rather to our perception of reality. "We live by a perceptual 'map' which is never reality itself."[41]

LISTENING

Nearly one hundred years ago in George Eliot's *Felix Holt, the Radical,* The Reverend Rufus Lyon counseled the hot-tempered hero: "Therefore I pray for a listening spirit, which is a great mark of grace. . . . The scornful nostril and the high head gather not the odors that lie on the track of truth."[42]

From a discussion of the process of perception and its intimate relationship to the process of communication, it seems obvious that although speech training must put great emphasis on skills of delivery (encoding and transmitting), it must also be concerned with listening. We may think of listening in terms of the general discussion of perception and specifically as auditory perception. Once again we may profitably divide auditory perception (listening) into hearing (sensation) and listening (interpretation).

Our disposition, set (or expectancy), and attention once again become critical even before the hearing or sensation is actually registered or received by the brain. The interpretation of this *hearing* is affected by our interest, motivations, and desires. When we think of speech as a communication and a perception process, we are also discussing listening. Listening is the most used of the communicative skills, and *good* listening is an integral part of the communication process; it is therefore an essential factor in *good* speaking. Surveys of communication habits indicate that man may spend as much as 60 to 75 percent of his time listening.[43]

Stuart Chase scolds Americans forthrightly:

> Listening is the other half of talking. If people stop listening, it is useless to talk—a point not always appreciated by talkers.
> Americans are not good listeners. In general they talk more than they listen. Competition in our culture puts a premium on self-expression, even if the individual has nothing to express. What he lacks in knowledge he tries to make up for by talking fast or pounding the table. And many of us, while ostensibly listening, are inwardly preparing a statement to stun the company when we get the floor.[44]

---

41 Ibid., p. 485.

42George Eliot, *Felix Holt, the Radical: The Personal Edition of George Eliot's Works* (New York: Doubleday & Company, Inc., 1901), p. 70.

43Ralph G. Nichols and Leonard A. Stevens, *Are You Listening?* (New York: McGraw-Hill Book Company, 1957), pp. 6–8.

44Stuart Chase, "Are You Listening?" *Reader's Digest,* December 1962, p. 80.

Robert Goyer indicates the following as factors and attributes of good, perceptive listening:

FACTORS
1. An adequate hearing acuity.
2. A recognition on the part of the listener of the problems and obstacles to overcome in order to listen effectively, including such things as improper attitude, boredom, fatigue, and the like.
3. A knowledge of the specific kind of listening situation and the listener's adaptation to it, including such kinds as casual listening and intent listening.
4. The relationship between listening and vocabulary.
5. The judging of what is heard—being able to think and analyze while listening.

ATTRIBUTES
1. A readiness to listen.
2. An ability to discriminate among sounds and ideas.
3. The capacity to give meanings to selected sounds.
4. The ability to relate meanings given to certain sounds to other experiences.
5. The ability to evaluate properly the medium and manner of the sound presentations.
6. The willingness to disregard prejudice.[45]

You listen with more than your ears, and you listen for more than sound—you listen with all appropriate senses to perceive the total situation or receive the total communication. This concept is far removed from a concept of listening that can be described as *auding*, which utilizes only an adequate hearing acuity. Cortright and Hinds have blended listening and perception in this way: "The listening process involves accurate perception and orientation, direction of attention toward digestion of the speaker's views, and integration of the meaning into objective concepts."[46]

In an article entitled "The Listening Spirit and the Conference Leader," Ernest D. Nathan attempted to diagram the process of perceptive listening and to develop functional definitions. His emphasis was on conference leadership, but the theory is equally applicable for almost all speech and communication situations (See Figure 1–22).[47]

[45]Robert S. Goyer, "Oral Communication: Studies in Listening," *Audio-Visual Communication Review*, 2, No. 4 (Fall 1954), 263–76; see also Sam Duker, *Listening: Bibliography* (New York: Scarecrow Press, Inc., 1964).

[46]Rupert L. Cortright and George L. Hinds, *Creative Discussion* (New York: The Macmillan Company, 1959), p. 117.

[47]Ernest D. Nathan, "The Listening Spirit and the Conference Leader," *Training Directors Journal*, 18, No. 1 (January 1964), 24.

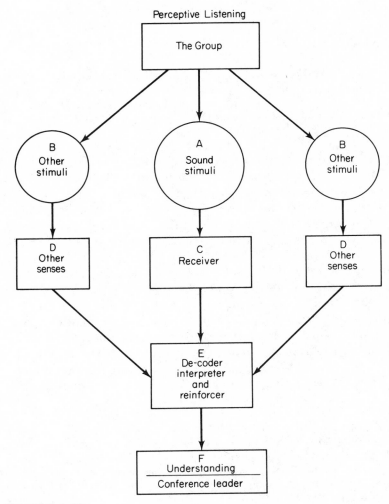

Perceptive Listening

FIGURE 1–22.

Key:

A. The stimulus, primarily sound, originates from some member of the conference group.

B. Other stimuli, such as bodily movements, facial and manual expressions, and external distractions join, reinforce, or even dilute the sound stimulus.

C. The audible stimuli strike the ear and are auded.

D. The nonaudible stimuli are directed to the other senses, such as sight, smell, touch, taste, fear, pain, balance, and so on.

E. Aided by a conscious effort on the part of the receiver to gain understanding, the various stimuli are conducted to the nervous system of the receiver, where they are decoded, interpreted, and reinforced by experience.

F. Decoded and reinforced, and combining the effects of all senses involved, the communication is completed, resulting in understanding in the terms intended by the sender of the stimuli.

31

Nathan concludes:

> Perceptive listening is a conscious, cognitive effort involving primarily
> the sense of hearing reinforced by other senses and leading to understand-
> ing. When perceptive listening is inspired by a sincere desire to understand,
> it becomes more than a sensory process. It is an attitude well expressed as
> "a listening spirit."[48]

Listening is a difficult process even under the most favorable conditions. One reason is that we think much faster than we talk. The
average rate of conversational speech of most Americans is around 125
words per minute, whereas it has been found that people can comprehend
speech at more than 300 words per minute without significant loss.[49]
The lag between speaking speed and listening speed is probably the cause
of our listening trouble.

A more important collection of obstacles to listening includes: *pre-
judging*, or jumping to the conclusion that the other person's meaning
is understood before it is fully expressed; *ambiguity*, or the possibility,
always present, that the idea expressed is open to more than one interpretation; and related to both of these, the *illusion* that effective communication has taken place. These obstacles are especially insidious because they are difficult to detect and, in some instances, seem to reinforce
the conviction of perceptive listening when, in fact, the opposite is the
case.

> If we hear something that opposes our most deeply rooted prejudices,
> notions, convictions, mores, or complexes, our brains may become over-
> stimulated, and not in a direction that leads to good listening. We men-
> tally plan a rebuttal to what we hear, formulate a question designed to
> embarrass the talker, or perhaps simply turn to thoughts that support our
> own feelings on the subject at hand.[50]

However, let us not forget that as a speaker, or sender, we are responsible to a large extent for both the attentive *hearing* and the
objective *listening* of the audience. An audience that is inattentive and
half-asleep may not be *hearing* very efficiently because of the speaker's
dull and monotonous voice or delivery pattern, or because the subject
itself is dull and monotonous, or both. The audience may not be *listening*
for the same reasons; however, *listening* is more closely related to subject,
organization of material, interest, and linguistic ability. In terms of
critical listening, the speaker has serious ethical responsibilities in regard

---

[48]Nathan, "The Listening Spirit and the Conference Leader," p. 25.
[49]Nichols and Stevens, *Are you Listening?* pp. 78–79.
[50]Ralph G. Nichols and Leonard A. Stevens, "Listening to People," *Harvard Business
Review*, 35, No. 5 (September 1957), 88.

to *stacking* his message organization and evidence, *name-calling,* and using abstract language of the *glittering-generality* variety. The devices might improve hearing or attending, but they make objective listening very difficult.

This distinction between hearing and listening, you will recall, is based on the perception process. *Auditory perception* is the general term and *hearing* is the sensating step, or sensation; *listening* is the interpretation. It behooves the speaker to take all of auditory perception into account when organizing and adapting his material, mood, and mode of delivery to a particular group of potential listeners. Those factors thought to play the most important role in listening comprehension were reported by Nichols.[51] They are critical in helping you better analyze your listeners for maximum adaptation. Some are more useful in evaluating your own listening habits. The factors are:

Intelligence
Reading comprehension
Recognition of correct English usage
Size of the listener's vocabulary
Ability to make inferences *draw conclusions*
Ability to structuralize a speech (that is, to see the organizational plan and
    the connection of the main points)
Listening for main ideas, not merely for specific facts
Use of special techniques while listening to improve concentration
Real interest in the subject discussed
Emotional adjustment to the speaker's thesis
Curiosity about the subject discussed
Physical fatigue of the listener
Audibility of the speaker
Speaker effectiveness
Admiration for the speaker
Respect for listening as a method of learning
Susceptibility to distraction
Sex of the listener (males are better listeners, on the average) *???*
Room ventilation and temperature
Use of only the English language at home
High-school scholastic achievement
High-school speech training
Experience in listening to difficult expository material

An interesting listening quiz and suggestions for identifying listening problems may be found in Barker's book, *Listening Behavior.*[52]

In a new book on listening Carl Weaver opines, "Perhaps listening

[51]Ralph G. Nichols, "Factors in Listening Comprehension," *Speech Monographs,* 15, No. 2 (1948), 161–62.
[52]Larry L. Barker, *Listening Behavior* (Englewood Cliffs, N.J.: Prentice-Hall, Inc., 1971).

cannot be *taught*, but many of us are convinced that it can be learned."[53]
Weaver makes ten suggestions for improving your listening capacity and
five suggestions for evaluating what you hear:

IMPROVING YOUR LISTENING CAPACITY
1. You can reflect the message to the talker.
2. You must guess the talker's intent or purpose.
3. You should strive to bring the quality of your habitual listening up to
   the level of your optimal capacity.
4. You should try to determine whether your referents for the words of the
   talker are about the same as his.
5. You should try to determine your purpose in every listening situation.
6. You should become aware of your own biases and attitudes.
7. You should learn to use your spare time well as you listen.
8. You should analyze your listening errors.
9. You should pay attention to the process of cognitive structuring as it
   occurs and to the time it takes.
10. You should learn as much as you can about the process of listening.[54]

EVALUATING WHAT YOU HEAR
1. You should get the whole story before evaluating it.
2. You should be alert to mistaken causal relations.
3. You should ask yourself whether the speaker has done his homework well.
4. You should ask yourself whether the opinions you hear are sound.
5. You should judge how much the speaker's biases are affecting his
   message.[55]

All speakers are entitled to some listening effort. In the rare case of a
required course that is notoriously dull and taught by an even duller
teacher, you may dramatically discover your listening responsibilities
as you fail the mid-semester examination!

Understanding language usage and subtle linguistic devices is quite
obviously an important part of critical listening; more will be said of
this element in relationship to good listening habits in Chapter 2.

Listening, then, may be defined *as a conscious cognitive effort involving
primarily the sense of hearing (reinforced by other senses) and leading to
interpretation and understanding.*

SUMMARY

Theoretically, human communication is capable of fantastic speeds. The
amount of communication we engage in is tremendous. Practices of

[53]Carl H. Weaver, *Human Listening, Processes and Behavior* (Indianapolis and New
York: The Bobbs-Merrill Co., Inc., 1972), p. xii; see also F. Eugene Binder and Edward
L. McGlone, "Experimental Evaluation of the Xerox Effective Listening Course,"
Western Speech, 35, No. 4 (1971), 264–70.

[54]Weaver, *Human Listening, Processes and Behavior*, p. 99.

[55]Ibid., p. 105.

government, industry, and colleges and universities reflect the growing importance of speech and communication training. The literature here discussed reflects the growing systemization and interdisciplinary character of the study of communication. The importance of speech training to college students in terms of (1) work in other courses, (2) learning, (3) study habits, and (4) grades and personality has been demonstrated experimentally. Intentional communication is defined as a transactional process involving a cognitive sorting, selecting, and sending of symbols in such a way as to help a listener elicit from his own mind a meaning or response similar to that intended by the communicator.

The processes of communication and perception are essential fields of knowledge for people who would meaningfully learn communication skills. The model suggested for analysis of the communication process (Figure 1–7) includes: (1) an idea or concept; (2) selecting and sorting; (3) encoding; (4) transmission; (5) receiving and decoding; (6) selecting and sorting; and (7) a reconstructed idea or concept. The element of feedback, or the return of some of the transmitted energy to the source, is vital to self-correction and audience analysis.

The study of perception as a process gives us much insight into the speech and communication act. Perception may be usefully divided into (1) sensation and (2) interpretation. The effect of past experience, knowledge, set, expectancy, wish, and desire have intense impact upon perception. Autistic thinking is the cause of much distortion in perception and therefore impedes communication. Perception is a function of internal as well as external signals or forces. Listening is an integral part of the communication and perceptual processes and is the most used of the communication skills. Listening may be defined as *a conscious cognitive effort involving primarily the sense of hearing (reinforced by other senses) and leading to interpretation and understanding.* The speaker must take all of auditory perception into account when organizing and adapting his material, mood, and mode of delivery to a particular group of potential listeners.

The point of view of this book is that communication should not be considered as a simple transfer or transmission of meaning from one mind to another. It is a transactional process intimately related to perceptual processes, and it involves the sorting, selecting, and sending of symbols in such a way as to help a listener elicit from his own mind a meaning similar to that contained in the mind of the communicator.

Speech Communication Principles

1. Human communication is a transactional process involving a cognitive sorting, selecting, and sharing of symbols in such a way as to

help another elicit a meaning or response from his own experiences similar to that intended by the source.

2. Interpersonal communication is a transactional process involving commonality of experience and mutuality of influence.

3. A large portion of a person's self-concept is shaped by interactions with people whom he considers significant to him.

4. Every person is the center of his own phenomenal field; the way he experiences and perceives it is his own reality.

5. A person's set, expectancy, or preparation to perceive has much to do with his level of perception as well as his individual acceptance of a stimulus.

6. Our life space, phenomenal field, and self-concept significantly affect the way we view or perceive all kinds of stimuli, ranging from optical illusions to complex nonverbal behavior.

7. Listening is a conscious cognitive effort involving primarily the sense of hearing (reinforced by other senses) and leading to interpretation and understanding.

A.   General Learning Outcomes

1. We should better understand the enormous complexity of the process of human communication.

2. We should gain a working understanding of the process nature of human communication and its transactional nature.

3. We should learn the factors and attributes of effective listening so that we may improve our own listening behavior.

4. We should learn the importance of speech communication training for our successful growth and development.

B.   Specific Learning Outcomes

1. We should be able in a five-minute report to explain and illustrate orally and pictorially the transactional and process nature of human communication.

2. We should be able to reproduce and explain in a three-page report the essential dimensions of any three of the models illustrated in Chapter 1.

3. We should be able to explain orally or in a short essay the relationship between the process of perception and the process of communication.

4. We should learn the attributes of effective listening and be able to apply them to a personal audit of our own listening behavior.

5. We should be able to relate the foregoing general and specific learning outcomes to the speech communication principles enumerated above.

C. Communication Competencies

1. We should develop an ability to adapt to feedback in a classroom communication situation to the satisfaction of peers who are familiar with the material in this chapter.

2. We should develop a sensitivity toward the role of self-image as it affects both sending and receiving signals in the process of communication.

3. We should be able to "see" the hidden messages in the perceptual tests of Chapter 1 and better assess the role of past experience in the communication of meaning.

4. We should develop better listening habits and a better monitoring system for our own verbal output.

5. We should be able to apply a communication model to a specific incident or interaction for greater insight into the process of communication and should be able to demonstrate this application orally and pictorially to the satisfaction of our instructor.

D. Study Projects and Tasks

1. Develop your own verbal-pictorial model of the human communication process (cf. Figure 1–23). See Appendix B for more ideas.

2. Apply one of the communication models to a specific incident, event, or interaction (cf. Figure 1–24); report (verbally and/or pictorially) what insights or lessons it yielded. Pay special attention to feedback.

3. Using the optical illusions of Chapter 1 or other perceptual anomalies you may find, test a few nonclass members and record their decoding behavior. Assess the reasons for the differences and be prepared to share your experiences in class. Is self-image involved?

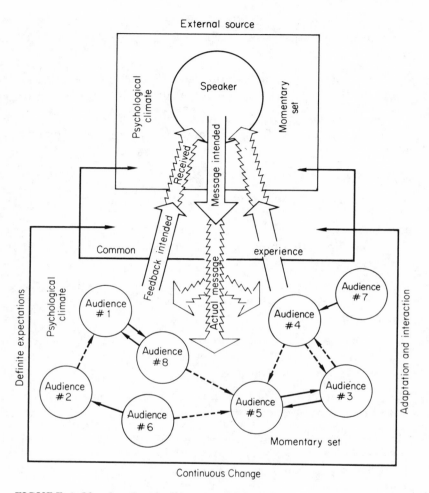

FIGURE 1–23. Speaker-Audience Model.*

4. Reread the various definitions of communication offered in Chapter 1 and be prepared for a classroom discussion on the drawbacks and merits of each.

5. With a classmate prepare an eight- to ten-minute dialogue in the form of an interview or role play for the purpose of introducing each other to the rest of the class (e.g., a job interview, a dialogue with an arresting officer, a doctor's appointment, a conversation with a friendly bartender, and so forth).

*From a student model by James Inglehart, Wayne State University.

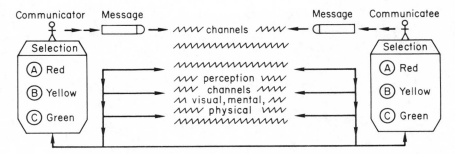

FIGURE 1–24. Traffic Light Communication Model.* Levels of Responsiveness and Receptibility.

Key:
Red—danger, stop
Yellow—caution
Green—go, clear passage

Message may be verbal, mental, kinesic

A., B., C., resulting from
  (1) situational-emergency
  (2) social-planned
  (3) personality value system—operational at times
  (4) psychological—operational at times

6. Prepare a seven- or eight-word original message and whisper it to one class member, who in turn whispers it to the next person. Have the last class member repeat the message aloud and compare it to the original. Discuss the results.

7. Read the following message once and count the *f*s. Compare notes with other class members and discuss any differences. Would an illiterate have as much trouble?

   The necessity of training farm hands for first-class farms in the fatherly handling of farm livestock is foremost in the minds of farm owners. Since the forefathers of the farm owners trained the farm hands for first-class farms in the fatherly handling of farm livestock, the farm owners feel they should carry on with the family tradition of training farm hands of first-class farms in the fatherly handling of farm livestock, because they believe it is the basis of good fundamental farm management.

*From a student model by Carol J. Meyer, Wayne State University.

8. Note how past experience interferes with this simple instruction on a double task. Connect all nine dots with four connecting straight lines. Discuss the implications for communication theory.

.   .   .   .

.   .   .   .

.   .   .   .

9. Check yourself on the following bad listening habits.* Then compare your list with those of other classmates. Discuss. Think of a specific person whom you feel is a bad listener. Check the inventory in a way that best describes his behavior. Discuss.

	FREQUENCY				
	Almost Always	Usually	Some-times	Seldom	Almost Never
1. Routinely calling the subject uninteresting	_____	_____	_____	_____	_____
2. Criticizing the speaker personally	_____	_____	_____	_____	_____
3. Getting over-stimulated by some point within the speech	_____	_____	_____	_____	_____
4. Listening primarily for facts instead of ideas	_____	_____	_____	_____	_____
5. Trying to outline everything	_____	_____	_____	_____	_____
6. Faking attentiveness to the speaker	_____	_____	_____	_____	_____
7. Tolerating or creating distractions	_____	_____	_____	_____	_____
8. Paying little attention to difficult expository material	_____	_____	_____	_____	_____
9. Letting emotion-laden words arouse personal antagonism	_____	_____	_____	_____	_____
10. Daydreaming	_____	_____	_____	_____	_____

*Adapted from the works of Ralph G. Nichols and Leonard A. Stevens cited earlier.

10. Read the Appendix speech, "Communication and the Survival of Democracy," and prepare to discuss the speaker's approach to providing for feedback in a truly participatory democracy. Make notes, by line number, of those specific lines and sections that are most relevant.

11. Prepare an oral report or essay attempting to prove or disprove any of the speech communication principles listed earlier.

12. Communication models often serve very specific purposes (e.g. instruction, prediction, research, classification, etc.). Study the models in Appendix B and try to determine the specific purpose of each. Evaluate their success. Prepare for a class discussion.

Chapter Two

Audience Psychology

Our emphasis in speech communication training typically involves casual, intentional, and generally passive audiences. However, the modern speaker is meeting more active, expressive, and aggressive collectiveness than ever before. In recent times we have known demonstrations, panics, riots, and other types of collective dynamics that challenge long-standing rhetorical advice and prescription. Most of our research and theorizing is predicated on relatively passive audiences and groups. Before discussing the more classic audience behavior models, some discussion of crowd phenomena is in order.

COLLECTIVE PHENOMENA

When a group of human beings, whatever its size, is hyperinterstimulated, it presents a need for a new and more systematic classification of collectivities and perhaps an entirely new model of interpersonal influence—a model involving contagion, regression, anonymity, suggestibility, violence, and other *active* dimensions not typically associated with more passive audiences.

A useful system of classification is provided by R. W. Brown (see

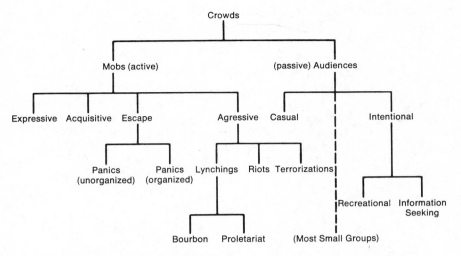

FIGURE 2–1.   Varieties of Crowds.
SOURCE: Adapted from R. W. Brown, "Mass Phenomena," in *The Handbook of Social Psychology*, Vol. 2 (Cambridge, Mass.: Addison-Wesley Publishing Co., 1954), pp. 833–76. (material in parenthesis added).

Figure 2–1).[1] *Crowds* becomes the generic term, which in turn is divided into two kinds: *mobs,* which are described as *active,* and *audiences,* described as passive. Mobs are divided according to overt behavior.

Another way of visualizing these differences is to supply an arbitrary universe—say, fifty people—and targets of behavior, with the bull's-eye representing the ultimate in *focus* and homogeneity (See Figure 2–2).

Mob Psychology

Without attempting to determine the predisposing causes of the Detroit riots of 1967 (the Kerner Commission speaks to this point), the precipitating or triggering causes indicate what social psychologists mean by contagion, regression, suggestibility, and violence.

It was 5 A.M. Daylight was beginning to show.
Lt. Raymond Good, night chief of the 10th (Livernois) Precinct Station, was riding to investigate a report of an unruly crowd and thought:
"It's going to be one hot July day."
Just how hot July 23, 1967, would be not even Good could imagine as his scout car stopped on Clairmount at 12th Street.

[1] R. W. Brown, "Mass Phenomena," in *The Handbook of Social Psychology*, vol. 2, ed. G. Lindzey (Cambridge, Mass.: Addison-Wesley Publishing Co., 1954), pp. 833–76; see also Stanley Milgram and Hans Toch, "Collective Behavior: Crowds and Social Movements," in *The Handbook of Social Psychology*, vol. 4, 2d ed., eds. G. Lindzey and E. Aronson (Cambridge, Mass.: Addison-Wesley Publishing Co., 1969), pp. 507–610.

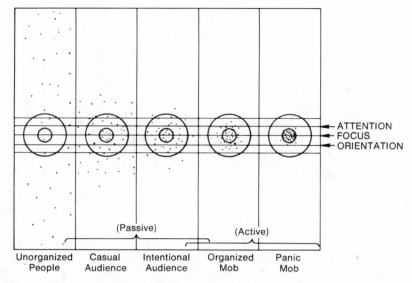

FIGURE 2–2.   Targets of Collective Behavior.

Good was about to witness the spark which ignited the five-day Detroit riot—the most devastating urban riot in the nation's history.

Before it was over 43 persons would be dead. Thousands of families would be homeless. More than $50 million in property would be destroyed.

Good, now a police inspector, described the events:

"We pulled up to the corner. A large crowd—maybe 200 or 250 people— was milling around on the southeast corner. They were watching and yelling things at our precinct cleanup crew, which was herding people out of the Economy Printing Co. building into a patrol wagon to take them to the station for booking.

"Our crew had raided a blind pig [illegal saloon] on the second floor of the building and arrested 83 persons. The raid had been made at 3:45 A.M. While some of the patrons were angry at being arrested, most of them were jovial because they knew they'd be out of jail quickly.

"Because of the large number it took us more than an hour to transport the 83 to the station. The noise attracted a large crowd from the neighborhood.

"It was a hot, muggy night. It wasn't unusual to have large numbers of people awake and even walking the streets in that area because of the heat.

"While the crowd was loud, they didn't look very mean. A few wastebaskets and other debris littered the street.

"Then a tall, thin young man in a green shirt (later we tagged him Mr. Greensleeves) came out of the crowd and started yelling, 'Get the cops off the street. The streets are ours.'

"He kept yelling and the crowd responded with catcalls. The youth walked across Clairmount in front of our car. I opened the right door and put one foot on the street to see him better as he moved toward the crowd, screaming and waving his arms.

"Then I saw stars. Someone behind me had thrown a piece of concrete and hit me above the right ear. I reached up and felt blood and a dandy bump. I got back into the car and told my driver, 'Get the hell out of here.'

"As we raced down 12th I glanced back and saw the crowd surge into the street. As we turned right on to Chicago Boulevard I radioed all other scout cars to stay out of the area and to rendezvous with me at Clairmount and the Lodge Freeway."[2]

Contagion and hyperinterstimulation are obvious in the events immediately preceding the riot. The subsequent looting and burning clearly indicate regression and perhaps the feeling of anonymity. An audience of onlookers can on occasion spontaneously become a mob. What a nightmare for a speaker attempting to "cool it" and what an opportunity for one bent on violence!

Inspector Good now believes, in retrospect, that one of the critical precipitating causes of the riot was "Mr. Greensleeves' " exhortation to the crowd at 12th and Clairmount. Almost immediately afterward, the crowd became a mob.

"If he hadn't been there urging them on, probably that crowd eventually would have dispersed on their own and gone back to bed," he said.

The fires of the riot were still smoldering when federal, state and city officials began searching for its causes.

"Mr. Greensleeves" remained unidentified for about two weeks after the riot. Later arrested and identified by Good, he was charged with inciting a riot and two counts of looting. Juries found him innocent on all three counts.

The riot seemed unbelievable to most Detroiters.[3]

While a panic may be an extreme example, it further clarifies the meaning of contagion, irrationality, and violence. The Chicago Iroquois Theatre fire of 1903, as related by the comedian Eddie Foy, who was on stage when it occurred, is a staggering real-life example.

"Fire!" . . . The crowd was beginning to surge toward the doors and already showing signs of a stampede. . . . They were falling into panic. . . . Especially in the gallery, they had gone mad.

The horror in the auditorium was beyond all description. . . . The fire escape ladders could not accommodate the crowd, and many fell or jumped to death on the pavement below. Some were not killed only because they landed on the cushion of bodies of those who had gone before. . . . Most of the dead were trampled or smothered. . . . In places on the stairways, . . . bodies were piled seven or eight feet deep. . . . The heel prints on the dead faces mutely testified to the cruel fact that human animals stricken by

[2]Don Tschirhart, *The Detroit Sunday News*, July 23, 1972, p.14f.
[3]Ibid.

terror are as mad and ruthless as stampeding cattle. Many bodies . . . had
the flesh trodden from their bones. . . .

From the start of the fire until all in the audience either escaped, died,
or lay maimed in the halls and alleys, took just eight minutes. In that 8
minutes more than 500 perished. . . . Subsequent deaths among the injured
brought the list up to 602."[4]

From the mob assaults of the French revolution so vividly described
by Gustave Le Bon to the college protests and race riots of recent times,
history obviously has recorded some very strange and frightening group
behavior. It is not our purpose here to evaluate these events as social
movements. Our interest, rather, is in mob behavior, whatever the issues that motivated it. E. A. Ross in 1913 wrote an impelling description
of crowd behavior that is still useful today.

> The crowd [mob] may generate moral fervor, but it never sheds lights. If
> at times it has furthered progress, it is because the mob serves as a battering-
> ram to raze some mouldering, bat-infested institution and clean the ground
> for something better. This better will be the creation of gifted individuals
> or of deliberative bodies, never of anonymous crowds. It is easier for masses
> to agree on a Nay than on a Yea. Hence crowds destroy despotisms, but
> never build free States; abolish evils, but never found works of beneficence.
> Essentially atavistic and sterile, the crowd [mob] ranks as the lowest of the
> forms of human association.[5]

Le Bon suggests that when a crowd reaches the focus and organization
of a mob there is a _psychological law of mental unity_ that comes into
play.[6] The participants are put into a sort of "collective mind" with a
loss of conscious personality; each thinks and behaves quite differently
from the way he would if acting alone. It is the same phenomenon that
E. D. Martin describes as "crowd mentality," a special collective mental
condition.[7] Martin believed this collective mind was classified with
dreams, delusions, and automatic behavior. It is as if the primitive ego
or id is unleashed and a mob, in Martin's words, becomes "a device for
indulging ourselves in a kind of temporary insanity by all going crazy
together."[8] The mob, for Martin and Le Bon alike, lurks under the
skin of us all. In this view mobs may be weapons of revenge. They are
always uncompromising about their demands and in no way respect in-

[4]From the book _Clowning Through Life_ by Eddie Foy and Alvin F. Harlow. Copyright, 1928, by E. P. Dutton & Co., Inc. Renewal, © 1956 by Alvin F. Harlow. Published by E. P. Dutton & Co., Inc., and used with their permission.
[5]E. A. Ross, _Social Psychology_ (New York: The Macmillan Co., 1913), pp. 56–57.
[6]Gustave Le Bon, _The Crowd_ (New York: The Viking Press, 1960), p. 26.
[7]E. D. Martin, _The Behavior of Crowds_ (New York & London: Harper & Bros., 1920),
pp. 4–5.
[8]Ibid., p. 37.

dividual dignity. Even when they achieve something, it is less a testament to their leadership than a consequence of their unbridled fury. In 1920 Martin wrote penetratingly and insightfully about mob behavior in words that have relevance even today:

> The crowd, in common with paranoia, uniformly shows the quality of "megalomania." Every crowd *boosts* for itself, lauds itself, gives itself airs, speaks with oracular finality, regards itself as morally superior and will, so far as it has the power, lord it over everyone. . . .
> Every organized crowd is jealous of its dignity and honor and is bent upon keeping up appearances. Nothing is more fatal to it than a successful assault upon its prestige. Every crowd, even the casual street mob, clothes the egoistic desires of its members or participants in terms of the loftiest moral motive. No crowd can afford to be laughed at."[9]

For Le Bon, Martin, E. A. Ross, and others, the mob is a collectivity in which people's normal reactions are subordinated to and superseded by unconscious desires and motivations. The major mechanisms leading up to a state of *collective mind* or *mob mentality* appear to be anonymity, contagion, and suggestibility. One gets lost in the press of the mob and loses much of his sense of responsibility. Through this anonymity comes an inflated feeling of power. Contagion was best illustrated in the panic attending the Iroquois Theatre fire described earlier, a kind of supersonic, infectious mayhem. A heightened state of suggestibility leads to precipitate action in an unthinking and uncritical way. Many of the restraining emotions are lost—fear is often gone in battle, pity in a riot or a lynching.

A full-blown concept of *collective mind* has, of course, many ethical and legal ramifications in terms of sanity and guilt or innocence. One can argue that stupidity, suggestibility, and irrationality exist in individuals as much as in mobs and that individuals vary in their degree of participation in mob action.[10] One can also argue, as has Floyd Allport, that mobs simply supply a form of *social facilitation* in stimulating individuals' desires[11]—creating a kind of heightened response merely from the sight and sound of others making similar movements.

A modern social psychologist, Roger Brown, argues that "something new is created. To describe this new thing, this 'emergent,' as a 'group mind' does not seem to be seriously misleading. It may be a degree more illuminating to say that what emerges in the crowd is a payoff matrix that does not exist for the members when they do not compose a crowd."[12]

[9]Ibid., pp. 74 and 83.
[10]R. H. Turner and L. M. Killian, *Collective Behavior* (Englewood Cliffs, N.J.: Prentice-Hall, Inc., 1957).
[11]Floyd N. Allport, *Social Psychology* (Cambridge, Mass.: Riverside Press, 1924).
[12]Roger Brown, *Social Psychology* (New York: The Free Press, 1965), p. 760.

There is still much to uncover about the behavior of crowds and mobs. In a sense, they add a new dimension to modern speech communication. Yet, they are certainly not a phenomenon new to this field, for as early as 1906 Walter Dill Scott wrote a pioneering public-speaking text in which he included a chapter on "Psychology of the Crowd and of the Audience."[13]

Audience Psychology

In Roger Brown's taxonomy of crowds (Figure 2–1) audiences are represented on the passive side of the diagram. There is far less emotionality and irrationality in a typical audience than in a mob; the "group mind" is nowhere near as evident and regressive acts are comparatively rare. Nevertheless there is a dynamic present even in very casually organized audiences. More formal audiences, such as classes of students, church groupings, and lecture assemblages, which are intentionally and purposefully organized, represent collectivities with more ascertainable dynamics. They may be information-seeking, recreational, or what Kimball Young calls *conversional*, such as the audience attracted to political rallies.[14]

Audiences, like mobs, can vary considerably in size; however, the small coacting group of six or less is thought special enough to be considered separately in Chapter 12, "Discussion: Cooperative Communication."

We are therefore most concerned with relatively formal, intentional audiences of roughly twenty or more people. We are primarily concerned with audiences that are present physically. When one is dealing with vast, unseen audiences as in the mass media one is, for the most part, beyond transactional, interpersonal influence and has need of a more sociological and political analysis of primary contacts (such as family and friends), secondary contacts (involving religious and political affiliations, occupational ties, etc), and definable *publics*. Nevertheless much of what is said here will also apply to the mass media audience. If the two-step flow hypothesis of Katz applies, that is, if opinion leaders take note of mass opinion and pass it along interpersonally, then it may apply very closely indeed.[15]

[13]Walter Dill Scott, *The Psychology of Public Speaking* (New York: Hinds, Hayden and Eldridge, 1906), Ch. 12.

[14]K. Young, *Social Psychology*, 3d ed. (New York: Appleton-Century-Crofts, 1958), p. 302.

[15]Elihu Katz, "The Two-Step Flow of Communication: An Up-to-Date Report on a Hypothesis," *Public Opinion Quarterly*, 21 (Spring 1957); see also Larry L. Barker and Robert J. Kibler, *Communication Behavior: Perspectives and Principles* (Englewood Cliffs, N.J.: Prentice-Hall, Inc., 1971).

An attempt at adapting the Ross transactional communication model (Figure 1–7), a dyadic model, to audience configurations follows. Mutual influence obviously presupposes a different kind of equation, as does also the speaker's assumptions about polarity, homogeneity, and the receiver's general orientation. A group of even eight or nine persons, much less twenty or more, would create an astronomical number of sub-group and individual relationships—hence the practical utility of the model shown in Figure 2–3.

Most of what was said about the Ross dyadic model in Chapter 1 directly applies here. The audience model involves quite obviously a larger potential for interstimulation and what goes with it; the problems of physical setting and feedback take on greater dimensions. Analysis of the audience by types and descriptive measures becomes in part an averaging process, and with that comes the realization that such generalizing inevitably fits some members of the audience poorly and others perhaps not at all. Accordingly, the model in Figure 2–3 shows some of the members outside of the larger audience concept.

The audience has frequently been considered as a statistical concept, that is, assembling a large amount of information about individuals into manageable form.[16]

Audiences can and have been classified into many general types such as organized-unorganized, unified, heterogeneous, apathetic, hostile, polarized, and bipolar. More will be said about types of audiences shortly. For the most part, we are talking about a fairly formal collection of people assembled with a specific intent in mind or for a specific purpose. Patterns of interaction are reasonably predictable in such groupings, given enough information.

Three of these patterns may be described as *polarization, interstimulation,* and *feedback-response. Polarization* describes unusually homogeneous audience attitudes. When two relatively homogeneous but opposing factions are present in an audience, it is referred to as *bipolar.* Debates often attract bipolar audiences. *Interstimulation* refers to some of the volatile behavior discussed under mobs and more specifically to Allport's concept of social facilitation. It involves ritual, suggestion, and the reinforcement one gets from similar and simultaneous behavior. When all of those around us are angry, we are apt to be angry; when all are happy, we are apt to be happy. *Feedback-response* refers to a special kind of reinforcement when it is a positive response to the efforts of the speaker; when it is negative it is quite another matter. If the speaker is strongly reinforced through positive feedback, he may become

[16]Theodore Clevenger, *Audience Analysis* (Indianapolis and New York: The Bobbs-Merrill Co., Inc., 1966), pp. 13–22.

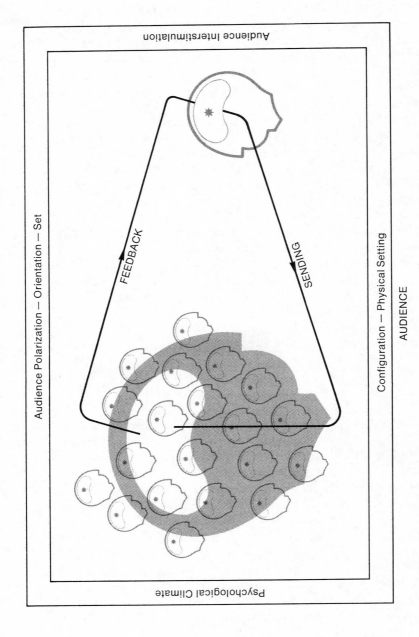

FIGURE 2-3. Ross Transactional Communication Model, as Adapted to Audience Configurations.

identified closely with some ideal. With strong interstimulation this identification may lead to exceptional, if only temporary, polarization among his listeners, an enviable situation only so long as the persuader can control it and live with the results over a period of time. A turned-on audience, let us recall, is only a few steps removed from a mob.

The classic categorization of audiences comes to us from H. L. Hollingworth. Hollingworth posited five types of audiences; his categories make sense not only in dyadic and small-group situations but also in more formal settings. The five types of audiences he labeled: (1) pedestrian, (2) discussion-passive, (3) selected, (4) concerted, and (5) organized. Hollingworth used the term *orientation,* by which he meant "the establishment of a pattern of attention, when the group is considered, or a set and direction of interest, when we consider the individuals comprising the group."[17]

The *pedestrian audience* is a transient audience such as exists among pedestrians on a busy street corner. No common ties or lines of communication bind the members of the audience and the speaker. The first step, that of catching everyone's attention, is crucial; how far the process goes beyond that varies with the purpose of the speaker.

The *discussion group* or *passive audience* is one whose first task is usually accomplished or guaranteed by rules of order. The persuader's initial problem is more likely to be the second step, that of holding attention or interest. How far the process goes again depends upon the occasion or the success of the persuader.

The *selected audience* is one in which the members are assembled for some common purpose, but not all are sympathetic to one another or to the speaker's point of view. Impression, persuasion, and direction characterize the speaker's undertaking here. *ex. jury, church*

The *concerted audience* is one in which the people assemble with a common, active purpose in mind, with sympathetic interest in a mutual enterprise, but with no clear division of labor or rigid organization of authority. A sense of conviction and delegation of authority are the speaker's chief responsibilities. *ex: do something about it (Taxes)*

The *organized audience* is an organized group with a rigid division of labor and authority supported by specific common purposes and interests, with tasks well learned and already assigned by authority of the leader. The persuader has only to issue instructions, since the audience is already persuaded. *ex: unions*

Before appearing before the audience, according to Hollingworth, the speaker ought to secure as full a knowledge as possible of the mode

[17]H. L. Hollingworth, *The Psychology of the Audience* (New York: American Book Co., 1935), p. 21.

and degree of the audience polarization or orientation, The speaker must be prepared to shift tactics if the first reactions of the audience show that his initial judgment was wrong.

In terms of the five fundamental tasks of a persuader, which Hollingworth describes as attention, interest, impression, conviction, and direction, we can get a better picture of what distinctions he saw among the five types of audiences. We shall have more to say of the five tasks in Part IV, "The Psychology of Persuasion." In Figure 2–4 we have listed the five tasks under the types of audiences to which they are most relevant, thus enabling us to see more clearly what Hollingworth is saying.

Pedestrian Audience	Discussion and Passive Audience	Selected Audience	Concerted Audience	Organized Audience
Attention	....	....	....	....
Interest	Interest	....	....	....
Impression	Impression	Impression	....	....
Conviction	Conviction	Conviction	Conviction	....
Direction	Direction	Direction	Direction	Direction

FIGURE 2–4. Hollingworth Typology of Audiences and Tasks.[18]

According to Hollingworth the craving for an audience represents one of man's fundamental needs. "Without an audience women relapse and men become unkempt." One of the most significant things about an individual is the type of audience that most readily motivates his or her thought and conduct. In his book Hollingworth gives the word *audience* an extended meaning. To have an audience in Hollingworth's usage means not only to be heard (though this is the dominant meaning), but also more generally to be the object of attention on the part of other human beings.[19]

Closely related to interpersonal communication as well as speaker-audience interaction is Hollingworth's observation that there is often a striking conflict between a person's need or craving for an audience and his fear of it. It is probably true that we seek a certain amount of confrontation or encounter and yet simultaneously resist it.

The *audience configuration* is thought to be an important aspect of collective behavior and audience analysis. For reasonably polarized or oriented formal audiences, the occasion and associated *ritual* may become an overwhelming part of the configuration. The speech communication student is well advised to take this observation to heart. The

18Ibid., p. 25.
19Ibid., p. 2.

Japanese auto worker who ritualistically does five minutes of company-coordinated calisthenics every morning, sings songs, and cheers his second-shift replacement is a different breed from most of the auto workers in Detroit.

Nevertheless, we take the rituals of our social clubs, veterans' organization, and churches well in stride. However, one had better be cautious and pragmatic about ritual where audiences are concerned. The old public-speaking adage against using foul language is probably a good one, especially where formal ritual is part of the configuration. The most foul-mouthed among us often become the purest of tongue in collectivities of the kind just described. Resentment is devastating for the blasphemer who misassesses the audience's temper. If a mob can become animalistic, some if not most audiences can in a flash become holier-than-thou! More will be said of verbal obscenity in Chapter 3, "Language Habits and Semantics."

The *physical setting* itself constitutes part of the occasion and ritual. The pulpit in a church adds something to the minister's message; in a like manner the raised dais in the House of Representatives imparts extra authority to the Speaker's words. The old Globe Theatre is no ordinary house! What we do with lighting, music, and pomp and circumstances are also part of the physical setting and ritual. The same message uttered in a church, a restaurant, or a fraternity house might be sacrilege in the first, rudeness in the second, and understatement in the third! People have different expectations for different settings as well as different situations. Proximity to the audience is also thought to be a factor. If you are on an elevated platform far removed from the first row of the audience, your style of delivery should be qualitatively different than if you are close to the group.

The *arrangement* of the audience also has an impact upon how it reacts to persuasion and influence. Although there is mixed evidence on the question, Furbay experimented with different seating patterns and related them to subsequent attitude shifts and retention of material. He found that audiences generally were more easily persuaded when seated in a scattered rather than a compact configuration.[20] In most of these experiments we are dealing with either fixed seating, recorded messages, or institutionalized environments where much of the "groupness" is at a minimum in the first place. It does appear that compactness of itself does not mean greater susceptibility to all types of messages. It is probably true that logical, factual-type persuasion is most effective when

[20]Albert L. Furbay, "The Influence of Scattered versus Compact Seating on Audience Response," *Speech Monographs*, 32, No. 2 (1965), 144–48; for a different view see G. L. Thomas and D. C. Ralph, "A Study of the Effect of Audience Proximity on Persuasion," *Speech Monographs*, 26 (1959), 300–307.

listeners are separated and emotional appeals most successful when listeners are closely compacted.

Several useful questions relating to *audience-message analysis* are suggested by Eisenson, Auer, and Irwin:

1. *What is the significance of the subject for the audience?* Is its interest in the subject only casual, or is it motivated by real needs and wants? How far has its thinking about the problem progressed?
2. *What does the audience know about the subject?* Does it have essential factual information, or only opinions and sentiments? Are its sources of information sound ones, unbiased and complete?
3. *What beliefs or prejudices does the audience have about the subject?* In either case, what are the probable sources or influences in the formation of these existing notions?
4. *What is the attitude of the audience toward the subject?* Is it possible to estimate the percentage who are favorable, neutral, or unfavorable toward the problem.[21]

Some *general descriptive measures* and factors worth considering in audience analysis are:

1. *Age.* It is obvious that an audience of ten-year-olds will call for considerably different preparation on the speaker's part than will a group of forty-year-olds, even if the subject is Little League baseball. Just a few children in an otherwise all-adult audience sometimes presents a problem. Even if you choose (or are advised) to ignore them, you can be certain that the *audience* will not ignore them and will establish norms of appropriateness and understanding in terms of the youngsters. A risque story is less well received when even a single child is present.

2. *Sex.* An audience of twenty men often differs considerably in outlook from an audience of twenty women. An audience of ten men and ten women is likewise different from either of the homogeneous audiences. An audience of nineteen men and one woman may cause a speaker to alter many of his jokes and examples, not necessarily *because* of the one woman but because of nineteen men's expectations that the speaker will be conscious of the one woman. Ignore the women in your audience and the men will be unhappy.

3. *Education.* A man's education is the sum total of his learning. Do not confuse schooling with education, for schooling is no guarantee of an education. There are many uneducated college graduates! Nevertheless formal schooling is in many cases a faster and more systematic way

[21]Jon Eisenson, J. Jeffery Auer, and John V. Irwin, *The Psychology of Communication* (New York:Appleton-Century-Crofts, 1963), p. 279.

of acquiring knowledge than other ways. A person's schooling level may therefore be useful information in planning your speech. Language and vocabulary should be adapted to your audience's educational level and previous schooling, as was suggested earlier. An audience with a highly technical education will require a different approach from one with a religious or a liberal arts background. Again, the problem of variable educational levels presents itself. Time invested in this kind of audience analysis is usually well spent.

4. *Occupation.* The procedure of typing a person by his occupation is as dangerous as classifying him according to schooling. Nevertheless, this information is often predictively useful. Income level and the things related to income can often be predicted by knowing the predominent occupation of your audience. Teachers can be expected to have college degrees, top management executives may have similar opinions about pieces of labor legislation, and so on.

5. *Primary group memberships.* Most of us belong to so many groups that prediction even for a uniform audience is often shaky at best. For example, an audience at a political convention may be 100 percent Republican or Democratic and yet may be split ever so many ways on other group memberships such as religion, ethnic group, and occupation not to mention key issues. However, the more you can learn about the groups an audience does or does not belong to, the more intelligently you can prepare your speech.

6. *Special interests.* Whatever our differences on some of our primary group memberships, we often find audiences highly polarized if there is some secondary or special issue that they all have in common. A small community with a winning high-school basketball team can unceremoniously ignore a guest speaker if he is unaware of this special interest. Sometimes these special interests are temporary, but a speaker will do well to look for those special interests that the audience *expects* him to know something about.

7. *Audience-subject relationships.* This part of your analysis concerns an audience's *knowledge* about your speech topic, its *experience* and *interest* in the subject, and its *attitude* toward your specific purpose. It is often valuable to know the extent of audience uniformity in respect to your subject.

Audiences are sometimes very firm in their beliefs, whatever their level of knowledge or experience. Specific methods of preparing strategy for these occasions are covered at length in Part Four. In general, an audience is interested or apathetic toward your speech *subject*, but attitude is a special dimension of interest in your *purpose*. A useful scale for determining the general audience attitude toward your speech purpose is as follows:

ATTITUDE SCALE

Hostile	Opposed	Uncertain	Cordial	Favorable
−2	−1	0	+1	+2

Your speech preparation and arrangement of material will be heavily dependent upon this kind of analysis.

SUMMARY

Collective behavior includes such varieties as that observed in *mobs, audiences,* and *small groups.* In R. W. Brown's taxonomy *crowds* becomes the generic term for collectives. Mobs are described as *active* and audiences as *passive.* Mobs are subdivided into four categories: expressive, acquisitive, escape (including panics) and aggressive (including lynchings, riots, terrorizations). Audiences are subdivided into casual and intentional (including recreational and information-seeking types).

When a crowd reaches the focus and organization of a mob, suggests Le Bon, there is a psychological law of mental unity or "collective mind" that makes a mob think and behave quite differently from the members acting individually. The major mechanisms operating to change the mob members' behavior appear to be anonymity, contagion, and suggestibility. Mobs supply a stimulation and facilitation of individual's repressed desires, a kind of heightened response from the sight and sound of others making similar movements.

In an audience the "group mind" is nowhere near as evident, regressive acts are less gross, and emotionality and irrationality are typically less pervasive. More formal audiences like classes of students, church groupings and lecture gatherings, which are intentionally and purposefully organized, represent collectivities with more ascertainable dynamics. Three reasonably predictable patterns of interaction are *polarization, interstimulation,* and *feedback-response.*

H. L. Hollingworth enumerates five types of audiences (1) pedestrian, (2) discussion-passive, (3) selected, (4) concerted, and (5) organized. In his view persuaders undertake five fundamental tasks (attention, interest, impression, conviction, and direction), all of which are necessary when speaking to nonpolarized pedestrian audiences and only one of which (direction) is necessary in speaking to highly polarized organized audiences.

Audience configuration considerations include ritual, physical setting, and seating arrangement.

Some general descriptive measures usually considered in analyzing an audience include age, sex, education, occupation, primary group memberships, special interests, and audience-subject relationships.

Speech Communication Principles

1. When a group of human beings, whatever its size, is hyperinter-stimulated, to understand it we need a model of interpersonal influence involving contagion, regression, anonymity, suggestibility, violence, and other active dimensions not typically associated with more passive audiences.

2. The major mechanisms influencing the psychology of mobs are anonymity, contagion, and suggestibility.

3. Mobs stimulate and facilitate the expression of individuals' suppressed desires, creating a kind of heightened response from the sight and sound of others making similar movements.

4. Polarization, interstimulation, and feedback-response are reasonably predictable patterns of interaction in collectivities.

5. Formal audiences that are intentionally and purposefully organized represent a collectivity with more ascertainable dynamics.

6. Distinctions between types of collectivities are critical to a reality-based theory of speech communication.

7. There appears to be a conflict between a person's need for an audience and his fear of it. We seek and yet resist a certain amount of confrontation or encounter.

8. For highly polarized or oriented formal audiences, the occasion and associated ritual often become an all-important part of the configuration.

9. Assuming some homogeneity, logical, factual-type messages are more effective when listeners are separated; physical closeness is more apt to enhance emotional appeals and messages.

A. General Learning Outcomes

1. We should be able to distinguish between crowds, mobs, and audiences, and develop insight into the roles such collectivities play in speech communication.

2. We should become familiar with the importance of audience analysis in terms of the configurations, seating arrangements, and audience characteristics that affect speech communication.

3. We should be able to explain the differences between dyadic and audience models of the communication process.

B. *Specific Learning Outcomes*

1. We should learn and be able to reproduce R. W. Brown's taxonomy of crowds.

2. We should learn and understand a collective behavior model involving contagion, regression, anonymity, suggestibility, violence, and other active dimensions not typically associated with more passive audiences.

3. We should learn of various types of audiences and patterns of interaction (e.g., polarization, interstimulation, and feedback-response).

4. We should understand the categories of audiences delineated by H. L. Hollingworth (i.e., pedestrian, discussion-passive, selected, concerted, and organized).

5. We should understand the general descriptive measures utilized in audience analysis and be able to explain their usefulness in preparing a message.

6. We should be able to relate the foregoing general and specific learning outcomes to the speech communication principles enumerated above.

C. *Communication Competencies*

1. We should be able to evaluate a real or hypothetical collectivity of people and determine whether it is a mob or audience and of what specific kind.

2. We should be able to develop an awareness of our own interstimulation in crowd situations, relate to the models described, and write an objective analysis of our own feelings and behavior.

3. We should be able to assess the general impact of occasion, arrangement, and ritual in most audience situations where we are not complete strangers.

4. We should be able to apply the general descriptive measures for audience analysis to the audience we will speak to and check our assessment against the facts as ultimately determined through class discussion and/or records.

D. Study Projects and Tasks

1. Observe live or televised collectivities of people until you find two clear-cut examples of (1) a mob and (2) an audience. Describe each in a page or less in terms of the given taxonomy.

2. Describe in one page a crowd situation with which you are familiar that approached the "crowd [mob] mentality" description of E. D. Martin.

3. Locate yourself near the center of an active collectivity (e.g., at a demonstration, revival meeting, athletic event, fight, political rally, or similar event) until you feel a sense of interstimulation (anonymity, contagion, suggestibility) or collective mind. Extricate yourself and write the most detailed introspective account that you can of how you felt, what impulses came over you, what seemed to cause these impulses, and how one might avoid them psychologically.

4. Attend the meeting of a relatively ritualized group (e.g., a church service, award ceremony, graduation, or funeral service) and write a short report on the role of ritual and audience arrangement in interstimulation and persuasion.

5. Prepare a two-minute speech to counterpersuade a hypothetical crowd of twenty-five. Assume your listeners are in a suggestible, active, aggressive, turbulent mood (for example, assume they are faced with a fire, flood, or other threatening situation that does not *really* warrant panic; or, alternatively, assume they comprise an ugly, angry, menacing mob whose actions are about to get out of hand). Some heckling might make this project more realistic.

6. Prepare a general or specific verbal-pictorial model of the communication process between an individual speaker and a mob (see Figure 1–7 for a suggested framework).

7. Prepare an oral report or essay attempting to prove or disprove any of the speech communication principles listed earlier.

8. The appendix speech, "Communication and the Survival of Democracy," was delivered by the president of the Speech Communication

Association to an audience of several hundred attending the association's annual convention. The speech was published for a still wider audience. Evaluate the speaker's analysis of his audience(s) as indicated by the speech. What specific lines (by number) support your evaluation?

Chapter Three

Language
Habits
and
Semantics

LANGUAGE AS CODE AND SYMBOL

We will consider language in the light of previous discussions of the communication and perceptual processes, namely, as code and symbol. In many respects, it is in the use of oral language that we need our most rigorous training, for there is an infinitely larger number of meanings available to the communicatee (the listener) in the oral situation than in the reader situation, due to the concomitant or simultaneous signals that are operative over and above words. Your voice, for example, is a wonderfully sensitive instrument that has a powerful influence upon the meaning the listener attaches both to the words and to the speaker himself. The correct use of voice is thus very important. "Right on!" is very difficult for white students to say with appropriate emotional character and voice.

The appearance of the speaker—his dress, movements, facial expressions, and use of gestures—represents another concomitant signal that obviously affects the decoding mechanism of the listener; this general category of visible codes will be referred to as body-action language and will be discussed along with voice in Part Two, "Nonverbal Communication."

Another less obvious point to be made is that these codes and signals are related in such a way as to seriously and fundamentally affect one another. Sometimes they work together and strengthen or reinforce the meaning intended by the speaker. Sometimes, however, they conflict with one another and distort the intended meaning to a point of confusion, suspicion, or frustration on the part of the listener. Consider the sloppy student giving a speech on the value of personal neatness or a professor speaking through a frozen grin while discussing the possibility of a student's failing his course. We often express actions contrary to what we really intend. The cause may be tension, emotional involvement, or simply poor speech training.

Let us now turn to the all-important symbols we call *words*, remembering that the concomitant codes and symbols previously discussed will affect their intended meaning over and above what is said here. Words are symbols that are conventionally agreed upon to represent certain things. They are convenient labels that help us to classify things. It is obvious that there are more things and concepts in the world than there are words. So you think a dog is a dog! Try these definitions:

Dog: a canine animal
Dog: a clamp used on a lathe
Dog: an andiron used in a fireplace
Dog: a worthless person
Dog: a kind of sandwich
Dog: to follow closely
Dog: to loaf on the job
Dogged: persistent
Dog-tired: exhausted
Dog days: hot, sultry weather

Cat: Felis catus
Cat: a carnivorous mammal
Cat: a strong tackle used to hoist an anchor
Cat: a type of boat (catamaran)
Cat: a whip (cat-o'-nine-tails)
Cat: a jazz musician
Cat: a form of tractor
Cat: a female gossip
Cat: a fish or bird
Cat: a man

Rat: a long-tailed rodent
Rat: a despicable, sneaky person
Rat: to betray one's associates ("rat on")
Rat: a pad of hair
Rat: to suspect treachery ("smell a rat")
Rat: to hunt rats with dogs
Rat: to work as a scab
Rat: to reverse one's position
Rat: to recant
Rat: a form of cheese (cheddar)

By way of further example, if each and every chair in the world had its own label, we would have nothing but dictionaries related to chairs.

Even with the general abstraction or classifying word *chair*, we have developed a large vocabulary of chair-words (for example, Windsor, Hitchcock, stuffed, swivel, rocking). In short, unless we used a limited number of words to represent an infinite number of things, we could hardly communicate at all. Despite our useful and necessary dictionaries, no word has real meaning except in the particular context in which it is used. Although the variation in meaning may not always be a serious one, the meaning will never be quite the same from one situation to another. This is because words do represent different meanings in different situations and because they do change when we take words for granted and think of them as actual things rather than as what they really are—representations of things. A good speaker must always ask himself, "What does *this* word mean to *this* audience in *this* situation, in *this* context, as used by *this* speaker at *this* time?"

A word may then be thought of as a representation or generalization having meaning according to its context. When we arrange words into the context (or syntax) of a sentence, we are really fitting generalizations together. The meaning of an English sentence is determined not by words alone but primarily by the total arrangement and sequence of the words within it. Even this meaning may be vague if its relationship to the larger paragraph or chapter is not known.

In one sense the communication pattern of a sentence is the systematic exclusion from the listener's attention of meanings he might attach that are *not* intended by the speaker. In short, it may define meanings *not* intended.

Two linguists, Donald J. Lloyd and Harry R. Warfel, illustrate this function clearly and simply. Let us use their sentence: THE YOUNG MAN AT THE CORNER WHO SEEMS VERY MILD BEATS HIS WIFE.

Beginning with *man*, let us use a circle to indicate all the possible meanings of *man* in all potential utterances:

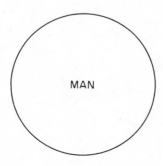

FIGURE 3–1.

We will take *the* as pointing out oné instance of *man*—whatever *man* means. We put a dot in the circle to stand for this one instance.

FIGURE 3–2.

The word *young*—whatever it means—has the force of cutting out of consideration all meanings of *man* that cannot accept the description *young:*

FIGURE 3–3.

The phrase *at the corner* cuts out of consideration all meanings of *man* that cannot be located in that bit of space:

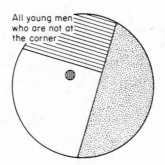

FIGURE 3–4.

The phrase *who seems very mild* cuts out all *young men* who do not *seem mild:*

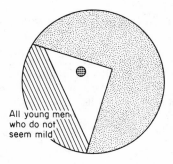

FIGURE 3–5.

The word *beats* cuts out all such men who *do not beat*—whatever *beat* means:

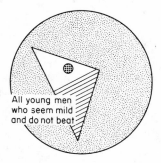

FIGURE 3–6.

The phrase *his wife* limits *beats* and by doing so puts a further limitation on *man*. It excludes all other objects of beating, such as *dogs, opponents,* or *rugs.*

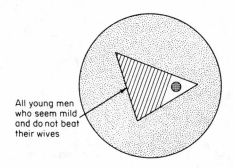

FIGURE 3–7.

This analysis of a sentence[1] shows how a writer or speaker utilizes arrangement and listener or reader attention to delimit meaning.

> The force of the pattern is to cut away meanings not intended. . . . Each word or word-group removes from consideration all instances of the key word that do not accept the qualification expressed in the word or in the group. The utterance reveals a successive removal from attention of the instances of the key word that are not affirmed by the successive elements in the sentence. It cuts a large and unmanageable area of meaning down to size. The whole sentence becomes the equivalent of what has traditionally been called a proper noun: a noun "used to designate a specific individual, place, etc." It is a marvelous operation.[2]

Eight black Wayne State University students did a language project for a speech psychology class in 1972 in which they compiled some eighty Black ghetto words and phrases unfamiliar to most nonghetto students. Five inner-city black students agreed on the definitions, although these may vary somewhat with changes in context and tone of voice. Test yourself:

Spade	A black
Ripe apples	Men with money for the taking
Crackers	White folks
Ofay	A white person
Bring ass to get ass	You'll have to come to me in order for us to fight
Your head going back home	Even if you straighten your hair it will still kink up if you go out in the rain
Slipping you into the dozens	Start talking about your family
Cholly	The white man
Funky	Anything that is truthful or dirty
Git-go	From the start
Caught up	Nothing more to gain
Cop some zees	Get some sleep
Burnt one on	Got drunk
Off your wood	Crazy
Jive	Kidding; false information
Gig	A job; a dance
Slammers	Prison

[1]Reprinted by permission of Alfred A. Knopf, Inc., from *American English in Its Cultural Setting* by Donald J. Lloyd and Harry R. Warfel. Copyright 1956 by Donald J. Lloyd and Harry R. Warfel.

[2]Lloyd and Warfel, *American English in Its Cultural Setting*, p. 109.

Nigger	Anybody that is not Caucasian
Finest vines	Nice clothes
Kicks	Shoes
Going up the side of your head	Being slapped around
Sendin' up kites	Writing letters
Magdaleen	A pure, straight woman
Stable	House of prostitution
Pushin'	Dope peddling
Bookin'	Horse betting
Charley fever	Trying to imitate the white man
Dinner pail	Going to work from 9 til 5
Quickies	Anything you can do to make money, legal or not
86	Get out or cut off
Chalked out	Died of a heart attack
Nursery	Reform school
Stabbin' horses to steal blankets	Barely making it, subsisting
Jigs	Nigger
Stir buggy	Jail-crazy (stir-crazy)
Kinky	Out of your mind
Six months to ride	Six months to live
Caper's cut	Percentage a lookout makes on a crime
Pill joint	Pool hall
Got into the life	Career of prostitution
Put the bleed	To blackmail
In a minute	After a while; at a later date
Brother	Male member of the black race
Bull skating	Being hypocritical; not down to earth and for real
Dude	Male member of black race; boyfriend
Jones	Type of narcotics, withdrawal symptoms, sexual desire
Ice	To put someone off to the side
Get chose	To be selected, as for a date
Get yo' grits together	Get your mind together
Thump	To fight
Love hand	Feeling for sex
Boss	Very acceptable, real good
Jam	45 rpm record or record album; a together song
It's a monster	Something so together as to be almost beyond comprehension
Rip off	To steal
Cop	To steal
Roscoe	A gun
Boon coon	Buddy, friend

Crib	Your home
Blow	To make a serious mistake, to err inexcusably, to mess up
Rags	Clothes
Ride	Car
Broom	To leave
Strides	Pants, trousers
Front off	To pretend, to humiliate
Pluck	Wine
Steam	Wine
Regroup	Reevaluate your situation and pursue a course of improvement; get it together again after it has fallen apart
Skull	Oral sex
Conkin' yo' head	Straightening your hair
Sister	Female member of the black race
For days	True, correct
Smoking	Really together
Stang	To rob
Cat	Any male
Pad	Your home
Scope	To look at
Dig it	To understand something and accept it
Right on	Giving of approval

The group of blacks that undertook this project believed that white students were in a sense intruding culturally when they used the phrase "Right on!" indicating a special emotional attachment to that phrase on the part of blacks. However, word habits change!

The *New York Amsterdam News,* one of the largest black-community newspapers, announced in 1967 that it would no longer use the word "Negro." It would henceforth identify Americans of African descent as Afro-Americans. The Negro Teachers Association of New York City became the African-American Teachers Association.[3] *Ebony* magazine surveyed its readers on the potent question of names or labels by asking them to indicate their preferences for the names *Afram, African-American, Afro-American, Black, Colored, Overseas African,* or *Negro.* The survey results are not reported as of this writing. However, a study by *The Michigan Chronicle* in August 1968 found that in the Detroit area the word "Afro-American" was preferred by its respondents.

Still later, the *Detroit News* polled 218 registered Negro voters in

[3]Lerone Bennett Jr., "What's In A Name?" *Ebony,* 23, No. 1, (November 1967), 46–54.

metropolitan Detroit, producing the following results in order of preference:

	Total Sample (N=218)	Age 21–39 (N=98)	Age 40+ (N=120)
Negro	32%	24%	36%
Afro-American	24	22	26
Black	16	19	13
Colored	16	19	14
Other	12	16	11

The "other" included replies such as "I'd rather be thought of just as a person," or "as an American."[4]

The word "black" indicates that time and context do make a difference. In a 1964 study by Ross and Maddox "black" was found to be offensive to 59 percent of the Negroes surveyed. In 1967 the youth section at the Black Power Conference in Newark led the debate against use of the word "Negro." "Negro" in the 1964 study offended only 15 percent of the blacks sampled. In the early 1950s, sensitive teachers found "African" was discriminatory to many Afro-American students. Ross and Maddox comment:

> The reasons for some of the racial potency attached to some words by Negroes are often difficult to understand, and perhaps it is even more difficult for the Negro to understand *why* the non-Negro should find them so difficult. In part this difficulty may be attributed to the fact that there was an almost complete lack of Negroes in some sections of the country previous to the migrations begun after World War I. Besides this, an outright discrimination for many years thereafter allowed for little feedback on Negro reaction to communications. For example, in 1913 a New York department store advertised shoes as "nigger brown," and right up to the 40s, we sold "Nigger-Hair Tobacco."[5]

In a 1973 language survey by Ross and Mosley in the Detroit metropolitan area preliminary data indicate additional change since 1968.[6] "Assuming an interracial communication situation (person-to-person, speaker, radio, TV), which of the following do you consider the most appropriate identification for a non-white?"

[4]"Negro, Colored or Black?" *The Detroit News*, Sept. 8, 1968, p. 1.

[5]G. A. Maddox and R. S. Ross, "Strong Words," *Childhood Education*, 45 (January 1969), pp. 260–64.

[6]R. S. Ross and A. Mosley," Identification Preferences" (research material, Wayne State University, 1973); see also R. Popa, "Black Is Beautiful to More Blacks, 2 at WSU Find," *Detroit News*, June 13, 1973, p. 25.

	Total Sample (N=300)	Age 18–39 (N=200)	Age 40+ (N=100)
Negro	14.3%	10 %	23%
Afro-American	14	15	12
Black	63	66.5	56
Colored	4	3.5	5
Other	4.7	5	4
	100.0%	100.0%	100%

The sensitive nature of language and collecting data about it was indicated by a refusal of many black subjects to be surveyed unless they could also react to "the most appropriate identification for a Caucasian?" These data are shown below:

	Total Sample (N=300)	Age 18–39 (N=200)	Age 40+ (N=100)
Caucasion	25%	23.5%	29%
European-American	9	8	10
White	57	61	50
Anglo	1	1	1
Other	8	6.5	10
	100%	100.0%	100%

A sample of 200 whites is now reported for comparison. This tabulation shows what whites prefer to be called, and what they think blacks prefer to be called.

	Total Sample (N=200)	Age 18–39 (N=100)	Age 40+ (N=100)
Caucasian	28%	30%	26%
European-American	8	4	12
White	58	62	54
Anglo	0	0	0
Other	6	4	8
	100%	100%	100%
Negro	20.5%	16%	25%
Afro-American	5.5	9	2
Black	49.5	59	40
Colored	9.5	2	17
Other	15	14	16
	100.0%	100%	100%

Note the change in reactions to the word "black." In 1964 it was offensive in almost any context to 59 percent of the Negro sample; 40

percent of the whites also found it offensive when used to describe Negroes (Maddox-Ross study). In 1973 63 percent of the Negroes preferred to be called blacks and 50 percent of the whites agreed (Ross-Mosley study). The differences between 1968 and 1973 show that "black" has now become the leading designation among blacks (16 percent preferred it in 1968 and 63 percent in 1973.

In a 1968 article entitled "Negro, Black or Afro-American?" John A. Morsell, then assistant executive director of the NAACP, discussed the semantic pitfalls attending the choice of an appropriate term:

> In point of fact, there is simply no other word [than Negro] we can use if we wish to speak solely and exclusively of persons of black African descent. Black Africans, New Guineans, aboriginal Australians, East Indians (especially the harijans) and a host of diverse racial and ethnic strains are all properly called "blacks," and "black" therefore fails the tests of exclusivity and specificity.
>
> "African-American" and "Afro-American" are equally deficient, since Ian Smith of Rhodesia is an African, as are President Nasser, the King of Morocco, and any of the thousands of Whites who hold citizenship in Nigeria, Ghana, Kenya, and other black African states. Should any of these, or their descendants, become United States citizens, they, too, would be "African-Americans."
>
> Only "Negro" possesses, by reason of years of wide and continued usage, a clear, specific and exclusive denotation: a person of black African origin or descent. Proponents of other names may object that it is a white man's word; but so is "black" and so is "African-American." All these are "white man's words," by virtue of their being English. Moreover, it should be recalled that "blacks" was the white man's first designation for black African; historical circumstances brought into common English use the Spanish word for black which is "Negro."
>
> The intolerance with which the cause of this or that designation is pressed carries a special danger. We have already been told by some of the more extreme advocates of "black" that it is to be more than just an ethnic term: it is to be an elite designation, reserved for only those whom the extremists deem worthy, without regard to skin color or anything else.
>
> Whether this absurdity gets very far or not, it is still a very likely prospect that, given de rigeur usage of "black," succeeding generations will indeed make darkness of skin an elite attribute which will irrevocably divide the Negro population. There could be no more ironic outcome of the generations of struggle against color prejudice than to find Negroes themselves split into rival camps on the basis of skin color.
>
> This danger is great enough, it seems to me, to justify reasonable men in combating any effort to restrict our usage to a single term, whatever it may be. Whites in particular should not, in an excess of fear less they offend, cater to a movement of intolerance and divisiveness.[7]

[7] John A. Morsell, "Negro, Black or Afro-American?" *New York Times*, July 20, 1968, p. 11. © 1968 by the New York Times Company. Reprinted by permission.

In light of the above studies and commentary, it is not difficult to understand why certain sensitivities exist and why the Negro may sometimes react negatively to words not intended to be derogatory. If Americans were more aware of the words and phrases likely to provoke hostility and more cautious in their usages, better communication between the races might result.

Were Confucius alive today, he might well be pained by our contemporary fascination with slang. He once said, "The first step in finding out the truth is to call things by their right names." The terms listed under "Slang Language" should be easy for you to recognize if their meanings don't change before publication. *Dates* become critical where meaning in language is concerned.

SLANG LANGUAGE

Bug	To irritate someone
Bug out	To disappear
Cop out	To plead guilty; to fail in an endeavor
Loser	A person who is unacceptable
Catch some rays	To sunbathe
Hang-up	A preoccupation or psychological block
Hung-up	Stymied
Kook	Eccentric person
Animal	A sloppy or uncouth person
Swinger	One who adopts the latest style or trend
Mod	Unconventional style of dress
Punt	To give up
Flake out	Go to sleep
Stay loose	To relax
Put on	To fool or bluff
Dig	To be in agreement; to understand
Cool it	Calm down
Turned-on	Excited
Up-tight	Tense, nervous
Put down	To deflate someone's ego
Gross	Ugly, nasty
Mover	An aggressive person
Cool	In vogue, admired
Freak out	To withdraw from rational behavior

Context obviously makes a difference; there are more standard meanings. Members of the drug subculture might translate many of these words still differently. When "bad" means good, "Confucius have problem."

Verbal obscenity is a part of the modern scene. Words can hurt us.

According to James Michener the National Guardsmen involved in the Kent State tragedy were particularly enraged by the obscenities shouted by female demonstrators. "To hear obscenities in common usage from girls who could have been their sisters produced a psychic shock which ran deep. To many of the Guardsmen these girls had removed themselves from any special category of 'women and children.' "[8]

The riots at the 1968 Democratic National Convention in Chicago likewise involved much obscenity and counterobscenity. Bowers and Ochs in *The Rhetoric of Agitation and Control* say flatly that "the tactic that probably prompted the 'police riot,' the violent suppression witnessed by millions on television, was the use of obscenity."[9]

How we treat verbal obscenity in rhetoric is a difficult and critical question. The ancient rhetoricians state clearly and without qualification that verbal obscenity should be rejected as a legitimate rhetorical strategy. J. Dan Rothwell, however, suggests a more up-to-date response:

> Neither denunciation nor suppression of its use is an adequate response to the fact of verbal obscenity; the students of rhetoric must seek to understand the purposes and effects of this rhetorical strategy. Despite centuries of negative criticism, verbal obscenity has become a more frequent rhetorical device. It is successful in creating attention, in discrediting an enemy, in provoking violence, in fostering identification, and in providing catharsis. Its effects are governed by a variety of circumstances which need to be understood more fully. It has precipitated a police riot, brutal beatings, and even death. Hoping it will go away will not make it so. It is time to accept verbal obscenity as a significant rhetorical device and help discover appropriate responses to its use."[10]

W. W. Bauer, a physician, put it well. "Words can be many things. They can be weapons. They can be messengers of peace. The right word can soothe like the soft touch of a gentle hand. The wrong word can lacerate like a sword. Even truth, unkindly or unskillfully spoken, can be as deadly as any poison."[11]

The emotional interpretations attached to language demand careful audience analysis and word selection on the part of the speaker. Words are not things or emotions, but we often act as if they were. Language

---

[8]James A. Michener, "Kent State: What Happened and Why," *Reader's Digest*, April 1971, p. 232; see also S. I. Hayakawa, "The Uses of Obscenity," *The Saturday Evening Post*, Spring 1972, p. 123.

[9]John Waite Bowers and Donovan J. Ochs, *The Rhetoric of Agitation and Control* (Reading, Mass.: Addison-Wesley Publishing Co., 1971), p. 70.

[10]Dan Rothwell, "Verbal Obscenity: Time for Second Thoughts," *Western Speech*, 35, No. 4 (1971), 242.

[11]W. W. Bauer, "The Bloodless Emergency," *This Week Magazine*, October 23, 1966, p. 25.

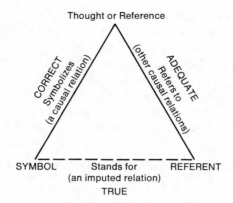

FIGURE 3-8.   Ogden and Richards Model

is by nature abstract and involves generalizations about concrete or real things.

ABSTRACTION

The heart of the difficulty with language is the confusion of the word with the thing for which it stands. The further we get from the referent the more problems of meaning that arise. Meaning is thought to involve three elements: a person having thoughts, a symbol (or sign), and a referent. The triangle of Ogden and Richards is a classic explanation (see Figure 3-8).[12]

When we receive a symbol or sign, it travels to our *thought or reference* center. As in our transactional communication model, our storehouse of experience is consulted to locate the thing or *referent* to which it refers. The triangle is represented as having no base to make the crucial point that the symbol and its referent are not *directly* related. The word is not the thing! You cannot sit on the word *chair* or write with the word *pencil!*

Line A indicates what a person hopefully perceives as a *correct* symbol, in this case the word *CHAIR*. Line B represents the cognitive selecting and sorting of knowledge and experience to hopefully locate an *adequate* referent. The broken line C makes the point that the *word* chair and a *real* chair are not the same. Clear communication calls for a referent,

[12]C. K. Ogden and I. A. Richards, *The Meaning of Meaning* (New York: Harcourt, Brace and Company, 1936, London: Routledge & Kegan Paul, Ltd.), p. 11.

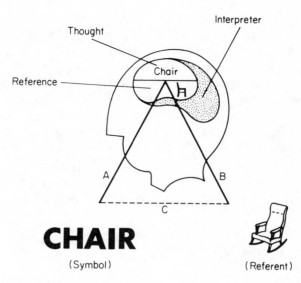

FIGURE 3-9. A Model of Meaning

a reference, and a symbol, which leads us to the subject of misuse of abstractions.

Abstracting is a process of thinking in which we selectively leave out details about concrete or real things. The nature of perception indicates that we are dealing with at least two factors, namely, (1) sensation and (2) interpretation of the stimuli impinging upon our senses. This interpretation is heavily controlled by our individual knowledge, experience, and emotional set. For this reason, as well as the limitations of our language system discussed previously, all language involves an element of abstraction.

The process of abstraction may be classified into levels. For example, we have cars, sportscars, and Corvettes. The Corvette is a first-order abstraction, that is, it is a very special, specific type of sportscar, which in turn is a type of car. As we move from lower- to higher-order abtractions, we tend to consider fewer and fewer details of the specific or original object. Another way of looking at abstracting is to consider first-hand observations as facts, but facts which may never be described in an absolutely complete way. If we become divorced from firsthand descriptions, we are in a different order of abstraction—inference. Most simply, an inference goes beyond what is observed. If an ambulance is in your driveway when you return home, you may say, "One of my family has been seriously hurt," This is an inference. You must go into the house to see if it is valid. Upon entering the house, you may find

a close friend excitedly telling your healthy family about his new business venture of converting station wagons into ambulances. Suppose
you have been told by a resort owner that the fishing is great on the
edge of some weeds. If you are a veteran fisherman, you will ask, "What
does 'great' mean?" You will want more than inferences, namely, descriptions of this great fishing ("Just this morning a fellow took five bass
in two hours"). Of course, in dealing with fishermen one might be just
a little suspicious of the reliability of the description (another inference).
One scholar put it this way: "The reliability of inferences depends on the
reliability of the descriptive premises, and description is more reliable
than inference."[13] When we are in the realm of inference, then, we are
dealing with probability rather than certainty.

SPECIFICITY

When we support our inferential statements with specific descriptive
statements and examples, we will not only be using more accurate, but
probably more interesting, language. The question of how much specificity to use is not always an easy one. For example, a physicist, in explaining atomic fission to us, might choose only terms that are closely
related to his referents—that is, highly specific, technical, and scientific
terms. He is in one sense using accurate language, but his message may
be very long (because of the detail) and for nonphysicists very difficult
to understand. Should he decide to eliminate detail in an effort to use
less time and to avoid technical language in an effort to sustain interest,
he will then lose precision of meaning; his listeners may attach a wider
range of meanings from their own experiences than he had intended,
and this might lead to serious distortion, confusion, or contradiction.

For the speaker, the answer to this dilemma is typically found in the
interest and previous knowledge of the audience. Just how important is
precision in relation to this subject and this audience? Is there a potential
danger involved, such as in a speech on drug prescriptions or hypodermic
injections to an audience of student nurses? Time is another factor
in resolving this prbolem. Classroom speeches will tend to be short, and
this fact alone may foster the problems of overgeneralization, lack of
specificity, and inaccuracy of meaning. It is probably true that it is easier
to give a long speech than a short one.

---

[13]Alfred Korzybski, *Science and Sanity* (Lancaster, Pa.: The Science Press Printing
Co., 1933), p. 479.

LANGUAGE AND PERSONALITY

Language and the particular character you give it through usage has obvious importance in terms of your message. However, language habits alone often convey our personality (or assumed personality) to the listener. For example, extreme cases of talkativeness or undertalkativeness are often indications of emotional maladjustment. This pattern may afflict all of us in moments of distress, peril, or unhappiness, but a consistent pattern may call for professional help. As was indicated in Chapter 1, the problem of autistic thinking, or interpreting communication only in terms of one's desires, is a serious problem; when practiced consistently, it is thought to be indicative of what the psychiatrist calls paranoia. One of the most characteristic language patterns of schizophrenics is an apparent confusion between words and things. The words are taken not as representations of reality, but as reality itself. For the schizophrenic, objective systematic abstraction is difficult, and he is extremely one-sided and opinionated. The sobering thought in discussing the extreme language habits of maladjusted people is that we are all guilty to some degree of doing all these things. It behooves us to be aware of our patterns lest we too represent a one-value world of words without referents. All "normal" speakers should ponder Wendell Johnson's compelling description of the linguistically irresponsible behavior of schizophrenics:

(1) An "emotional flatness," an unresponsive, poker-faced air of detachment; (2) a grotesque confusion of sense and nonsense, essentially the same tone of voice, facial expression, and general manner being employed in making sensible remarks as in uttering the purest gibberish; (3) an apparent lack of self-criticism, a striking failure to show any glimmer of curiosity about whether the listener understands or agrees; and (4) a general confusion or identification of level of abstraction, as though all levels were one and the same, there being no apparent differentiation between higher and lower orders of inference and between inference and description.[14]

If the last paragraph frightened you just a little, this is a healthy sign, for your powers of evaluation had to go beyond just the words. Remember that your language habits reflect your personality. We shall now examine some practical suggestions for improving your language and avoiding

[14] Wendell Johnson, *People in Quandaries* (New York: Harper & Row, Publishers, 1946), p. 275.

linguistic behavior patterns that convey unintended and undesirable meanings.

IMPROVING YOUR LANGUAGE HABITS AND SEMANTICS *Study meaning of words*

Almost any good course in speech, whatever its context (radio, television, public speaking, persuasion, semantics, rhetoric, correction, theater, communication, discussion, or debate), puts a high premium on language habits. The instructor will criticize you diligently, for he knows that proper language habits will make it easier for you to adjust to the linguistic demands of college life.

Reading and listening, when done systematically, will help improve your language behavior. In both reading and listening, you are essentially involved in the receiving and decoding function of communication. Critical, objective listening and reading habits have been an intimate part in the training of almost all famous speakers.[15]

When reading or listening to a speech, try to determine what the words mean to the speaker and how the timing of the communication might alter the meaning. All the communication signals and cues have to be considered in critical listening; as was discussed earlier, the non-word signals (gestures, visual aids, vocal emphasis, and others) are an intimate part of the message. The way in which an idea is stated cannot really be divorced from the idea itself. Perhaps the most important aspect of listening, as well as reading, pertains to the listener's awareness of his own beliefs, prejudices, or lack of knowledge; *what* we believe profoundly influences our ability to perceive objectively. This is not to suggest that one should not believe anything. Were this the case, we might never make any kind of a necessary decision. The point is simply to know more precisely *what* you believe and be aware of its role in your listening and reading habits.

It should be evident to you by this time that it is literally impossible for a person to "say exactly what he means." Much of our language behavior is what S. I. Hayakawa calls presymbolic[16]—that is, it may function even without recognizable speech or perhaps with symbols that approach the character of an idiom. A grunt from my office partner at 8:00 A.M. means "Good morning, it's good to see you." When you pass a friend

---

[15]See W. N. Brigance, ed., *History and Criticism of American Public Address* (New York: McGraw-Hill Book Company, 1943) , p. vii.

[16]S. I. Hayakawa, *Language in Thought and Action* (New York: Harcourt, Brace & World, Inc., 1949), p. 77.

on the street and he says "Hi," how does this really differ from "How are you?" Does "Nice day" mean just that and no more?

A favorite illustration of many teachers regarding this point concerns a man staring dejectedly at a very flat tire. A smiling farmer comes up and asks "Got a flat tire?" If we take his words in an absolutely literal sense his communication appears stupid indeed and we might answer, "Can't you see, birdbrain?" A famous psychiatrist interprets the words "Got a flat tire?" as follows:

> Hello—I see you are in trouble. I'm a stranger to you but I might be your friend now that I have a chance to be if I had any assurance that my friendship would be welcomed. Are you approachable? Are you a decent fellow? Would you appreciate it if I helped you? I would like to do so but I don't want to be rebuffed. This is what my voice sounds like. What does your voice sound like?[17]

When language is used in a presymbolic sense, we have to look considerably beyond the actual words to get the real meaning intended. We must take precautions to see that in our efforts to become alert, critical listeners, we do not become so literal-minded that we mistake tact and social grace for inaneness, hypocrisy, or stupidity. Much of what we refer to as small talk is in part presymbolic language. In the interest of being an objective and honest receiver or listener, we must strive to distinguish presymbolic from symbolic language.

Let us now look at some specific actions you might take as a communicative and responsible speaker to improve your use of language.

SEMANTICS AND GENERAL SEMANTICS

In the view of S. I. Hayakawa *semantics* may be defined as

> (1) in modern logic, the study of the laws and conditions under which signs and symbols, including words, may be said to be meaningful; semiotic [pertaining to signs]; and (2) the study of the relation between words and things, later extended into the study of the relations between language, thought and behavior, that is, how human action is influenced by words, whether spoken by others or to oneself in thought; significs. The word was originally used to mean (3) in philology, the historical study of changes in the meaning of words; semasiology [study of semantic change].[18]

[17]Karl Menninger, *Love Against Hate* (New York: Harcourt, Brace & World, Inc., 1942), pp. 268–69.

[18]S. I. Hayakawa, *Language, Meaning and Maturity* (New York: Harper & Row, Publishers, 1954), p. 19.

Semantics is specifically and primarily involved with meaning. Other areas and disciplines interested in language have typically not shown the same concern for meaning. *Linguistics*, until recently with the advent of psycholinguistics and social linguistics, has been primarily interested in structural description and the science of language. It includes phonetics, phonemics, morphology, and syntax. *Philology* is primarily interested in the study of written records, authenticity, and form. *English* is primarily interested in language in terms of rules for combining words into sentences and all that goes with syntax. Other areas have even more obvious interests in language: *anthropology*, as a reflection of culture; *engineering*, in terms of information theory and cybernetics; *philosophy*, *psychology*, and others. *Speech communication* has shown the broadest interest in denotation, connotation, style, phonology, and non-verbal signals, including meanings, semantics, and general semantics.

The term *general semantics* is credited to Alfred Korzybski and is amplified in his book *Science and Sanity*.[19] If semantics concerns primarily meaning and changes in meaning, general semantics extends these concepts to include relationships between symbols and behavior. Korzybski was interested in man's total response to his environment, particularly how man evaluates and uses language and how language affects his attitudes, feelings, and behavior. It was Korzybski's thesis that much of the misunderstanding in the world was caused by too dogmatic an internalization of basic Aristotelian logic assumptions, particularly in the human social realm. Since understanding and objective communication are heavily dependent upon the relationship between language and reality, it follows for Korzybski, that any system that was oversimplified in this way presented a real threat to one's psychological and emotional flexibility, maturity, and sanity.

To offset bad habits of language and evaluation Korzybski suggests three fundamental principles that he thought of as essentially non-Aristotelian. These are based on an analogy between language and the reality it represents and a map and the territory it represents. (1) A map is *not* the territory; that is, words are not things. (2) A map does not represent *all* of the territory; one cannot say *everything* about anything. (3) A map is self-reflexive; a map should include a map of the map of the map, etc.[20] That we use words to talk about words is another example of self-reflexiveness.

If in formal logic we speak of a:

19Korzybski, *Science and Sanity*.

20For an excellent discussion of semantics see Hayakawa, *Language, Meaning and Maturity*; see also *Language in Thought and Action*, and Stuart Chase, *The Tyranny of Words* (New York: Harcourt, Brace & Co., 1938).

1. *Law of identity,* a thing is what it is, a man is a man,
2. *Law of excluded middle,* anything is either A or non-A, true or not true, either or, two value,
3. *Law of noncontradiction,* something cannot be both A and non-A, true and not true.

then general semantics postulates:

(1) *the principle of nonidentity,*
(2) *the principle of nonallness, and,*
(3) *the principle of self-reflexiveness*

Some examples of how the general semanticist would have us modify formal logic are shown in Figure 3–10.

The propositional nature of language can be a problem in some language systems. That is, even absurd statements can be grammatically correct (e.g., "red is green"). The rules of formal logic have an obvious utility, as we shall see in Chapter 11, "The Logical Supports of Persuasion." The problem is that because of the propositional nature of language one might become too literal-minded and develop an evaluational rigidity that leads ultimately to poor logic, poor language habits, emotional imbalance, and misunderstanding. The general semantics principles combat such dangers by allowing a communicator to evaluate his own evaluative process through the following kinds of checks or rules.

The *is problem* is related to the principles of nonidentity. Simply stated, words are *not* things even though we obviously must use them as substitutes. The map is not the territory, as anyone who has ever been misled by an old map can readily tell you. You cannot write with the word *pencil.* Hayakawa comments that the injunction to "call a spade a spade" is profoundly misleading because it implies that we call it a spade because that's what it is. Language and thought are not identical. Words are not the things signified (the referents). Dictionaries do *not* give the referents, but only the meanings that people have given to words!

The *et cetera rule* is related to the principle of nonallness. In a sense this also refers to the consciousness of abstracting—an awareness that you are leaving something out. One cannot say everything or the last word on a given matter—there is always more to be said. A practical implication is that the good speaker should leave his listeners with the impression that he has not attempted to say the last word on a subject. He should avoid alienating his listeners by not appearing to be a naive know-it-all, blinded by zeal, bias, or prejudice.

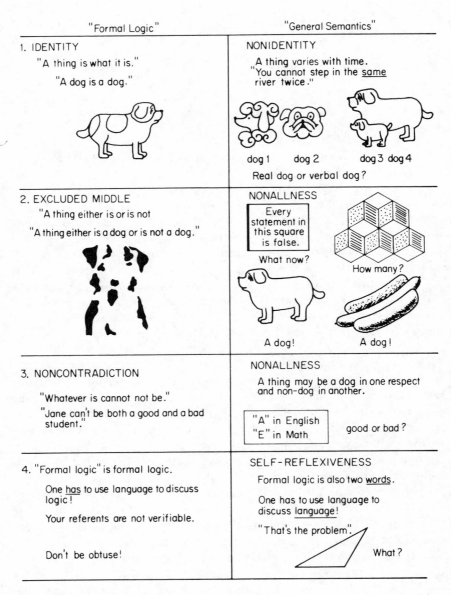

FIGURE 3-10.

The *indexing rule* relates to overstatement and overgeneralization. All Democrats are not alike, nor are all Republicans alike. This rule would have us *think* in terms of, if not actually index, Democrat[1], Democrat[2], Democrat[3], and so on. It is an admonition against taking stereotypes seriously and failing to appreciate individual differences.

One of the most prevalent communication faults on the part of student speakers is spurious generalization. This is the problem of selectively leaving out details and arriving at an overstatement or concluding after only a cursory examination that a thing is true beyond any shadow of doubt. If upon driving into Detroit for the first time you (1) witnessed a serious accident, (2) observed a truck exceeding the speed limit, and (3) got a dented fender in a busy intersection, you might be tempted to draw some strong conclusions, and speak in strong language about the character of Detroit drivers. However, an examination of comparative safety records, driver education programs, and driver insurance rates would be minimal prerequisites for any intelligent discussion about Detroit drivers. Even then you might want to hedge your generalizations by noting that Detroit has more cars per capita than any other city in the world.

A violently antiunion student speaker opened one of his class speeches with the words "Unions are ruining this country. I am going to prove to you that they are entirely corrupt and more dangerous than the Communist Party." The sound of this language was enough for his opponents to throw up an emotional communication barrier so that not much persuasion took place. The most interesting part of this story is that it was the pro-management people who were most critical of his speech. Even when a sophisticated audience largely agrees with your point of view, it can be offended by extreme overstatement and overgeneralization, for these are indications of immaturity, emotional insecurity, or stupidity.

The irony and tyranny of overgeneralization is that it is usually not intended—it seems so obvious that all Detroit drivers are crazy! When a person speaks from firsthand experience in a sincere and friendly voice without being aware or conscious of his faulty abstracting or generalizing, we are faced with a serious problem. The speaker carries an ethical responsibility proportionate to his reputation. Perhaps this is why sophisticated men of high ethical qualities are often accused of qualifying things to the point of vagueness—which itself raises the ethical question as to how much you can qualify before you in effect completely dodge your obligations and responsibilities. The communication problems of generalization are complicated, frustrating, and often dangerous for the speaker. Once this fact is clearly understood, you have already solved much of the practical problem, for it is in being *aware* or conscious of abstracting and generalizing that we find the beginnings of the checks and balances that inhibit overstatement and reckless generalization. A practical way of implementing this awareness is to qualify and index statements with great care.

Dating your language is another form of indexing worthy of a special rule. The date of an event often significantly affects the meaning a listener will attach to it. "At last the Japanese people have taken the actions that will restore their rightful dignity." Certainly we would attach different meanings to this hypothetical statement by the Emperor of Japan according to whether it was uttered on:

January 7, 1925 (No special significance)
December 7, 1941 (Pearl Harbor)
September 2, 1945 (Surrender of Japan)
July 1, 1968 (Return of Okinawa)

A favorite exam question of one psychology professor was "What are Thorndike's laws of learning?" The challenging character of this question is evident from the fact that Thorndike changed his mind about some of his laws of learning and made this clear in his writings only after 1930. If the student had read only his pre-1930 writings, he would inevitably give the wrong answer.

When we respond to words or language apart from meaning and in an almost automatic, emotional way, we are guilty of *signal response*. If we can delay signal responses even a split second, we may get closer to the referents by understanding the total context. Did he *really* intend what I'm thinking? Was it just poor word choice? Am I a little oversensitive?

The *either-or response* is a type of dead-level abstracting that indicates that one's language habits are concealing differences of degree. The despot or demagogue uses this device with regularity. All of us in moments of frustration or desperation seem to revert to "They're all no good," "You're either for me or against me," or "You never will understand." When we routinely use words like *all, nobody, everybody*, and *never* we are guilty of a false-to-fact use of language. The speaker guilty of these exaggerations runs great risks of creating resentment, particularly among sophisticated audiences.

An extremely irritating form of this either-or, dead-level abstracting is something we might call *arrogant dismissal*. Irving Lee illustrates it most clearly in the following pattern of disagreement:

> The mood of dismissal, in which a man makes it clear that he wishes to go no farther, to talk no more about something which is to him impossible, unthinkable, wrong, unnecessary, or just plain out of the question. He has spoken and there is little use in trying to make him see otherwise. If he has his way there will be no more discussion on the matter. "It won't work and that's all there is to it. . . . I refuse to listen to any more of this nonsense. . . . Anybody who comes to such a conclusion has something wrong

with him. . . . We've never worked that way before and we aren't going to start."[21]

People who consistently engage in this kind of behavior are considered by Wendell Johnson to have serious "quandries." Simplistic language like this usually reflects simplistic thinking or a high degree of emotional involvement.

Finally (and that itself is a dangerous word), try to think like the listener; try to understand your subject and position from *his* point of view. Audience analysis is a critical part of public speaking. Knowing what you think is equally important. If you do not care what the audience thinks, are not very sure of your own purpose, and are unaware of your preferences, your beliefs, and your word meanings, you are in for a difficult and frustrating series of speeches. The meaning of any speech is really in the mind of the listener. You must so manipulate your language to help him select and sort from his word representations something approximating your purpose.

> Humpty-Dumpty said: "There's glory for you." "I don't know what you mean by 'glory,' " Alice said. Humpty-Dumpty smiled contemptuously. "Of course you don't—till I tell you." . . . "But 'glory' doesn't mean 'a nice knock-down argument,' " Alice objected. "When I use a word," Humpty-Dumpty said in a rather scornful tone, "It means just what I choose it to mean, neither more nor less."[22]

SUMMARY

Language has been discussed primarily in the context of code and symbol. Oral language calls for more rigorous training than other forms because of the larger number of concomitant signals. Voice, for example, has a powerful influence upon meaning. A speaker's appearance and his gestures represent still other concomitant signals that affect the listeners.

Words are a form of symbol. A word is a generally agreed upon representation of a thing. There are obviously more things and concepts in the world than there are words, so a word may be thought of as a representation or generalization having meaning according to its context. A speaker should ask himself, "What does *this* word mean to *this* audience in *this* situation, in *this* context, as used by *this* speaker at *this* time?" A good sentence systematically excludes from the listener's at-

[21]Irving J. Lee, *How to Talk with People* (New York: Harper & Row, Publishers, 1952), p. 46.
[22]Lewis Carroll, *Through the Looking-Glass* (Cleveland: The World Publishing Company, 1946), p. 245.

tention meanings he might attach that are not intended by the speaker—in short, it qualifies by defining meanings *not* intended.

How we should approach verbal obscenity in rhetoric is a difficult problem. The ancient rhetoricians believed that verbal obscenity should be rejected as a rhetorical strategy, but recent commentators are beginning to question this view.

Abstraction is that process of thinking in which we selectively leave out details about concrete or real things. The heart of the difficulty with language is the confusion of the word with the thing for which it stands. The further we get from the referent, the more problems of meaning that arise. Short speeches may foster overgeneralization. This is why short speeches often call for more preparation than long ones.

Language habits reflect your personality. Seriously maladjusted people can often be identified by their language habits. Speech courses, together with attentive reading and listening, will help you learn proper language behavior.

The *way* in which you say a thing is often as important as *what* you say. The listener as well as the speaker should be aware of his own beliefs, prejudices, or lack of knowledge. It is almost impossible to say *exactly* what you mean. We must take precautions not to become so literal-minded that we mistake tact and social grace for hypocrisy or stupidity. We must strive to distinguish presymbolic from symbolic language.

Semantics may be defined as the study of the laws and conditions under which signs and symbols may be said to be meaningful. It is the study of the relationship between words and things and, further, how human action is influenced by words. Of the many disciplines and fields related to semantics, *speech communication* has shown the broadest interest in denotation, connotation, style, phonology, nonverbal signals, and so on, including meanings, semantics, and general semantics. Semantics concerns primarily meaning and changes in meaning; general semantics extends these concepts to include relationships between symbols and behavior. Alfred Korzybski is the founder of general semantics. It was his thesis that much misunderstanding in the world was caused by overly dogmatic internalization of formal logic, particularly in the social realm. Korzybski postulated three principles designed to offset bad habits of evaluation. These were based on an analogy he drew between language and the reality it represents and a map and the territory is represents. (1) A map *is* not the territory; that is, words are not things. (2) A map does not represent *all* of the territory; one cannot say everything about anything. (3) A map is self-reflexive; that is, a map should include a map of the map, of the map, etc. These postulates are known as the principles of (1) *nonidentity*, (2) *nonallness*, and (3) *self-reflexiveness*.

The propositional nature of language can be a problem in some language systems. If one becomes too literal-minded and evaluationally rigid, logic language habits may be impaired and misunderstanding and emotional imbalance may result. Such dangers may be combated through sufficient appreciation of the *is* problem, the need for indexing and dating one's statements, and the need to avoid signal responses and either-or responses.

Sophisticated audiences are offended by overstatement and overgeneralization, even when they agree with the speaker's point of view. The speaker carries a tremendous ethical responsibility. It is in being conscious of abstraction, generalization, and semantics that we begin to meet our ethical responsibilities. Qualify your statements appropriately. Try to think like the listener. Select your language so as to help the listener select and sort from his word representations something approximating your meaning.

Speech Communication Principles

1. Despite the existence of dictionaries, which are both useful and necessary, no word has real meaning except in the particular context in which it is used.

2. Part of the communication pattern of a good sentence consists in the systematic exclusion from the listener's attention of meanings not intended by the speaker.

3. There is an emotional dimension to words. Words can hurt us.

4. The heart of the difficulty with language is the confusion of the word with the thing for which it stands: words are not their referents; one cannot say everything about anything; we use words to talk about words (self-reflexiveness).

5. Language habits often convey our personality (or assumed personality) to the listener.

6. It is literally impossible for a person to "say exactly what he means."

7. Much of our language behavior is presymbolic; we must look beyond the words for the meaning.

8. The date of an event or statement often significantly affects the meaning a listener will attach to it.

9. If one becomes too literal-minded and evaluationally rigid, he will likely display poor logic, bad language habits, misunderstanding, and even emotional imbalance.

A. *General Learning Outcomes*

   1. We should learn the cardinal importance of language habits and semantics as they relate to meaning and one's total communication effectiveness.

   2. We should learn about the sensitive nature of words and language segments and their impact upon human behavior and understanding.

   3. We should learn that language habits affect and reflect our personality.

   4. We should learn that unless we develop a consciousness of abstraction, generalization, and semantics, we are not meeting the ethical responsibilities of an educated communicator.

B. *Specific Learning Outcomes*

   1. We should learn and be able to illustrate the emotional and cultural dimension of words through personal experience.

   2. We should learn and be able to illustrate the role of context in relation to meaning.

   3. We should learn and be able to reproduce the triangle of Ogden and Richards.

   4. We should learn the difference between presymbolic and symbolic language and be able to produce several examples showing why the difference is important.

   5. We should learn the three basic principles of general semantics and be able to define and illustrate each in a short oral or written report.

   6. We should be able to relate the foregoing general and specific learning outcomes to the speech communication principles enumerated above.

C. *Communication Competencies*

   1. We should be able to apply, in a ten-minute dialogue, the test of context before determining language meaning to the satisfaction of an audience of fifteen to twenty-five who are familiar with the context of this chapter.

   2. We should develop a sensitivity toward words and language as they affect meaning and interpersonal communication to the satisfaction of the rest of the class and/or the instructor.

3. Our language behavior should be characterized by awareness of the *is* problem and the *et cetera* and indexing rules.

4. Our listening and critical behavior should be characterized by a more objective and flexible language sensitivity than usually pertains.

5. We should learn to look for meanings in people, not just symbols.

D. *Study Projects and Tasks*

1. Collect two examples showing context confusion that caused language to mean different things to different people.

2. On one page list five words or short language segments that "turn you off" (almost regardless of context) and try to explain why.

3. Interview a person of a different race or culture (or subculture) regarding the language he finds most offensive. Report results in one page or less.

4. Find an advertisement or commercial that you feel is racially or culturally debasing (linguistically) and explain why.

5. Language can be quite tricky when it deliberately takes advantage of its propositional function, context, and the receiver's experience. See if you can answer and untangle the following. Discuss.

   a. How many members of each species did Moses take aboard the Ark? _____

   b. If you take 2 apples from 3 apples, how many do you have? _____

   c. How many outs are there in an inning in baseball? _____

   d. Can a man living in North Carolina be buried west of the Mississippi? _____

   e. Can a man in South Carolina marry his widow's sister? _____

   f. If a farmer lost all but nine of his seventeen sheep, how many would he have? _____

   g. If a doctor told you to take three pills, one every half-hour, how many hours would they last? _____

   h. Does England have a Fourth of July? _____

   i. How many birthdays does a man have in his average lifetime? _____

   j. How many months have 28 days? _____

6. Some of you will have more trouble with the following test items* than others. Find out why. What does it tell us about language?

A. A "gas head" is a person who has a:
1. fast car.
2. stable of "lace."
3. "process."
4. habit of stealing cars.
5. long jail record for arson.

B. If a man is called a "blood," then he is a:
1. fighter.
2. Mexican-American.
3. Negro.
4. hungry hemophile.
5. redman or Indian.

C. A "handkerchief head" is:
1. a cool cat.
2. a porter.
3. an Uncle Tom.
4. a hoddi.
5. a preacher.

D. "Jive" is to "stiff" as "konk" is to:
1. lame.
2. weird.
3. screw.
4. blast.
5. pimp.

E. If a man is called a "splib," he is:
1. a scrupulous narcotics pusher.
2. a fast-talking social worker.
3. a white trying to be black.
4. a brother.
5. somebody of little or no importance

F. "Out of sight" is a phrase akin to:
1. "Blind Lemon Jefferson."
2. "somethin' else."
3. "pullin' up."
4. "out of mind."
5. "lay it on me."

G. "Deuce and a quarter" is similar to:
1. a card and a coin.
2. a Negro and a hustle.
3. a car.
4. twenty-seven cents.
5. an after-hours joint.

H. "Mountain Oysters" and "Guts" are closely related to:
1. the Bowery Boys.
2. inveterate lovers of swine.
3. Bayou and Delta Valley fishermen.
4. a West Virginia ridge runner with a six-string guitar.
5. none of these.

7. Prepare an oral report or essay, attempting to prove or disprove any of the speech communication principles listed earlier.

8. Examine the speech in the appendix, "Communication and the Survival of Democracy," and indicate by line number those language segments that you find difficult or "heavy." Suggest alternative ways of saying the same thing before a group of college freshmen.

*Adapted from the Dove Counterbalance General Intelligence test.

Chapter Four

Emotion
and
Confidence

Eight years of empirical and survey observation at Wayne State University indicate that beginning speech communication students consider speech fright (or what is often called stage fright) a serious problem.[1] More than three-fourths of an average public-speaking class indicate concern. One-fourth of the typical class prefer special treatment in the form of instructor conferences, desensitization, or specific reading assignments. Baird and Knower reported a survey of various college speaking groups in which 60 to 75 percent of the students admitted that they were bothered by nervousness in speaking; 35 percent considered it a severe problem.[2] E. C. Buehler has reported a survey of 1750 students and 77 public-speaking teachers. On a scale of factor importance, the students ranked self-confidence first.[3] When a pattern of fear response extends across all or nearly all interpersonal relationships involving oral communication, it may be referred to as

[1]R. S. Ross and W. J. Osborne, "Survey of Incidence of Stage Fright" (unpublished research material, Wayne State University, 1968).

[2]A. C. Baird and F. H. Knower, *Essentials of General Speech* (New York: McGraw-Hill Book Company, 1968), p. 34

[3]E. C. Buehler, "Progress Report of Survey of Individual Attitudes and Concepts Concerning Elements Which Make for Effective Speaking" (mimeographed report, University of Kansas, August 1958).

reticence. According to research at the Pennsylvania State University, this figure could reach 5 percent of a class.[4]

Psychologists and speech communication scholars also stress the difference between a general proneness to experience anxiety and a kind of temporary, particular anxiety of the moment.[5] It is the latter type we are most interested in where public speaking and small-group communication are concerned. That the levels of anxiety and kinds of experience that provoke it may also vary in conversation, small-group, or public speaking has also been considered. Scales for the measurement of these various communication-related anxiety states are being developed.[6] Some of these are illustrated at the end of this chapter.

One conclusion of all the surveys and much of the research is that many of you will suffer some temporary form of speech fright of varying intensity in different communication situations. Page's research argues that measured anxiety is clearly related to your expectations or anticipation of anxiety for various speech communication situations.[7] The person who experiences reticence about all interpersonal communication is defined by Phillips as "a person for whom anxiety about participation in oral communication outweighs his projection of gain from the situation."[8] McCroskey calls the phenomenon "communication apprehension."[9] Most of you will find, other things being equal, that the more formal audience situations provoke the most speech fright.

If it is true that "misery loves company" or that there is "safety in numbers," then it may be reassuring to know that you are certainly not alone. Even professional performers report startling emotional reactions before some public performances. Some personal reports of actors about the emotional problems of performing are quite vivid:

> It's really not fun, acting. Always that tremendous fear. . . . Do you know that before a performance sometimes Laurence Olivier goes back to the foyer and, to release his tension, swears at the audience? Some actors even stick pins in themselves.
>
> *Jane Fonda*

[4]G. M. Phillips, "Reticence: Pathology of the Normal Speaker," *Speech Monographs*, 25, No. 1 (March 1968), 44.

[5]Douglas H. Lamb designates the first "A-Trait" and the second "A-State" in "Speech Anxiety: Towards a Theoretical Conceptualization and Preliminary Scale Development," *Speech Monographs*, 39, No. 1 (March 1972), 62–67.

[6]James C. McCroskey, "Measures of Communication-Bound Anxiety," *Speech Monographs*, 37, No. 4 (November 1970), 269–77.

[7]William T. Page, "The Development of a Test to Measure Anticipated Communicative Anxiety," in *Bibliographic Annual in Speech Communication*, ed. Ned A. Shearer (New York: Speech Communication Association, 1971), p. 99.

[8]Phillips, "Reticence," p. 40.

[9]McCroskey, "Measures of Communication-Bound Anxiety," p. 270.

Acting is a way to overcome your shyness every night. The writer creates a strong, confident person, and that's what you become—unfortunately, only for the moment.

Shirley Booth

Acting scares me senseless. I hate everything I do. Even if it's a crummy radio show with a script, I throw up, I tell ya—it's the equivalent of going voluntarily to hell.

Judy Holliday[10]

The fact that audiences do not view your fright as seriously as you do indicates that you do not appear and sound as bad as you feel; this should be reassuring. Whether your fear is readily apparent or not, the result may be the same. The consequences of such emotional involvement are not very different from other fright-producing situations. Internally you may feel a dryness in the mouth, a rapid heartbeat, a sinking feeling in the stomach, even difficulty with visceral control. Generally observable behavior patterns in excessively frightened people are reported in a study by Clevenger and King.[11] They suggest three general factors or categories of symptoms:

FIDGETINESS	INHIBITION	AUTONOMIA
1. Shuffles feet	1. Deadpan	1. Moistens lips
2. Sways	2. Knees tremble	2. Plays with something
3. Swings arms	3. Hands in pocket	3. Blushes
4. Arms stiff	4. Face pale	4. Breathes heavily
5. Lacks eye contact	5. Returns to seat while speaking	5. Swallows repeatedly
6. Paces back and forth	6. Tense face	
	7. Hands tremble	

A study of other dimensions of the experience, intelligence, and personality of students who suffered from speech fright indicated the following conclusion:

1. They have not engaged in as much platform speaking activity.
2. They have not participated as much in extracurricular and social activities.
3. They have difficulty in always making an adequate social adjustment.
4. They tend to have less linguistic ability.

[10]Phyllis Battelle, "Stars Give Their Views on Acting as a Career," *The Detroit News*, December 6, 1961.

[11]Theodore Clevenger, Jr., and Thomas R. King, "A Factor Analysis of the Visible Symptoms of Stage Fright," *Speech Monographs*, 28, No. 4 (November 1961), 296; see also T. Clevenger, "A Synthesis of Experimental Research in Stage Fright," *Quarterly Journal of Speech*, 45 (1959), 134–45.

5. They have less interest in activities which involve verbal self-expression and in work involving the evaluation and supervision of others.[12]

The study further indicated through testing that these same students did not differ significantly from the others in terms of the following:

1. General intelligence.
2. Quantitative reasoning ability.
3. The more important aspects of personality.
4. Interest in the fields of science, mechanics, nature, and business.

While you are pondering these symptoms and aspects of fright, you should realize that speech courses do help with this all-too-common problem. On a ten-point scale of speech-fright intensity, Henrikson discovered that at the end of the course the students made an average gain (more confidence) of 6.67 points.[13] Actual speaking experience was considered a major factor in gaining confidence.

In most studies involving specific techniques to help students with anxiety problems, all forms of counseling, group therapy, and group desensitization were found to be helpful.[14] A general state of anxiousness beyond the normal speech communication contexts discussed here (but including these) seems most amenable to a form of "insight" counseling and group therapy. The "desensitization" approach proved effective for the typical temporary public-speaking form of fright.[15] *Desensitization* is a form of emotional re-education involving deep relaxation.[16] Some speech communication departments have developed desensitization laboratories and programs of help. One such program is described by Gordon Paul:

> During the first treatment hour, a maximum of 10 minutes was spent exploring the history and current status of the subject's problem. Five to 10 minutes were spent explaining the rationale and course of treatment. Each subject was told that his emotional reactions were the result of previous experiences with persons and situations, and that these inappropriate

[12]Gordon M. Law and Boyd V. Sheets, "The Relations of Psychometric Factors to Stage Fright," *Speech Monographs*, 18, No. 4 (November 1951), 266–71.

[13]E. Henrikson, "Some Effects on Stage Fright of a Course in Speech," *Quarterly Journal of Speech*, 29, No. 4 (December 1943), 491.

[14]Donald H. Meichenbaum, J. Barnard Gilmore, and Al Fedoravious, "Group Insight Versus Group Desensitization in Treating Speech Anxiety," *Journal of Consulting and Clinical Psychology*, 36, No. 3 (1971), 410–21; see also J. C. McCroskey, D. C. Ralph, and J. E. Barrick, "The Effect of Systematic Desensitization for the Reduction of Interpersonal Communicative Apprehension," *Speech Teacher*, 19, (1970), 32–36.

[15]Meichenbaum et al., "Group Insight," p. 419.

[16]J. Wolpe, *Psychotherapy for Reciprocal Inhibition* (Stanford, Calif.: Stanford University Press, 1958).

emotional reactions could be unlearned by first determining the situations in which he becomes progressively more anxious, building a hierarchy from the least to the most anxious situations associated with giving a speech, and then repeatedly visualizing these situations while deeply relaxed. The subject was also told that relaxation was beneficial because the muscle systems of the body could not be both tense and relaxed at the same time, and that by proceeding gradually up the hierarchy, the previous anxiety-provoking situations would become associated with relaxation, thus desensitizing the anxiety.[17]

In the subsequent four or five sessions time was spent constructing a "spatial-temporal anxiety hierarchy" involving speech communication situations ranging from reading alone to giving a speech before an audience. Subjects also received training and practice in "progressive relaxation," a technique involving muscle relaxation exercises. Modern laboratories are equipped with soft lights and appropriate relaxation music. The latter sessions involved presenting two to eleven of the disturbing situations to a relaxed subject. The items might be presented two to ten times for a period of three to thirty seconds. The subjects were aroused from their deep relaxation and asked to discuss their reactions and images.

An important question you may ask is, "Even if I overcome this problem for this class, using whatever help I can get (perhaps just reading the rest of this chapter), will my speech communication training carry over and help me in another situation?" Several researchers have explored this question, and their findings are also reassuring. This is the psychological and learning problem referred to as *transfer*. In a study by S. F. Paulson, speakers were taken from their regular class and made to speak before a strange class audience. The results of an adjustment inventory test indicated no decrease in confidence scores; it was concluded that a transfer of training did take place.[18] It is likewise encouraging to note that about three-fourths of a group of students at Penn State defined as *reticent* indicated noticeable positive effects on their out-of-class oral behavior after ten weeks of speech training.[19]

To a great extent man is afraid of what he does not understand. Young children may be paralyzed with fear during a severe electrical storm until their mother or father explains what causes the thunder and lightning. Even afterwards the child will experience fear, but not of a paralyzing nature. Loud noises make all people jump and frighten

[17]Gordon L. Paul, *Insight vs. Desensitization in Psychotherapy* (Stanford, Calif.: Stanford University Press, 1966) p. 20.

[18]Stanley F. Paulson, "Changes in Confidence During a Period of Speech Training: Transfer of Training and Comparison of Improved and Nonimproved Groups on the Bell Adjustment Inventory," *Speech Monographs*, 18, No. 4 (November 1951), 260–65.

[19]G. M. Phillips, "Reticence," p. 49.

oldsters and youngsters alike, but knowledge and understanding of what causes the loud noises make it possible for us to stop jumping *between* noises.

Because we are dealing with the symptoms and causes of an emotional reaction, we will be better able to control emotion if we know in some detail what it is and how it operates.

THE NATURE OF EMOTION

In 1884 the famous psychologist William James presented us with a relatively simple and extremely useful theory of emotion. One year later, Carl Lange, who had worked independently of James, derived a strikingly similar thesis. The theory is now referred to as the James-Lange theory of emotion. Although there is controversy over this theory in some academic circles, the theory has great practical value for speakers.

> Our natural way of thinking about . . . emotions is that the mental perception of some fact excites the mental affection called the emotion [e.g., fear] and that this later state of mind gives rise to the bodily expression. My thesis on the contrary is that the bodily changes follow directly the perception of the exciting fact [stimulus] and that our feeling [awareness] of the same changes as they occur *is* the emotion.[20]

The gist of the above is that it is awareness of our *reactions* to a frightening situation that is the *real* emotion. James's favorite illustration of this theory was that of a man coming upon a bear in the woods. In a nonscientific way, we might say the bear triggers the emotion of fear. Not so, for according to James our body reacts almost automatically to the bear. Our natural survival devices take over to prepare us for an emergency. Our muscles tense for better agility, our heartbeat and breathing quicken to provide larger supplies of fuel, our glands secrete fluids to sharpen our senses and give us emergency energy. All of this happens in a blinding instant. Then we become aware of our bodily reactions. We sense our heavy breathing, our muscles tense to the point of trembling, perhaps even a surge of adrenalin into our body system. It is this *awareness* of these reactions that frightens us; in other words, that is the emotion. Of course, the bear still has a lot to do with our condition! To tell you that if you understand clearly all the physiological reactions described above you've eliminated the bear is ridiculous. However, this knowledge and understanding, other things being equal, *will* help you

---

[20]William James and Carl Lange, *The Emotions* (Baltimore: The Williams & Wilkins Co., 1922), Vol. 1, p. 12. (Emphasis added.)

better control what action you take and thereby considerably improve your chance for survival. This is what we mean by emotional or speech-fright control, and this is the reason we use the term *control* rather than *eliminate* when speaking of fear.

In the same manner that our fear of the bear is caused not by the bear itself but our *awareness* of our bodily reactions to the bear, we can say that in speech fright it is our *awareness* of these internal and external signs that provides us with the emotion, or at least a reinforcement of the emotion, and may therefore become the cause of a large part of our trouble. The speech situation, though obviously less dangerous, poses a more difficult problem. Nature's physiological provisions typically prepare us for flight or fight, so that we either flee from the bear or attack him. The speech situation obviously inhibits the utilization of survival-tactics, for you can neither attack the audience nor run for the woods. The problem is to drain off some of this excess energy while holding your ground and facing a fear-provoking stimulus (the audience). In your favor is the fact that there are no recorded instances of an audience eating a speaker!

The point of the bear story is to help you better understand the nature of emotion, for understanding and knowledge almost always promote emotional adjustment. There is a second lesson closely related to the first that may be of even more use to you. It is the principle of *objectification*. Intellectualization, objectification, or detailed explanation may destroy or at least take the edge off emotion. Let us imagine a great lover who, when kissing his beloved, decided to analyze objectively exactly what he was doing. A former student, reporting on one of his own objectification experiments, reported, "You know, Doc, it takes all the kick out of it!" By the same reasoning, detailed intellectualization of the speech-fright experiences should help take some of the "kick" out of them. A veteran speech psychologist, Dr. Knower, refers to this phenomenon as a *law* of stage-fright control:

> Anything that increases the efficiency of intellectual control or reduces the intensity of emotional responses helps develop confidence in the speech situation.[21]

Have you ever asked yourself, "Why do my arms and hands tremble? Why do I have that sinking feeling in my stomach?" The issue is not *whether* you experience these things, but rather *why*? If you do ask why and answer, "Because I'm scared to death," you probably only add to the emotion. This is the time to apply both the James-Lange theory of emotion and the principle of objectification. Remember that the emotion

---

[21]Baird and Knower, *Essentials of General Speech*, p. 38.

is primarily the result of your *awareness* of your own bodily reactions and that an objective explanation of the physiological experiences will take the edge off of your awareness.

Let us take the case of the trembling extremities. Skeletal muscles are usually arranged in antagonistic groups, one of which opposes the other. The muscles located on the inside (anterior) surface of the arm and forearm are called *flexors*; those located on the back or outside (posterior) surface are called *extensors*. The flexors bend or draw up your arm, the extensors extend or straighten the arm. When either set of muscles contracts, the opposing set undergoes relaxation—but not complete relaxation, for there is a *tone* to skeletal muscles, which gives them a certain firmness and maintains a slight, steady pull upon their attachments.[22] Suppose you *will* or direct your forearm to rise (as in the diagram— try it). Your flexor muscles contract and the extensor muscles on the other side of your arm are forced to relax. If you will your arm to straighten out, the antagonistic muscles simply reverse functions. Now try something more interesting. Put your arm in about the position of the picture; will it to stay there and at the same time will both sets of muscles to contract at the same time. If you are really working at it, you will notice a tremble in your arm. If you extend your fingers, the tremble is usually quite evident in the hands. You have just produced a state very similar to the trembling that takes place in speech fright. Your real emotion, acting as it was intended, increases the natural tension of your antagonistic muscles and causes the same kind of trembling. You will still experience some trembling and you will still be aware of it, but theoretically, at least, not in exactly the same way as before. You now have increased your knowledge about this phenomenon. Other things being equal, you are better equipped both consciously and subconsciously to adjust to the event when it occurs. Some of the "kick" has been taken out of it. Although the lightning still startles you, you're

[22]Diana Clifford Kimber, Carolyn E. Gray, and Caroline E. Stackpole, *Textbook of Anatomy and Physiology*, 11th ed. (New York: The Macmillan Company, 1946), p. 103.

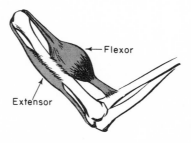

FIGURE 4–1.   Antagonistic Muscles of the Arm and Forearm.

somewhat better off because science has explained *what* it is. Most important, your behavior may change qualitatively in a direction more acceptable to social custom.

A detailed and vivid description of the bodily reaction to threatening situations is provided by W. B. Cannon. These were his conclusions, based upon animal experimentation.

> The adrenalin in the blood is increased . . . which causes strong, rapid heartbeat, suspended activity of the stomach and intestines, wide opening of the air passages in the lungs, release of sugar from the liver, delay of muscle fatigue, free perspiration, dilation of the pupils of the eyes, more red corpuscles to carry oxygen, faster blood coagulation, and increased blood pressure.[23]

The sinking feeling in the stomach that we experience under duress can be physiologically explained in great detail. When faced with a fear-provoking situation, the body calls upon its glandular secretions, notably adrenalin, for emergency energy. These secretions chemically interfere with and literally halt the digestive system. This process tends to make the stomach contract and produces the sensation typically referred to as a "sinking feeling." At the same time, we also become aware of many lesser concomitant reactions, such as a rapidly beating heart (for added circulation) and heavier breathing (for extra oxygen fuel), that help prepare the body for survival. Seaching for these rational explanations should help you maintain perspective and psychological equilibrium. We are often afraid of things simply because we do not understand them.

The famous psychologist Edward Titchener was one of the early theorists who suggested that several emotions could not exist together. He believed that although they could follow one another very closely, they could not coincide. We might say that most people cannot experience two opposite or different types of emotional reactions at the same time. For example, at that instant when you are boiling mad you are probably not afraid. This is not to suggest that you freely substitute anger for your fright, but you may already have observed that when a speaker is really wrapped up or immersed in his subject, he will tend to be less frightened by the platform situation. This in part helps explain our almost instinctive compensatory actions to ward off fright situations. This is why we whistle while walking through a dark alley. We are acting "as if" we are unafraid—perhaps happy, indignant, or angry. Acting "as if" has helped all of us through emotionally charged situations. It is healthy to whistle in the dark; it is often the difference between

---

[23]W. B. Cannon, *Bodily Changes in Pain, Hunger, Fear, and Rage* (Boston: Charles T. Branford Co., 1953), p. 368.

poise and panic. Your choice of a speech topic may therefore be important to you emotionally as well as rhetorically. If you are excited or can become excited about your subject, you are making theory work for you—a kind of natural and intelligent whistling in the dark.

CONTROLLING EMOTION

The preceding section on the nature of emotion has already indicated some of the principles useful in controlling speech fright. Let us talk about some specific actions you can take to further implement the theory.

Understand Emotion

Remember that emotion is primarily the result of *your awareness* of your own bodily reactions. An analysis of these reactions should help control fright. Emotion loses its intensity under examination and objectification. Face up to your problems and get the facts straight. It is healthy to talk objectively about your fright; your instructor is a good listener. Let him help you talk it out. Thus you will meet your fright on a conscious level where you have the most control. If your mouth feels dry, find out why. If your knees shake, find out why. If you feel faint, find out why. The *why* is usually rather mundane, dull, and unexciting, but it is extremely logical and objective. Should inordinate speech fright persist, you may find it useful to review this entire chapter at a later date.

Utilize Excess Tension

It should be clear from the previous discussion, particularly the bear story, that we direct our actions most usefully once we break the wall of tension with the first step. Actual physical movement—either away from the bear at full speed or toward him in Davy Crockett style—bursts the dam of tension. In your speech situation you are in no real danger. You have primarily the problem of releasing, burning, or draining off some of the extra energy that your body dutifully provides. Once again, the *first* step is very important. Bodily activity will help you utilize your extra energy or tension. This is evidenced by expectant fathers who pace the floor rather than stay put.

In the speaking situation you might be concerned about how your activity looks and what it communicates to the audience. The strategy here is very simple—plan and direct some of your gross bodily movement in advance—not in a stereotyped way, but nevertheless systematically, complete with options. For example, at the close of your introduction or perhaps at a transition between points, you might plan on moving a step to the side or raising a book or card for emphasis. You have the option to select the precise time and action, depending upon how natural it seems and how tense you are. Another very natural kind of activity is that associated with visual aids. The communication values of visual aids are almost self-evident, but their value as emotion-controlling devices may not be so obvious. If you comment on a picture, demonstrate an object, or write on a blackboard, you have to make perfectly natural movements in the process. This is an excellent way to utilize excess energy. It is the same reason you will probably be asked to give a demonstration or visual-aid speech early in the semester. The lesson is obvious: use planned and directed activity freely as a means of utilizing excess tension and energy.

There are some pre-speech physical actions that can help you reduce your tension and relax. A brisk walk has helped many an athlete unwind. Even moderate exercises are in order. Of course you cannot do push-ups in the classroom, but deep breathing is possible. Lifting or pressing your chair has been successfully prescribed by speech teachers. Isometric exercises are inconspicuous and should help. A yawn is a natural outlet so long as you do not look *too* relaxed! A certain amount of repetition may also be a useful pre-speech exercise. If the journey from your chair to the speaker's platform seems like the last mile, rehearse this activity in an empty classroom or in measured distances at home. Keep rehearsing it until you sense a monotony in the repetition. College debaters often inadvertently repeat certain strategies and argument patterns so zealously in practice that they run a very real risk of becoming stale when presenting the same ideas in actual debate. Football teams have had similar experience. The point here is that monotonous repetition may help us drain off that keyed-up feeling.

Good health and a reasonable amount of rest are necessary for sound emotional adjustment; speech and communication demand both because so much energy is involved. Assuming an understanding of and a willingness to utilize the suggestions above, a moderate amount of repression of external behavior may then also be in order to help you get started. By repression we mean a form of mental discipline in which you literally force yourself to get on with the business at hand. This is by no means a form of final adjustment, because continued repression would result in extreme fatigue and possible emotional disintegration. However, it is neither unusual nor abnormal to use moderate repression of external behavior as a first step in reaching adjustment.

Redirect Your Attention

Let your emotions work for you when you can. In moments of strain, redirect your attention to other things and bring more tolerable emotions to focus. It is a form of distraction. You try to become so involved in one thing that you are less aware of the other. Psychologists call this compensation. In a speech situation one very obvious and natural avenue of distraction from your fright is an absorbing or vital interest in your subject. If you can get excited about your subject or develop a positive desire to communicate, you will often find your fright diminishing. If you can find humor in your task or in your reactions to it, you may have found a very healthy distraction.

You can redirect your attention in terms of the audience by concentrating on the smiling and pleasant faces for moral support. Most of your audiences are after all supportive. Research indicates that it is true, at least in persuasive speeches, that unfavorable feedback may result in some deterioration of adequate bodily movement, fluency, and the like.[24] One professor reported that he started to overcome his speech fright when he began concentrating on the sleeping faces. He may have been substituting anger or he may have decided his fear was a little ridiculous if he was talking only to himself.

One can overdo this form of compensation. Take care not to so concentrate on redirecting your attention that you lose sight of the real purpose of your total effort—communication.

Protect Your Memory

Our memory like our perceptions may became less dependable under severe forms of emotional duress.[25] It is also a fact that beginning speakers are often frightened, or the initial cause of fright is reinforced, by just the thought of forgetting their speech. It apparently becomes a vicious circle—speech fright becomes a cause of forgetting and the thought of forgetting a cause or reinforcer of speech fright.

As with redirecting attention, your subject or topic may have an important part to play. The more you know about a subject and the more enthusiastic and excited you are, the less likely you are to forget

[24]Philip P. Amato and Terry H. Ostermeier, "The Effect of Audience Feedback on the Beginning Public Speaker," *The Speech Teacher*, 16, no. 1 (January 1967), 56–60.

[25]James T. Freeman, "Set Versus Perceptual Defense: A Confirmation," *Journal of Abnormal Social Psychology*, 51 (1955), 710–12.

your material. Your attitude toward your subject, your involvement in it, and your eagerness to communicate it are all related to memory.

In terms of preparation the key word for memory protection is *system*. We remember better, we learn better, and we speak better if the material we're dealing with is systematically or serially arranged. Your organization of material can significantly affect your ability to remember. More will be said about rhetorical organization in later chapters. The point here is simply that it is easier to remember a list of twenty automobile names grouped according to some system (that is, according to manufacturer, size, horsepower, and so on) than one in a random order. Have you ever noticed how rapidly you can learn the names of baseball players? Obviously it is because of the system of positions; if you do not know the positions, you will be slower at learning the names. Find a natural and meaningful order (to you) of your speech materials, and you will find it much easier to remember what comes next. Your audience, incidentally, will probably find your material easier to follow.

One of the most effective memory aids is a visual aid. If you are explaining how an internal combustion engine works, it is obviously easier to remember functions and parts if you have the engine to point to. If your speech deals with numbers and statistics, a large card with the numbers listed and identified takes considerable pressure off your memory. An occasional speech note with testimony, statistics, or other details tucked in your pocket as a safety precaution is also helpful, even if it is not used. Just the knowledge that you have such a backstop is often worth more than the material on the cards. Some of the best speeches are delivered from a visual outline. All the major points and supporting statements are put on large cardboard visual aids in much the same way as one might put notes on 3 × 5 file cards. They serve much the same function, except that now you get credit for using visual aids instead of being criticized for being too dependent upon your notes. A visual-outline speech or chalk talk, in which you use the blackboard, is an exercise your instructor may wish to prescribe to help you learn the value of visual aids both as mnemonic devices and as agents for clarity.

Despite all the protection you can give your memory, all speakers occasionally experience the frustration of "blank out" or momentary forgetting. A good question is, "What do I do now?" If you have ever watched youngsters delivering memorized poems or salutations at an elementary school convocation, you have heard the children forget their materials. You probably also noticed that they almost instinctively keep repeating the last line they *do* remember in a frantic effort to go back and rerail their memory. This effort may help, but the prompter often has a busy day also. Word-for-word memorization is really not a very intelligent "system," because it cannot relate so many small, unrelated parts.

Where word-for-word memorization is concerned, the lesson for you as a speaker should be obvious. However, the principle of repeating the last thing you do remember is still a useful concept. The practical application here is to *review* the material you have just covered. If your memory failure is toward the end of your speech, you can *summarize* the key points you have made. Practical experience indicates that these techniques do help you reawaken your memory. One student who found these suggestions useful formulated his own rule: "When in doubt, summarize." If you blank out before you have really said anything your summary had better not start, "In summary," or "In review"!

Evaluate Your Communication Role

We talked earlier of a professor who felt less speech fright when he discovered that most of his class was asleep. With all due respect to student audiences, an honest appraisal is that they are not eagerly leaning forward, straining with every muscle to record for all time the wisdom you are about to impart. Professors know this and so should you. Audiences may on occasion be lively, but more often than not this is due to the efforts of the speaker. Experienced speakers and teachers live for those eager audience moments. Be objective about your audience. An analysis of speech-rating charts, particularly the write-in comments, indicates a sympathy toward the speaker in the form of commiseration. This means that if the audience is listening at all, it is rooting for you.

However important your speech message, it will probably not be recorded for posterity. If every speaker in a class of 25 gives 10 speeches, any particular speech is 1 out of 250. If it is reassuring to be part of the crowd, then relax. Be realistic about your speech goals and their effect upon the audience.

Think of your speech in terms of the communication process discussed in Chapter 1 and realize the worthy purpose of speech training. Instead of worrying about what damage your ego may suffer, be afraid of *not* being able to motivate an audience to listen. Commiserate with Adlai Stevenson as you read his remarks about campaigning for the presidency in 1952.

> You must emerge, bright and bubbling with wisdom and well-being, every morning at 8 o'clock, just in time for a charming and profound breakfast talk, shake hands with hundreds, often literally thousands, of people, make several inspiring, newsworthy speeches during the day, confer with political leaders along the way and with your staff all the time, write at every chance, think if possible, read mail and newspapers, talk on the telephone, talk to everybody, dictate, receive delegations, eat, with decorum—and discretion!—and ride

through city after city on the back of an open car, smiling until your mouth is dehydrated by the wind, waving until the blood runs out of your arm.

Then, you bounce gaily, confidently, masterfully into great howling halls, shaved and all made up for television with the right color shirt and tie—I always forgot—and a manuscript so defaced with chicken tracks and last minute jottings that you couldn't follow it, even if the spotlights weren't blinding and even if the still photographers didn't shoot you in the eye every time you looked at them. Then all you have to do is make a great, imperishable speech, get out through the pressing crowds with a few score autographs, your clothes intact, your hands bruised, and back to the hotel—in time to see a few important people.

But the real work has just commenced—two or three, sometimes four, hours of frenzied writing and editing of the next day's immortal mouthings so you can get something to the stenographers, so they can get something to the mimeograph machines, so they can get something to the reporters, so they can get something to their papers by deadline time.

The next day is the same. But I gained weight on it. And it's as tenacious as a campaign deficit!

And, too, there is mirth mingled with the misery all along the way. They shout, "Good old Ad-lie!" If you run for office and have a slightly unusual name, let me advise you either to change it before you start, or be prepared to take other people's word for it. And I shall not soon forget about the woman in the crowd in San Francisco who reached into the car to shake hands with me, and not long after discovered that she had lost her diamond ring. Nor will I forget the warm welcome I received on a whistle stop in Bethlehem, Pa., and my thanks to "the people of Allentown." My only hope is that *they* forget it! Again, out West, I warmly endorsed the impressive chairman of a meeting as a candidate for Congress, only to discover that he was not running for Congress or anything else.[26]

Finally, evaluate your communication role in a total sense. Your speeches will be lost among hundreds of other speeches; your audience is generally sympathetic; your instructor is trained to be alert to your problems; and the rhetorical and psychological research in speech has given us reliable methods and knowledge to help you learn. Have faith in hard-earned experience and knowledge; have faith in the goodness of people; have faith in yourself.

SUMMARY

Most beginning speech students (60 to 75 percent) admit that they are bothered by nervousness. About 35 percent consider it a severe problem. Professional performers report similar feelings of tension. It is significant

[26]Bill Adler, "Adlai Stevenson's Wit," *This Week Magazine*, September 12, 1965, p. 5. Reprinted from *This Week Magazine*. Copyrighted 1965 by the United Newspaper Corporation. Reprinted with the permission of the author and his agents, Scott Meredith Literary Agency, Inc., 580 Fifth Ave., New York, New York 10036.

that reports indicate you do not *appear* and *sound* as bad as you *feel*. Research also indicates that the frightened people do not differ from the confident minority in very basic ways such as intelligence and the important aspects of personality and that students do gain confidence during a course in speech and are able to transfer this learning to other situations.

Understanding the nature of emotion is useful because it helps us objectify our feelings and reactions. The James-Lange theory of emotion suggests essentially that it is our awareness of our *reactions* to a frightening situation that is the *real* emotion. Emotion is a good and necessary phenomenon. The problem is one of control. An understanding of the physiological reactions helps us to control our emotions. Objectification of the emotional reactions tends to take the edge off emotion, making it easier to control. An increase in intellectual activity helps reduce emotional intensity. We are afraid of what we do not understand.

Most people cannot experience two different types of emotional reactions at the same time. If you are excited or can become excited about your subject, you are making theory work for you—a kind of natural and intelligent whistling in the dark.

Some specific suggestions for controlling emotion involve:

1. Understanding emotion and the principle that objectification and intellectualization reduce tension.
2. The utilization of excess tension by planning and directing some of your gross bodily activity in advance of the speech situation.
3. The redirecting of your attention to more pleasant emotions to let your emotions work for you.
4. The protecting of your memory through logical systems of organization, visual aids, and pre-set psychological options or alternatives.
5. An honest evaluation of your communication role and situation and a faith in knowledge, the goodness of people, the interest of your instructor, and yourself.
6. Concentrate on the message more than yourself.

Lastly, when at your wit's end, remember that there is no recorded experience of an audience having eaten a speaker!

Speech Communication Principles

1. Most beginning speech students admit that they are bothered by nervousness.

2. Nervousness is not as apparent to the audience as it is to the speaker.

3. Nervous student speakers do not differ from the confident majority in intelligence and other important personality traits.

4. Generally observable behavior patterns in extreme cases of speech fright include fidgetiness, inhibition, and autonomia.

5. It is our awareness of our *reactions* to a frightening situation that is the *real* emotion.

6. An understanding of physiological reactions helps us control emotion.

7. Objectification of emotional reactions tends to reduce their intensity.

8. An increase in intellectual activity helps reduce emotional intensity.

9. Most people cannot experience two different types of emotional reactions at the same time.

10. Speech communication courses that require practice speeches help alleviate speech fright.

A. *General Learning Outcomes*

1. We should learn about the nature of human emotion and its relationship to confidence.

2. We should learn the basic principles for alleviating and controlling speech fright.

B. *Specific Learning Outcomes*

1. We should learn that nervousness is a common problem among beginning speakers.

2. We should learn that frightened people do not differ from the confident majority in terms of intelligence and other important personality characteristics.

3. We should learn that students do gain confidence during a course in speech.

4. Those experiencing excessive fright should learn, and be able to explain, the nature of emotion to their instructor in a twenty-minute conference.

5. We should be able to relate the foregoing general and specific learning outcomes to the speech communication principles enumerated above.

C. *Communication Competencies*

1. We should be able to give a five-minute extemporaneous speech before an audience of twelve to thirty-five in such a manner that our anxiety does not seriously interfere with our sense of communication so far as the *audience* is concerned.

2. We should learn to be a sympathetic and emotionally reinforcing listener for obviously frightened speakers through an appreciation of the material in this chapter.

D. *Study Projects and Tasks*

1. Prepare a five-minute extemporaneous speech in which you explain or demonstrate how to do something (e.g., driving a golf ball, serving a tennis ball, swinging a bat, casting a fly, lifting a weight, skiing and so forth). Make sure you can do it; practice before coming to class.

2. Prepare a five-minute extemporaneous speech describing some exciting event you witnessed or participated in (e.g., a race you won, an accident, the big game, a close call, a big fish, a fight, a surprise present, your lucky day, and so forth). Make sure you really were excited about or involved with the event so that your enthusiasm helps you look forward to telling the story.

3. Assess your speech anxiety level with the following inventory.* If you check twelve or more items and feel up-tight, it would probably be a good idea to confer with your instructor. You're probably not the only one. . . .

Check only those statements which you feel apply to you in an abnormal or extraordinary degree.

_____ 1. Audiences seem bored when I speak.
_____ 2. I feel dazed when speaking.
_____ 3. I am continually afraid of making some embarrassing or silly slip of the tongue.
_____ 4. My face feels frozen while speaking.

*Adapted from the research of H. Gilkenson by R. S. Ross and W. J. Osborne, Wayne State University.

_____ 5. I have a deep sense of personal worthlessness while facing an audience.

_____ 6. Owing to fear, I cannot think clearly on my feet.

_____ 7. While preparing my speech I am in a constant state of anxiety.

_____ 8. I feel exhausted after addressing a group.

_____ 9. My hands tremble when I try to handle objects on the platform.

_____ 10. I am almost overwhelmed by a desire to escape.

_____ 11. I am in constant fear of forgetting my speech.

_____ 12. I dislike using my body and voice expressively.

_____ 13. I feel disgusted with myself after trying to address a group of people.

_____ 14. I feel tense and stiff while speaking.

_____ 15. I am so frightened that I scarcely know what I'm saying.

_____ 16. I hurry while speaking to get through and out of sight.

_____ 17. I prefer to have notes on the platform in case I forget what I'm saying.

_____ 18. My mind becomes blank before an audience and I am scarcely able to continue.

_____ 19. I particularly dread speaking before a group that opposes my point of view.

_____ 20. It is difficult for me to search my mind calmly for the right word to express my thoughts.

_____ 21. My voice sounds strange to me when I address a group.

_____ 22. My thoughts become confused and jumbled when I speak before an audience.

_____ 23. I am completely demoralized when suddenly called upon to speak.

_____ 24. I find it extremely difficult to look at my audience while speaking.

_____ 25. I am terrified at the thought of speaking before a group of people.

_____ 26. I become so confused at times that I lose the thread of my thinking.

_____ 27. My posture feels strained and unnatural.

_____ 28. Fear of forgetting causes me to jumble my speech at times.

_____ 29. I am fearful and tense all the time while I am speaking before a group of people.

_____ 30. I feel awkward.

_____ 31. I am afraid the audience will discover my self-consciousness.

_____ 32. I am afraid my thoughts will leave me.

_____ 33. I feel confused while speaking.

_____ 34. I never feel I have anything worth saying to an audience.

_____ 35. I feel that I am not making a favorable impression when I speak.

_____ 36. I feel depressed after addressing a group.

_____ 37. I always avoid speaking in public if possible.

_____ 38. I become flustered when something unexpected occurs.

_____ 39. Although I talk fluently with friends, I am at a loss for words on the platform.

_____ 40. My voice sounds as though it belongs to someone else.

_____ 41. At the conclusion of the speech I feel that I have failed.

4. Prepare an oral report or essay attempting to prove or disprove any of the speech communication principles listed earlier.

5. Evaluate the speech-fright or anxiety problems that might pertain to some of the suggestions for participatory democracy in the appendix speech, "Communication and the Survival of Democracy" (e.g., lines 262–265; 269–286, and 361–374).

PART TWO

NONVERBAL COMMUNICATION

Receivers decode communication in terms of the total stimulus presented. Experts have estimated that verbal messages even in face-to-face transactions carry no more than 35 percent of the social meaning.[1]

When a gesture that means "come here" in America means "go away" in Italy, we begin to sense the problem. There is evidence that in our own culture black and white job interviewees behave quite differently nonverbally, even though their intent is the same.[2] Dubner suggests that white people "run white" and blacks "run black."[3] Time, especially CPT, WPT, and clock time, appears to say different things to different people nonverbally.[4] Perhaps a culture or subculture creates its own system of nonverbal communication.

There are then many dimensions of nonverbal communication besides those of time and space (what Hall calls proxemics). Time talks and space speaks.[5] Body movements have been studied in terms of revealing how much

[1]Randall Harrison, "Nonverbal Communication: Explorations into Time, Space, Action, and Object," In *Dimensions in Communication*, eds. J. H. Campbell and H. W. Hepler (Belmont, Calif.: Wadsworth Publishing Co., Inc., 1970), p. 285.
[2]William Kloman, " E. T. Hall and the Human Space Bubble," *Horizon*, 9 (Autumn 1967), 43.
[3]Frances S. Dubner, "Nonverbal Aspects of Black English," *Southern Speech Communication Journal*, 37, No. 4 (Summer 1972), 366.
[4]*CPT*, Colored People's Time; *WPT*, White People's Time.
[5]Edward T. Hall, *The Silent Language* (Garden City, New York: Doubleday & Co., Inc., 1959).

FIGURE II–1. Source: Photography by Guy Morrison, Bloomfield Hills, Michigan.

112

you like or dislike another person.[6] Note how meanings change when dress codes are in or out of sync with their historical period (see Figure II–1).

In addition to dress, some of the more obvious kinds of body action language are expressed by your posture, facial expression, hair style, breathing rate, and gestures. According to Bernard Gunther, the body *talks* and its message is how you really are, not how you think you are.[7]

One attempt at classifying all these nonverbal cues suggests three categories of language: *sign* language for the typical stereotyped gestures; *action* language for the nonstandard general body movements (most of those above); and *object* language for the message suggested by material things such as your choice of clothes, hair style, car, and so on.[8] An elaborate system of notation for nonverbal movements called kinesics[9] has been devised, and popular writers now speak of *Body Language*.[10]

In addition to the body action and related dimensions to be discussed in Chapter 5, voice or paralanguage[11] has been identified as a significant nonverbal cue. The way we project our voices is related not only to our mood and message but also to the distance or space between us and the audience. E. T. Hall's scale should be useful for speech communication students:

1. *Very close*   Soft whisper;top secret
   (3 in. to 6 in.)
2. *Close*   Audible whisper; very confidential
   (8 in. to 12 in.)
3. *Near*   Indoors, soft voice; outdoors, full
   (12 in. to 20 in.)   voice; confidential
4. *Neutral*   Soft voice; low volume; personal sub-
   (20 in. to 36 in.)   ject matter
5. *Neutral*   Full voice; information of a non-per-
   (4½ ft. to 5 ft.)   sonal nature
6. *Public distance*   Full voice with slight loudness; public
   (5½ ft. to 8 ft.)   information for others to hear
7. *Across the room*   Loud voice, talking to a group
   (8 ft. to 20 ft.)
8. *Stretching the limits*   Hailing distance; departures[12]
   of distance
   (20 ft. to 24 ft. indoors;
   up to 100 ft. outdoors)

[6]Albert Mehrabian, "Significance of Posture and Position in the Communication of Attitude and Status Relationships," *Psychological Bulletin*, 71 (1969), 359–72; see also Albert Mehrabian, *Silent Messages* (Belmont, Calif.: Wadsworth Publishing Co., Inc., 1971).

[7]Bernard Gunther, *Sense Relaxation: Below Your Mind* (New York: Collier Books, 1968), p. 90.

[8]Jurgen Ruesch, "Nonverbal Language and Therapy," in *Communication and Culture*, ed. Alfred G. Smith (New York: Holt, Rinehart and Winston, Inc., 1966).

[9]R. L. Birdwhistell, "Background to Kinesics," *ETC.*, 13, no. 1 (1955); R. Birdwhistell, *Introduction to Kinesics: An Annotation System for Analysis of Body Motion and Gesture* (Washington, D.C.: Foreign Service Institute, Dept. of State, 1952); and R. L. Birdwhistell, *Kinesics and Context: Essays in Body Motion Communication*, ed. Barton Jones (Philadelphia: University of Pennsylvania Press, 1970).

[10]Julius Fast, *Body Language* (New York: M. Evans and Co., dist. by Philadelphia: Lippincott, 1970).

[11]Mark L. Knapp, *Nonverbal Communication in Human Interaction* (New York: Holt, Rinehart and Winston, Inc., 1972), p. 7.

[12]Hall, *Silent Language*, pp. 208–9.

In addition to the obvious stereotyped vocal cues (i.e., voices that are tough, effeminate, sexy, and so on), there now is evidence that one's *social status* can be reasonably determined (apart from language) by cues in the voice alone.[13] Because of the importance of this subject matter we devote all of Chapter 6 to a discussion of voice and articulation.

Except in isolation, nonverbal cues are quite accurate in conveying ideas, particularly emotional concepts like love and hate. Yet there is also evidence that people display quite different physical patterns of response in various emotion-producing situations. In some speech communication situations our voices and our actions speak so loudly that our words are often unheard or surely not very persuasive.

It would appear that one cannot avoid acting nonverbally indefinitely and therefore we inevitably communicate, at least nonverbally. That our non-verbal behavior may unintentionally contradict our verbal message should provide food for thought for speakers. We express our attitudes through our body action, voice and articulation patterns, objects we wear or own, our treatment of time and space, and through language and thoughtfully pre-pared messages. The speech communication act is, as Keltner puts it, "a multimedia process of almost infinite dimensions."[14]

Making the nonverbal process work for us to reinforce and enhance our messages is the major objective of Chapters 5 and 6.

A general review of the hoped-for *learning outcomes* that should result from a close reading of Part Two, particularly when related to class proj-ects and performances, follows. A more specific set of learning outcomes or lesson objectives and communication competencies, along with creative, relevant projects and tasks, is appended to each chapter.

We should learn that the nonverbal cues, that is, what our audience sees and hears apart from words, profoundly affect what it decodes or abstracts from our message.

We should learn the practical elements and standards of bodily action and facial expression as they relate to communication.

We should learn again that "meaning" is in the eyes, ears, and other senses of the receiver, but even more it is also in his store of experience, knowledge, feelings, attitudes, and emotions.

We should learn of the communication impact of the nonverbal cues of voice and articulation.

We should learn the practical dimensions of the vocal and articulatory processes and pronunciation as they relate to communication.

We should learn that receivers decode messages in terms of the total stimulus presented, that speech communication is a multimedia process.

---

[13] James D. Moe, "Listener Judgments of Status Cues in Speech: A Replication and Extension," *Speech Monographs*, 39, no. 2 (1972), 144–47.

[14] John W. Keltner, *Interpersonal Speech Communication* (Belmont, Calif.: Wadsworth Publishing Co., Inc., 1970), p. 110.

Chapter Five

Body Action Language

THE ROLE OF BODILY EXPRESSION

In Chapter 1 we learned that the receiver decodes the communication in terms of the total stimulus presented to him. What your audience sees may seriously affect what they decode or abstract from what you say. In clever pantomime the communication is sometimes much clearer and more emphatic than when the actor speaks. Body action language may therefore play an important part in the total impression made by the speaker.

Unconscious Nonverbal Communication

We constantly use bodily action in our everyday conversation. It is a definite part of our communication system. The way a person walks at a given moment may demonstrate his mood more adequately than do his words.

A speaker deciding to repress all bodily action as a means of trying to avoid looking awkward usually succeeds in communicating even more awkwardness and actually looking more unnatural and ridiculous. In addition, such repression may lead to poor emotional control. A lack of action often makes the message less clear. There is no point in trying to avoid or repress bodily action and many good reasons to try to understand it, control it, and use it.

Communication by Stereotypes

The communication of stereotyped or stylized facial expressions and gestures has been studied experimentally. Landis performed an experiment designed to discover whether reported emotions were accompanied by definite and easily recognized facial expressions. A series of photographs were taken of his subjects while they were actually being exposed to various emotion-producing situations, not simply portraying emotions as an actor would. After comparing the reactions of many subjects Landis reported:

> With no verbal report of a given emotion did a muscle, group of muscles, or expression occur with sufficient frequency to be considered characteristic of that emotion. There is no expression typically associated with any verbal report.[1]

A study similar to the one described above was conducted by Feleky, but with one vital difference: the photographs of emotions were artificially portrayed or acted. The experimenter found in this case a remarkable agreement on the description of the poses, indicating that we may interpret an individual's emotional state with reasonable accuracy from a posed photograph.[2]

A study with more specific conclusions was conducted by Knower and Dusenbury. The design of the study was almost identical to Feleky's. Knower and Dusenbury concluded:

1. Interpretation of the facial expression of emotional tendencies and attitudes may be made with a high degree of reliability.
2. There are significant individual and group differences in ability correctly to interpret facial expressions of the emotions.
3. Women are more accurate in the interpretation of facial expressions of the emotions than men.
4. Patterns of facial expressions extended in time, as on a short, moving picture, are judged more accurately than are still photographs of the same emotional tendencies.

[1]C. Landis, "Experimental Studies of the Emotions: The Work of Cannon and Others," in *Great Experiments in Psychology*, ed. Henry E. Garrett (New York: Appleton-Century-Crofts, 1941), p. 331; for an interesting discussion of the nonverbal role of the face and eyes, see also Mark L. Knapp, *Nonverbal Communication in Human Interaction* (New York: Holt, Rinehart and Winston, Inc., 1972). pp. 119–46.

[2]Garrett, *Great Experiments in Psychology*, p. 330; see also J. Frois Wittman, "The Judgment of Facial Expression," *Journal of Experimental Psychology*, 13 (1930), 113–51.

5. Accuracy in the interpretation of facial expression of the emotions is influenced by the conditions under which such expressions are judged.[3]

A more recent study by Williams and Tolch[4] indicated that there are two basic dimensions in the perception of stimulated facial expressions, *general-evaluation* and *dynamism*. By *general-evaluation* is meant a viewer's assessment of those characteristics of an expression that reveal such qualities as goodness, gratefulness, kindness, and the like. *Dynamism* involves an assessment of qualities such as active-passive, fast-slow, interesting-boring, and so on. Simulated facial expressions based only on these two dimensions were successfully differentiated by viewers. However, a simulated "no message—neutral" expression introduced into the study was usually perceived as having both *evaluative* and *dynamic* qualities.

Schlosbery suggests in his studies that facial expression can be assessed in terms of what he calls pleasantness-unpleasantness, sleep-tension, and rejection-attention.[5]

In one study Moe and Savage cut up pictures of stereotyped emotions (e.g., terror, love, hate) and asked students to look at the hand and face gestures separately. Recognition or identification was higher in both cases, indicating that there are reasonably stylized expressions of the hands as well as the face.[6]

As far as communication (recognition) is concerned in these experiments, we can say that simulated or stereotyped emotions can be perceived or identified with some reliability while real emotions cannot be judged with any certainty.

Good actors and capable speakers appear to communicate emotions with regularity. The actor has the play, the set, the other actors, and the stylized conceptions of the audience to help him. If the cause of whatever emotion the actor is portraying is also perceived (for example, a gun and fear), the communication pattern is easier to follow.

Although certain peripheral patterns or expressions have become stylized, we still have a potential barrier to communication, for these patterns may vary so much from person to person, from sender to re-

[3]D. Dusenbury and F. H. Knower, "Experimental Studies of the Symbolism of Action and Voice—I: A Study of the Specificity of Meaning in Facial Expression," *Quarterly Journal of Speech*, 24, No. 3 (1938), 435.

[4]F. Williams and J. Tolch, "Communication by Facial Expression," *The Journal of Communication*, 15, No. 1 (March 1965), 17; see also J. Tolch, "The Problem of Language and Accuracy in Identification of Facial Expression," *Central States Speech Journal*, 14 (February 1963).

[5]Harold Schlosbery, "Three Dimensions of Emotion," *The Psychological Review*, 61 (1954), 81–88.

[6]J. Moe and N. Savage, "Recognizability of Emotions as Expressed by Facial Expressions and Hand Gestures" (unpublished pilot study, Speech 0726, Wayne State University, 1967).

ceiver, that except perhaps in skilled acting it remains difficult to communicate the precise emotion intended.

In review, our research into portrayal and recognition of emotional
states such as anger, love, and fear has shown that we do rely on learned
action habits to decode at least these highly abstract messages. The expression on the face of a person photographed as he is being stuck with
a needle may be incorrectly identified as portraying love. If the viewer
also sees the needle or stimulus, however, his chances of identifying the
emotion are much better. If a person is asked to act as though he is in
great pain, viewers usually get the message.

As explained in the introduction to Part Two, certain cultures and
groups have action patterns that are stereotyped in ways different from
our own. For the Japanese, a smile does not indicate amusement, but
rather politeness.[7] American Indians had an elaborate sign language that
the pioneers had to learn before they could communicate with them
effectively.

These observations lead to the question of how much stereotype or
formalism a speaker should use. One needs enough stereotype to be
understood, but not so much as to appear artificial. American speech
education in the nineteenth century suffered through a highly mechanical
approach. This was a period of flamboyant language and highly stylized
gestures. Delsarte, a French scholar, contributed a system of gesture during this time that contained some eighty-one gestures for practically all
parts of the body, including specific ones for the nose, eyebrows, and feet.
In answer to this elocutionary movement, the famous School of Expression
of S. S. Curry was born. This view taught that "every action of face or
hand . . . is simply an outward effect of an inward condition. Any motion
or tone that is otherwise is not expression."[8] In other words, a speaker
should be so saturated with his subject that his expression is always
dynamic and spontaneous. At present we recognize that communicative
bodily action does rely on certain learned general stereotypes that we
use in natural and relatively spontaneous ways.

The conclusion of all this research is that "meaning" is in the eyes, ears,
and other senses of the receiver, but even more it is in his store of experience, knowledge, feelings, attitudes, and emotions.

Empathy

If your instructor runs his fingernails sharply across the blackboard,
you probably cringe and literally grit your teeth. If you've ever huddled

[7]Weston LaBarre, "The Cultural Basis of Emotions and Gestures," *Journal of Personality*, 16, no. 1 (1947), 49–69.

[8]S. S. Curry, *Foundations of Expression* (Boston: The Expression Co., 1920), p. 10.

in the stands alternately shivering and cheering as the Detroit Lions made a goal-line stand against the Green Bay Packers or the Dallas Cowboys, you can understand empathy. If you have ever seen a youngster take a violent and bruising fall, you probably "felt" the pain as you projected your own consciousness into the youngster's action. This projection of consciousness is the essence of empathic response. Empathy therefore involves a muscular reaction, and an audience imitates in part the actions of the speaker. When a speaker appears mortally afraid and tense, the audience dies a little. When he acts tired, the audience feels tired or bored. When he paces the floor like a caged lion, the audience usually tires before he does. The speaker should take the audience into account when considering his bodily action. He should attempt to use that kind and amount of action that will help achieve his speech's purpose.

Emotion

In Chapter 4 we noted that a prolonged repression of normal physical outlets could result in emotional disintegration. One can drain off pent-up tension by bodily action. That is often why some speakers pace the floor or incessantly fidget. Instead of actions that are distracting, use meaningful bodily action that will help you control your speech fright at the same time it helps communicate your message.

THE ELEMENTS OF BODILY ACTION

These elements are the actual physical behavior patterns that make up the total bodily action. While the elements most often occur simultaneously, we are separating them here for purposes of elucidation.

General Impression

The general impression you create is a synthesis not only of all the elements that are communicated to your audience but also of the phenomena over which you may not always have control—for example, the lighting, the building, the platform, the person who introduces you, and other such factors. However, there are relatively simple things over which you *do* have some control and which may contribute in a major way to your general impression. The problem of dress is one of these. In considering what to wear, the watchword is *appropriate*. You do not want to appear conspicuous and yet you do wish to live up to the expectations of dress the audience has for its speakers. Your physical and psychological comfort affect your bodily action. If the audience remembers your leotard instead of your speech, you can draw your own conclusion. It goes without saying that, as with appropriate dress, one's general impression is better if he is personally neat, washed, and combed.

The dimension of time, or chronemics, is another element over which you have some control. Seldom are you in trouble for being early, but occasionally you may get in trouble for being late! One famous American general who had risen from the ranks claimed that one of the secrets of his success was always being fifteen minutes early for appointments. Almost every appraisal or interview form includes an assessment of the subject's dependability, which often translates into his attitude toward being on time.

Another problem is whether to address the audience from a sitting or a standing position. Some small informal audiences may prefer that you sit while speaking to them, and you might feel conspicuous standing on a platform with only three or four people at your feet. However, some small groups are actually insulted if the speaker sits. The general impression they get, apparently, is that they are not considered important enough for a stand-up speech. A lot depends upon how well you know the group and how well they know you. As a general rule there is less risk in standing, even before a very small group. If the audience should appear uncomfortable, it is much easier to sit down after a speech has started than to stand up. Through observations made in an "Effective Supervision" course (in which eight to twelve students, typically foremen, formally rated the teachers), the evaluations of the otherwise generally equal instructors favored those who stood while speaking.

All bodily action elements contribute to the general impression. The more important elements are discussed below.

Posture

Posture is an integral part of your general impression not only from the point of view of empathy and what the audience infers but also in terms of your own reactions to yourself. Whether you slouch and cower or whether you stand with military bearing affects your outlook and sense of power or control over yourself. Acting "as if" can affect your actions. The earlier discussion of empathy indicated that a slouching posture can tire the audience as quickly as it can the speaker.

In general, good posture involves the distribution of body weight in a comfortable and poised way consistent with the impression desired by the speaker. You should be erect without looking stiff, comfortable without appearing limp. Your bearing should be alert, self-possessed, and communicative. Good posture and poise are a kind of studied non-chalance. The great danger, as with all studied bodily action, is one of appearing artificial, conspicuous, or out of phase.

A satisfactory standing position should be a balanced one in which, for example, a sudden push would allow you to recover quickly. Your feet should be fairly close together, with one foot slightly ahead of the other. Keep your hips straight, shoulders back, and chin in. Experiment in looking for a poised, natural speaking stance. There is no one way that is right for every speech! The stance you finally select will have to be modified to meet changing speech circumstances, such as the size and nature of the audience, the formality of the occasion, and so on.

Walking

Actors have long known the importance of gait and walk in expressing various moods and degrees of emphasis. The *femme fatale* has a walk that clearly communicates her role; the sneaky villain also has a stereo-typed walk. The child about to be spanked has a considerably different walk from the same child on his way to the movies. Zsa-Zsa, a sexy crea-ture with an undulating walk and a come-hither look in her eyes, com-plains that all men are after the "same thing" and none respects her mind. Which part of the message is to be believed, the verbal or the nonverbal?

Walking may serve as a form of physical punctuation. Transitions and pauses may be reinforced with a few steps to the side, emphasis with a step forward. As does the actor, the speaker wishes to appear natural, not awkward. If your walking is inept, ungraceful, or mechanical, it will distract from its intended purpose; if it is random, it will distract from the general speech purpose.

Walking also has empathic qualities for the audience. It can afford physical relief to a suffering audience. By the same token, too much walking can literally wear an audience out. A certain amount of devised, purposeful walking is often helpful in affording an outlet for muscular tension for both the speaker and the audience.

The question of the amount and kind of walking desirable involves the same considerations that affect all bodily action: the subject, the speaker, the size of the audience, the formality of the occasion, and so on. In general, the more formal the speech, the less pronounced your walking should be. The larger the audience, the more definite your steps may be.

One should also remember that walking, like all bodily action, starts before you actually start to speak. When you leave your chair to approach the speaker's stand, your communication has already begun; nor are you finished until you have walked off the platform.

Facial Expression

In the studies on the portrayal and recognition of emotion already discussed, most of the pictures taken were of the facial expressions of the people involved in the experiments. This was because the researchers thought the face was the most expressive and quickly altered part of our anatomy. This may very well be the case. We have all heard of "the face that launched a thousand ships," and that "the eyes are the mirror of the soul"; maybe some of you have even heard of the old song entitled "Your Lips Tell Me 'No, No,' But There's 'Yes, Yes,' in Your Eyes."

The problem is that the speaker may inadvertently use stereotyped facial expressions or ones unsuitable to the subject. A girl in a speech class once had a temporary facial tic so that her eye uncontrollably winked at about sixty-second intervals when she was speaking. Even after the class discovered that it was a tic, the signal confusion was alarming. Once she learned to blink both eyes, most of the problem was solved. The blink of one eye (wink) has a highly specialized, stereotyped meaning. The wink of two eyes simultaneously (blink) has no stereotyped meaning (unless done in rapid succession) and was not confusing or particularly distracting. An emotionally tense person may tighten his jaw and unconsciously assume a crocodile grin. This usually passes as he relaxes, but the first few moments of a serious speech by a grinning speaker can be most perplexing.

The eyes, at least in relatively small audiences, are vehicles of much communication, as was indicated with the wink example. Right or wrong, audiences are wary of shifty eyes. "He avoids my eyes" is a frequent classroom criticism. The audience expects to be looked at—not incessantly stared at, but occasionally looked at. Direct, forthright delivery (directness) is defined by many, and not unrealistically, as based on eye contact.

Simply stated, the lessons to be learned are: (1) avoid inadvertent or inappropriate facial stereotypes; (2) make eye contact with the audience; and (3) free your natural and spontaneous facial expressions so that they may reinforce your message.

Gestures

In discussing gestures, we shall be concerned primarily with the hands and arms, but always keep in mind that you gesture with your entire body and personality. In a very general way, all people use gestures for two rhetorical purposes—to reinforce a concept or to help describe something.

Reinforcing Gestures. It seems natural to clench your fist or perhaps even pound the lectern when trying to communicate a strong feeling. This reinforces and gives emphasis to your words. In rejecting or disagreeing verbally, one might routinely turn his palms down or out. In pleading or appealing, one might naturally turn his palms up or in. These types of gestures reinforce through emphasis; others reinforce through a kind of suggestion. In communicating a scolding attitude toward the other political party, one might wag his finger in much the same way that the stereotyped teacher does. Speakers may reinforce a division or separation of points by using first one hand ("On the one hand it can be said . . .") and then the other. Or it may be that only one hand is used, and the speaker may with a vertical palm suggest several divisions or categories as he slices the air, moving his hand on a level plane from left to right. No two people use these reinforcing gestures exactly alike, but the general stereotype is usually recognizable.

Descriptive Gestures. When asked to describe the size or shape of something, it is natural to use your hands to indicate the dimensions. A circular staircase would be difficult to describe to a person who had never seen one if you could not use your hands. All descriptive gestures are in some part also reinforcing and emphatic. The fellow describing his blind date with his gestures communicates more than just size and shape; we might, for example, quickly infer his approval or disapproval.

STANDARDS OF GOOD BODILY ACTION

Appropriateness

Your subject, your particular physiology and personality, and, most important, the size and nature of the audience are the determinants of appropriate bodily action. A very formal subject, particularly if connected with a formal occasion and a small, older audience, would generally call for poised but relatively restricted bodily action. The grandiose movement and grand sweep of the arms would be out of place. Other things being equal, the larger the audience, the more gross and unrestricted your bodily action may become.

For most speakers the problem is one of too little bodily action, whatever the speech occasion. When you are finally free of your inhibitions, however, remember to match your bodily actions to the expectations of the audience.

Variety

Any bodily action, but particularly gestures, should be varied occasionally; otherwise the routineness may call attention to itself and not only cease to carry meaning but also become a distraction. A speaker who pounds the table for *every* point he makes, regardless of its importance, soon loses the reinforcing effect of that gesture. A random or meaningful gesture used in moderation does not harm your communication, but if it is repeated again and again, even though not really a reinforcing or descriptive gesture, it is no longer a random gesture and may interfere with the message. Monotony of action, whether meaningful or not, is usually distracting. All of us tend to repeat our favorite gestures, and these mannerisms often reflect our personalities. We must periodically ask ourselves if we are overworking some gestures and if our bodily actions really reflect the kind of personality we would like to project. Part of the problem is that we are typically unaware of overdoing a favorite gesture, particularly if it is used primarily as a tension release. Your instructor will feed back this information so that you can correct this distracting monotony.

Physical Coordination

Physical coordination means the integration of all parts of the body in expressing yourself. You can appear quite ridiculous by locking your elbows to your sides and moving only your forearms and hands. The whole body is always involved in any bodily action. A literal detachment will make you appear mechanical.

Verbal Coordination

By verbal coordination is meant the synchronization of words and action to achieve maximum reinforcement of the message. This is a timing problem that is primarily related to rehearsed or "canned" bodily action. A lack of coordination can be quite humorous. Try saying "Uncle Sam needs *you*," but instead of pointing on the word *you*, wait three seconds more and then point!

Dynamic Bodily Action

By dynamic bodily action is meant the projection of a lively, animated, vigorous sense of communication. The use of bodily action should be essentially spontaneous; that is, the mechanics of bodily action should be determined by extemporaneous thoughts and impulses. To become dynamic and spontaneous in your bodily action you sometimes have to prime the pump by including some speech details that require bodily action, such as visual aids and demonstrations that require description of shape or size and imitations of people or animals.

SUMMARY

What your audience sees profoundly affects what it decodes or abstracts from what you say. Much unconscious bodily action accompanies most speeches. A lack of action often makes the message less clear. There is therefore no point in trying to avoid or repress bodily action and many good reasons to try to understand it, control it, and use it.

Receivers decode communication in terms of the total stimulus presented. Body action language may carry as much as 65 percent of the social meaning.

Research into the portrayal and recognition of emotional states such as anger, love, and fear has shown that we do rely on learned action habits to decode at least these highly abstract messages. Certain cultures and groups have action patterns that are stereotyped in ways different from our own. We should use stereotype to be understood, but not so much as to appear artificial.

In general a speaker should be so saturated with his subject and audience that his body action language will be both dynamic and spontaneous. It is also evident that we communicate through many learned action stereotypes that a speaker must utilize.

Empathy involves a muscular reaction in which the audience imitates in part the actions of the speaker. A speaker should adapt his bodily action to the empathic requirements and expectations of his audience.

Prolonged repression of normal bodily action can result in emotional disintegration. One should use meaningful bodily action to help control speech fright as well as to communicate the message.

The *general impression* is a synthesis of all the action elements that are communicated to an audience. Your dress should be appropriate for the occasion and in keeping with the expectations of the audience.

Promptness in arriving is also an important consideration: seldom are we offensive by being early.

If there is any question about the advisability of standing or sitting, you should probably stand.

Posture is an integral part of your impression not only in terms of what the audience infers cognitively and empathically but also in terms of your own perceptions and reactions to yourself. Good posture and poise present a picture of studied nonchalance. The great danger is in appearing artificial, conspicuous, or out of phase.

Walking is an important method in expressing various moods and degrees of emphasis. It serves as a form of physical punctuation for the speaker. Walking also has empathic value for the audience. It can afford physical relief to a cramped or suffering audience.

The recommendations for good facial expression are: (1) avoid inadvertent or inappropriate facial stereotypes; (2) make eye contact with the audience; (3) free your natural and spontaneous expressions so that they may reinforce your message.

Some gestures are used primarily to emphasize or reinforce parts of the message. These are the *reinforcing* gestures. Others are used primarily to describe the shape or size of objects and are called *descriptive* gestures.

The standards of good bodily action call for: (1) *appropriateness* to your subject, your particular physiology and personality, and the size and nature of the audience; (2) *variety of* bodily action, so that monotony does not cause a loss of the reinforcing effect; (3) *physical and* (4) *verbal coordination,* which involve correct timing and the use of the entire body in an integrated way; and (5) *dynamic and spontaneous projection* of a lively, animated sense of communication.

Speech Communication Principles

1. Receivers decode communication in terms of the total stimulus presented. A large amount of social meaning is conveyed by the nonverbal cues.

2. Cultures and subcultures create their own forms of nonverbal communication.

3. Except in isolation, nonverbal cues accurately communicate most emotional concepts.

4. Our actions may speak so loudly that our verbal codes are meaningless.

5. We express our attitudes through bodily action, the objects we wear and own, and our treatment of time and space.

6. Much of our nonverbal communication is expressed unconsciously.

7. The communication of simulated or stereotyped emotions can be perceived or identified with some reliability.

8. Real emotions, apart from the total stimulus, are difficult to identify perceptually.

9. Empathy involves a muscular reaction in which the audience imitates, in part, the actions of the speaker.

10. Promptness is admired in our culture; seldom are we offensive by being early.

11. Good posture and poise take the form of studied nonchalance.

A. *General Learning Outcomes*

1. We should learn that nonverbal cues profoundly affect what an audience decodes and abstracts from what we say.

2. We should learn the standards for determining appropriate bodily action and facial expressions as they relate to communication.

3. We should learn that we *cannot avoid* communicating, at least nonverbally.

4. We should learn that we express attitudes through bodily action, what we wear and own, and our treatment of time and space.

B. *Specific Learning Outcomes*

1. We should become sensitive to concealed unconscious messages as revealed by nonverbal cues and be able to describe the messages.

2. We should become sensitive to the fact that cultures and subcultures vary in their use of nonverbal signs and cues.

3. We should be able to relate the meanings conveyed in nonverbal communication to the process nature of human communication, as described in Chapter 1.

4. We should learn that simulated or stereotyped nonverbal emotional cues can be perceived with considerable reliability, though real emotions may be easily misread.

5. We should learn the difference between reinforcing and descriptive gestures and be able to illustrate several of each.

6. We should learn the standards of good bodily action: appropriateness; variety; coordination; and a dynamic projection of a lively sense of communication.

7. We should be able to relate the foregoing general and specific learning outcomes to the speech communication principles enumerated above.

C. *Communication Competencies*

1. We should learn to take time requirements seriously and start and close formal speech communication exercises on time.

2. We should learn to adapt our bodily action to the empathic requirements and expectations of an audience of fifteen to twenty-five students who are familiar with the content of this chapter.

3. We should be able to use bodily action to help control speech fright as well as to communicate a message.

4. We should learn to adapt our dress to the appropriate style for our subject and audience.

5. We should learn to use movement on the platform as a form of physical punctuation as well as for empathic relief.

6. We should learn to apply the lessons relating to good facial expression: avoid inappropriate facial stereotypes, make eye contact, and be natural.

D. *Study Projects and Tasks*

1. Develop a two-minute pantomine using no props in which you try to communicate an emotion (e.g., fear, love, rage). Let the class feedback be the measure of your effectiveness.

2. Watch a television show, the first half with only the picture and and the second half with only the sound. Describe, on one page for class discussion, the effects of having no verbal and no visual input.

3. Prepare a one-minute empathic pantomime in which through

bodily action you elicit an empathic response (e.g., walking and fatigue, lifting and strain, falling and pain, taste and ecstasy, and so forth).

4. Take turns trying to communicate the following messages through body action language:
    a. Don't blame me.
    b. I'm the piano tuner.
    c. She (he) is really quite something.
    d. Will you walk with me?
    e. Oh, George, let's not park here. (Oh, Gladys, let's park here.)

5. Prepare a two- to four-minute descriptive speech that requires considerable bodily action (e.g., shooting the rapids, water skiing, ski jumping, the big-game play, the close race, the big storm, a frightening episode, a close call, an embarrassing moment).

6. Observe the nonverbal behavior of a speaker (e.g., instructor, preacher, lecturer, student) and comment upon his effectiveness (e.g., appropriateness, variety, coordination, dynamism).

7. What nonverbal communication problems, if any, do you see attendant upon the solutions offered for a more participatory democracy in the appendix speech, "Communication and the Survival of Democracy"?

Chapter Six

Voice
and
Articulation

VOICE AND PERSONALITY

An expert in voice and diction training once said, "Bluntly stated, one may have a dull, uninteresting, or unpleasant voice because his voice is defective or improperly used; but he may also have such a voice because he is a dull, uninteresting, or unpleasant person."[1] He goes on to point out that vocal training, like all speech training, cannot take place in a vacuum, that it proceeds in intimate relationship with one's total personality. Just as personality affects voice, voice improvement may affect personality.

In any event, the voice contributes much to the total communication signal. It may be that it is the single most important code we emit. The studies on voice and social status discussed earlier (see p. 114) indicate the importance and the communication potential in this nonverbal code. Just as with pantomime, we have certain long-standing stereotypes that we take for granted. We recognize certain radio roles as voice stereotypes—

[1]Virgil A. Anderson, *Training the Speaking Voice* (New York: Oxford University Press, Inc., 1942), p. xvii.

"mean character," "hero," "sissy," "dunce." The very great danger is that one might assume an artificial or affected voice on a permanent basis. Of course, we all occasionally fail to match the voice we "put on" with the situation in which we find ourselves. Listen to yourself on occasion. If you sound "arty" when talking about fertilizer, it may just be that your voice habits are altering your personality in ways that will seriously affect your communication.

The discussion above leads to the question of what is abnormal or defective speech. Charles Van Riper, a highly respected speech clinician, put it quite clearly: "Speech is defective when it deviates so far from the speech of other people that it calls attention to itself, interferes with communication, or causes its possessor to be maladjusted."[2] Speech is defective when it is *conspicuous, unintelligible,* or *unpleasant.* Van Riper explains that not all deviations constitute defects:

> A child of three who says "wabbit" for "rabbit" has no speech defect, but the adult of fifty who uses that pronunciation would have one because it would be a real deviation from the pronunciation of other adults. If you said *deze, doze,* and *dem* for *these, those,* and *them* in a hobo jungle, none of the other vagrants would notice. If you used the same sounds in a talk to a P.T.A. meeting a good many ears would prickle.[3]

We are not totally consistent in our voice and articulation patterns; we vary, adjust, and adapt to moods, subjects, and people, as indeed we should. It is when our deviations become conspicuous in ways damaging to our intended communication that we have problems.

We do have many deviations that are not defects in a clinical sense yet do call for some personal remedial action. Some common problems that are usually quickly adjusted through normal speech training are fast rate, wrong pitch, loudness, and certain functional articulation disorders such as the substitution of a *d* sound for *th* sound (*dese* for *these*). However, there are physiological and functional disorders that may call for the services of a qualified speech correctionist. Your instructor is in a position to determine your needs. The physiological aspects refer to any uncorrected organic conditions such as cleft palate, malocclusion of the teeth, or enlarged tonsils, which *may* cause conspicuous deviations. The functional disorders are those caused by habitual misuse of all or part of the voice and articulation mechanisms—poor breathing, tight jaw, lazy lips. The majority of articulation problems are functional—that is, they are simply bad habits.

[2]Charles Van Riper, *Speech Correction* (5th ed.) (Englewood Cliffs, N.J.: Prentice-Hall, Inc., 1972), p. 29.
[3]Ibid.

THE VOCAL PROCESS

The vocal process involves organs of the body whose primary function is physiological. We use muscles and bones that have as their first responsibility respiration, mastication, and swallowing. In using or retraining these organs for speech, therefore, we must take care not to create a radical perversion of the physiological functions. That physical moods or states such as exhaustion or inebriation cause noticeable physical variations is obvious. That these same and related states affect the sound of the noise and notes produced is also obvious. This combination of noise and musical notes is voice, and voice is a large part of the stuff of which communication is made. For these reasons, a brief physiological description of the speech organs is necessary.

In order to produce modifiable sound, a mechanism with certain functions and characteristics is necessary. In almost any musical instrument, an *energy source* is the first prerequisite, whether it be a violin bow or a saxophone player's lungs. The second requisite is a *vibrator,* such as the violin string or the saxophone reed. The third function involves strengthening or building up the resultant sound; this is called *resonation*. The resonators of the violin are the hollow body and the texture of the materials, whereas the primarily metal texture of the saxophone produces a sound easily distinguishable from a violin. When one alters or modifies the size, shape, and texture of the resonating agents in some recognizable, consistent, or pleasing way, we call it music. Let us now analyze the human vocal process in the same terms.

The Energy Source

The breathing machinery is our energy source for voice production (phonation). The primary purpose of this machinery is to bring oxygen into the lungs as a source of fuel for the body and also to expel the waste gases. The various physical demands of the body noticeably affect this machinery. When running we need more energy (oxygen), and therefore our breathing becomes harder or faster. Speech after running the hundred-yard dash is difficult.

We normally speak on exhalation rather than inhalation. Thus we are quite apt to notice a heavier than usual inhalation cycle, particularly if it is public speech and we are under some emotional load. According to the James-Lange theory (see p. 96), the awareness of an unexplained physical reaction such as this one might lead to speech fright and may in fact *be* emotion. It is normal for the inhalation effort to be different in public speaking for the reasons indicated. We should of course make every effort for our breathing machinery or energy source to operate as efficiently as possible. This involves good posture, comfortable clothes, ventilation, bodily rest, and an understanding of the unexpected inhalation variations that are the source of much speech fright.

The Vibrator

The vocal cords within the larynx or Adam's apple are the vibrating agents. The larynx, located on top of the trachea or windpipe, has a flap called the epiglottis, which closes when you swallow. The air is forced up the trachea through the vocal cords in the larynx and causes them to vibrate, producing sound. Figure 6–1 shows clearly the trachea and the esophagus. Probably all of us have had the experience of food going down the "wrong throat," which is usually the result of swallowing food at the instant of starting phonation. Because speech is an overlaid function, it is not too unusual for this to happen. You are really asking the epiglottis to be both opened and closed at the same time. A physical problem such as this is normally taken care of naturally by the body's defense systems. You automatically cough and expel the food or liquid from your windpipe. However, if this happens during a speech, the psychological impact may be quite frightening. The dangers of chewing gum or throat lozenges while speaking are evident. The embarrassment is not worth whatever relaxation the chewing affords.

The Resonators

The sound produced by the action of the energy source and the vibrator now permeates the entire head, so that the head then becomes an agent of resonation. We said earlier that sound changes as the resonators vary in size, shape, and texture. The cavities in your head are quite readily altered. For example, the size and shape of your aural cavity are changed as you open your mouth or shift your tongue position. If you hold your nose, you immediately notice a change in vocal quality. This is because a certain amount of sound escapes through your nose when you speak. The nasal cavity is controlled and changed by the action of the tongue and soft palate. The sinuses in your head also are resonators; when their texture and size is changed, as during a head cold, you are quickly aware of voice changes. We recognize people by their voices in large part because of the inherent qualities of their resonators, but it is also evident that we have considerable control over resonation if we work at it. This is demonstrated by people who make a living at imitating other people's voices.

The Modifiers

The resonated sound is now more precisely modified, interrupted, and delineated in conventionalized segments, which we may call speech. The modifying agents are the lips, teeth, tongue, jaw, and soft palate. Their function is most recognizable in the consonant interruptions. Try to say the word *pill* without bringing your lips together. The *p* demands a specific kind of labial modification; so do other letters like *b* or *m*. The consonants are really voiceless except for certain mechanical noises that may go with them, such as the hissing of an *s*. The vowels carry the voice. The consonants are known through the alteration and specific interruptions of those vowels by the modifying agents, namely the lips, teeth, tongue, jaw, and palate. The importance of the modifiers to articulation is self-evident. If there are physiological defects, such as defective teeth or cleft palate, acceptable enunciation may be difficult until one has

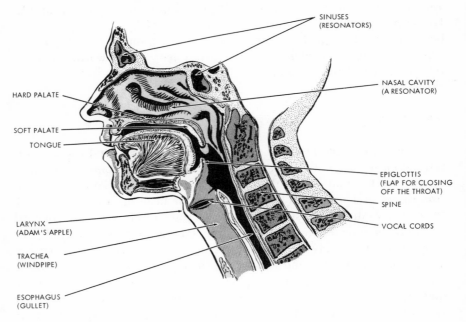

FIGURE 6–1. Where Speech Sounds Are Formed.

surgery or has been taught to compensate by a qualified speech patholo-gist. Faulty enunciation is more commonly caused by lack of knowledge, lazy speech habits, or, on occasion, overly precise habits.

VARIABLE CHARACTERISTICS OF VOICE

There are certain attributes of voice that you can vary in easily dis-tinguished ways and over which you have considerable control. You can change your *rate* or speed of utterance; you can adjust your *loudness* almost as you would that of a radio; you can speak at different *pitch* levels; and you can alter the overtones or partial tones, which represent a kind of *quality* control often referred to as *timbre* or *vocal color*.

Rate

There are test passages devised for actually measuring your verbal speed in wpm's (words per minute).[4] In general, a rate in excess of 185 wpm is too rapid for a normal public speaking situation, and a rate of less than 140 wpm is too slow.[5] The problem of measurement is complex, for cer-tain communications utilize a very rapid rate and others a slow or mixed rate. A further problem is that words and sounds are not truly separately formed units but tend to flow from one sound to another; this affects both articulation and pronunciation. Take the phrase "Did you eat?" If really speeded up, it becomes, "Jeet." This process is called *assimilation*. The length of sound or tones is also a factor, as are pauses, phrasing, and general rhythm patterns.

The duration of sounds and words normally varies with emotional moods. We typically use tones of relatively short or even staccato duration when expressing anger and more prolonged tones for expressing love. Good speakers tend to have a longer average duration of words than do poor speakers. A poor speaker is more apt to use staccato speech con-sistently.

A person's use of pauses and phrases is also a factor in his rate of speaking. The "meaningful pause" is no idle jest; it has much to do with our communication. Phrases are selected groups of words that typically form a fragmentary thought unit. In oral speech you have much more

[4]F. L. Darley, "A Normative Study of Oral Reading Rate" (Master's thesis, State University of Iowa, 1940).

[5]Grant Fairbanks, *Voice and Articulation Drillbook* (New York: Harper & Row, Publishers, 1960), p. 115. Some authorities argue that since listening rates may be 400–800 wpm, a public speaking rate of 200 wpm is not unrealistic.

flexibility than grammar permits in written communication. You should be guided by the fine shades of meaning you wish to express, rather than by mechanical rules. The pauses occur between the words and phrases, and the number and duration of pauses seriously alter the expression or meaning. The complexity and nature of your speech material should also affect your decisions on phrases and pauses. If you were to use a long pause after a phrase for emphasis, fine, but if the phrase were relatively inane you might appear ridiculous. If you were to use long pauses in a random manner not related to meaning (not an uncommon error), you then *confuse* your audience. The short pauses generally indicate that there is more to come. If you routinely use a rather intermediate length pause without consistently relating it to what you are saying, you run the added danger of monotony. Be sure that your speech pattern of pauses and phrases does not take on a fixed pattern or rhythm that interferes with your communication.

Rhythm patterns really involve all the variable characteristics of voice. Excessively recurring pitch and volume patterns also contribute to the singsong, pause-phrase problem so prevalent among improperly trained speakers.

Loudness

A very common fault among beginning speakers is an improper projecting of the voice to the audience. They either project more volume than the situation calls for or, even more typically, they do not project enough. It is essential that your audience be able to hear you. Loudness refers to the magnitude of the total signal. You may think of this generally as volume, but speech science indicates that volume is so intimately related to pitch that the term may be misleading. Your volume is easier to raise as your pitch goes up. Futhermore, it is possible to speak with more force or intensity without proportionately altering your volume. If your duration of tones is too short, you may not be getting adequate loudness simply because the mechanism has not been given a chance to produce for you; this may be caused by a restricted energy source or breathing apparatus, but most likely it is related to your pitch selection. More will be said of this in the following discussion on pitch.

The psychological reasons for this common lack of projection involve a form of avoidance of the speech situation. You tend to *withdraw* from threatening situations. Poor projection is a logical and normal device when you cannot really run away. It may also be a form of *repression*; you hold yourself in check emotionally to get through the ordeal. Once again, loudness suffers. It is almost as if speaking with a soft, barely audible voice is the next best thing to not being in the speech situation at all.

Your audience will help you adjust your loudness. Look at them for feedback signs. Are they straining to hear? Are they withdrawing?

Much of what we call vocal variety is related to loudness. The force with which you utter certain phrases or words is a form of oral punctuation and can add much to understanding. The manner in which force is applied is also a factor. You may use a lot of oral exclamation marks or you may, through intensity, figuratively underline many words. In the latter case the intensity could go either way; that is, the contrast or variety is important. An audible whisper can be powerful nonverbal as well as verbal emphasis under some speech situations. These are some of the loudness dimensions of vocal variety.

Pitch

The frequency of vibration of the vocal cords determines the measurements of the sound wave. The frequency of vibrations in a sound wave is *pitch*. More simply, pitch refers to a tonal position on a musical scale. When we speak, we typically range through a variety of pitches, which are normally distributed in terms of usage. That is, if we were to plot the number, we would find a central pitch about which the others vary in relatively predictable frequencies. The typical musical range may include two octaves. The problem of *optimum* pitch level for a given person is a complex one. To locate your best general pitch level often involves a compromise between mechanical vocal efficiency and what is generally accepted as being pleasing or appropriate. For example, if your *optimum* pitch is exceptionally high for a man in our culture, you may wish to lower your *habitual* pitch level even though you may lose some vocal efficiency. If you lower your pitch unreasonably, this loss of vocal efficiency shows up as inflexible pitch or lack of variety and may also result in an impairment of loudness.

For most people, optimum pitch should be the habitual or central pitch. Our optimum pitch is not infrequently found a little below the habitual or normal pitch due to tensions that restrict the apparatus. Young men may so deliberately strive for very low voices that the reverse is occasionally true.

Trying to locate your optimum pitch from the viewpoint of vocal efficiency alone is fun (if not always entirely reliable). With the aid of a piano, determine in relation to middle-C the lowest and highest note you can sing without a complete loss of quality. This interval is your singing *range*. "The average voice will be found to perform best when the speaking level is at approximately the midpoint of the lowest octave of the singing range."[6] The next step is to try to locate your habitual or most frequently used pitch by a sample of normal speech. Hit the piano keys in the vicinity of the optimum pitch already located as you speak or read until you get a kind of blend or synthesis. You will then have a rough idea as to whether or not your present general pitch level is adequate.

It is obvious that you could speak at your best all-around pitch and be terribly monotonous if you became a "Johnny-one-note" who lacked pitch variety in the form of *shifts* or *inflections*. A shift is a pitch change that occurs between independent sounds or phonations; an inflection is a pitch change without interruption of a given phonation.

Quality

Voice quality is a product modification and modulation of the vocal cord tone by the resonators. It is that attribute of tone and sound waves which enables us to discriminate between two sounds that are otherwise alike in pitch, duration, and loudness.[7]

Other things being equal, we can still easily distinguish the excessively nasal, breathy, or harsh voice. In addition to these, we are able to make nonverbal distinctions of a much more subtle nature: for example, we recognize the voice of a person sincerely touched by a tribute or the voice of a person who is suppressing anger. Emotional moods affect voice quality and may have a profound effect upon emphasis and meaning. In this context, voice quality is often referred to as *timbre*.

Quality is considered defective when it is routinely deviate and when the deviations detract from the message or meaning. Certain organic disorders, such as a cleft palate, or nasal obstructions, can cause these defects. Emotional moods may also result in quality deviations which, even if temporary, appear as defects. There are, in addition, the strictly temporary, organic insufficiencies caused by head colds, sore throats, and the like. However, we are primarily interested here in nonorganic, functional defects—in other words, with faulty habits.

Some of the more common voice-quality problems are nasality, breathiness, and harshness.

---

[6]Anderson, *Training the Speaking Voice*, p. 368. For women the average is just under middle-C;for men it is one octave lower.
[7]Fairbanks, *Voice and Articulation Drillbook*, chs. 1 and 15.

Nasality. This problem is caused by an excess of nasal resonance particularly for nonnasal voiced sounds. The vowels are most noticeably deviate. Aside from other organic defects, the problem is typically caused by not opening the mouth wide enough or by improper use of the soft palate or tongue. The factor of assimilation also plays a role here. A person may excessively run the nasal sounds right into following vowels, or when the vowel precedes the nasal consonant, he may have initiated the nasal resonance too early, that is, during the phonation of the vowel. This is called assimilated nasality and is one of the more frequent bad habits to guard against. Opening the mouth wider and a firmer tongue action help control the initiation and termination of nasal resonance.

Breathiness. If your vocal cords do not draw close enough together during phonation, an excess of unvocalized air escapes, giving your voice a breathy or aspirated quality. Functional reasons for this phenomenon may be related to faulty breathing habits (see p. 132), insufficient loudness, or too low a pitch level. Improper or too frequent inhalation, often caused by deviate-rate characteristics, may be at fault. Insufficient loudness automatically causes more unvocalized air to escape. A whisper is obviously breathy; on the other hand, it is practically impossible to emit a really loud tone that is breathy. The role of pitch is related in that if you are straining for an unusually low pitch, you may affect both loudness and larynx control, either of which can cause breathiness.

Frequent temporary causes of breathiness are overexertion, emotional strain, illness, and on occasion certain affectations thought to be desirable.

Harshness. Harshness is meant here to include also huskiness, hoarseness, and throatiness. These terms and more are specifically defined by voice scientists, but for our purposes we may think of all these as describing a rasping, unmusical quality. We all do it frequently when grunting, growling, or when suffering from a sore throat after cheering at a football game.

A chronic harshness is often organically caused and should call for diagnosis by both a qualified speech pathologist and a physician. The most frequent functional cause is a routine misuse of voice, which, if serious enough, can lead to organic pathologies. This misuse is typically accompanied by tension in the laryngeal muscles, which may be caused by general tension and emotional load (see Chapter 4) or by a speaker's too frequent attempts to show strain, emotion, or earnestness in his communication. He actually constricts his throat while attempting to project loudness (particularly at low pitches) at the same time. This results in a stridently harsh quality often referred to as "clergyman's throat."

General tenseness is probably the most common functional cause of a consistently harsh vocal quality.

THE ARTICULATORY PROCESS

The Organs of Articulation

The word *articulation* refers in general to a mobile joining or fitting of things together. For example, the bones and cartilages in your elbow are said to articulate. The word is well suited to the action of the speech organs as they interact with one another and help fit or join the various sound units into agreed-upon patterns that we call speech. This articulating of bones, muscles, teeth, and so on is obviously amenable to training. Just as the musician, typist, and surgeon must learn certain motor skills and habits pertinent to the articulating of the knuckles, bones, and cartilages in their hands, so too must the speaker develop good skills and habits with his articulating mechanisms. If a musician is lazy with his fingers, it qualitatively decreases the beauty or acceptability of his effort. If a typist is careless about the use or consistent placement of her fingers, it may cost her a job. Your habits and training in articulation of such organs as teeth, tongue, lips, palate, and jaw are of great importance to you also.

Articulation where dialect-related should be adapted to groups and situations to some extent, particularly if you are a part of those groups. Many students have developed two dialects to facilitate communication. Whatever the utility of such adaptation, take care that you don't develop poor, unplanned articulations of a primarily mechanical nature. These might call adverse attention to yourself regardless of the situation. You may wish on occasion to test or make an inventory of your articulation habits to be sure you are not becoming careless. A short articulation test is supplied at the close of this chapter.

Common Articulatory Faults

Some of the more common causes of slovenly articulation in a mechanical sense are: (1) locked jaw, (2) lazy lips, and (3) mushy mouth.

Locked Jaw. The speaker simply will not open his mouth wide enough. His jaw is tight and seems locked in position. He talks through his teeth and nose because the sound has to get out somehow. His projection is curtailed; his resonance is mismatched; his vowel quality is particularly impaired. This may in part be caused by tension and speech fright, but the admonition is the same—unlock your jaw, open your mouth!

Lazy Lips. In this case the lips are so tight or so slack that in either condition they do not adequately shape the mouth opening for proper vowel resonation or for the proper articulation of the labial or lip consonants (*p, b, m, w, f, and v*). The rule is simple: allow your lips to perform their necessary functions. The visual lack of lip action is also disconcerting to many listeners. Unless you are a ventriloquist, free your lips.

Mushy Mouth. This problem is caused primarily by feeble or sluggish tongue activity. Because the tongue is our most important articulation organ, you may foul up a large part of your speech if you are guilty of this fault. The fine shades of tone between vowels are obviously in jeopardy, since the tongue position in large part decides the shape and size of the aural cavity. Many consonants also depend heavily upon vigorous and precise tongue action. A *th* sound (*th*ese) easily becomes a *d* sound (*d*ese) if the tongue is lazy and does not move forward far enough to actually articulate with the teeth. Other consonants such as *d, l, r,* and *s* also call for vigorous and specific tongue action. If your tongue action is slack, languid, drooping, and feeble, you will be afflicted with mushy mouth. A vigorous and firm tongue action where you can feel your tongue articulate with your teeth on the appropriate sounds is your best safeguard against this problem.

A check of your articulation habits may be made by referring to the phonetic and diagnostic sentence inventory found under "Study Projects and Tasks" at the end of this chapter.

PRONUNCIATION

Pronunciation is the act of expressing the sounds and accents of words so that they conform with accepted standards. In addition to aiding understanding, appropriate pronunciation has much to do with the way an audience evaluates and judges a speaker. Adapting and relating to varying standards and groups to which you may belong again points up the utility of bidialectation. In old Milwaukee the word *theater* was typically pronounced "the-*ay*-ter," a compromised carry-over from the German pronunciation of "das Theater" (tay-*ah*-ter). In Detroit we hear "the-*uh*-ter." Some localities may say "drammer" for "drama." The in-

valuable dictionary is a little awkward on some pronunications because there are three generally accepted dialects in the United States
(eastern, southern, and general American). The most prevalent dialect
is general American, and our dictionaries and national mass media are
geared to this dialect. That there are others is obvious.

The problem of showing desired or different pronunciation of a word
on paper is awkward at best. One way is to agree upon and memorize a
common code of symbols based strictly upon sound and free of un-
phonetic spelling. Thus, the International Phonetic Alphabet was born.
It has one symbol for every different sound in the language. The news
services use a system of respelling similar to what was used earlier in
this section. Dictionaries use diacritical marks and relatively stable words
as pronouncing criteria. Accent or stress is indicated as primary (') or
secondary (,).

EXAMPLES OF PRONOUNCING SYSTEMS

Word	Diacritical System	International Phonetic System	Respelling System
chaotic	/kā-'ät-ik/	[ke'atɪk]	kay-otic
theatre	/'thē-ət-ər/	['θiətɚ]	the-uh-ter
nativity	/nə-'tiv-ət-ē/	[ne'trvətr]	nay-tiv-ity

A guide to pronunciation and the dictionary diacritical system is carefully explained in the introduction to any good dictionary[8] and is well
worth your reading.

The principal sounds of our culture in the alphabet of the International Phonetic Association (IPA) are listed below; also shown are the
written symbols used from our spelling alphabet, key words with the
sound in italics, the diacritic symbols, and (for the vowels and diphthongs)
the name we give the sound.

Some of the more common pronunciation errors in the English
language are improper stress, errors in spelling-phonetics (pronouncing
words as they are spelled), sound substitutions, sound additions, sound
reversals, and sound subtractions. The system of indicating pronunciation
shown on pages 143–145 is used by permission from Webster's Eighth
New Collegiate Dictionary, © 1973 by G. & C. Merriam Co., Publishers
of the Merriam-Webster Dictionaries.

---

[8]See especially *Webster's Eighth New Collegiate Dictionary* (Springfield, Mass.: G. &
C. Merriam Company, 1973).

PHONETIC ALPHABET
CONSONANTS

Phonetic Symbol	Written Symbol	Word	Diacritic Symbol	Sound Name
[p]	p	*p*ip	p	
[b]	b	*b*e	b	
[m]	m	*m*e	m	
[t]	t	*t*ea	t	
[d]	d	*d*o	d	
[n]	n	*n*o	n	
[k]	k	*k*ill	k	
[g]	g	*g*o	g	
[ŋ]	ng	si*ng*	ŋ	
[θ]	th	*th*ink	th	
[ð]	th	*th*is	*th*	
[f]	f	*f*or	f	
[v]	v	*v*ile	v	
[s]	s	*s*ip	s	
[z]	z	*z*oo	z	
[ʃ]	sh	*sh*oe	sh	
[ʒ]	zh	a*z*ure	zh	
[tʃ]	ch	pic*t*ure	ch	
[dʒ]	j	*j*udge	j	
[r]	r	*r*are	r	
[l]	l	*l*ove	l	
[h]	h	*h*im	h	
[w]	w	*w*it	w	
[hw]	wh	*wh*en	hw	
[j]	y	*y*es	y	

VOWELS

Phonetic Symbol	Written Symbol	Word	Diacritic Symbol	Sound Name
[i]	ee	s*e*nior	ē	long e
[ɪ]	i	s*i*t	i	short i
[e]	a	ch*a*otic	ā	half-long a; long a
[eɪ]	a	d*a*y	ā	long a
[ɛ]	e	b*e*t	e	short e
[æ]	a	c*a*t	a	short a
[ɑ]	a	f*a*ther	ä	two-dot a
[ɔ]	o	*o*ught	ȯ	circumflex o
[oʊ]	o	g*o*	ō	long o

[u̇]	oo	t*oo*k	u̇	short double o
[u]	u	t*oo*	ü	long double o
[ʌ]	u	s*u*n	'ə	short u
[ə]	a	*a*bove	,ə	short u
[ɝ]	ea	h*ea*rd	'ər	"er" sound
[ɚ]	er	pe*r*cent	,ər	"er" sound

DIPHTHONGS

[ju]	u	use	yü	half-long u
[au̇]	ou	out	au̇	
[aɪ]	i	ice	ī	long i
[ɔɪ]	oi	oil	oi	

IMPROPER STRESS

prag'matist instead of pragmatist
super'fluous instead of su'perfluous
com'parable instead of 'comparable
tele'graphy instead of te'legraphy

ERRORS OF SPELLING-PHONETICS

salmon/'sal-mən/	instead of	/'sam-ən/
rancid/'ran-kid/	instead of	/'ran (t)-səd/
hearth/hürth/	instead of	/'härth/
zoologist/'zü-alə•jəst/	instead of	/zō-'äl-ə-jəst, zə-'wäl-/

SOUND SUBSTITUTIONS

just/jist/	instead of	/'jəst/
tremendous/tri-'men-jəs/	instead of	/tri-'men-dəs/
sieve/sēv/	instead of	/'siv/
ask/äsk/	instead of	/'ask/
catch/kēch/	instead of	/'kach, 'kech/
heinous/'he-nəs/	instead of	/'hā-nəs/

SOUND ADDITIONS

elm/'el-əm/	instead of	/'elm/
film/'fil-əm/	instead of	/'film/
umbrella/əm-bər-'rel-ä/	instead of	/,əm-'brel-ə/
wash/'wȯrsh/	instead of	/'wȯsh/
athlete/'ath-ə-lēt/	instead of	/'ath-,lēt/
indict/in-'dīkt/	instead of	/in-'dīt/

Sound Reversals

larynx/'lar-ningks/	instead of	/'lar-iŋ (k)s/
cavalry/'kal-vərē/	instead of	/'kav-əl-rē
perspiration/'pres-pi-rā-shən/	instead of	/ˌpər-spə-'rā-shən, pər-'sprā
tragedy (trăd'ĕjĭ)/'trad-əjē/	instead of	/'traj-əd-ē/

Sound Subtractions

popular (pŏp'lēr)/'päp-lər/	instead of	/'päp-yə-lər/
eighth/'āt/	instead of	/'ātth/
geography/'jäg-rə-fē/	instead of	/jē-'äg-rə-fē/
history (his'trĭ)/'his-trē/	instead of	/'his-t (ə-)rē/
picture/'pich-ər/	instead of	/'pik-chər/

SUMMARY

Your voice contributes much to your nonverbal and total communication signal; it may be the most important code you emit. Voice and articulation are thought to be defective when they deviate so far from the norm that they call undue attention to themselves.

Some common problems are fast rate, wrong pitch, loudness, and faulty articulation.

The vocal process involves: an *energy* source, or our breathing machinery; a *vibrator*, or our vocal cords; *resonators* such as the cavities in our heads; and, finally, *modifiers* such as our lips, teeth, tongue, jaw, and palate. The alteration or modification of the size, shape, and texture of these agents is the primary factor involved in producing speech.

There are certain attributes of voice over which you have considerable control. These are *rate, loudness, pitch,* and *quality.* The rate characteristic is influenced by assimilation, duration, pauses, phrases, and rhythm. Loudness includes considerations of intensity, volume, and vocal variety. Pitch includes considerations of central, habitual, and optimum levels and range. Quality factors considered most critical are nasality, breathiness, and harshness.

Articulation involves the interacting of the speech organs as they help fit or join the various sound units into agreed-upon patterns that we call speech. Your habits and training of such organs as teeth, tongue, lips, palate, and jaw are of great importance to proper articulation. Some of the more common mechanical faults are *lazy lips, locked jaw,* and *mushy mouth.*

Pronunciation is the act of expressing the sounds and accents of words so that they are best adapted to your total communication. There are three general dialects in the United States: eastern, southern, and general American. Our mass media and dictionaries are geared to the general American dialect.

The problem of showing different pronunciations in print is solved in part through pronouncing systems such as the International Phonetic Association alphabet, respelling, and the diacritical mark system; the last is preferred by our dictionaries.

Some of the more common pronunciation errors in the English language are *improper stress, spelling-phonetics, sound substitutions, sound additions, sound reversals,* and *sound subtractions.*

Speech Communication Principles

1. The way we project our voices is related not only to our mood and message but also to the distance or space between us and the audience.

2. Our social status is communicated by cues in the voice.

3. We express our attitudes through our voice and articulation.

4. Just as personality affects voice, voice improvement may affect personality.

5. Speech is defective when it is conspicuous, unintelligible, or unpleasant.

6. The majority of articulation problems are functional, that is, matters of habit.

7. The vocal process involves organs of the body whose primary function is physiological.

8. Good speakers tend to have a longer duration of words than poor speakers.

9. For most people, optimum pitch should be the habitual or central pitch.

10. A chronic harshness is most often organically caused.

11. Articulation, where dialect-related, should be adapted to groups and situations to some extent, especially when you are a part of those groups.

12. The most prevalent dialect is general American.

13. Your voice contributes much to your nonverbal and total communication signal. It may be the most important code you emit.

A. *General Learning Outcomes*

   1. We should learn the communication impact of the nonverbal cues of voice and articulation.

   2. We should learn the practical dimensions of the vocal and articulatory processes and of pronunciation as they relate to communication.

B. *Specific Learning Outcomes*

   1. We should learn to describe and explain the vocal process in terms of *energy source, vibrator, resonator,* and *modifiers.*

   2. We should learn to describe and explain the variable attributes of voice: *rate, loudness, pitch,* and *quality.*

   3. We should learn and be able to apply some of the various pronouncing systems: International Phonetic Association alphabet, respelling, and the diacritical mark system.

   4. We should learn to identify the more common pronunciation errors in the English language: improper stress; spelling phonetics; sound substitutions; sound additions; sound reversals; and sound subtractions.

   5. We should learn to identify the common articulatory faults of locked jaw, lazy lips, and mushy mouth.

   6. We should be able to relate the foregoing general and specific learning outcomes to the speech communication principles enumerated above.

C. *Communication Competencies*

   1. We should be able to adjust in a short oral exercise our vocal rate, volume, pitch, and quality to the satisfaction of an audience of fifteen to twenty-five students who are familiar with the content of this chapter.

   2. We should be able to employ one of the pronouncing systems

in such a way that our pronunciations generally agree with those of our instructor.

3. We should be able to understand and correct our own pronunciation errors in terms of the six common errors through ten-minute drill and practice sessions.

4. We should be able to discover our own optimum pitch and learn to adjust (if necessary) our habitual or central pitch.

5. We should be able to adjust our articulation in a short oral exercise to the satisfaction of an audience of fifteen to twenty-five students who are familiar with the content of this chapter.

D. *Study Projects and Tasks*

1. Record your voice for five minutes, one-half while reading, the other half while speaking impromptu; do a written report and inventory of your voice and articulation in accordance with the advice given in this chapter.

2. Record your voice, as above, and then write a report on the personality you think others might associate with it. Record it again, attempting to portray a different personality through voice and articulation alone. Write a brief, second report explaining your success or lack of it.

3. Locate a piano, and following the advice of this chapter find your *optimum* pitch and compare it to your habitual pitch. Report any wide variations to your instructor.

4. Select a 100–300-word poem, scene from a play, novel, or other material for an oral presentation to the class. Prepare a short extemporaneous introduction for the material and practice to sharpen your voice, articulation, and pronunciation. Prepare for class feedback. See the readings appended at the end of this chapter.

5. In two or three well-chosen sentences write a characterization for each member of the class based upon your impressions derived primarily from his voice and articulation habits. Your instructor may wish to read some of these aloud (anonymously).

6. Prepare an oral report or essay attempting to prove or disprove any of the speech communication principles enumerated earlier.

7. Pair off with another class member and take the following

phonetic inventory. Using either the form provided or a description based on the material in this chapter, report the areas in which you feel you would like to improve.

ARTICULATION INVENTORY

The following phonetic inventory and diagnostic sentences are taken from a drill book by the late Grant Fairbanks, an outstanding voice scientist.* Each sentence tests a particular sound as listed on the phonetic inventory.

PHONETIC INVENTORY

TYPE OF ERROR

	Substitution	Omission	Distortion	Slighting
1. [i]	. . .	. . .	. . .	. . .
2. [ɪ]	. . .	. . .	. . .	. . .
3. [eɪ]	. . .	. . .	. . .	. . .
4. [ɛ]	. . .	. . .	. . .	. . .
5. [æ]	. . .	. . .	. . .	. . .
6. [ʌ]	. . .	. . .	. . .	. . .
7. [ɑ]	. . .	. . .	. . .	. . .
8. [ɔ]	. . .	. . .	. . .	. . .
9. [oʊ]	. . .	. . .	. . .	. . .
10. [ʊ]	. . .	. . .	. . .	. . .
11. [u]	. . .	. . .	. . .	. . .
12. [ju]	. . .	. . .	. . .	. . .
13. [aʊ]	. . .	. . .	. . .	. . .
14. [aɪ]	. . .	. . .	. . .	. . .
15. [ɔɪ]	. . .	. . .	. . .	. . .
16. [ɝ]	. . .	. . .	. . .	. . .
17. [ɚ]	. . .	. . .	. . .	. . .
18. [r]	. . .	. . .	. . .	. . .
19. [l]	. . .	. . .	. . .	. . .
20. [m]	. . .	. . .	. . .	. . .
21. [n]	. . .	. . .	. . .	. . .
22. [ŋ]	. . .	. . .	. . .	. . .
23. [j]	. . .	. . .	. . .	. . .
24. [w]	. . .	. . .	. . .	. . .
25. [hw]	. . .	. . .	. . .	. . .
26. [h]	. . .	. . .	. . .	. . .

*Form 2, "Phonetic Inventory—Sentences for Phonetic Inventory" from *Voice and Articulation Drillbook*, Second Edition, by Grant Fairbanks. Copyright © 1960 by Grant Fairbanks. By permission of Harper & Row, Publishers, Incorporated.

PHONETIC INVENTORY

TYPE OF ERROR

	Substitution	Omission	Distortion	Slighting
27. [p]	...	...	...	...
28. [b]	...	...	...	...
29. [t]	...	...	...	...
30. [d]	...	...	...	...
31. [k]	...	...	...	...
32. [g]	...	...	...	...
33. [f]	...	...	...	...
34. [v]	...	...	...	...
35. [θ]	...	...	...	...
36. [ð]	...	...	...	...
37. [s]	...	...	...	...
38. [z]	...	...	...	...
39. [ʃ]	...	...	...	...
40. [ʒ]	...	...	...	...
41. [tʃ]	...	...	...	...
42. [dʒ]	...			

SENTENCES FOR PHONETIC INVENTORY

1. Some people reason that seeing is believing. They feel they are frequently deceived.
2. Bill saw a big pickerel swimming in the ripples. He licked his lips in anticipation of a delicious fish dinner.
3. The agent remained away all day. Late at night he made his way to the place where the sailors stayed.
4. Special regulations were necessary to help the selling of eggs. Several Senators expressed pleasure.
5. Sally banged the black sedan into a taxicab. It was badly damaged by the crash.
6. I am unable to understand my Uncle Gus. He mutters and mumbles about nothing.
7. John started across the yard toward the barn. His father remarked calmly that he'd better not wander too far.
8. Is Shaw the author of "Walking on the Lawn"? I thought it was Walter Hall.
9. Don't go home alone in the snow. You'll be cold and soaked and half-frozen.
10. Captain Hook pushed through the bushes to the brook. From where he stood it looked like an ambush.
11. As a rule we go canoeing in the forenoon. The pool is too cool in June.
12. Hugh refused to join the musicians' union. His excuse was viewed with amusement.
13. Fowler wants to plow all the ground around his house. Somehow I doubt if the council will allow it.

14. The tile workers were fighting for higher prices and more time off. They tried to drive back the strike-breakers.
15. The boys toiled noisily in the boiling sun. They enjoyed the work that Ray avoided.
16. First the girls turned on the furnace. Then they worked on burning the dirty curtains.
17. I'll undertake it sooner or later. Perhaps after another summer is over, in September or October.
18. Our barn is covered with brilliant red roses. The broad crimson roof draws admiring crowds from far and near.
19. Lawyer Clack held his little felt hat and his black gloves in his lap. He silently placed the will on the table.
20. Mr. Miller had climbed many mountains, but the chasm before him was the mightiest in his memory.
21. Laden down by their burdens, Dan and Ned ran from the barn into the open. The tornado was not far distant.
22. The monks had no inkling that anything was wrong. Suddenly the strong tones of the gong rang out.
23. Did you ever speculate on the uses of the familiar onion? On the value of a yellow yam?
24. Wait until the weather is warm. Then everyone will want to walk in the woods.
25. "What is that?" he whispered. Somewhere from the left came the whistle of a bobwhite.
26. Hurry back, anyhow, Harry. It will help if you only hear half the re-hearsal.
27. Part way up the slope above the pool was a popular camping spot. Many people stopped there for picnic suppers.
28. The British were not bothered about the robbery. They believed they could bribe the Arab to betray his tribe.
29. After waiting for twenty minutes the train left the station. The excited recruits sat and talked all night.
30. The doll's red dress was soiled and muddy, but the ragged child hugged it adoringly.
31. Old Katy had a particular dislike for hawks and crows. She calls them "wicked creatures."
32. The big dog began to dig under the log. Gary forgot his hunger and grabbed his gun.
33. "For breakfast," said father, "I find that coffee is the staff of life. Grape-fruit is a food for infants."
34. I believe I'll save this heavy veil. The vogue might be revived eventually.
35. We thought that the theory was pathetic, but we had faith that something would lead to the truth.
36. My father finds it hard to breathe in this weather. Even the heather withers.
37. The successful student does not assume that class exercise is sufficient. He also practices by himself outside.
38. My cousin's play, "The Zero Zone," is amusing, but it won't be chosen for a prize because it doesn't deserve it.
39. The fishing ship was in shallows near the shore. In one motion a wave crushed it on the shoal.

40. I make no allusion to sabotage, but an explosion near that garage is unusual.
41. Mitchell was a righteous old bachelor. He watched for a chance to chase the children out of his orchard.
42. All but Judge Johnson pledged allegiance to the legislation. He objected that it was unjust to the soldiers.

8. What are the major differences between a written message and a spoken one? Use the speech in the appendix, "Communication and the Survival of Democracy," as a case in point (e.g., judge it in terms of meaning, clarity, and interest).

9. Find four words that are relatively new to you in the appendix speech. Show how to pronounce them using the diacritical marking system and the respelling system.

10. Selected practice readings:
    a. *Pompeii* (anon.)
    b. *If—* by Rudyard Kipling.
    c. For a more typical message, you might prefer to select a paragraph or two from the model speech in the appendix.

POMPEII

Roll back the tide of many hundreds of years. At the foot of vine-clad Vesuvius stands a royal city. Like all cities, both ancient and modern, there exists a number of contrasts, particularly between the splendid palaces of the royalty and the simple dwellings of the plebeians.

Despite the contrasts, life is happy, unhurried. The stately Roman walks the lordly streets, or banquets in the palaces of splendor, or dines simply in a modest home. There is the bustle of busy thousands; you may hear it along the thronged quays; it rises from the amphitheatre and the forum. And there is the sense of quieter moments along the less frequented streets. As a whole, it is the home of luxury, of gaiety, and of joy. The togaed royalty drowns itself in dissipation, the lion roars over the martyred Christian, and the bleeding body of the gladiator dies at the beck of applauding spectators. Little by little the senses are deadened in riotous living. It is a careless, a dreaming, a devoted city.

Lo! There is blackness on the horizon, and the earthquake is rioting in the bowels of the mountain! Listen! A roar! A crash! And the very foundations of the eternal hills are belched forth in a sea of fire! Woe for that fated city! The torrent comes surging like the mad ocean! It boils above wall and tower, palace and fountain, engulfing a screaming, scuttling mass of people! There is hardly time for escape! Many are caught unaware in their beds and are suffocated by the fire and ash that settles over the city. Pompeii, once a city of luxury, of gaiety, and of joy, becomes a massive tomb.

—An adaptation from an anonymous writer

IF—
by Rudyard Kipling
If you can keep your head when all about you
    Are losing theirs and blaming it on you;
If you can trust yourself when all men doubt you,
    But make allowance for their doubting too;
If you can wait and not be tired by waiting,
    Or, being lied about, don't deal in lies,
Or, being hated, don't give way to hating,
    And yet don't look too good, nor talk too wise;

If you can dream—and not make dreams your master;
    If you can think—and not make thoughts your aim;
If you can meet with triumph and disaster
    And treat those two impostors just the same;
If you can bear to hear the truth you've spoken
    Twisted by knaves to make a trap for fools,
Or watch the things you gave your life to broken,
    And stoop and build'em up with wornout tools;

If you can make one heap of all your winnings
    And risk it on one turn of pitch-and-toss,
And lose, and start again at your beginnings
    And never breathe a word about your loss;
If you can force your heart and nerve and sinew
    To serve your turn long after they are gone,
And so hold on when there is nothing in you
    Except the Will which says to them "Hold on";

If you can talk with crowds and keep your virtue,
    Or walk with kings—nor lose the common touch;
If neither foes nor loving friends can hurt you;
    If all men count with you, but none too much;
If you can fill the unforgiving minute
    With sixty seconds' worth of distance run—
Yours is the Earth and everything that's in it,
    And—which is more—you'll be a Man, my son!

SOURCE: "If," Copyright 1910 by Rudyard Kipling, from the book *Rudyard Kipling's Verse*: definitive edition. Reprinted by permission of Doubleday & Company, Inc., and Mrs. George Bambridge.

PART THREE

MESSAGE PREPARATION

Speech messages, like machines, musical scores, and fine art, have a classifiable structure and internal consistency. Learning to systematically prepare speech messages is similar to the labor of the engineer, the artist, or the composer. This is not to say that there is no elusive and critical artistry in these persons' works, but all true masters are quick to point out the overwhelming importance of training, of practice, of purpose, and of structure.

In Parts I and II we learned that speech communication can be verbal, nonverbal, related to signs, related to time, space, actions, and objects, intentional or accidental, and, of course, rhetorical. In Part III we are primarily concerned with intentional, rhetorical, written, and verbal symbols, that is, a carefully planned message purpose and a carefully arranged and organized outline to carry out your general and specific purposes. The message is still the crux of all speech communication. Part III is designed not only to assist you in intelligently preparing messages but also to make you more able critics of the messages with which we are daily bombarded.

Purpose and delivery are crucially important in all areas of speech communication, but especially so in public speaking, hence the emphasis of Chapter 7. It's a little like having a specific and realizable goal. If you don't know *where* you're going, how will you know *when* you're there? If you don't know what your purpose is, how will you know if you've achieved it? More to the point, perhaps—how will you go about preparing, organizing, and presenting your message?

Fundamental to the structuring of messages around a purpose is a knowledge of location of materials, note-taking techniques, arrangement of materials, the mechanics of outlining, means of achieving clarity and interest, types of supporting materials, and audio-visual aids. These topics, among others, are the subjects of Chapters 8 and 9. More will be said about the special psychological arrangement of primarily persuasive messages in Part IV.

A well-organized message and outline should help give you the confidence born of the knowledge that you've done your homework and that you've got a system. The systematic structure should make it easier for you to remember your material and easier for the audience to understand and retain it.

A general review of the hoped-for learning outcomes that will result from a close reading of Part III, particularly when related to class projects and performances, follows. A more specific set of learning outcomes and communication competencies, together with relevant projects and tasks, is appended to each chapter.

We should learn the fundamentals of message preparation so that we are able to structure our own messages and to criticize more knowledgeably those of others.

We should learn the general purposes and goals of speaking.

We should learn the four principle types of delivery and when to employ each.

We should learn how and where to locate materials for our speech.

We should learn to differentiate the standard ways of organizing ideas.

We should learn the major systems for arranging parts of a message.

We should learn about the rhetorical principles of unity, coherence, and emphasis.

We should learn the six basic principles of outlining message materials.

We should learn three principles of learning and how they are related to message preparation.

We should learn the basic forms of support in terms of clarity and interest.

We should learn how to relate audio-visual aids to the "cone of experience."

Chapter Seven

Purpose and Delivery in Speech Communication

GENERAL PURPOSES FOR SPEAKING

In previous chapters we have discussed some general theory and knowledge essential to intelligent, objective speech and communication, namely, the process of communication, language, collective behavior, emotion and its relation to confidence, and nonverbal communication. In this chapter we will study the general purposes for speaking and the various ways of delivering a speech. The specific ways of preparing and outlining a speech will be explained and illustrated in Chapters 8 and 9.

The insurance agent who comes to your door with policy in hand is primarily interested in selling you the policy. Even though he may present an armload of objective and practical information to indicate the risks of not having insurance and to describe how the policy works, his general purpose is to persuade. A speech billed as an "Informative Talk on the Arts" may turn out to be a highly derogatory piece of persuasion on abstraction or abstract painting, although most of the material may be truly informative and perhaps very entertaining. These examples illustrate the difficulty of intelligently dividing the purposes for speaking into even the apparently obvious ones of informing, persuading, and entertaining. It is probably true that there is no such thing as a purely informative, purely persuasive, or even purely entertaining speech. Even the most overgeneralized, flamboyant oratory probably conveys at least a smidgeon of information. Entertainment, from court jesters to comedy players, has for ages been the vehicle of subtle and effective persuasion. And some very effective persuasive speeches have had the sound or ring of informative talks; some, in fact, were compositionally almost all information.

The sheer number of informative, entertaining, or persuasive elements does not alone determine the kind of speech or speaker purpose with which we are dealing. The arrangement of the material, the information level of the audience, the speaker's style and vocal adaptation, and many more factors must be taken into consideration.

With the above paragraphs as qualifiers, let us become a little more arbitrary. Educationally, it is practical and useful to discuss these various purposes one at a time. If your instructor asks you to prepare an informative speech for the next class and you state your purpose as being "to inform the class why they should join the Republican party," you had better be prepared for criticism. He will probably suggest that you save the subject for the persuasive speech assignment and that you then more accurately state your purpose as being "to persuade the class to join the Republican party." You might use as your purpose "to inform the class about the history of the Republican party." The speech then becomes essentially informative or persuasive depending upon the treatment and emphasis you use. Certainly this *could* be an excellent, *essentially* informative speech subject.

It might be said that your real purpose is known in terms of the primary reaction you want from your audience. The general purposes for speaking may be stated as follows:

THE GENERAL PURPOSES FOR SPEAKING

Purpose	*Goals*
To inform	Clarity
	Interest
	Understanding
To persuade	Belief
	Action
	Stimulation
To entertain	Interest
	Enjoyment
	Humor

To Inform

One of the most frequent purposes for speaking is to inform people of something about which you either have more knowledge than they do or know in a different or more specific way. This is the purpose of a typing teacher who is showing students how to approach the keyboard. The teacher or instructor also lectures primarily to inform. The speaker who would inform has the obligation of making his information or instruction clear and interesting as well as easy for the audience to learn, remember, and apply. To achieve these goals, a speaker should know something of how man learns (this will be discussed in detail in Chapter 9). Briefly, a man learns through his previous knowledge and experience, and he learns more easily when material is arranged in some meaningful sequence or serial order. He remembers better because of reinforcement (enhancing the message through repetition), verbal emphasis, organization, effective use of voice, and similar techniques. The primary goal in informative speaking is *audience understanding*; the key principles involved are *clarity, interest,* and *organization of material.*

To Persuade

The general goals of a speech to persuade involve getting people to believe something, getting people to do something, and stimulating or inspiring people to a higher level of enthusiasm and devotion.

These divisions (belief, action, and stimulation), like the general purposes for speaking, often overlap and are not easily discernible at first glance. When no immediate action is being called for, the speaker may be attempting to convince or to induce *belief.* This might be illustrated by persuasive speeches, such as "Foreign Policy," "The Threat of Fascism," or "Uphold the United Nations." No specific and immediate action or performance is asked of the audience. Rather, the audience is asked to agree with the speaker and to believe and be convinced. This assumes that the audience does not typically have the power to act except in some remote or distantly related way. If the audience were the Congress of the United States, these could become action purposes.

When the audience is asked to do something specific immediately following the speech, the purpose is one of *action.* A speech asking for donations to the Red Cross that is concluded by passing a container for contributions among the audience is an obvious example. Electioneering speeches asking people to vote or to sign petitions are further examples. Most sales talks are action speeches—even though the TV announcer does not really expect you to run out and buy a Chevrolet at 11:30 P.M. Nevertheless, the action is typically specific and typically available in the very near future.

When a speaker is seeking a higher degree of audience involvement, enthusiasm, or devotion on issues and beliefs that the audience already holds, his purpose is one of *inspiration* or *stimulation.* One example might be a speech for party unity at a political convention after the nominee has been selected. In short, the purpose of stimulation is found in those situations where the speaker is: (1) not trying to change any basic attitudes, but rather to reinforce them; (2) not trying to prove anything, but rather to remind his listeners; or (3) not calling for any special or unique action, but inspiring his listeners to a more enthusiastic fulfillment of the actions to which they are already committed.

To Entertain

When your purpose in speaking is to help people escape from reality and you sincerely desire that they enjoy themselves, your general purpose is to entertain. The "fun," after-dinner, or radio-television speeches are the most typical examples. These speeches involve jokes, stories, and a variety of humor depending upon the experience, skill, and personality of both the speaker and his audience. In a speech solely to entertain, the audience should preferably understand that purpose and be genuinely encouraged to relax and enjoy themselves.

A word of warning is in order for both beginning and experienced speakers. Other things being equal, the speech to entertain is the most difficult kind of speech to give! The feedback is more rapid and far less subtle. There is little doubt when a funny story or joke does not succeed. The effect on the speaker is often demoralizing, and the presentation and adaptation of the rest of the speech may suffer. Practice is critical.

TYPES OF DELIVERY

The four principal ways of delivering a speech are (1) by reading from a manuscript, (2) by memorization, (3) by impromptu delivery, and (4) by speaking extemporaneously. The subject and the occasion are the primary determinants of which one or which combination of types should be used at a given time.

Reading from Manuscript

In this type of delivery the speaker presents his subject by reading a completely written out, verbatim manuscript to the audience. Fortunately, the subjects and occasions that demand this method of delivery and preparation are few, for this is probably the most difficult of all the types of delivery; however, such occasions are on the increase. An important policy speech by the United States Secretary of State may be dissected word by word by foreign governments; therefore, it will call for maximum accuracy in wording and a minimum of opportunity for misstatement. Our mass media make further demands on a speaker's flexibility. Very often a copy of the manuscript is obtained in advance of the speech so that the newspapers can print or quote the speech almost before it has been delivered. When such a speaker deviates from his manuscript, he invites trouble and confusion. Certain highly complicated and technical subjects demanding absolute accuracy may call for manuscript reading. Very rigid and inflexible time limits may also necessitate reading from a manuscript so that the speech does not exceed the allotted time; this is especially important in radio and television broadcasts.

The problems of this type of delivery, even for a classroom speech, should be obvious. The preparation must be painfully accurate, but, worse, there is little chance for spontaneity or for momentary adaptation or adjustment of the material to the ever changing demands of the audience. The actual delivery, except for very exceptional readers, is hamstrung by a lack of eye contact and directness; the speaker's eyes are typically glued to his manuscript, except for furtive glances into outer space, which only cause him to lose his place. This embarrassment may cause him to retrench, by which he loses emphasis and vocal variety. A lively sense of communication is almost impossible to maintain in this situation—and for some the word is *dull*.

One of the real ironies in speech training is that the beginner, apparently in an effort to avoid the inevitable confrontation with the audience, may use the manuscript as something to hide behind. This only delays his self-development, because it usually results in an unsuccessful audience experience, which is extremely frustrating to the beginner.

Yet even with all the problems attendant upon this type of delivery, we find ourselves in a world demanding more and more dependence on manuscripts.

When writing a manuscript to be read orally to an audience, we have to make some fundamental stylistic changes in the actual writing. The language of a writer, for example, is less direct. He uses *a person, people, the reader*; a speaker uses *I, you, they,* and the like. The other differences are not as obvious at first glance. Although we might remember to extemporize in short, simple sentences, our tendency is to write in longer, more complex ones. When we are doing literary writing (that is, material that will be read silently by the receiver), we have less problem with this style, for the receiver can go back and reread and review. But in a speech, the necessity for shorter, less complex sentences is critical, as is the use of more repetition, restatement, and reinforcement. Remember, the listener cannot stop and go back over the material or use a dictionary like a reader can. The style of the spoken word must be instantly intelligible to the listener. This requires more illustrations, examples, analogies, contrasts, and vividness than the style for a written essay. The secret is to write "out loud."

The actual delivery of the speech from a manuscript is equally special. Normal eye contact and vocal patterns are often disrupted. In addition, the manuscript itself may be a problem if the lighting is bad or your vision otherwise impaired. A fan has been known to foul up a speaker. The position of the manuscript also creates problems. You may either hold your manuscript in your hand at about waist level or put it on a lectern. In one case, you inhibit your hand gestures; in the other, you hide most of your body. In either method, the problem is to let your eyes drop to the paper while keeping the head erect.

Most good manuscript reading involves a generous amount of memorization, but partial memorization only—that is, language groups held together for you by meaning. This permits you more time to look at the audience. When your memory gives out, you refer back to the manuscript for the cue that allows you to move on to the next memorized language group. The problem is trying to find your place! Marginal notes, underlinings, and various markings can assist you here. The real insurance is an intimate understanding of your message and practice, practice, practice. To effect real oral communication, you must learn to spend considerably more time looking at your audience than at your manuscript.

The problems of voice may also be acute. Most people do not read well without practice and training; that is why we have courses in interpretative reading. Beginners may singsong, use stress and inflection separate from meaning, or project a withdrawal tendency in a sonorous, unbroken monotone. The varying of rate, loudness, pitch, and quality, along with the judicious use of pauses, is essential in manuscript reading. It is most critical to keep these vocal variations closely coupled to the meanings involved. The secret is to try to develop a *wide eye-voice span*. (For a more extensive discussion of voice, see Chapter 6.)

Memorization

Occasionally an effective speech is delivered from memory (that is, a carefully written speech, every single word of which is committed to memory). Except among actors, who work so hard at sounding spontaneous despite exact memorization, there is little justification for a completely memorized speech. The effort required in a word-for-word memorization is enormous. The delivery, except by professional actors, is typically stilted, rhythmical and impersonal, and the method allows for no easy adaptation of material to the audience. However, just as in reading from a manuscript, many frightened beginners will undertake this enormous task. This method can induce real panic if memory does fail. There is literally neither a place to go nor a specific thing to do. The gradeschooler repeating a memorized poem is in far better shape than most speakers, for he has a prompter. Moreover, it is only a poem, not his own personal message, that is in jeopardy.

This is not to say that you should not memorize *parts* of your speech. A dramatic introduction, a conclusion making use of poetry, a piece of testimony, and a complicated group of statistics (when visual aids are unavailable or awkward) are all likely passages for memorization.

Impromptu Delivery

When you are asked to speak on the spur of the moment, without advance notice or time for detailed preparation, this type of speaking is called impromptu. Typically, however, you will not be asked to make even an impromptu speech unless you have some general subject-matter preparation, if only by reason of your special knowledge, experience, or training. If you have some special experience or expertise that makes you vulnerable to unexpected requests for a "few words," you had better carry at least a mental outline with you at all times. In this way you cut the risks of being caught completely off guard. A student from Kenya once observed that even in the most informal gatherings he was routinely asked to explain something about Kenya, his reaction to America, and the like. On these occasions, he eventually found himself in a true speaking situation as more and more people gathered around and he did more and more of the talking. To improve these presentations, he prepared several highly adaptable speech outlines, committed the outlines to memory, and then tried to anticipate each situation and group in which he was apt to find himself. He explained that he has become so adept at this that he is now disappointed if he *isn't* asked to say a few words. People are amazed at his fluent and well-organized "impromptu" remarks!

Your instructor may give you some experience in impromptu speaking by simply stating two or three speech topics, telling you to choose one topic, take a minute to collect your wits, and then start talking. If you find yourself in this or any other impromptu or potentially impromptu situation, here are some general rules that may help you:

1. Anticipate the situation. Try to avoid a true impromptu speech by figuring the odds on the likelihood of your being called upon and on what topic you will be speaking.

2. Relate the topic under consideration to your experience. You will tend to speak more easily and confidently about that with which you have had specific experience.
3. When in doubt, summarize. There may be moments when you lose the thread of what you were saying or where you were going. At this moment, a quick review or summary often restores perspective and allows your mind to retrack.
4. Be brief! The less impromptu exposure, the less chance for you to become incoherent.
5. Quit when you are ahead! All too often a man makes a good impromptu speech and then, either because he feels he has not said enough or because his momentary success has given him confidence, he continues to ramble on and on until he eventually dissipates whatever communication he had achieved.
6. If you really have nothing to say, then don't speak! Better to be thought a fool than to open your mouth and remove all doubt.

Extemporaneous Delivery

The extemporaneous method of speaking involves the preparation of a thorough but flexible outline, the cataloging of a wealth of potentially usable material, and the use of a basic or general outline, which is either memorized or carried by the speaker. The language and wording of the speech are adaptable, as is the use of speech materials and details.

In this method the emphasis is on knowing your subject and knowing your audience. It typically means collecting a lot more material than you will need. Thus, if one illustration or piece of evidence does not satisfy your audience, you will immediately be able to select another. If one strategy of organization is unclear, you will need a predetermined alternative to adapt to the audience confusion of the moment.

The chief and obvious advantage of extemporaneous preparation and delivery is that it gives you the flexibility and adaptability essential to an audience- and communication-sensitive speaker. You are able to respond successfully to the communication problems as they develop. You are thinking on your feet in the best sense of the term.

In general, extemporaneous delivery is most effective when given from a brief but meaningful outline, which is carried either in your head or your hand and supported by thorough preparation. This is the type of preparation and delivery expected of you except in those special exercises your instructor may announce.

CHARACTERISTICS OF GOOD DELIVERY

In the preceding section it was noted that extemporaneous delivery gives you potentially a more thorough understanding of your subject and the words you use and further that it gives you a flexibility of thought, adaptability of material, and a meaningful sensitivity (or *empathy*) toward your listeners. These are the essential qualities of good conversation and interpersonal communication. These same qualities should be manifest in all good speeches as well. The speaker who seeks to inspire need not sound artificial or take on the style of high elocution. A speaker can be eloquent without sounding like an oracle. On the other hand, adapting conversational qualities to public speaking does not mean employing a matter-of-fact voice, poor preparation, or careless language.

A very great speech teacher, James A. Winans, once put it this way: "It is not true that a public speech to be conversational need sound like conversation. Conventional differences may make it sound very different."[1] We are seeking the best qualities and moods of conversation, not a stylized version of conversation.

Research studies reveal that the characteristics most often associated with effective speaking include:

1. Clear organization leading to a meaningful conclusion.
2. A definiteness of concept and preciseness in language and wording.
3. A clear, distinct, and pleasant voice and articulation.
4. A forthright sense of communication indicated by some direct eye contact.
5. An alertness of body and mind, indicating enthusiasm.
6. A controlled yet flexible use of bodily activity, which enhances or reinforces meaning.

CHARACTERISTICS OF BAD DELIVERY

Speech studies undertaken to determine just what specific aspects of delivery are unpleasant, ineffective, or actually annoying to audiences are most useful in helping us recognize effective delivery.[2] Those aspects actually considered annoying include:

1. Evident lack of preparation and knowledge.
2. A dangling conclusion, in which the speaker seems unable or unwilling to close and simply repeats himself.
3. A mumbling of words leading to indistinct speech.
4. A general vagueness, indefiniteness, and lack of clarity.
5. Poor reading or delivery from manuscript (monotonous, stiff, indirect).
6. Superfluous verbalizations of such inserts as "ah," "er," and "uh."
7. Excessive mispronunciation and grammatical mistakes.

[1] James A. Winans, *Speech Making* (New York: Appleton-Century Crofts, 1938), p. 17.
[2] S. R. Toussaint, "A Study of the Annoying Characteristics and Practices of Public Speakers (doctoral dissertation, University of Wisconsin, 1938); see also Alan H. Monroe, "Measurement and Analysis of Audience Reaction to Student Speakers Studied in Attitude Changes," *Bulletin of Purdue University Studies in Higher Education*, 32, 1937.

✓8. A loss of temper over relatively routine disturbances or interruptions.

Other aspects of delivery that lead to ineffective speaking include:

1. A stiffness or rigidity of bodily action.
2. An avoidance of the audience by refusing to look at them.
3. A weak, indistinct, or monotonous voice.
4. Excessive nervousness or fidgeting.
5. An evident lack of enthusiasm.

SUMMARY

The general purposes of speaking are to inform, to persuade, and to entertain. Many speeches combine these purposes and are difficult to classify. The degree of information, entertainment, or persuasion in a speech does not alone indicate the speaker's purpose; we must also consider the arrangement of the material, the information level of the audience, and the speaker's style and vocal adaptation. It may be said that the real purpose is known in terms of the primary reaction desired from your audience. The primary goal in informative speaking is audience understanding. The key principles are clarity, interest, and organization of material. In a speech to persuade, the speaker tries to make people *believe* something, urges them to *do* something, or attempts to *stimulate* them to a higher level of enthusiasm. The goals of a speech to entertain are to help people escape from reality and to enjoy themselves without the threat of some hidden agenda or meaning.

The four principal ways of delivering a speech are by reading from a manuscript, by memorization, by impromptu delivery, and by extemporaneous speaking. In manuscript delivery the speaker presents his subject by reading a completely written speech verbatim to the audience. In memorization the speaker commits every word of his manuscript to memory. Impromptu delivery involves being asked to speak on the spur of the moment without advance notice or time for detailed preparation. In the extemporaneous method a thorough but flexible outline is prepared, a wealth of potentially usable material is cataloged, and a basic general outline is either memorized or carried by the speaker; the language and wording of such a speech may be specific, but they are always adaptable to circumstances, as is the use of speech materials and details.

The characteristics of good delivery include: a conversational quality; a definiteness of concept, wording, and pronunciation; a clear, pleasant voice and articulation; direct eye contact; enthusiasm; and a controlled yet flexible use of bodily action.

The characteristics of bad delivery include: evident lack of preparation; dangling conclusions; mumbling; vagueness; stiff reading; excess verbalizations; mispronunciation; loss of temper; rigid bodily action; lack of eye contact; weak voice; fidgeting; and an evident lack of enthusiasm.

Speech Communication Principles

1. The real purpose of a message is determined by the primary reaction you want from your audience.

2. The primary goal of an informative message is audience understanding; the key factors are clarity, interest, and organization.

3. The primary goals of a persuasive message are to make people *believe* something, *do* something, or *stimulate* them to a higher level of enthusiasm.

4. Many speeches combine the general purposes and are difficult to classify both by the speaker and the receiver.

5. Assuming a message of some intrinsic worth, the method of delivery and its concomitant ethical proof significantly affect how we perceive the source.

A. General Learning Outcomes

1. We should learn the general purposes and goals of speaking to better structure our own messages and to become a more able critic of others.

2. We should learn the four principle types of delivery and when each is appropriate.

3. We should learn the characteristics associated with good delivery and bad delivery.

B. Specific Learning Outcomes

1. We should learn to distinguish between speech purposes that are primarily informative, persuasive, and entertaining.

2. We should learn to describe and compare *extemporaneous* delivery to the other three types (reading from a manuscript, memorization, and impromptu).

3. We should become familiar with the characteristics associated with good delivery—namely, a conversational quality, a definiteness of concept, wording, and pronunciation, a clear, pleasant voice and articulation, direct eye contact, enthusiasm, and a controlled yet flexible use of bodily action.

4. We should become familiar with the characteristics associated with bad delivery—namely, an evident lack of preparation, dangling conclusions, mumbling, vagueness, stiff reading, excess verbalizations, mispronunciation, loss of temper, rigid bodily action, lack of eye contact, a weak voice, fidgeting, and an evident lack of enthusiasm.

5. We should learn the general rules for managing well in impromptu speaking situations.

6. We should be able to relate the foregoing general and specific learning outcomes to the speech communication principles enumerated above.

C. *Communication Competencies*

1. We should learn and be able to explain the conditions under which a message should be delivered by reading and the problems and limitations of manuscript reading.

2. We should learn the general rules for impromptu speaking and be able to apply them successfully in one or two short classroom exercises.

3. We should learn to identify, while observing speech behavior, those characteristics associated with bad (and good) delivery.

4. We should be able to distinguish the general and specific purposes of oral and written messages.

D. *Study Projects and Tasks*

1. Write out, word for word, a two- to-three minute message in your best oral style. Then rehearse and prepare it for reading from a manuscript.

2. Observe a speaker (live, radio, or TV) for at least fifteen to thirty minutes. On two separate sheets of paper note the characteristics of good and bad delivery that you have observed.

3. From newspapers and magazines select and clip items that are clearly (1) informative, (2) persuasive, (3) entertaining, or (4) a combination of these and identify the general and specific purposes of each.

4. Your instructor will assign you two numbers at random from 1 to 50. These refer to the numbered impromptu topics below. Review the suggestions on page 163 for making good impromptu speeches, choose one of the two topics, take thirty seconds to prepare, and speak impromptu for one minute before the class.

   1. Animals I Have Known
   2. The Most Valuable Modern Invention
   3. A Mystery I Never Solved
   4. Things I Want to Learn
   5. Learning to Dance
   6. Learning to Swim
   7. My First "Public Appearance"
   8. "It Pays to Advertise"
   9. Learning to Play Golf
   10. My Hobby
   11. What To Do on a Rainy Day
   12. The Radio or Television Program I Like Best
   13. My Favorite Character in Fiction
   14. Improvements I Would Suggest for This School
   15. How I Taught Someone to Drive
   16. How I Got Out of a Difficult Situation
   17. The Most Important Story in This Week's News
   18. Charisma
   19. Improvements I Would Suggest for This City
   20. A Joke That Didn't Come Off
   21. My Favorite Relative
   22. My Pet Superstition
   23. Styles Have Changed
   24. Books Worth Buying
   25. Something I Do Well
   26. "Pride Goeth Before a Fall"
   27. The Best Purchase I Ever Made
   28. The Music I Like Best
   29. My Last Vacation
   30. Why I Like (Do Not Like) to Live in This State
   31. A Buying Experience!
   32. " 'Tis More Blessed to Give . . . "
   33. The Time That It Paid to Disobey
   34. A Selling Experience!
   35. My Green Thumb
   36. A Camping Experience
   37. The First Money I Ever Earned
   38. An Embarrassing Moment

39. The Popular Radio or Television Program I Like Least
40. Propaganda
41. Spiritual Aspects of Nature
42. Beauty Justifies Itself
43. Censorship in American Life
44. Where There Is a Will There's Always a Way
45. The Time I Won
46. An Obnoxious Character
47. God Is Dead
48. An Unforgettable Moment
49. The Love of My Life
50. Honesty Is the Best Policy

5. Prepare an oral report or essay attempting to prove or disprove any of the speech communication principles listed earlier.

6. Determine the general and specific purposes of the speech in the appendix. Indicate support for your opinion by citing specific line members.

7. In what style do you think the speech in the appendix was actually delivered? Why? Which of the four types would be your second choice? Why? What are the hazards of each type? (The audience was composed of several hundred people attending the annual convention of the Speech Communication Association in Chicago, 1972.)

Chapter Eight

Preparing and Organizing the Message

PREPARING THE SPEECH

In Chapter 7 we discussed the *general* purposes of speaking, namely, to inform, to persuade, and to entertain. In this chapter we are concerned with the *specific* purpose, the specific audience, and methods of locating, organizing, and outlining materials.

The Specific Purpose

The specific purpose is the specified *outcome, objective,* or *response* that your speech is supposed to achieve. A teacher, for example, talks in terms of lesson plans (outlines); the specific purpose is typically called a learning outcome (desired objective or response). A geometry teacher has the general purpose of *informing* (about geometry). His specific purpose or learning outcome for a given class might be to inform the class about the applications of geometry to map and chart reading.

If you are interested in flying, you might start your speech preparation with the general idea (purpose) of informing the class about flying. It is obvious that the general subject of flying is far too big a subject or goal for a short speech. You will want to restrict your subject to what you can reasonably cover in the time available. You might state your specific purpose as follows: to inform the class about the principle of aerodynamics that allows a wing to "lift." Or you might talk about weapon and propeller synchronization in World War I Jennys. The more specifically you can state just exactly what it is you are trying to say or do, the more systematic and intelligent will be your preparation and your communication. In some speeches to persuade you may not wish to state your purpose to the audience orally; however, in terms of preparation and outlining, you should always start with a clear, precise statement of your specific purpose.

The Audience

Close on the heels of your specific purpose should come a careful consideration of your audience. In fact, if you know your audience, you should really be considering your specific purpose and audience at the same time. Most often one knows the general type of audience he will meet (for example, businessmen, teachers, housewives). In the case of your classroom speeches, you will have an opportunity to know the specific audience. The introduction speeches give you a marvelous opportunity to gain insights into your specific audience.

Suppose your specific purpose were "to explain the five managerial functions of planning, organizing, controlling, coordinating, and communicating to an audience of management personnel." Your preparation and organization would be different if in checking on your specific management audience you discovered that they were executive vice-presidents rather than first-line foremen. These principles apply to both groups, but the application might vary widely. You might revise your specific purpose in the light of this important audience factor so that the purpose became "to explain the five managerial functions of planning, organizing, controlling, coordinating, and communicating to an audience of *executive-level* personnel."

Pertinent factors to be considered before you can most efficiently and intelligently collect speech materials are the occasion, the environment, and the general descriptive measures of an audience (size, age, education, and other factors are discussed in detail in Chapter 2).

The speech subject, the language you use, the clothes you wear—all these and many other matters are often directly related to the purpose of the gathering. The question in part is, "Why have I been chosen to speak?" Are you a second or third choice? Are you being paid? Is this a special meeting called for the express purpose of hearing you? Did the audience pay for this experience? Were they forced to come? Is this perhaps a regular meeting in which they routinely ask interesting people to speak to them? Are you the headline attraction, or are there other events or speakers on the program? If so, when, in what order, and for how long does each person speak? All these questions are critical to a speaker's preparation for and adaptation to an audience.

A speaker should if possible know the special rules, habits, rituals, and practices he is likely to encounter. For example, organizations such as the Kiwanis, Rotary, Lions, Eagles, and Elks have relatively standard meeting formats. Many of these same organizations have certain "fun" rituals, which, though great sport if you are forewarned, can also be a nightmare if you are caught unaware. A speaker was once fined $1 before saying his first word because he was wearing a red necktie! Know your occasion so well that you can predict these things and actually work them into your preparation.

Part of the occasion is the inevitable speech of introduction. (If you *are* the introducer, read Chapter 14 now.) A bad speech of introduction can make life very difficult for the speaker. Seldom does the introducer mean any harm; quite the contrary, his lengthy speech is meant to be complimentary. He may even be so enthusiastic about your subject that he will give part of your speech for you. The chairman or introducer almost always asks the speaker for help, and the novice or incautious speaker almost always answers with a blush, "Oh, it doesn't really matter." But it *does* matter, so *do* give him help. He will appreciate it and you will cut down your risks at the same time. On one occasion, a speaker was asked to give a ten-minute critique on a championship debate held before a business audience. His university public relations department had sent a standard release to the chairman of the debate. This release consisted of about four pages of biographical material, including a careful listing of every award and publication with which the speaker had ever been associated. You can guess what happened. The well-intentioned chairman read off every word and took ten embarrassing minutes to do it. This terrifying experience for the critique speaker evoked the somber comment, "Make a careful study of the occasion and then expect the worst!"

Closely related to the occasion is the location and arrangement, that is, of the room or building in which the speech will be made. The same speech delivered in a church, a restaurant, or a fraternity house will be altered communicatively by the location alone. People have different expectations for different types of buildings. Your proximity to the audience is also a factor. If you are on an elevated platform far removed from the first row of the audience, the style of your delivery should be qualitatively different than if you are close to the group. The seating arrangement of the audience also makes a difference, as we learned in Chapter 2.[1]

Another environmental factor is the use of a public-address (P.A.) system. If you do have a P.A. system, it may importantly affect the way in which you use your visual aids. Most microphones will fade if you get more than two feet away from them. It is a good idea to check such things *before* you speak. The noise level of the room is often a problem, as are the lighting and ventilation. Many of these circumstances can be controlled (or at least better adapted to) if you merely consider them early enough.

Effectiveness of visual aids is closely related to all these practical environmental factors. The size of the visual aid should be related to the size of the room and the size of the audience. A chart big enough for a group of 25 may be hopelessly small for a group of 300. A series of slides may be useless if the room will not darken, and a tape recording may not be audible in a room filled with echoes.

The time for which the speech is scheduled may make a difference. Occasionally A.M. and P.M. have been falsely assumed. The concept of "company time" versus "our time" often pertains, and a speaker might regulate not only the content but the length of his speech accordingly. It has been observed that industrial and business audiences are often more generous when they are listening on company time. The message is, of course, most critical. The audience-message analysis discussed in Chapter 2 is highly pertinent. Some practical questions are: (1) what is the significance of the subject for the audience? (2) what does the audience know about the subject? (3) what beliefs or prejudices does the audience have about the subject? and (4) what is the attitude of the audience toward the subject?

Some general descriptive measures discussed in Chapter 2 that may aid you in analyzing your audience are: age, sex, education, occupation, primary group memberships, and special interests.

Locating Materials

Once you have thoroughly considered your specific purpose and have related it to the analysis of audience and occasion, you are ready to start locating and collecting the materials that will constitute the speech itself. Obviously this collection of speech details should be closely related to

[1]Albert L. Furbay, "The Influence of Scattered Versus Compact Seating on Audience Response," *Speech Monographs*, 32, No. 2 (June 1965), 144–48.

your specific audience as well as to your specific purpose. The question now is, "Where do I find these materials?"

Your own knowledge and experience may give you a head start. Conversations with knowledgeable people can be invaluable. However, any serious interviewing or corresponding should usually be preceded by some modicum of reading and observing. The purpose of starting your more formal research early is to help you better understand what the important questions are. If, for example, you were going to interview an electrical engineering professor on "Information Theory," you would be well advised to browse through one or two of the classic books or articles in the field to get the maximum value out of the interview. The same would be true if you were going to interview a speech professor on such subjects as "Semantics," "Psycholinguistics," or "Congruency." Your probable question right now is, "Where do I find these sources to browse through?"

The Library. The simplest answer is your *library card catalog.* This obvious source represents a vast treasure-house óf information, so take advantage of it. Almost every library has the *Reader's Guide to Periodical Literature.* This source lists magazine articles by author, title, and subject matter. It is typically bound into annual volumes and is located in the reference section of the library. You use it much as you would the library card catalog. You may also look through the *Cumulative Book Index* and its predecessor, the *United States Catalog*; these sources do for books approximately what the *Reader's Guide* does for magazines. The *Book Index* is arranged according to author, title, and subject. While in the library, see if it has the *New York Times Index.* This is the only complete newspaper index in the United States and can be a real time-saver for you. There is also an *Index to the Times* of London, England.

A good set of general encyclopedias (such as *Britannica, Americana, New International*) and special ones (such as the *International Encyclopedia of the Social Sciences, Catholic Encyclopedia, Jewish Encyclopedia,* and the *Encyclopedia of Religion and Ethics*) is found in many libraries and very often presents the best short statement on a given subject to be found anywhere. These encyclopedias are typically kept current by annual supplements called yearbooks.

When in need of statistics and short statements of factual data, see *The Statesman's Yearbook, The World Almanac and Book of Facts,* and *The Statistical Abstract of the United States.* Smaller general encyclopedia such as the *Columbia* or *Everyman's* will also give compact statements and facts.

To learn more about the authority you may wish to discuss, interview, or quote in a speech, consult some of the better-known directories and biographical dictionaries, such as *Who's Who in America, Who's Who in*

American Education, Who's Who in Engineering, American Men of Science, and the *Directory of American Scholars.* For prominent Americans of former years, see *Who Was Who in America, The Dictionary of American Biography, Lippincott's Biographical Dictionary,* and *The National Cyclopedia of American Biography.*

Most professional or trade associations publish journals of their own. Some of these organizations are the American Bar Association, the American Bankers' Association, the American Medical Association, the Speech Communication Association, the American Psychological Association, and the American Federation of Labor. Many of the journals emanating from these organizations are indexed by special publications often available in your library (for example, *The Agricultural Index, The Art Index, Index to Legal Periodicals, Index Medicus, Psychological Abstracts,* and many more).

In addition to the *Statistical Abstract of the United States,* mentioned earlier, other government publications can be excellent sources of speech materials. The *Commerce Yearbook* and the *Monthly Labor Report* provide much valuable information. The *Congressional Record* is an especially fertile source for speech students. It includes a daily report of the House and Senate debates indexed according to subjects, names of bills, and congressmen, and an appendix with related articles and speeches from outside of Congress.

Other sources of materials are the thousands of organizations that issue pamphlets and reports, often at no cost. You can write directly to these organizations for information and in some cases receive a speech outline or manuscript in the return mail (for example, Planned Parenthood League, Inc., the World Peace Foundation, the American Institute of Banking, and the AFL-CIO). If you would like to know the addresses of these or other organizations, refer to the *World Almanac* under the heading "Associations and Societies in the United States."

If you cannot find enough information in the sources already cited, or if you would like to *start out* with a printed bibliography on your subject, you may obtain in some libraries a bibliography on bibliographies—an index of bibliographies called the *Bibliographic Index.* Check with your librarian for this material.

Conversation and Interview. Another way to gather materials is to converse with people about your selected topic, sort of "try it out" on somebody. If the somebody has first- or second-hand experience with your topic, you may be in real luck. If there are people on your campus or in your locality who are known experts on your topic and who are available for consultation, you may be able to turn from conversation to a more formal interview. If you embark on interviewing, always do some preliminary research so you can frame clear and succinct questions to your subject, who, after all, may be a very busy person. Explain early in the conversation why you want his opinion or information so that he does not think you are invading his privacy without good reason. On the same note, avoid loaded or biased questions (even though you may have a bias) and try to be objective throughout. Remember to note any sources he mentions. Listen carefully, letting your subject do most of the talking. You won't locate materials or learn very much if you dominate the conversation.

Note Taking

While you are reading and absorbing all the materials discovered through the devices discussed above, you must consider problems of selecting, sorting, evaluating, and finally recording the material. It will become evident that you need an almost mechanical system of taking notes if you are not to be overwhelmed by the sheer amount of information available to you. The problem of not remembering exactly what you read or where you read it is frustrating indeed, but if this failure of memory is serious enough to prompt a return trip to the library, you have lost preparation time as well.

A very general "yes-no" selection of your potential major sources is usually possible after rapid browsing or scanning. After this preliminary rough sorting, you are ready to record the details that are most likely to support your specific purpose and to coordinate with your audience analysis. One more general consideration is in order before you actually write things down. You may wish to revise, alter, or enrich your specific purpose as a result of your browsing and the subsequent important guidelines that emerge in terms of kinds of materials, issues, causes, or perhaps in your order of presentation. In other words, devise tentative categories or classifications. You can add, delete, or subdivide later as your search becomes more specific. This will also give you a head start on the eventual organizing and outlining of the speech itself.

Now you should start taking systematic notes. The emphasis is on the word *system*. As long as you have done the rough sorting suggested above and are not taking notes purposelessly or haphazardly, you may use any system that is workable for you. The most common system for library searches involves the use of 3 × 5 or 4 × 6 file cards. You may have noticed debaters actually carrying small metal file cases filled with cards arranged either alphabetically or according to the issues pertinent to their debate subject. You should keep only one subject, source, classification, and note on each card. The big advantage over a notebook is that you can rearrange file cards and thus reclassify or subclassify very easily. This shuffling of cards is very useful when you are actually ready to organize and outline your speech.

The next problem is what to write on the card. If you have a general source that you "may or may not" wish to use later, a short summary in your own words may be in order. You will then be better able at a later time to decide whether you wish to reread the article. If you find a statement by an authority that you may wish to use, take it down verbatim and put quotation marks around it. Be sure to get the authority's name and qualifications recorded. In transcribing testimony or statistics, make sure you record the date. It is a well-known fact that people change their minds. If you insert explanations or interpretations of your own, put brackets around the words so that at a later date you will not confuse your words with those of your sources.

In your English class you may have been schooled in a system of taking notes for a source theme. It should be useful here. Whether you use classifications at the top of the card or footnotes at the bottom will depend in part upon your training and preferences as well as the nature of your specific purpose and subject. Some samples are shown in Figures 8–1 through 8–4.

ORGANIZING THE SPEECH

One can start his thinking about organization in terms of the specific ideas and speech details he has collected or in terms of the general parts into which speeches can conveniently be divided. Let us first look at some useful principles for organizing the raw materials and then analyze ways of dividing or arranging the parts of a speech.

(Subject) *Creativity*   (Classification) *Mental Functions*

1. Absorptive—the ability to observe, and to apply attention.
2. Retentive—the ability to memorize and to recall.
3. Reasoning—the ability to analyze and to judge.
4. Creative—the ability to visualize, to foresee, and to generate ideas.

Source: Alex F. Osborn, *Applied Imagination,* 3rd ed. (New York: Charles Scribner's Sons, 1963), p. 1.

FIGURE 8–1.

Methods of Organizing Ideas

Chronological Method. In this method your materials are arranged according to the order in which a number of events took place. In discussing "Life on Earth," we would probably take the periods chronologically: (1) Archeozoic, (2) Proterozoic, (3) Paleozoic, (4) Mesozoic, (5) Cenozoic, and (6) Present. Most historical subjects lend themselves readily to this method; so do processes of a sequential, 1–2–3 order, such as film developing. Remember, however, that these subjects may be handled in different ways. History is often more interesting and meaningful if discussed topically.

Topical Method. In this method the material is ordered according to general topics or classifications of knowledge. To continue the example of history, we might concentrate on the history of religion, war, govern-

---

(Subject) *Prehistoric Man*   (Classification)   *Dinosaurs*

". . . you will often see cartoons showing cave men being chased by dinosaurs. But this could never have happened. The physical anthropologists tell us which bones are the bones of the prehistoric men who lived in caves. The paleontologists tell us which bones are the bones of the giant reptiles. The geologists tell us that the human bones come from layers of earth that are 50,000 years old, and the dinosaur bones come from rocks 150,000,000 years old."

Source: Donald Barr, *Primitive Man* (New York: Wonder Books, 1961), p. 10.

FIGURE 8–2.

(Subject) *Problem Solving*   (Classification)   *General*
         Systems   *Background*

Chapter 2 (Reasoning) of this book covers four special readings, including some special problems. Included are the following: 1. Reasoning in Humans; 2. An Exper. Sty. of P. S.; 3. The Sol. of Prac. Probs.; 4. Prob. Sol. Proc. of Col. students. [Looks impressive]

Source: T. L. Harris, and W. E. Schwahn, *The Learning Process* (New York: Oxford University Press, 1961), pp. 29–79.

FIGURE 8–3.

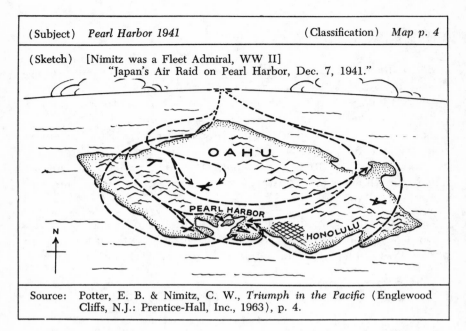

(Subject)   *Pearl Harbor 1941*   (Classification)   *Map p. 4*

(Sketch)   [Nimitz was a Fleet Admiral, WW II]
            "Japan's Air Raid on Pearl Harbor, Dec. 7, 1941."

Source: Potter, E. B. & Nimitz, C. W., *Triumph in the Pacific* (Englewood
          Cliffs, N.J.: Prentice-Hall, Inc., 1963), p. 4.

FIGURE 8–4.

ment, education, or science. The topical importance may or may not
violate chronology and is a very useful way to start breaking down very
broad topics. One can, for example, look at integration of the races in a
myriad of topical ways—educationally, socially, militarily, and eco-
nomically, for example. Similarly, a city may be described topically in
terms of its industry, employment opportunities, recreational facilities,
schools, climate, and so on.

Logical Method. This method involves generally accepted or obvious
cause-and-effect relationship, whether we are talking about the fall of the
Japanese empire or the building of a house or a boat. When the order is
natural or inherent in the subject or when the association of ideas is
self-evident, it may be convenient to organize our speech materials accordingly. This method differs from the topical in that subpoints almost always illustrate or explain that to which they are subordinate
unless the audience already knows the logical relationship. Thorough-
going audience analysis is imperative before using this method.

Difficulty Method. For some subjects, particularly those of a technical nature, it may be advantageous to organize your materials according
to an ease index or difficulty order, that is, proceeding from the easiest
aspect to the most difficult or complex. In discussing general principles
of electricity, we might arrange a series of ideas as follows:

1. The flashlight.
2. Switches.
3. Dry cells.
4. Light bulbs in a series.

5. Light bulbs in parallel.
6. Electromagnets.
7. Current and electrons.

Spatial Method. This method is particularly useful in certain types of geographical or physical-order subjects. In a speech about the United Nations one might first describe each building, then discuss the offices in each building one floor at a time, that is, organize the ideas spatially. It could also be done topically if the audience were familiar with the general political structure of the United Nations. In discussing " Nationalism in Africa," one might use geographical space and simply divide the ideas from north to south and east to west. It is obvious that chronological history might also be a useful method.

Need-plan Method. This method involves the organization of materials according to problems (needs) and solutions (plans). An affirmative debate team concerned with a resolution on government health programs will typically divide its material into these two general categories. The first speaker will concentrate on the various needs in our present situation or in our present programs. The second speaker will discuss the various plans and indicate why one is better than the others. The needs can be subdivided into many useful types, such as economic needs, health needs, and social needs.

Methods of Arranging the Parts

Various sets of terms refer to the *parts* of a speech: *Beginning, Middle,* and *End; Introduction, Body,* and *Conclusion;* or, in a more classical vein, *Proem, Statement, Argument,* and *Epilogue.* Other *parts* are the speech details and ideas you have already collected and perhaps partially organized into one or more of the sequences discussed in the last section.

Before analyzing these parts, let us look at certain rhetorical principles that have a bearing on the ordering and arranging of the parts. They are *unity, coherence,* and *emphasis.*

Unity. In discussing tragic drama, Aristotle once said that a play must be so constructed that omission of any part damages the whole, and that each part of the plot must contribute to making inevitable the purpose or end of the play. By analogy, he said, it must have a total unity in the same manner as a living organism. We still use the term *organic unity* to express this concept. With regard to a speech it means that the material should be unified to the point that it can be summarized in a single statement of purpose. In some speeches it takes the form of a resolution or proposition that is forthrightly announced; in other cases, for purposes of strategy, such a proposition might be left unstated; but in all cases the speaker must understand his purpose if the speech is to have unity. This consciousness of specific purpose helps the speaker evaluate the materials and ideas during preparation. The arrangement of the parts of a speech should be so unified that there is a welding of audience, speaker, and purpose.

Coherence. Coherence refers to the specific sequence of the parts of the speech; it therefore involves the various methods of ordering and arranging ideas and speech details already considered. To *cohere* is to be connected by a common principle or relationship. It involves the logically consistent subordination of ideas. The actual connecting of the various parts and ideas of a speech is done through words or phrases. Unlike the writer, the speaker cannot go back and recheck the text to locate a lost thread of meaning. Thus he must be especially careful of his connectives, often repeating and clearly labeling them. Coherence must therefore always involve the audience. A speaker may lose his audience when going from one point to another by assuming that the audience will see the connection, because the relationship or subordination of ideas is logically consistent to him.

To achieve coherence, we must carefully consider the connecting words of transition. Some of the types of links or connectives possible in our language are as follows:

TYPES OF CONNECTIVES[2]

1. *Indicating time:*	previously, formerly, at an earlier period, anterior, contemporary, at the same moment, in the same period, throughout this period, during this time, meanwhile, in the meantime, upon this, then, by that time, already, now, since then, after this, thereafter, in the end, at last, at length, at a later time, henceforth, now that.
2. *Making evident:*	thereof, thereby, thereto, therein, therefrom, in this case, in such a case, at such times, on such occasions, under these circumstances, in all this, in connection with this, together with this, here again.
3. *Returning to purpose:*	to continue, to return, to report, to resume, along with . . . , as I have said, then, now, again, once more, at any rate, at all events.
4. *Making reference:*	in point of, with respect to, as related to, concerning, as for.

[2]For a discussion of connectives see Glen E. Mills, *Putting a Message Together* (Indianapolis and New York: The Bobbs-Merrill Co., Inc., 1972), p. 26.

5. *Citing:*	for instance, for example, to illustrate, by way of illustration, another case, a case in point is . . . , under this head.
6. *Excepting:*	with this exception, this exception made, except for this, waiving this question, leaving this out of account . . . , excluded, exclusive of . . . , irrespective of . . . , excluding this point.
7. *Summarizing:*	to sum up, to recapitulate, on the whole, briefly, in a word, in brief, in short, we have traced . . . , as we have seen, up to this point, yes, no.
8. *Concluding:*	to conclude, finally, lastly, in conclusion, last of all.
9. *Explaining:*	that is, to explain, in other words, this is as much as to say, that amounts to saying.
10. *Marking a change in tone or in point of view:*	at least, seriously, in all seriousness, jesting aside, to speak frankly, for my part, in another sense, as a matter of fact, in fact, to come to the point, in general, of course, you see, as the matter stands, as things are.
11. *Comparing:*	parallel with . . . , allied to . . . , comparable to . . . , from another point of view, in the same category, in like manner, in the same way, similarly, likewise, as similar view, yet more important, of less importance, next in importance, in contrast with this, conversely.
12. *Emphasizing:*	indeed, moreover, add to this, futhermore, besides, further, even without this, in addition to this, all the more, even more, into the bargain, especially, in particular, how much more, yet again, above all, best of all, most of all.
13. *Judging:*	so, therefore, consequently, accordingly, thus, hence, then, in consequence, as a result, the result is, we conclude, because of this, for this reason, this being true, such being the case, under these circumstances, what follows.
14. *Conceding:*	certainly, indeed, it is time, to be sure, it must be granted, I admit, true, granted, admitting the force of . . . , no doubt, doubtless.
15. *Opposing:*	yet, still, nevertheless, however, on the other hand, at the same time, none the less, only, even so, in spite of this, the fact is . . . , after all.
16. *Refuting:*	otherwise, else, were this not so, on no other supposition, on the contrary, no, never, hardly.

Emphasis. Emphasis involves the location, space, form, and order you give your most important ideas. Should you put your most important idea first, last, or in a climactic order? Does the amount of space you give the idea affect emphasis? (Your main point ordinarily is not buried under some minor subpoint.) Since a number of really important ideas may compete for attention, to which should you give the most emphasis? These questions can be best answered in terms of your subject, your knowledge, your audience, and the occasion. Location, space, form, and order do make a difference and do affect emphasis. The function of emphasis is to use these devices in harmony with the relative importance assigned to each part or idea in your speech.

Systems of Arrangement. Aristotle used the Greek word *taxis,* which denotes division or arrangement, to explain what he thought was the most obvious and logical arrangement of parts or elements of a speech, particularly a persuasive or argumentative speech. He felt that the following elements were most closely related to the thinking habits of man: Proem (Introduction), Statement, Argument, and Epilogue (Conclusion).[3] For Aristotle the proem and epilogue are primarily used as aids for memory and attention. The main *body* of the speech is the statement of purpose and the proofs or *argument.*

In the twentieth century H. L. Hollingworth[4] posited the fundamental tasks or steps of a speech as being attention, interest, impression, conviction, and direction. Just as Aristotle suggested that for some occasions a proem or attention step was less necessary, so too does Hollingworth explain the shortening or actual elimination of some of the elements as the audience becomes more selected, organized, concerted, or polarized.

In still more recent times Alan H. Monroe,[5] a speech psychologist, has suggested that the fundamental elements are attention, need, satisfaction, visualization, and action. Like Hollingworth, Monroe believes that the emphasis given each element depends upon the audience's disposition and knowledge as well as the nature of the speech. A speech to inform might use only three elements, while a speech to persuade might call for all five.

These systems and many more are very useful in that they point up the complicated interaction of subject, audience, speaker, and arrangement. Any system is undoubtedly an understatement or a dangerous generalization in terms of unbelievably complex communication problems.

That other divisions or participations are possible is evident. The *general* purpose of your speech (to persuade, to inform, or to entertain) will dictate how much of a system you will need to include under the general divisions of introduction, body, and conclusion. For example, in Chapter 9 a special system of organizing is recommended that borrows not only from the systems above but also from learning theories; it in-

    [3]Lane Cooper, *The Rhetoric of Aristotle* (New York: Appleton-Century-Crofts, 1932), pp. 220–40.
    [4]H. L. Hollingworth, *The Psychology of the Audience* (New York: American Book Company, 1935), pp. 19–32.
    [5]Alan H. Monroe, *Principles and Types of Speech* (Glenview, Ill.: Scott, Foresman & Company, 1967).

cludes attention, overview, information, and review. In Chapter 10, several useful systems are discussed and illustrated, one of which is a combination of attention, need, plan, objections, reinforcement, and action. Let us view these elements in terms of the more common arrangement of introduction, body, conclusion.

SOME GENERAL SYSTEMS OF ARRANGEMENT

Proem	Attention	Attention	Attention Overview	Attention	*Introduction*
Statement	Interest	Need		Need	
Argument	Impression	Satisfaction	Information	Plan	*Body*
	Conviction	Visualization		Objections	
Epilogue	Direction	Action	Review	Reinforcement Action	*Conclusion*

More will be said about these specific organizational patterns in related chapters. We will now look at the general requirements of a good introduction, body, and conclusion.

Introduction. The preceding analysis of systems indicates that in all cases gaining the listeners' attention is an important requirement in the beginning of a speech. We also learned in the discussions of emphasis and arrangement that the number of attention devices to be utilized depends on what attention level the audience has already achieved. In other words, if the listeners are on the edge of their seats and in a state of readiness to hear what you have to say, a lengthy introduction designed to arouse attention would be superfluous. More will be said about attention in Chapter 10.

Arousing attention is only one requirement of an introduction. Your introduction should also strive to establish or reaffirm good will between you, the group you represent, and the audience. In those rare cases where good will is hard to come by (i.e., when facing a hostile audience), then perhaps "establishing a climate for a fair hearing" is the most you can hope for. For example, Adlai Stevenson used humor to establish rapport with a tough Labor Day audience in 1952: "When I was a boy I never had much sympathy for a holiday speaker. He was just a kind of interruption between hot dogs, a fly in the lemonade."

Certain terms or language may be either vague or unknown, and *not* to define them is to confuse the audience (for example, cybernetics, carcinoma, data processing, method acting, afram, and so forth). In some situations, a function of the introduction is *orientation*; the speaker must sometimes supply certain background explanations or definitions to promote audience comprehension of the main body. A brief historical sketch often helps an audience gain perspective and orientation. A good example is John F. Kennedy's opening address to a conference on African culture in New York City on June 28, 1959.

> Some 2,500 years ago the Greek historian Herodotus described Africa south of the Sahara as a land of "horned asses, of dog-faced creatures, the creatures without heads, whom the Libyans declared to have eyes in their breasts, and many other far less fabulous beasts." Apparently when Herodotus found himself short on facts, he didn't hesitate to use imagination—which may be why he is called the first historian.
>
> But we must not be too critical of Herodotus. Until very recently, for most Americans, Africa was Trader Horn, Tarzan, and tom-tom drums. We are only now beginning to discover that Africa, unlike our comic strip stereotypes, is a land of rich variety—of noble and ancient cultures, some primitive, some highly sophisticated; of vital and gifted people, who are only now crossing the threshold into the modern world.

The introduction seeks to make your purpose clear; it is often a kind of preview of what is to follow in the main body. This involves a certain amount of repetition, but remember that an *audience*, unlike a *reader*, cannot go back to a previous page. Therefore more repetition is called for.

In sum, the general functions of an introduction are: (1) to secure *attention*; (2) to establish *good will*; (3) to assure a *fair hearing*; (4) to *orient* your audience to the subject; and (5) to make your *purpose* clear.

You can achieve good introductions in many different ways; however, all of them should ideally be related to both the subject and the situation. An unusual story describing your tribulations in getting to the meeting is acceptable, especially if you can relate it to your subject. Humorous anecdotes may also be useful. Although the research is inconclusive on this point, most experts generally agree that if you are going to use jokes they should be in some way related to the subject or situation.

As an illustration of all the functions and requirements of a good introduction, let us quote from the 1961 Inaugural Address of John F. Kennedy:

My fellow citizens:

Attention	We observe today not a victory of party but a celebration of freedom—symbolizing an end as well as a beginning—signifying renewal as well as change. For I have sworn before you and Almighty God the same solemn oath our forebears prescribed nearly a century and three-quarters ago.

Orientation and Good Will	The world is very different now. For man holds in his mortal hands the power to abolish all forms of human poverty and to abolish all forms of human life. And, yet, the same revolutionary beliefs for which our forebears fought are still at issue around the globe—the belief that the rights of man come not from the generosity of the state but from the hand of God.
Fair Hearing	We dare not forget today that we are the heirs of that first revolution. Let the word go forth from this time and place, to friend and foe alike, that the torch has been passed to a new generation of Americans—born in this century, tempered by war, disciplined by a cold and bitter peace, proud of our ancient heritage—and unwilling to witness or permit the slow undoing of those human rights to which this nation has always been committed, and to which we are committed today.
Purpose	Let every nation know, whether it wish us well or ill, that we shall pay any price, bear any burden, meet any hardship, support any friend, or oppose any foe in order to assure the survival and success of liberty.
	This much we pledge—and more.

Another powerful example of a good introduction is taken from a 1959 speech by Richard Nixon, then Vice-President of the United States, entitled "The Heart of the American Ideal." The speech was given to a Russian audience attending the opening of the American National Exhibition in Moscow.

Attention	I am honored on behalf of President Eisenhower to open this American exhibition in Moscow.
Good Will	Mrs. Nixon and I were among the many thousands of Americans who were privileged to visit the splendid Soviet exhibition in New York, and we want to take this opportunity to congratulate the people of the U.S.S.R. for the great achievements and progress so magnificently portrayed by your exhibition.
Fair Hearing	We, in turn, hope that many thousands of Soviet citizens will take advantage of this opportunity to learn about life in the United States by visiting our exhibition. Of course, we both realize that no exhibition can portray a complete picture of all aspects of life in great nations like the U.S.S.R. and the United States.

*Orientation
(Preview)*

Among the questions which some might raise with regard to
our exhibition are these: To what extent does this exhibition accurately present life in the United States as
it really is? Can only the wealthy people afford the things
exhibited here? What about the inequality, the injustice, the
other weaknesses which are supposed to be inevitable in a
capitalist society?

Purpose

As Mr. Khrushchev often says: "You can't leave a word out
of a song." Consequently, in the limited time I have, I
would like to try to answer some of those questions so that
you may get an accurate picture of what America is really
like.

In still more specific terms, an introduction may utilize appreciation,
personal reference, quotations, humor, related stories or experiences, and
so on. When the purpose is relatively obvious and the speaker and subject well known, a related story, incident, or narrative with built-in attention often serves to reinforce the purpose and give a fresh orientation.

Booker T. Washington's introduction to his address at the Atlanta
exposition is a case in point.[6]

Attention

Mr. President and Gentlemen of the Board of Directors and
Citizens: One-third of the population of the South is of
the Negro race. No enterprise seeking the material, civil,
or moral welfare of this section can disregard this element
of our population and reach the highest success.

Good Will

I but convey to you, Mr. President and Directors, the sentiment of the masses of my race when I say that in no way
have the value and manhood of the American Negro been
more fittingly and generously recognized than by the managers of this magnificent Exposition at every stage of its
progress. It is a recognition that will do more to cement the
friendship of the two races than any occurrence since the
dawn of our freedom.

Fair Hearing

Not only this, but the opportunity here afforded will
awaken among us a new era of industrial progress. Ignorant
and inexperienced, it is not strange that in the first years of
our new life we began at the top instead of at the bottom;
that a seat in Congress or the state legislature was more
sought than real estate or industrial skill; that the political
convention or stump speaking had more attractions than
starting a dairy farm or truck garden.

[6]Quoted in A. Craig Baird, *American Public Addresses: 1740–1952* (New York:
Mc-Graw-Hill Book Company, 1956), p. 189.

	A ship lost at sea for many days suddenly sighted a friendly vessel. From the mast of the unfortunate vessel was seen a signal, "Water, water; we die of thirst!" The answer from the friendly vessel at once came back, "Cast down your

Orientation

A ship lost at sea for many days suddenly sighted a friendly vessel. From the mast of the unfortunate vessel was seen a signal, "Water, water; we die of thirst!" The answer from the friendly vessel at once came back, "Cast down your bucket where you are." And a third and fourth signal for water was answered, "Cast down your bucket where you are." The captain of the distressed vessel, at last heeding the injunction, cast down his bucket, and it came up full of fresh, sparkling water from the mouth of the Amazon River.

Purpose

To those of my race who depend on bettering their condition in a foreign land or who underestimate the importance of cultivating friendly relations with the Southern white man, who is their next door neighbor, I would say: "Cast down your bucket where you are"—cast it down in making friends in every manly way of the people of all races by whom we are surrounded.

During World War II, President Roosevelt also used a story in one of his introductions to the many appeals he made for the purchase of war bonds.[7]

> Once upon a time, a few years ago, there was a city in our Middle West which was threatened by a destructive flood in a great river. The waters had risen to the top of the banks. Every man, woman, and child in that city was called upon to fill sandbags in order to defend their homes against the rising waters. For many days and nights destruction and death stared them in the face. As a result of the grim, determined community effort, that city still stands. Those people kept the levees above the peak of the flood. All of them joined together in the desperate job that had to be done —businessmen, workers, farmers, and doctors, and preachers—people of all races.
>
> To me that town is a living symbol of what community cooperation can accomplish.

Body. The major discussion of the speech material takes place here. This is where the bulk of the information or argument is located. All the previous discussions of organization, rhetorical principles, and arrangement come into focus here. Typical forms of the body will subsequently be explained and illustrated in the next section, "Mechanics of Outlining," and the next chapter, "Presenting Information." Some special arrangement systems will also be discussed in Part IV, "The Psychology of Persuasion."

Conclusion. The words from the arrangement chart on p. 185 are *direction, action, review,* and *reinforcement*; we could add *visualization, restatement,* and *summary.* These are devices all calculated to rekindle attention and to assist the memory. You will recall that it was Aristotle

restatement, and *summary.* These devices are calculated to rekindle attention and to assist memory. You will recall that it was Aristotle who suggested that the major purpose of the conclusion was to help the memory.

The conclusion is generally shorter than either the introduction or the body. It may and generally should include a short summary for clarity and reinforcement. In some cases it will call for explicit directions wherever certain actions are part of the speaker's purpose. When your purpose has been inspiration, you may need a more impressive conclusion. Some of the devices suggested in the discussion on introductions (impressive quotation, incident, or experience) are applicable here. A classic conclusion of the inspirational type was provided by Martin Luther King Jr., in his famous speech in support of civil rights legislation before an estimated 200,000 people.

> So let freedom ring—from the prodigious hilltops of New Hampshire, let freedom ring; from the mighty mountains of New York, let freedom ring— from the heightening Alleghenies of Pennsylvania!
>
> Let freedom ring from the snowcapped Rockies of Colorado!
>
> Let freedom ring from the curvaceous slopes of California!
>
> But not only that; let freedom ring from Stone Mountain of Georgia!
>
> Let freedom ring from Lookout Mountain of Tennessee!
>
> Let freedom ring from every hill and mole hill of Mississippi. From every mountainside, let freedom ring, and when this happens . . .
>
> When we allow freedom to ring, when we let it ring from every village and every hamlet, from every state and every city, we will be able to speed up that day when all of God's children, black men and white men, Jews and Gentiles, Protestants and Catholics, will be able to join hands and sing in the words of the old Negro spiritual, "Free at last! thank God almighty, we are free at last!"[8]

Most important, make it evident when you are finished; carefully consider your exit lines. It is frustrating to an audience and awkward for a speaker who does not know when he is going to finish. This is the dangling or never-ending conclusion caused either by the "ham actor" in all of us or by improper preparation, which leaves you with so many things to tie together that you literally cannot conclude in any unified manner. The lessons are obvious. Prepare your conclusion as carefully as the rest of your speech. It serves as a good check on organic unity. And quit while you are ahead. Do not let an audience so mesmerize you that you ruin a good speech by an overly long or overly dramatic conclusion.

Mechanics of Outlining

Where to Start. You might start by rereading the material just previous to this section! The mechanics can be hollow indeed if they are

---

[8]Quoted in Robert T. Oliver and Eugene E. White, *Selected Speeches from American History* (Boston: Allyn and Bacon, 1966), pp. 289–94.

not enriched with an understanding of: (1) subject, audience, and occasion analysis; (2) methods of locating materials; and (3) methods of organization and arrangement.

The outline is to a speech what a blueprint is to a house. A good, clear outline can help you discover mistakes, weaknesses, and unnecessary information *before* you speak, just as the builder or architect can often save costly mistakes by taking a hard look at his plans before he starts to build the house.

Begin by reviewing your specific purpose for speaking, which may evolve into a proposition or a thesis. This review serves to narrow and unify the subject matter further and should result in a precise summary statement of purpose. Your statement of purpose attempts to capture the gist of the entire speech in one sentence, but should not be confused with a title or a general subject area, although they may be closely related.

Start your serious outlining with the body of the speech. The introduction and conclusion, though very important, are nevertheless only enrichers, preparers, or reinforcers of the content-loaded main body. State your main points or ideas in terms of your purpose and locate your supporting material under the appropriate main points. After roughing out the body of your speech, proceed to outline the introduction and conclusion.

Your rough outline should eventually evolve into a complete sentence outline. This will force you to *think* your way through the material and help avoid embarrassing moments on the platform. The sentence outline will also make it easier for your instructor to evaluate and help you with your speech planning. If you intend to use the speech again or if others may have to speak from it, the value of filing a complete sentence outline becomes obvious. After this kind of thorough outlining, you may prefer to redo the outline in a topical or key-word form for actual use on the platform. An outline is an aid to clear, orderly thinking. It is a blueprint of the speech.

Principles of Outlining. Mills suggests six principles that apply in all cases: simplicity, coordination, subordination, discreteness, progression (or sequence), and symbolization.[9]

Simplicity means that each numbered or lettered statement should contain only one concept or idea.

WRONG

I. I should like to cover the following major steps in musical theory:
    A. The kinds of notes and the musical staff.
    B. Methods of counting and the relation of these to an instrument.

[9]Mills, *Putting a Message Together*, pp. 26–28.

RIGHT
I. I should like to cover the following major steps in musical theory:
    A. The kinds of notes.
    B. The musical staff.
    C. Methods of counting the notes.
    D. Relation of these to an instrument.

Coordination means that a subordinate list of topics must have a common relationship.

WRONG

A. Manufacturing companies in Detroit:
    1. General Motors Corporation.
    2. Ford Motor Company.
    3. Chrysler Corporation.
    4. American Motors Corporation
    5. Campbell Ewald Advertising Company.
    6. American Automobile Association.
    7. Benedict and Moore Insurance

RIGHT
A. Manufacturing companies in Detroit:
    1. General Motors Corporation.
    2. Ford Motor Company.
    3. Chrysler Corporation.
    4. American Motors Corporation
B. Service companies in Detroit:
    1. Campbell Ewald Advertising Company.
    2. American Automobile Association.
    3. Benedict and Moore Insurance

Subordination means that related lesser points supporting a general category or statement should be so indicated in your outline, usually by the amount of indentation. Items of equal import should be given equal billing.

WRONG

A. Learning to type.
    1. Preliminary preparation.
    2. Addressing the keyboard.
    3. Practice exercises.
    4. First-level maintenance.
        a. Unsticking the strikers.
        b. Cleaning the keys.
        c. Replacing the ribbon.
    5. Selecting a typewriter.
        a. Mechanical machines.
        b. Electrical machines.
        c. Kinds of type.

RIGHT
A. Learning to type.
    1. Preliminary preparation.
    2. Addressing the keyboard.
    3. Practice exercises.
B. First-level maintenance.
    1. Unsticking the strikers.
    2. Cleaning the keys.
    3. Replacing the ribbon.
C. Selecting a typewriter.
    1. Mechanical machines.
    2. Electrical machines.
    3. Kinds of type.

Discreteness means that each item in an outline should be able to stand alone. It should be a distinct point and not overlap with others.

WRONG
A. Tennis tips.
    1. The serve.
    3. The forehand stroke.
    3. The backhand stroke.
    4. Various shots.

RIGHT
A. Tennis tips.
    1. The serve.
    2. The forehand stroke.
    3. The backhand stroke.
    4. Volley shots.
    5. Approach shots.
    6. The overhead shot.

Progression refers to arranging coordinate items in some sort of normal or natural sequence such as chronology, time, genre, space, and so on. Keep them in sequence and don't switch patterns. A difficulty sequence is a good example.

WRONG
A. Principles of electricity.
    1. Current and electrons.
    2. Light bulbs in parallel.
    3. Light bulbs in a series.
    4. Dry cells.
    5. The flashlight.
    6. Switches.

RIGHT
A. Principles of electricity.
    1. The flashlight.
    2. Switches.
    3. Dry cells.
    4. Light bulbs in a series.
    5. Light bulbs in parallel.
    6. Current and electrons.

Symbolization means that similar symbols (I, 1, A, b, and so on) should represent items or points of comparable importance. The symbol and its indentation should indicate relative importance in terms of subordination. Usually main points are Roman numerals, major subpoints are capital letters, minor subpoints are Arabic numerals, and so on. Symbolization is concerned with outline headings and forms.

Logical outlining involves (1) subdivisions of ideas and (2) subheadings for amplification or support. If a topic is divided, there should be two or more parts. In other words, if you are going to have a *1*, you should also have a *2*; if you are going to have an *A*, you should also have a *B*. If your *2* or *B* is not important to your speech, the first point should be incorporated into its superior heading. For example:

    A. Wagon trains.
       1. Role in development of West.

becomes

    A. Wagon trains as factor in development of West.

The numbers and letters used as labels must be consistent. Let your symbols clearly show the relationship of main ideas to each other and the relationship of subpoints to main points. Do not extend any portion of any statement beyond its symbol.

The standard system of symbols and indentations is as follows:

OUTLINE FORM

  I. _____
    A. _____
      1. _____
        a. _____
        b. _____
          (1) _____
          (2) _____
      2. _____
    B. _____
  II. _____

The number of main points you may have in a speech is open to some debate. If you use more than four or five, your listeners will have difficulty relating the points to one another and retention becomes more difficult. Your main points, in order to be true main points and not subdivisions, should be of approximately equal weight or importance. Each main point should be carefully and completely worded and should contribute to the central purpose of the speech. The order or sequencing of your main points should be such that it facilitates retention, logical development, motivation, and understanding.

The format of your outline may vary with your purpose and your instructor's preference. You may use *Introduction, Body,* and *Conclusion* or some of the other formats discussed previously. In any case you should probably capitalize, but not number, such words as *Introduction,*

Body, and *Conclusion,* and perhaps put other words such as *attention, overview, need* and *reinforcement* in the margins.

Types of Outlines. The complete sentence outline is the most detailed and specific of all the forms. All main and minor points are written out as complete sentences so that their relationship to one another is graphically clear. In all probability, however, your first try at outlining a given speech will be in a topical, skeleton form. The phrases or groups of words that carry the essential meanings are typically written as grammatically incomplete sentences. The disadvantage of the topical outline is that your memory may fail you and the topics may suddenly be difficult to visualize as complete sentences or thoughts. Its advantages are fewer notes, more extempore potential, and quick comprehension—*if* you are thoroughly familiar with the concepts involved. A key-word outline is an abbreviated topical outline. In terms of indentation and symbols it looks the same as the complete sentence outline. The key-word outline is usually easier to remember and greatly facilitates extemporaneous resequencing of ideas when the situation calls for such adaptation.

Combinations of these forms are often advisable when you are speaking on a subject with which you are thoroughly familiar. The main points might be complete sentences, the subpoints phrases, and the sub-subpoints key words.

Some actual student examples illustrating variations and the use of symbols and indentations follow. The marginal notes in parentheses indicate other systems of arrangement. Two different ways of arranging or organizing the same material are shown in Appendix C (e.g., "The Role of the Manager").

OUR FUTURE FIVE WONDERS[10]

General End:	To inform.
Specific Purpose:	To inform the class of the future five wonders of the world and to explain their functions and how they differ from the old seven wonders.

Introduction

I. Let me briefly remind you of the seven wonders of the Ancient World. (Pictures)
    A. The Great Pyramid of Cheops.
    B. The Hanging Gardens of Babylon.
(Attention)   C. The Tomb of Mausolus.
(Interest)   D. The Temple of Diana at Ephesus.
    E. The Colossus of Rhodes.
    F. Phidias' Statue of Zeus.
    G. The Pharos of Alexandria.

[10]From a student speech by Gary Carotta, Wayne State University.

II. The future wonders which I will explain are as
follows:

    A. Australia's Snowy Mountains Scheme.
    B. The United States' Chesapeake Bay Bridge
       Tunnel.
    C. The Netherland's Delta Plan.
    D. The United States' New York Narrows Bridge.
    E. The Mont Blanc Tunnel Between France and
       Italy.

Body

I. Each of the future wonders will be of real benefit to
man.
    A. The Snowy Mountains Scheme will provide an
       additional 650 billion gallons of water per year
       in the Australian desert.
         1. This will be done by forcing the wasted
           water of the Snowy River through the
           mountains in long tunnels.
         2. This project will cost $1 billion.
         3. This project will consist of many facilities.

            a. 9 major dams.
            b. 10 power stations.
            c. 100 miles of tunnels.
            d. 80 miles of aqueducts.
    B. The Chesapeake Bay Bridge Tunnel will con-
       nect Norfolk, Va., with the Delmarva Peninsula.
         1. Travel time will be thirty minutes.
         2. Longest span over exposed navigable
           water.
            a. Both tunnels and bridges are used
               (diagram).
            b. It is 17.6 miles long.
            c. It will cost $140 million.
    C. The Netherlands' Delta Plan will prevent
       ocean storms from overrunning the land (map).
         1. Prevent damage to property and life.
         2. Prevent salting of fertile land as in 1953.
         3. Five massive dams will cut off the sea
           arms.
            a. This is first attempt to hold back this
               much sea.
            b. The cost will be $750 million.
    D. The U.S. N.Y. Narrows Bridge will cross the
       narrows at the entrance to N.Y. harbor.
         1. The world's longest suspension span, 4260
           feet.
         2. The world's largest and most expensive
           bridge.
            a. Will have 12 traffic lanes.

            b. One granite block weighs 410,000
               tons.

    c. Can be seen 20 miles at sea.

    d. Will cost $325 million.

E. The French-Italian Mont Blanc Tunnel will permit travel *under* the Alps.

    1. The tunnel was a joint venture.

      a. French drilling company.

      b. Italian drilling company.

    2. The first all-year route from Paris to Rome.

      a. Cuts distance by 140 miles.

      b. Cuts time from a day of mountain roads to fifteen minutes' tunnel time.

    3. A brilliantly coordinated engineering feat.

II. Modern wonders of the world are more incredible than the old.

    A. Modern wonders have beauty.

    B. Modern wonders have a utility the ancient did not.

Conclusion

I. These new five wonders have practical and useful purposes for man.

    A. Snowy Mountains Scheme will make Australia's desert lands places of lush vegetation.

    B. Chesapeake Bay Bridge Tunnel will enable man to travel more easily from Norfolk to the Delmarva Peninsula.

(Review)
(Reinforcement)

    C. The Netherlands' Delta Plan will secure the land from the damaging storms of the sea.

    D. The New York Narrows Bridge will allow traffic to cross the entrance of New York Harbor.

    E. The Mont Blanc Tunnel will allow travel through the Alps all year around.

II. These constructions are more wondrous than the ancient ones.

    A. Ancient wonders were noted primarily for art, size, and beauty.

    B. The modern wonders each have all of these plus unchallenged utility.

A shorter topical and key word form of outline is illustrated below:

THE LEFT WING[11]

General End:	To inform and entertain.
Specific Purpose:	To inform the audience about left-handed people, their problems, theories as to why some people are left-handed, and what is being done to help them.

[11]From a student speech by Robert Willard, Wayne State University.

Introduction

I. Are you one of those people who have been described as temperamental, unstable, unintelligent,
pugnacious, or, in a word, left-handed?

II. Even if you are not, you should know some facts
about this persecuted group.

               A. Their number.

(Attention)   B. Their difficulties.

(Overview)   C. Assistance given.

               D. Theories as to why.

Body

I. Who are the Southpaws?

    A. Number.

        1. ¼ North Am. originally left-handed.

        2. Schools report an 8% increase.

(Information)   B. Some are famous.

        1. Present-day lefties.

        2. Historic lefties.

II. Southpaw advantages and disadvantages.

    A. Advantages

        1. Mirror writing.

        2. Sports.

    B. Disadvantages.

        1. Eating.

        2. Musical instruments.

        3. Knitting.

        4. Office machines.

III. Help for left-handers.

    A. The Association for the Protection of Rights of
Left-Handers.

        1. Oaths.

        2. Saluting.

        3. Fellowship.

    B. Manufactured goods for lefties.

        1. Golf clubs.

(Visualization)   2. Musical instruments.

        3. Reversed turnstiles.

    C. Theories concerning Southpaws.

        1. Cerebral dominance.

        2. Inherited.

        3. Present opinion.

           a. Surveys.

           b. Tests.

Conclusion

I. If you are left-handed be comforted in that:

    A. Though your numbers are small you are not in-
ferior.

(Review)   B. Your disadvantages are being reduced.
       C. The theories make you more interesting.
       D. Society is trying to help.
  II. You righties should now have a right attitude about the left wing.

SUMMARY

One of the most important aspects of preparing, organizing, and out-lining a speech is to achieve a clear understanding and statement of your *specific purpose*, that is, the outcome, objective, or response that your speech is supposed to accomplish. Of almost equal importance is a careful consideration of the audience and situational factors. The relationships between audience and subject as well as between audience and speaker are other critical factors.

When you have thoroughly considered your specific purpose and have related it to an analysis of audience and occasion, you are ready to start locating and collecting the materials that will constitute the speech itself. This chapter provides an extensive list of sources and procedures for making the task much easier than it may at first appear. Taking notes from your readings and sources should be done systematically, neces-sitating only a minimum of rereading and returning to the library. Use of file cards rather than a notebook will also facilitate the eventual or-ganizing and arranging of the various parts of the speech.

The principal ways of organizing ideas for speech purposes are by the chronological, topical, spatial, logical, difficulty, and need-plan methods. The arrangement of the parts of a speech (beginning, middle, end; intro-duction, body, conclusion; and other variations) is related to your general end as well as your specific purpose. These are all closely interwoven and can usually be coordinated with a simple introduction-body-conclusion system. The rhetorical principles of unity, coherence, and emphasis also have a strong bearing on the arrangement of the parts.

The general functions of a good introduction are: (1) to secure atten-tion; (2) to establish good will; (3) to assure a fair hearing; (4) to orient your audience to the subject; and (5) to make your purpose clear.

The conclusion is generally shorter than either the introduction or the body. It may, and generally should, include a short summary for clarity and reinforcement. In some cases it will call for explicit directions whenever certain actions are part of the speaker's purpose. It is important to make it evident when you are through; carefully consider your exit lines. It is frustrating to an audience and awkward for a speaker who does not know when to finish. Prepare your conclusion as carefully as the rest of your speech; it is a good check on organic unity; remember to "quit when you're ahead." Never ruin a good speech by an overly long or overly dramatic conclusion.

An outline is an aid to clear, orderly thinking. It is a blueprint of the speech. Useful principles of outlining that apply in all cases include simplicity, coordination, subordination, discreteness, progression, and symbolization.

Start your serious outlining with the body of the speech. State your main points or ideas in terms of your purpose and locate your supporting material under the appropriate main points. After roughing out the body of your speech, proceed to outline the introduction and conclusion. Your rough outline should eventually evolve into a complete sentence outline. After completion of a thorough outline, you may then redo it in a topical or key-word form for actual use on the platform.

Your outline numbers and letters used as labels must be consistent. Let your symbols clearly show the relationship of main ideas to one another and the relationship of subpoints to main points. Let each division have at least two headings and do not extend any portion of any statement beyond its symbol. The number of main points in a speech should seldom go beyond four or five. Your main points should be of approximately equal weight or importance. Each main point should be carefully worded and should contribute to the central purpose of the speech. The order or sequencing of your main points should be such that it facilitates retention, logical development, motivation, and understanding.

Speech Communication Principles

1. Unity, or a consciousness of specific purpose, helps us to evaluate the materials and ideas during preparation of a message. The arrangement of the parts should be so unified that there is a welding of audience, source, and purpose.

2. Coherence: messages are more clearly transmitted when organized according to some pragmatic, natural order (e.g., chronologically, topically, spatially, logically, difficulty).

3. Emphasis: arranging your message parts systematically makes for ease of preparation, presentation, and better audience impact (e.g., introduction, body, conclusion).

4. One should consider, if possible, his specific purpose and audience analysis at the same time.

5. The style of your message and its delivery should be related to the location and arrangement of the setting as well as the content and audience.

6. There is a commonly held set of rules for mechanically outlining messages that can measurably improve preparation and evaluation (e.g., simplicity, coordination, subordination, discreteness, progression, and symbolization).

A. *General Learning Outcomes*

1. We should learn how and where to locate materials for message preparation.

2. We should learn to differentiate the standard ways of organizing ideas.

3. We should learn the systems for arranging the parts of a message.

4. We should learn the rhetorical principles of unity, coherence, and emphasis.

5. We should learn the basic principles of outlining a message.

B. *Specific Learning Outcomes*

1. We should learn how to use the basic resources of a library in message preparation: the *Readers' Guide to Periodical Literature,* the *Cumulative Book Index,* the *United States Catalog,* and related publications.

2. We should learn at least six methods of organizing materials: chronological; topical; logical; difficulty; spatial; and need-plan.

3. We should learn to prepare and test our messages in terms of unity of purpose, coherence and sequencing of the parts, and the emphasis given the most important ideas.

4. We should learn to arrange messages using introduction-body-conclusion and attention-overview-information-review.

5. We should learn the functions and requirements of a good speech introduction: attention; good will; fair hearing; orientation; and purpose.

6. We should learn the six mechanical rules of outlining: sim-

plicity, coordination, subordination, discreteness, progression, and symbolization.

7. We should be able to relate the foregoing general and specific learning outcomes to the speech communication principles above.

C. *Communication Competencies*

1. We should be able to prepare an intelligent two- to three-page speech outline that passes the mechanical, organizational, and rhetorical tests discussed in this chapter.

2. We should be able to critically outline the oral messages of another for purposes of evaluating the speaker's message strategy and preparation.

3. We should be able to deliver a two- to four-minute speech extemporaneously from an outline in such a way that an audience is not distracted by the use of notes.

4. We should be able to locate materials through standard library references for a three- to four-page speech outline.

D. *Study Projects and Tasks*

1. Prepare a detailed outline (see the models in this chapter) for a two- to four-minute, one- or two-point speech. After your instructor has evaluated it, reduce it to a key-word outline for actually delivering the speech to the class. In general, choose topics that are primarily explanatory or informative (rather than persuasive or entertaining).

2. Make simple one-page, main-point outlines of your classmates' speeches and give them to your instructor who will feed them back to the speaker for insight into his organizational effectiveness.

3. Prepare only the *introduction* to a five- to ten-minute speech that you might use later. Make your general and specific purposes clear and try to achieve all of the functions of a good introduction (e.g., attention, good will, fair hearing, orientation, purpose). (See the model outlines in this chapter.)

4. Prepare an oral report or essay attempting to prove or disprove any of the speech communication principles listed earlier.

5. Read the speech in the appendix, "Communication and the Survival of Democracy." Using introduction-body-conclusion and Roman numerals for main points, outline the speech through the Arabic numerals (1, 2, 3 . . .) only.

6. Evaluate the introduction part of the speech in the appendix using the five functions discussed in this chapter as criteria. Indicate by line number where each criterion is met (e.g., attention, good will, fair hearing, orientation of audience, clarity of purpose).

7. Evaluate the speech in the appendix in terms of the organization method used; justify your opinion (e.g., chronological, topical, spatial, logical, difficulty, need-plan).

8. Evaluate the appendix speech in terms of the rhetorical principles of unity, coherence, and emphasis.

9. Locate six types of connectives by line number from the appendix. See pages 182–183 for examples of connectives.

Chapter Nine

Presenting Information

HOW WE LEARN

One of the most frequent reasons for speaking or communicating is to inform people about something. In a sense you play the role of a teacher; you have the obligation of presenting your material not only in a clear and interesting way but also in the way that makes it easiest for your audience to learn, remember, and apply the information. To achieve these goals we need to know something of the way in which man learns.

From Known to Unknown

In Chapter 1 we learned that man understands a message primarily as he brings his previous experience and knowledge to bear on the stimulus. It follows that a teacher or speaker must arrange and select his material so that he best utilizes the knowledge and experience the audience already has. In describing or explaining something, the rule might be stated: go from the known to the unknown. For example, in trying to explain the relationship between wire size and electric current, an electrician compared the rule for selection of size to a garden hose (known) and the excess strain put upon it when one restricted the opening with the nozzle. Having once burst a garden hose by turning the nozzle off, the writer understood his explanation. It was clear, interesting, and easy to apply.

On the assumption that everybody knows the size of an English sparrow, a robin, and a crow, bird watchers typically relate the size of all unknown or unidentified birds to one of these three. This simple relating of known to unknown has made the communicating and sharing of much information far less frustrating for serious bird watchers.

Serial Learning

As we learned in previous chapters, people tend to learn more readily when things are arranged sequentially or in some serial order, especially when they are aware of the order. We teach youngsters addition and subtraction before multiplication and division. Though we could start with algebra, it is deemed more efficient to use a sequencing based upon difficulty, partial-responses, and cumulative effect. In history courses, we often use a chronological order; at other times, an order or sequence based on social issues might be preferable.

The particular ordering of the parts to be learned is based upon the previous knowledge of the audience, the complexity of the subject, and the specific information or skill the speaker wishes to impart. Typically, the audience is said to be learning (serially) when it is able to connect each portion of the sequence to the one that comes immediately after it.[1] In learning to drive a car, one must learn a great many specifics, but he has not really learned to *drive* until clutching, braking, steering, and other operations are so connected that the necessity of one arouses automatically the next appropriate action.

Reinforcement

Perhaps in an education or psychology course you have heard the expression *S R X*. In discussing the involved subject of learning, theorists use *S* to stand for stimulus, *R* for response, and *X* for reinforcement. This *X* may be a reward for responding in the desired way, a punishment, some form of known association, or perhaps some form of repetition. The exact nature and mode of operation of reinforcement is highly complex and is the subject of considerable academic debate. For some

[1]J. A. McGeoch and A. L. Irion, *The Psychology of Human Learning*, 2d ed. (New York: David McKay Co., Inc., 1952), p. 89.

theorists SR is explanation enough, so long as there is some form of time-related proximity or what they refer to as temporal contiguity.[2]

For the speech and communication theorist, both temporal contiguity and reinforcement have great practical usefulness. The previous discussion of the advantages of serial learning and relating new information to things already known is an application of temporal contiguity. The teacher who "feeds back" criticism by a smile, a frown, or a high grade is practicing reinforcement. So is the drill sergeant with a really loud voice. This enhancement of a desired response is an application or reinforcement, whether it be by repetition, loud voice, or some other form of emphasis.

A most interesting communication experiment regarding the relative effectiveness of various modes of emphasis was conducted by Dr. Raymond Ehrensberger. A fifteen-minute speech was delivered to various audiences in what may be described as a relatively neutral mode of emphasis; experimental speeches on the same subject to similar audiences made much use of various kinds of emphasis. All twenty-one audiences were given tests on the material covered in the speeches to see which kind of treatment effected the greatest retention.

Some of the primary devices of emphasis studied were:

 1. Verbal emphasis ("now get this," and so on, preceding a remark).
 2. Three distributed repetitions.
 3. Immediate repetition early in the speech.
 4. Speaking slowly (half the normal rate).
 5. Immediate repetitions late in the speech.
 6. Pauses.
 7. Gestures (hand and index finger only).
 8. Four distributed repetitions.
 9. Two distributed repetitions.
10. Soft voice (aspirate).
11. Forceful voice (almost bombastic).

An analysis of the retention test results is shown below. The numbers represent the percentage of right answers (of 100 items) that each specific audience scored. When the difference between a specific experimental mode of emphasis and the neutral treatment is greater than might be expected by chance, it is referred to as a significant or very significant difference.

This is strong evidence of the value of emphasis, whether verbal, vocal, gestural, organizational, or some combination of the above. However, some serious warnings are also implied for the speakers. You will note that while three repetitions was a very significant factor in retention,

[2]McGoech and Irion, *The Psychology of Human Learning*, p. 46.

four repetitions fell off considerably and two appeared to cause no effect. Although the results of one limited experiment in no way suggest that three is a magic number, they do imply that too much repetition is as bad as too little. All of us have grown weary of certain TV commercials that continually repeat the product name. By the same token, you have probably learned to appreciate the teacher who repeats and reviews things often enough, making it easier to understand and to recall the important items. It is also interesting to note that voice volume made a difference in this experiment. Although this does not mean that we should never use a loud voice, it does demonstrate that a loud voice under certain communication circumstances may actually interfere with retention and recall of information. In sum, take care not to overdo a good thing or to draw superspecific rules from limited experiences. Reinforcement in the form of verbal, vocal, gestural, and organizational emphasis can be a real asset to the speaker presenting information—so long as he is careful to adapt the amount and kind of reinforcement to his particular subject, situation, and audience.

THE RELATIVE EFFECTIVENESS OF A MODE OF EMPHASIS COMPARED TO A NEUTRAL TREATMENT*

Rank	Device	Experimental Mode % Right Answers	Neutral Mode % Right Answers	Statistical Analysis†
1	"Now get this" (verbal emphasis)	86	53.2	Very significant difference
2	Three distributed repetitions	78	51.4	Very significant difference
3	Repeat (early in speech)	72	50.7	Very significant difference
4	Slow	76	59.8	Very significant difference
5	Repeat (late in speech)	67	50.7	Very significant
6	Pause	69	55.4	Very significant difference
7	Gesture	66	53.2	Very significant difference
8	Four distributed repetitions	60	51.4	Significant difference
9	Two distributed repetitions	58	51.4	No real difference
10	Soft voice	56	55.4	No real difference
11	Loud voice	51	59.8	Significant negative difference

*R. Ehrensberger, "An Experimental Study of the Relative Effectiveness of Certain Forms of Emphasis in Public Speaking," *Speech Monographs*, 12, No. 2 (1945), 94–111.
†Very significant difference = 1% level of significance; significant difference = 5% level; no real difference = below the 5% level; significant negative difference = 5% level favoring neutral mode.

PRIMARY OBJECTIVES

One of the primary objectives in presenting information is *clarity*; we utilize what we know about the psychology of learning to facilitate understanding. Perhaps not quite so evident is the fact that an audience's *interest* or motivation to learn may importantly affect how much it retains or remembers. The third primary principle is *organization*.

Achieving Clarity

The scope of your purpose (the amount of information you wish to cover in a given period of time) is a vital factor in clarity, as are the organization of the material and the choice of language. The use of audio-visual aids represents still another method of enhancing clarity. These special factors will be discussed later; this section is primarily concerned with verbal forms of clarity.

Illustration or Example. An education major who was also a student teacher had as her specific purpose "to inform the class of the basic principles of overcoming discipline problems in the fourth grade." She could have explained "projections of insecurity and overt cognitive intellectualization assistance from an interacting teacher." The class was fortunate because she elected instead to draw specific examples from her own experience to illustrate and make clear the profound problems of discipline, and this approach was much more interesting. She opened her speech by describing an experience involving George Z. and his persistence in putting gum in little girls' hair. She followed this with the story of Bernard B., who, though a gifted child, took a special delight in swearing. Next she explained the psychological reasons for such behavior, the things not to do, and the proper principles of discipline to apply. In a sense the whole speech was an extended example that served the purpose of making her point clear. The more detail and the more vivid the incident, the more interesting it generally is. Very often verbal illustration can be efficiently enhanced through tangible examples like pictures or actual objects (perhaps a recording of Bernard B.'s language).

If your subject is one with which you have had no firsthand experience, you can often draw your examples from people who have. An excellent speech on aerial acrobatics was delivered by a student who had never been in an airplane but who used examples drawn from the actual experiences of three veteran stunt pilots.

An illustration or example may be hypothetical (that is, a made-up or contrived story that is reasonable and fair to the facts). It usually starts, "Suppose you were flying at 10,000 feet . . ." or "put yourself in this predicament. . . ." The hypothetical example does not carry the proof of a real or factual illustration, but it does have the attribute of adaptability to the point being made, since you may tell it as you please. The major problem is an ethical one. Make sure the hypothetical example is never taken for a factual one, and make sure it is plausible and consistent with known facts.

Illustration or example represents a powerful, efficient way of clarifying and supporting a point. In choosing your illustrations, make sure that they are truly related to the point being made and that they are representative. An example out of context or a very real example that is an exception to the general rule only inhibits clarity in the long run. In addition to being reasonable and fair, your illustrations and examples should contain enough specific details and excitement to add to the interest of the subject.

Analogy or Comparison. Analogy is often the most useful device a teacher or speaker can use in making a point vivid and clear. Its use substantiates the learning theory discussed earlier, in that the nature of analogy is to point out similarities between something already known or understood and that which is not (in other words, going from the known to the unknown). If we were trying to give meaning to the minuscule size of a molecule or the gigantic size of our galaxy, the following analogies should be both vivid and useful.

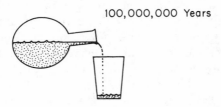

100,000,000 Years

FIGURE 9-1. If *molecules* of water were poured into a drinking glass at one per second, it would take 100,000,000 years to fill it.

At 186,000 miles per second light travels 6,000,000,000,000 miles a year or 250,000,000 times around the earth. At this rate we could reach the sun in 8½ minutes, the next nearest star in 4½ years. If we started at age 20, moving at light speed we would be 80 before we reached the star Aldebaran. The really distant stars in our galaxy would take us thousands of years to reach!

Abraham Lincoln made good use of analogy and comparison not only for vivid clarification but also for persuasion. During the Civil War there were those who loudly criticized his method of conducting the war. At that time, a tightrope walker named Blondin became famous for walking and for riding a two-wheel bicycle on a rope strung across Niagara Falls.

In explaining the dangerous position of the nation, Lincoln directed the following analogy at his critics:

> Gentlemen. I want you to suppose a case for a moment. Suppose that all the property you were worth was in gold, and you had put it in the hands of Blondin, the famous rope-walker, to carry across the Niagara Falls on a tightrope. Would you shake the rope while he was passing over it, or keep shouting to him, "Blondin, stoop a little more! Go a little faster!" No, I am sure you would not. You would hold your breath as well as your tongue, and keep your hands off until he was safely over. Now the government is in the same situation. It is carrying an immense weight across a stormy ocean. Untold treasures are in its hands. It is doing the best it can. Don't badger it! Just keep still, and it will get you safely over.[3]

A junior high school principal made his point most vivid through an analogy:

> Someone has pointed out that a pig of iron is worth $5.00; if it is made into horseshoes, it is worth $10.50; if it has been refined and tempered and shaped into needles, it is worth $3,500; but if it has been fashioned into balance springs for watches, it is worth $25,000. How much more spectacularly does the value of an individual increase when he is given good surroundings, good training, and a challenge to his skills and spirit! The measure of success of a school is the extent to which it makes possible the maximum development of the potentialities of the individuals within it.[4]

Statistics. The use of figures or numbers to help make a point more clear or specific is not as simple as it may seem. Statistics are frequently used to support a point in a persuasive speech, but they are only powerful evidence if they are (1) meaningful to the audience and (2) related to the point under consideration. However, when statistics are overly precise and complicated, we may cloud rather than clarify an issue. Have you ever been given directions like the following by a local resident: "You go down Norfolk Street exactly 3.2 miles to Baker Street, then 2.4 miles to a Y intersection, turn about 120° on Charlie Street for .3 of a mile, then right for 150 yards and you're there." Some specifics are most helpful, but not these! Even if you *were* able to keep them straight, you would probably cause an accident by watching your odometer instead of the road. Of course, the other extreme is: "You go up Norfolk quite a little piece and than a couple of miles or so on Baker to a kind of wide angle left turn and then . . ." A "little" piece and a "fur" piece can vary by a good many miles.

By themselves, statistics are abstract. Make them more concrete by relating them to known things. To say that South America has serious economic problems because the average family income is $150 per year is reasonably clear, but it is clearer when this figure is compared to the

---

[3]Quoted in *Town Meeting,* 11 (October 11, 1945), 24.
[4]Roy E. Vannette, *Barnum Junior High School Student Handbook*, 13th ed. (Birmingham, Mich.: Parent-Teachers Association, 1964).

$8400 of the United States or when shown that $150 comes to only 41¢ a day.

We live more and more by predictive statistics. From Univac's vote predictions to insurance rates, from the number of cancerous agents in a carton of cigarettes to the average number of cavities in a given group of children, we are involved in an age of specific, predictive statistics. We have learned to combine statistics with analogies or comparisons to make sense out of the astronomical numbers of outer space. We also express speed as Mach 1, 2, or 3 instead of in miles per hour and distance in terms of light years.

The use of statistics can give a speech a sense of specificity and precision if we remember to relate the statistics to known things and to make them meaningful to the audience.

Testimony. Like statistics, testimony has great use in speeches to persuade but is also valuable for the sake of clarity. In a speech to inform it may add considerable *interest* to what might otherwise be straight explanation.

In describing the course of events on D-day in Europe, one might more vividly express the story by a series of datelines and statements from a dozen G.I.s who hit the beaches:

> *0400*, Pvt. Johnson: "There were ships and little boats and men all tangled up in one maze of confusion."
> *0430*, Pvt. Sandrin: "The men coming down the cargo nets to the LCIs (Landing Craft Infantry) seemed to be 20 feet from the deck one minute and a step away the next."
> *0500*, Pvt. Brown: "The LCI to our left just seemed to evaporate."
> *0600*, Sgt. Glover: "Where the hell is the air cover?"
> *2300*, Lt. Rucks: "This has been the longest day of my life."

The explanation of events is often clearer and more impressive through the use of testimony. More will be said of this subject under "Authority" in Chapter 11.

Restatement. Restatement is more than simple repetition. It is saying the same thing in a different way. This is particularly useful if the material is complex or the vocabulary specialized. The value of restatement in terms of learning theory, particularly the concept of reinforcement, was made evident earlier in this chapter.

If you were to reread Chapter 1 of this book, you would find the process of communication defined in many different ways, all trying to say the same thing. One descriptive definition was a whole page long, another consisted of a short paragraph, another reduced the definition essentially to encoding and decoding. This is an example of restatement for clarity. If it was not clear one time because of sentence structure or another because of vocabulary, you were given still more choices. If you understood all the definitions at first glance, fine. Assuming that it was not too extended, this repetition should have reinforced the learning. To restate the point of this clarity factor—it involves more than simple repetition, it includes saying the same thing in different ways for reinforcement of learning, and it is particularly useful if the subject is complex or if the vocabulary may be specialized or strange to the audience.

Developing Interest

The second of the two primary principles in presenting a speech to inform, *interest* refers to the motivation of the audience to want to listen or learn. The problem is to hold the attention of your audience while you are practicing all the clarity suggestions just discussed. What are the categories of things that tend to interest all of us? How can they be applied to your subject in such a way as to motivate the audience to pay attention and want to learn? Much of a speaker's *interest* is of course dependent upon his style of delivery and his use of vocal variety; however, we are here concerned primarily with speech content. Some of the more useful qualities of content that stimulate interest are as follows:

Specificity. When a speaker says, "Let me give you an example of what I mean by dog-tired," you probably pay closer attention than if he were simply to give you some general, academic explanation. Suppose he used the following example:

> The men of hurricane Camille's Red Cross rescue group thought after two days of forced march through wreckage-strewn coastal areas that they were dog-tired. Then they saw the remote victims of the storm who seemed to be moving on sheer instinct and determination alone. They staggered through their broken homes with drooping shoulders, so physically drained that it seemed to take every last ounce of strength to put one foot in front of the other.

Specificity, reality, or concreteness are more interesting than vague generalities or the abstract. Instead of saying, "A boy was run over," be specific. Call him by name; indicate his age; identify the car. "Mark Scott, age 6, dashed into the street to greet his mother approaching from the other side and was dashed to the pavement by a 1974 Thunderbird traveling at the 30-mile speed limit."

Conflict. The TV westerns always seem to pit "bad guys" against "good guys." This conflict and fighting pay off in viewer interest. Can you imagine a Bonanza story without conflict, uncertainty, or antagonism? Sports contests, even when you know that U.S.C. will surely beat Otterbein College, still conjure up interest. Disagreement and opposition have elected and destroyed many a politician, but almost always in an interesting way! If in your examples, illustrations, and explanation, you can utilize the factor of conflict without seeming to set up sham or mock battles, your speech should have added interest for the audience.

Novelty. That which is novel is different, unusual, contrasting, or strange. Of course, if the subject is so unique that a listener cannot relate it to his previous knowledge and experience, interest may actually be lost rather than gained.

Novelty is not limited to uniqueness or oddness, however. Relatively average things become novel if the world about them is in contrast. At one time a bikini bathing suit would have been an interesting novelty, primarily because of its contrast to other more conservative swimsuits. In our time a girl would probably gain more attention wearing one of the old-fashioned neck-to-ankle suits of the early 1900s or an ultra-modern "topless." Of course, as one student put it, "It depends on the girl." New Yorkers find nothing unusual or novel about their tall sky-scrapers, but a visitor might himself become a novelty to the natives by his trancelike stares into the low clouds that hide the Empire State Building from view.

The unusual, the contrasting, the unique, the strange, the rare, and the generally different things in life are more interesting than the run-of-the-mill. Let your examples, analogies, and explanations be novel for added audience interest.

Curiosity. One of the more marvelous and exasperating aspects of young children is the seemingly endless questions they persistently ask about an infinity of subjects. Grown children (men) are not really much different, except that they may become a little more specialized about the subjects and the questions they ask. Man seems to have a compulsion to find out what lies around the corner or beyond the stars. Each new discovery in space now leads to suspense about what the universe is really like and to the big question, "Is there life out there?"

Unanswered questions, uncertainty, suspense—these are the ingredients that may be effectively utilized by speakers to arouse curiosity and there-by enhance interest.

Immediacy. By immediacy is meant those matters of the moment or specific occasion that will quickly arouse and arrest attention and interest when related to a speaker's subject. A company training director has the uncanny ability to memorize names of people along with other pertinent facts after just one informal meeting. He once startled a group of forty executives on the second day of a course by randomly calling off their names throughout a two-hour period: "Mr. William Sandy, what do you think of. . . ." Needless to say, interest was high. You never knew when he would call your name, cite your job description, and ask your opinion.

A reference to a previous speaker or some incident that is proximate and known to the audience may have similar effects in garnering interest. In a speech to businessmen in Grand Rapids, Michigan, a speaker noticed several members of his audience staring out the window at the falling snow, probably through apprehension more than a lack of interest. In any event, he too looked toward the window, paused, and commented, "Misery loves company. We have 18 inches of snow in Detroit and you have 42 inches. The weather man is predicting clearing skies in the next few hours." The audience seemed more interested after that. Not only had a distraction been acknowledged, but the audience felt more closely attuned to the speaker.

Learning about the speech occasion, the audience, the last-minute headlines, and all similar matters of the moment is time well spent in trying to devise methods of making your speech interesting.

Humor. If you feel you do not tell a joke well or find it difficult to be a humorous speaker, perhaps you need not be too concerned. The limited speech research on the impact of humor on an audience seems to indicate that at least in *persuasive* speeches it does not make any difference. In a study by P. E. Lull[5] it was found that audiences listening to humorous and nonhumorous speeches on socialized medicine were equally persuaded by both speeches and in both directions of the attitude scale. D. Kilpela had the same results with a more recent study using government health insurance as the topic.[6] Both methods were effective, but they did not vary significantly in effectiveness. A series of studies by Gruner produced similar results, except that humor seemed to enhance the character ratings of the speaker.[7] This was supported in a study by Kennedy, who also found that "subjects viewed the humorous introductory speech as significantly more effective, enjoyable, and interesting."[8] A study by J. Douglas Gibb comparing humorous and nonhumorous *informative* lectures did show significantly better student *retention* of the humorous lecture.[9] Lull and Kilpela were quick to point out, however, that the type of humor in their studies may not have been of a real

[5]P. E. Lull, "The Effectiveness of Humor in Persuasive Speeches," *Speech Monographs*, 7 (1940), 26–40.

[6]Donald Kilpela, "An Experimental Study of the Effects of Humor on Persuasion" (Master's thesis, Wayne State University, 1961).

[7]C. Gruner, "Effect of Humor on Speaker Ethos and Audience Information Gain," *Journal of Communication*, 17, No. 3 (1967), 228–33.

[8]Allan J. Kennedy, "The Effect of Humor upon Source Credibility," *Speech Communication Association Abstracts*, 1972, p. 10.

[9]J. Douglas Gibb, "An Experimental Comparison of the Humorous Lecture and the Nonhumorous Lecture in Informative Speaking" (Master's thesis, University of Utah, 1964).

professional nature. In other words, a Bob Hope or a Bill Cosby might indeed have produced significant persuasive results. In any event, funny anecdotes (if told well and in good taste) have probably helped many an otherwise dull speaker, subject, or audience.

If you do decide to try humor in the form of anecdotes for interest, make it as professional as possible. There is no feeling quite so desperate as that which comes upon viewing a poker-faced audience after you have told your best joke. Make sure that the anecdote is related to either the subject or the occasion; make sure you can tell it fluently; make sure you remember the punch line, and make sure it is not offensive to your audience. The best advice of all—try it out on a small group of your friends first. In other words, *practice.*

Vital Factors. If while reading this book you had the FM radio playing and suddenly the announcer broke in to say, "Alert! Alert! Please turn to your Conelrad frequencies at the civilian defense white triangles on your radio dial," you would undoubtedly stop your reading and turn the dial as instructed. The reason is obvious. Staying alive, protecting your loved ones, defending your home—all these are things of vital concern to you, and you are interested because you have to be.

Vital factors, if truly vital, will arrest attention through personal involvement. Those things that affect our self-preservation, reputation, property, sources of livelihood, freedoms are truly vital factors. More will be said about the role of each of these factors in Part IV, "The Psychology of Persuasion."

Figures of Speech. Figures of speech are metaphorical statements that can add interest, spunk, and delight to your message. That they may create confusion if used to excess should also be considered. A description of the major types of figures of speech with examples of each, follows:

Anadiplosis:	a sentence beginning with the last word or words of the one immediately preceding it. "There can be no such thing as a peaceable secession. Peaceable secession is an utter impossibility."—D. Webster
Anaphora:	consecutive clauses or sentences beginning with the same word. "Give me liberty or give me death!" —P. Henry "Why the outgoing President's felicitation on the indorsement? Why the delay of a reargument? Why the incom-

ing President's advance exhortation in favor of the decision?"—A. Lincoln

Epanalepsus: repeating the end of one sentence or clause at the beginning of the next one.
"All for one; one for all."

Epanodos: the same word appearing at both ends of a statement.
"Satan cannot cast out Satan."—H. E. Fosdick
"Genius always attracts genius."—A. Carnegie

Paromasia: the recurrence of the same letter, syllable, or word; word play, rhymes, and puns.
"Noah. . . . Ah no!"
"Amen. . . . Ah men!"
"This very little is more than too much."—J. Hoskins.

Polyptoton: a repetition of words of the same lineage that differ in their endings.
"Forsaken by all friends and forsaking all comfort."—J. Hoskins
"When better automobiles are built, Buick will build them."

Metaphor: implied comparsion: not farfetched, mixed, or inappropriate to the context.
"Fiery temper, thirsty sword."
"I have but one lamp by which my feet are guided, and that is the lamp of experience."—P. Henry

Metonymy: substituting the name of an item associated with a larger concept for the concept.
"Sword" for war.
"Brass" for military officers.

Synecdoche: the use of a part for the whole or the whole for a part or parts.
"Blamed by many tongues."
"All hands on deck."
"She wears a jewelry store."

Hyperbole: exaggeration; antithesis of understatement.
"Ichabod Crane's arms dangled a mile out of his coat sleeves!"—W. Irving

Asyndeton: words, phrases, clauses, or sentences occuring in a series without connectives.
"I came. I saw. I conquered."—Julius Caesar

Apostrophe:	direct address to imaginary or absent beings. "Hope, tell me, what hast thou to hope for?"—D. Webster at Bunker Hill.
Paralipsis:	a counterfeit statement or amplification in which one says he will not say something but then does so at length. "My friends, it is my pride that in all my years of service to the cause of Ireland I have never said one unkind, uncharitable word, not even about Tories and Orangemen, lying, unscrupulous, reactionary scoundrels and bigots though they be."—Irish Nationalist Orator.
Alliteration:	the use of words beginning with the same letter. "Over stock and stone." "Through thick and thin."
Simile:	comparison with "like"or "as." "The present administration is bobbing around like a cork in a stormy sea."—T. Dewey
Allusion:	a casual, undocumented use of an associated idea. "He failed in spite of herculean effort."
Reference:	a statement that gives the gist of the idea and credits the source. "As Shakespeare had Antony say of ambition . . ."
Personification:	treating the inanimate as animate. ". . . when the feet of barbarism should trample on the tombs of her consuls." —D. Webster
Prosopopoeia:	having the dead speak. "If Washington were here, he would say . . ."
Paradox:	a seemingly self-contradictory or absurd statement. "We'll teach these natives democracy even if we have to shoot every last one of them."—*Teahouse of the August Moon*
Catachresis:	somewhat abusive phraseology, stronger than metaphor, involving the use of an incompatible word. "He threatened me a good turn." "I am not guilty of such virtues."
Euphemism:	a mild, inoffensive substitute for a "bad" word.

"Grandpa passed away."
"It smells [stinks]."

Onomatopoeia: words that imitate the sounds to which
                       they refer.
                       "Buzz," "snarl," "tintinnabulation."

Oxymoron: use of incongruous details.
                       "Cruel kindness."
                       "Make haste slowly."

Antimetabole: an inverted sentence.
                       "Just to exercise his might, mighty to
                       perform his justice."[10]

Organizing Effectively

The learning theory previously discussed should have provided you with the rationale and background material to organize information effectively. What does it tell us? It tells us of the need for grabbing the listener's attention early and motivating him to continue listening; it tells us of the value of serially or sequentially ordered material; it tells us of the need for reinforcement and for preparing states of readiness to learn or listen.

One durable and effective method of organizing informative material that roughly meets the requirements above was voiced by the gifted speaker Chauncey Depew, the late state senator from New York: first, tell them what you're going to tell them; second, tell them; and third, tell them you've told them. We merely add the concept of an early attention step to motivate a desire to listen and then revise the language to better suit our purposes as follows: *attention, overview, information,* and *review.*

The interest factors discussed earlier are all excellent suggestions for gaining attention. Your immediate purpose is to create a desire on the part of listeners to hear more about the information you have to offer. If the audience is already highly motivated, your attention step becomes proportionately less important.

In a recent student speech "to inform the class about some of the sociological problems facing India," the speaker opened with the following (*attention* and *interest*): "Did you know that half of the world's population is illiterate and that one-third of this half lives in India? Did you know that over three hundred languages are spoken in India? That fourteen thousand babies a day are born in India?" He then proceeded to elaborate each of his three points in order. He gave us the detailed *information.* At the close of the speech, he repeated the

[10]Adapted from Glen E. Mills, *Putting a Message Together*, 2d ed., copyright © 1972 by The Bobbs-Merrill Company, Inc., reprinted by permission of the publisher.

three facets indicated in the overview, but in addition he briefly summarized some of the salient details from the *information* step. In other words, he *reviewed* the speech, or "told 'em what he told 'em." The amount of summary detail you put into your *review* will depend upon the complexity of the subject, the time allotted, and your purpose. In some speeches you may prefer a brief synthesis of what you have tried to say, in others perhaps some conclusions that adequately *review* your speech.

The reinforcement value of this development is obvious. Once more, remember that a listener cannot go back and reread or review. The speaker therefore has the obligation to be sure the learning is communicated. Toward this end, an occasional internal summary, review, or preview in the *information* step may facilitate clarity. A study by Fred Miller clearly shows that, other things being equal, audiences listening to well-organized speeches score higher on retention tests than do those hearing poorly organized speeches.[11]

Organization, the third primary principle of presenting information, may thus be systematically enhanced by following the four-part development scheme based upon learning theory: *attention, overview, information*, and *review*. A model outline showing this type of organization follows. The second version illustrates a slightly more detailed outline of the same material using *introduction, body*, and *conclusion* as its method of organization.

Similar informative outlines again demonstrating the two recommended ways of organizing the same informative material are shown in Appendix C (The Dietary Laws of the Jewish People).

INTRODUCTION TO MUSIC

General End: To inform.
Specific Purpose: To state and explain the fundamental concepts of musical theory.

Attention

   I. Play a few bars of music on the violin. (Demonstration)
  II. Poke fun at the music majors in the class.

Overview

   I. The kinds of notes.
  II. The musical staff.

11Fred Miller, "An Experiment to Determine the Effect Organization Has on the Immediate and Delayed Recall of Information" (Master's thesis, Miami University, Ohio, 1966); see also E. C. Thompson, Jr., "An Experimental Investigation of the Relative Effectiveness of Organizational Structure in Oral Communication," *Speech Monographs*, 27 (1960), 94.

III. Methods of counting the notes.

IV. Relation of these to an instrument.

Information

I. The kinds of notes.
   A. Neutral notes, A-B-C-D-E-F-G.
   B. Sharp notes, $\frac{1}{2}$ tone up.
   C. Flat notes, $\frac{1}{2}$ tone down.

II. Explanation of the musical staff.
   A. The treble clef and melody.
      1. Contains 5 lines, E-G-B-D-F.
      2. Contains 4 spaces, F-A-C-E.
   B. The bass clef and rhythm.
      1. Contains 5 lines, G-B-D-F-A.
      2. Contains 4 spaces, A-C-E-G.

III. Methods of counting the notes.
   A. Whole note gets 4 beats.
   B. Half-note gets 2 beats.
   C. Quarter-note gets 1 beat.
   D. Eighth-note gets $\frac{1}{2}$ beat.

IV. Relation of these points to a musical keyboard.
   A. The notes (whether neutral, sharp, or flat) correspond with the lines and spaces in the staff.
   B. The position of the notes on the staff determines what note or key is to be played on the musical instrument.
   C. The type of counting the note receives tells how long the note is played on the instrument.

Review

I. I have tried to make clear the following four factors of musical theory:
   A. The kinds of notes.
   B. The musical staff.
   C. Methods of counting the notes.
   D. Relating the theory to an instrument.

II. Now you can start writing your own music or at least sneer at the music majors.

INTRODUCTION TO MUSIC[12]

General End: To inform.

Specific Purpose: To state and explain the fundamental concepts of musical theory.

Introduction

I. Play a few bars of music on a violin. (Demonstration)

[12]From a student speech by Gary Carotta, Wayne State University.

A. "I wish I really was good at this."
B. I can't teach you to play an instrument in this short speech, but perhaps I can review musical theory so that you'll feel superior to the three music majors in this class.
II. I should like to cover the following major steps in musical theory:
   A. The kinds of notes.
   B. The musical staff.
   C. Methods of counting the notes.
   D. Relation of these to an instrument.

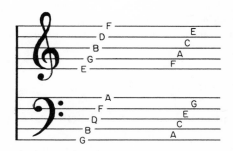

FIGURE 9–2.

Body

I. The kinds of notes.
   A. Neutral notes, A-B-C-D-E-F-G.
   B. Sharp notes, ½ tone up.
   C. Flat notes, ½ tone down.
      (A demonstration and a piano keyboard were introduced here.)
II. Explanation of the musical staff.
   A. The treble clef and melody.
      1. Contains 5 lines, E-G-B-D-F.
      2. Contains 4 spaces, F-A-C-E.
         (A visual aid was shown here.)
   B. The bass clef and rhythm.
      1. Contains 5 lines, G-B-D-F-A.
      2. Contains 4 spaces, A-C-E-G.
         (A visual aid was shown here.)
III. Methods of counting the notes.
   A. Whole note gets 4 beats.
   B. Half-note gets 2 beats.
   C. Quarter-note gets 1 beat.
   D. Eighth-note gets ½ beat.
      (A blackboard sketch and demonstration were used here.)
IV. Relation of these points to a musical keyboard.
   (The piano keyboard was displayed here.)
   A. The notes (whether neutral, sharp, or flat) correspond with the lines and spaces in the staff.

B. The position of the notes on the staff determines what note or key is to be played on the musical instrument.
C. The type of counting the note receives tells how long the note is played on the instrument.
(A short demonstration here.)

Conclusion

I. I have tried to make clear the following four factors of musical theory:
   A. The kinds of notes.
   B. The musical staff.
   C. Methods of counting the notes.
   D. Relating the theory to an instrument.
II. Now you can start writing your own music or at least sneer at the music majors.

AUDIO-VISUAL AIDS

Teaching or learning aids are used to help make a subject clear, to motivate interest, and to reinforce the message. On all counts they represent a value to the speaker although not without some hazards and problems. The question of what kind of aid to use in what situation is critical. The role of *demonstration* as an aid is especially important to beginning speakers, because teachers almost always ask for a demonstration speech, in part because it causes you to move and thereby work off excess tension. This section will relate the use of audio-visual aids to audience involvement and will indicate the special role of demonstration.

The Cone of Experience and Types of Aids

Dr. Edgar Dale, an expert on using teaching aids, has given us a theoretical model for classifying these aids in terms of audience involvement—namely, telling, showing, and doing.[13] The model grades experience and audience involvement according to the degree of abstractness. Those aids that allow the audience to "do" or experience something are more concrete than those aids that simply "show" something, and "telling" is the most abstract form. Hollingworth[14] thinks of this ladder of abstraction as being ordered in terms of interestingness—that is, the direct, purposeful experience would be the most interesting. Dale is quick to

[13]From *Audio-Visual Methods in Teaching*, Third Edition, by Edgar Dale. Copyright 1946, 1954, 1969 by Holt, Rinehart and Winston, Inc. Reprinted by permission of Holt, Rinehart and Winston, Inc.

[14]H. L. Hollingworth, *The Psychology of the Audience* (New York: American Book Company, 1935), p. 73.

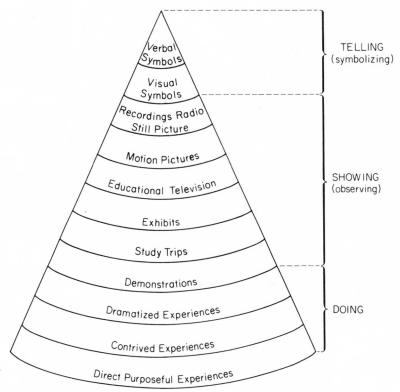

FIGURE 9–3.

point out the danger of too arbitrary a hierarchical order based on either interestingness or learning, since the other aspects of a speech situation are so variable. Audience response is affected by the previous experience of the audience, the kind of speech subject and its amenability to teaching aids, the oral ability of the speaker to visualize with word pictures, the real purpose of the speaker, and the interest level of the audience. The specific devices in the cone of experience are as follows:[15]

At the top of the cone (the "telling" area) are included the visual symbols that aid the audience. These are things such as graphs, charts, cartoons, diagrams, flat pictures, and blackboard sketches.

Some typical forms of graphs that a speaker might use include pictograms (Figures 9–4 and 9–5), bar graphs (Figure 9–6), area diagrams (Figure 9–7), and line graphs (Figure 9–8).

Some typical forms of charts include organization charts (Figure 9–9), stream or tree charts (Figures 9–10 and 9–11), and tabular charts (Figure 9–12).

[15]Dale, *Audio-Visual Methods in Teaching*, p. 39.

In the middle of the cone (the "showing" area) are included recordings, motion pictures, exhibits, field trips, and demonstrations. All these items except the last are self-explanatory (more will be said about demonstration in the next section). These are the devices that bring the audience closer to reality than the mere telling, but still not to the real personal involvement found in doing.

The bottom of the cone (the "doing" part) involves contrived experiences and dramatic participation. These would include LINK trainers for pilots, antigravity simulations for astronauts, and other models of mock-ups, as well as the personal involvement caused by semidramatic experiences like role playing or working on case-study problems. Perhaps in grade school you played a Pilgrim landing on Plymouth Rock, an angel at Bethlehem, or Paul Revere. In management training programs today, some of our top executives are once again role-playing, except that now it is an irate foreman, a shop steward, or an unhappy manager that is portrayed. Why? Because it is thought that this contrived slice of life gets the person more involved in the lesson and more closely approaches the reality of true experience.

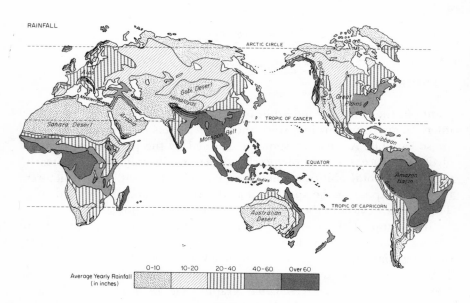

FIGURE 9–4. Pictogram (Pictorial Statistics: Rainfall).[16]

[16]From *The Golden Book Encyclopedia of National Science*, Volume 3. Edited by Herbert S. Zim. © Copyright 1962 by Western Publishing Company, Inc.

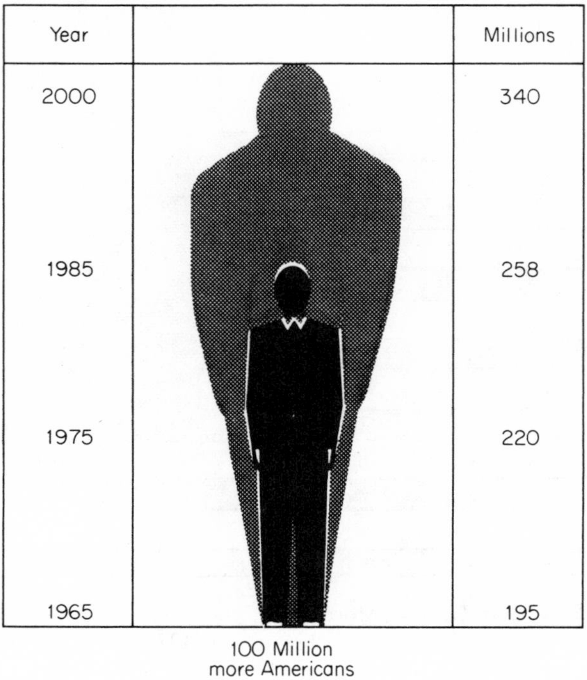

Year		Millions
2000		340
1985		258
1975		220
1965		195

100 Million
more Americans

FIGURE 9–5. Pictogram.

The Special Role of Demonstration

The demonstration aspect of teaching aids is especially important in a speech class because this is typically an early type of assigned exercise or informative speech. A demonstration speech reduces anxiety and at the same time enhances the presentation of information. The purpose of a demonstration is to show how a skill, a procedure, a process, or a device is used so that it may aid the audience in learning the skill or acquiring the knowledge. A demonstration combines showing with telling. Many grade-school systems have sessions called "show and tell." These are essentially demonstration exercises and are excellent early speech training if conducted by teachers with some basic speech experience.

The value of using demonstration is that the audience can learn by actually seeing. The demonstration helps the speaker remember his material; it appeals to several senses; it reinforces the message; it saves time; finally, it has dramatic appeal and is more concrete than just telling.

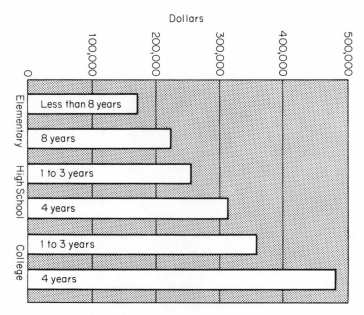

FIGURE 9–6.   Bar Graph: More Education, More Income, Lifetime Earnings of Males by Years in School.[17]

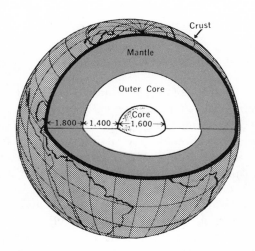

FIGURE 9–7.   Area Diagram Showing the Four Zones of the Earth's Interior.[18]

[17]"More Education, More Income," *200 Million Americans*, U.S. Department of Commerce, Bureau of the Census, November 1967, p. 55.

[18]Special permission granted by *My Weekly Reader*, No. 5, published by Xerox Education Publications, © Xerox Corporation, 1964.

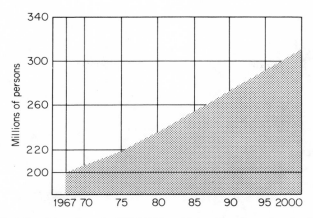

FIGURE 9–8. Line Graph: 100 Million More Americans by the Year 2000.[19]

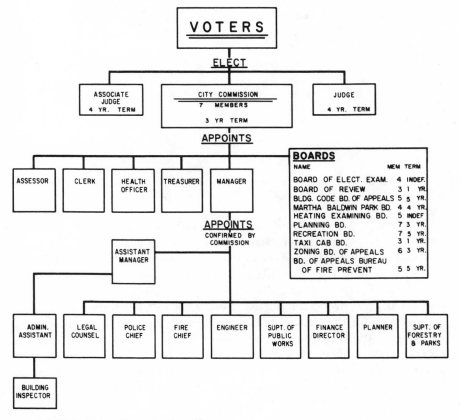

FIGURE 9–9. Organization Chart.

[19]"100 Million More Americans by the Year 2000," U.S. Department of Commerce, Bureau of the Census, November 1967, p. 8.

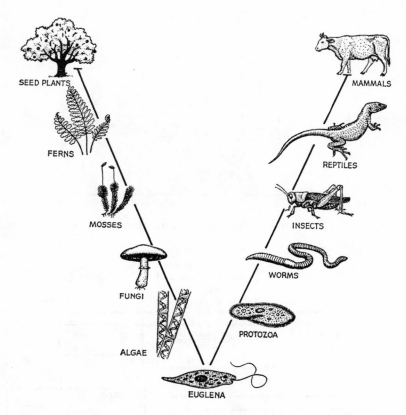

FIGURE 9–10.   Stream or Tree Chart (Plant Life Is Represented on the
Left Side of the "V," Animal Life on the Right).[20]

The best way to introduce some of the hazards of demonstration is by
examples of demonstrations that did not work as planned. A few years
ago many commercials were not taped as they are now. In a Westinghouse
commercial Betty Furness while gracefully swishing between refrigerator
doors, which were rhythmically opening and closing, had a door close
on part of her lovely, full-skirted dress. Miss Furness finished the commercial without the bottom half of her dress! The point is she finished
the speech. We can draw a lesson from this, but first let us recall another. Do you remember when an announcer tied a Timex watch to the
propeller of an outboard motor, lowered it into a fifty-gallon drum full of
water, and started the engine? When the motor was withdrawn, the
watch was gone. The camera panned down into the drum and there be-

[20]Truman J. Moon, Paul B. Mann, and James H. Otto, *Modern Biology* (New York:
Henry Holt and Company, 1947), p. 249. Reproduced by special permission of Holt,
Rinehart and Winston, Inc.

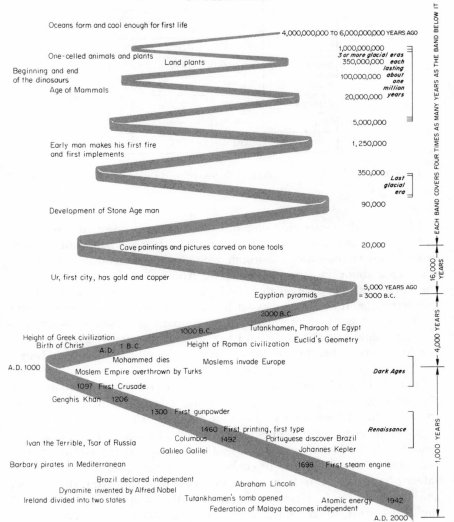

FIGURE 9–11.   Stream of Time Chart.[21]

fore millions of viewers was a very dead watch badly in need of re-assembly! What would you have done? Incidentally, due to a poised handling of this difficult situation, Timex sales actually went up, not down. Sometimes these demonstrations can actually be dangerous. On the late show one of the team added water to a bottle of pills they were selling, and then shook it to liven-up the demonstration. It blew up only moments after it was out of his hand!

[21]Margaret Bevans, ed., *The Golden Treasury of Knowledge* (New York: Golden Press, Inc., 1961), p. 621.

Name	Total sample 300	Age 18-39 sample 200	Age 40+ sample 100
Negro	14.3%	10%	23%
Afro-American	14%	15%	12%
Black	63%	66.5%	56%
Colored	4%	3.5%	5%
Other	4.7%	5%	4%
	100%	100%	100%

FIGURE 9–12. Tabular Chart (Negro Identification Preferences, 1973).[22]

Classroom demonstrations are just as much fun and often can be just as hazardous. A student once demonstrated a tear-gas pencil in an over-heated, poorly ventilated classroom with the temperature outside about zero. Talk about audience involvement! Another student, demonstrating the toughness of unbreakable, bulletproof glass, dropped it on the concrete floor. It did not break—it literally exploded. This produced one badly shaken speaker, although a glass company spokesman informed us at a later date that the chances of the angle of impact, the temperature, the force, and other factors being perfectly coordinated (which caused the shattering) were about 1 in 10,000.

The obvious questions are "What can I do to reduce the probability of things going wrong?" and "If something does go wrong in spite of careful planning, what do I do at that moment of truth?"

The answer to the first question is careful planning. Plan exactly *how* you will do it. Make sure you have *all* your equipment and have it in the right sequence. Be sure it *works* in your practice sessions. Emphasize safety precautions. Check for conditions that may vary from the practice session (for example, electric current). Finally, be sure *you* can do it. A flight instructor was teaching cadets the principles of airfoil and how an airplane wing develops lift. To demonstrate, he put a piece of $8\frac{1}{2} \times 11$ paper between his lower lip and his chin. He then blew over it, creating a partial vacuum on the top of the paper, which caused the paper to rise or lift. A new instructor who had observed this demonstration rushed to the next class with no time for practice. Confident that he could do it, he proceeded to blow—with no movement from the paper and with an audience of well-disciplined cadets trying not to explode with laughter. There are some moments when defeat is so very evident.

The answer to the second question, "What if it happens anyway?" is

[22]"Black Is Beautiful to More Blacks, 2 at WSU Find," *Detroit News*, June 13, 1973, p. 25.

again part of planning. More specifically, calculate the magnitude and nature of the risk and then plan emergency alternative procedures for every foul-up you can think of. This is very necessary. You have no time to protect yourself when it does happen, and the shock of the confusion may cause you to react emotionally rather than rationally.

Pilots of high-speed aircraft have long talked of calculated risk and alternate procedures. There are preplanned procedures to meet preclassified emergencies. If two engines go out, what do you do? Talk it over? NO, go to alternate plan two on a prearranged signal thereby cutting confusion and perhaps saving your life. There simply isn't time to do it any other way.

The student with the unbreakable glass had a calculated risk of 1 in 10,000. One can hardly blame him for being lax in planning alternate procedures. These are probably better odds than a pedestrian has on the Los Angeles freeway. Nevertheless he could have had two pieces of glass, just as you should always have two bulbs for your slide or movie projector. Extra equipment or spare parts are only part of the answer. The real problem is what you will say. Plan your communication strategy very carefully. *When and if the glass should break I will say* . . . *"the odds on that happening were 1 in 10,000. Let me prove it by beating the next piece of glass with this hammer."* If the next piece breaks you may have to resort to an alternate plan involving prayer. You can't win them all!

Some Practical Rules

Using Aids

1. Never obstruct the vision of your audience; make sure the lectern or stand is out of the way; try not to stand in front of your materials.
2. Use your aids to reinforce, not to distract; introduce them when pertinent, not before (unless for attention).
3. Talk to the audience; "talk" to your visual aid only when you wish the audience to look at it.
4. Make sure you thoroughly understand your own visual aid—precisely how and when you intend to use it; orient your audience to the aid (for example, "This is a top view").

Preparing Aids

1. Relate your choice of aids to the "cone of experience," a careful audience analysis, your subject, and your specific purpose.
2. Make a visual aid readily visible. Is it big enough? Are the lines heavy and dark enough (one-eighth to one-half inch thick)?
3. Make each visual aid comprehensible. Do not put too much detail or too many ideas on one aid. Clearly label all the significant parts. Let it be

simple enough so that you will be able easily and quickly to orient the audience to the aid.

4. Organize the aid systematically to make it easier for you to recall your speech material.

SUMMARY

Presenting information orally to an audience is similar to the task of a teacher. Teaching is a science as well as an art and involves the serious evaluation and application of learning theory. This same learning theory is therefore useful to any speaker who would attempt to inform. Three critical lessons involve: (1) relating new information to that which an audience already knows; (2) ordering the material in some serial progression that makes it easier for people to follow and relate the significant points; (3) reinforcing or enhancing the message and the response through prudent repetition, verbal emphasis, organization, and voice—connoting importance, reward, punishment, and the like. The final lesson from learning theory is that there appears to be a point of diminishing returns with all these devices, this point being related essentially and integrally to the specific and total communication circumstance involved.

The primary principles in informative speaking are clarity, interest, and organization. The factors of clarity are illustration or example, analogy or comparison, statistics, testimony, and restatement. The factors of interest are specificity, conflict, novelty, curiosity, immediacy, humor, and things that are of vital importance to the audience. The method of achieving psychologically sound organization involves: (1) gaining *attention*; (2) preparing the audience through a preview or *overview*; (3) giving the detailed *information*; and (4) *reviewing* the significant points for added reinforcement.

Using teaching aids is a vital part of public speaking, particularly when the goal is clarity. Edgar Dale's cone of experience gives us a good theoretical model for classifying these aids in terms of audience involvement—namely, *telling, showing,* and *doing.* The model helps us make decisions about our selection and use of aids by grading visual aids according to abstractness.

Some typical forms of graphs that a speaker might use are pictograms, bar graphs, area diagrams, and line graphs. Some typical forms of charts include organization charts, stream or tree charts, and tabular charts.

Demonstration is a special form of teaching aid for the speech student. The purpose of a demonstration is to show how a skill, procedure, process, or device is used so that it may aid the audience in learning the skill or acquiring the knowledge. A demonstration combines showing with telling. It appeals to several senses, reinforces the message, saves time, is more concrete than just telling, has dramatic appeal, and helps the speaker remember his material and burn off nervous energy.

The practical rules for reducing the hazards of demonstrations all involve planning in advance. (1) Calculate the risks involved. (2) Devise alternate procedures, including what you will say if something goes wrong. (3) Utilize practice runs to make sure you can do it.

The general rules for using all teaching aids are: (1) Make sure your audience can see your aids, and (2) select the proper aids to meet the specific requirements of your subject, purpose, and audience.

Speech Communication Principles

1. A message sender is most effective when he so arranges and selects his material as to best utilize the knowledge and experience of his receivers. We learn by relating the known to the unknown.

2. People tend to understand and learn more readily when messages are arranged sequentially or in some serial order.

3. Message reinforcement in the form of verbal, vocal, gestural, and organizational emphasis enhances audience comprehension.

4. An audience's *interest* or motivation to learn may significantly affect how much they retain or remember.

5. The cone of experience (telling, showing, doing) allows us to select and evaluate audio-visual aids according to level of abstractness.

6. A psychologically sound organizational structure for an informative message should include: (1) gaining *attention*; (2) preparing the audience through a preview or *overview*; (3) giving the detailed *information*; and (4) *reviewing* the significant points for added reinforcement.

A. General Learning Outcomes

1. We should learn three basic learning principles and their relationship to message preparation.

2. We should learn the basic forms of support (ways of supporting a main point in an outline) in terms of message clarity and interest.

3. We should learn how to relate the choosing and using of audio-visual aids to the cone of experience.

B. *Specific Learning Outcomes*

1. We should learn to make informative messages *clear* by relating new information to an audience's previous knowledge and experience (known to unknown).

2. We should learn to make informative messages *clear* by arranging messages sequentially or in some serial order.

3. We should learn to make informative messages *clear* by organizational repetition, restatement, and reinforcement.

4. We should learn to make informative messages *clear* and more *interesting* through the use of the forms of support: illustration, analogy, statistics, and testimony.

5. We should learn to make informative messages *interesting* through the use of specificity, conflict, novelty, curiosity, immediacy, humor, vital factors, and figures of speech.

6. We should learn to make informative messages *clear* and *interesting* through the use of visual aids, specifically, graphs and charts.

7. We should learn the purposes, planning, and special hazards of the demonstration speech.

8. We should learn to organize informational messages according to the learning sequence of *attention, overview, information,* and *review* (see models).

9. We should be able to relate the foregoing general and specific learning outcomes to the speech communication principles above.

C. *Communication Competencies*

1. We should be able to prepare an intelligent, detailed two-to three-page outline for a five- to eight-minute speech to inform that meets the message preparation tests of Part III (Chapters 7, 8, and 9).

2. In a speech to inform we should be able to prepare and effectively utilize visual aids of the graph and chart variety so that they meet the tests of Chapter 9.

3. We should be able to give a two- to four-minute demonstration

speech that is both clear and interesting to the audience and the instructor.

4. We should be able to evaluate critically the use of forms of support by other students for purposes of clarity and interest.

D. *Study Projects and Tasks*

1. Prepare a detailed two- to three-page outline for a four- to six-minute speech to inform that meets the message preparation tests of Part III (see models).

2. Prepare visual aids to accompany a four- to six-minute speech to inform that are designed to enhance clarity and interest.

3. Prepare a three- to four-minute speech to teach through demonstration that involves some audience participation and/or performance (e.g., demonstrating knot tying, basic tennis shots, a dance step, crewel, basic golf, or reading aloud, working a calculator, working a slide rule, setting points, sketching a landscape, a card trick, shooting dice, solving a puzzle, tying a bow tie, folding a flag, walking like a model). Do a careful demonstration for your listeners to follow; check difficulties and give personal help. Be specific about the items or steps of the process you most want them to remember.

4. Prepare a one- to two-minute demonstration of a simple but interesting process. It need not involve audience performance as does project 3 above.

5. Prepare an informative talk on your favorite hobby. Use visual aids and/or demonstration.

6. Practice critically evaluating your classmates using the criteria suggested on the following classroom rating scale (Figure 9–13). Your instructor may wish to collect the forms, remove the evaluators' names, and feed back the information to the speakers.

7. Prepare an oral report or essay attempting to prove or disprove any of the speech communication principles listed earlier.

8. Analyze the speech in the appendix, "Communication and the Survival of Democracy," and locate, if possible, one example (by line number) of each of the following types of support: illustration, analogy, statistics, and testimony.

9. Analyze the speech in the appendix, and locate, if possible, one example (by line number) of each of the following factors of

WAYNE STATE UNIVERSITY
College of Liberal Arts
Department of Speech Communication

R. S. Ross, Ph. D.

CLASSROOM RATING SCALE

1-2	3-4-5	6-7
Weak	Average	Strong

	Speaking Order	1	2	3	4	5	6	7	8	9	10	11	12
Course														
Project														
Professor														
Date														
Language														
Organization														
Voice-Articulation														
Bodily Action														
Adaptation of Material to Audience														
General Effect														
Total of Scale Scores														
Rank Order (Best Speaker 1; No Ties)														

COMMENTS

FIGURE 9–13.

interest: specificity, conflict, novelty, curiosity, immediacy, humor, vital factors, figure of speech.

10. Analyze the speech in the appendix and locate (by line numbers) attempts at clarity through repetition, restatement, and reinforcement.

11. Analyze the speech in the appendix and discuss how the speaker used the basic learning principles of (1) going from the known to the unknown, (2) serial order, and (3) reinforcement.

12. Design a visual aid for the speech in the appendix and explain your rationale in terms of the principles discussed in this chapter.

PART FOUR

THE
PSYCHOLOGY
OF
PERSUASION

In persuading people, we are primarily concerned with alteration of attitudes. "Does oral argument (speech) affect attitudes?" is a fair question. For centuries we have answered "yes," based on our subjective observations of speakers and audiences.

Many teachers, after a particularly exasperating day, may conclude that nothing happened to the minds of their students. We do have scientific evidence that some teaching appears to have little effect on student attitudes. As early as 1927, Donald Young found, after measuring class attitudes, that his course in American Race Problems had no effect upon the racial prejudices of his students at the University of Pennsylvania.[1] If Young's lectures and assignments are to be considered oral argument and persuasion, and if he measured the right attitudes at the right time, then we had better take a closer look at the question of oral persuasion and its effects upon attitudes.

In 1935 F. H. Knower reported specific insights into this question in a study that has become a classic in speech research. Some of the questions he asked in designing his study were these:

1. Is it possible to produce a significant change in attitude by argumentative stimulation?

[1]"Some Effects of a Course in American Race Problems on the Race Prejudices of 450 Undergraduates," *Journal of Abnormal and Social Psychology*, 22 (1927), 235–42.

2. Is an attitude more markedly changed by an argument which is predominantly factual and logical or one which is predominantly emotional?
3. Does an individual more markedly change his attitude when he hears an argument from a speaker while a member of an audience composed of, individuals who hold approximately the same attitude, or while alone in a room with the speaker who presents the argument to him?
4. Is there any difference in the effect of an argument on the change of an attitude in persons of different sex?[2]

This study was carried on in 1931 during the prohibition period in our history. The attitudes experimented with were in regard to this issue. The study was completed before antiprohibition feeling reached its height after the presidential campaign of 1932.

Knower constructed four carefully tested speeches. Two favored maintaining prohibition (dry speeches) and two opposed it (wet speeches). One wet and one dry speech were predominantly factual and logical; the other speech on each side of the issue was an emotional appeal speech. The latter type can be defined as one in which suggestion is employed; stereotypes, sanctions, and taboos are used; vivid illustrations are presented; and appeals to emotions are designed to submerge the listener's critical reactions. In the factual appeal evidence and logical reasoning were brought to the support of contentions and a general attempt was made to arouse rather than stifle critical reactions.

The 607 experimental subjects were first tested to determine their *attitudes before* being exposed to the speeches. They were then divided and grouped into a great many combinations with respect to four speeches (for example, the wet subjects were divided from the dry subjects). The dry-subject group was split and half given a logical appeal and half an emotional appeal. The group receiving the emotional appeal was further split, half hearing the appeal as members of an audience and half individually. It is to Knower's credit that despite all this subdividing no subject served in the experiment more than once.

Of all the carefully drawn conclusions, the most important in a general sense is that (1) 60 percent of the experimental group made a positive change in attitude, demonstrating that oral argument does affect attitude! Of almost equal importance was his discovery that (2) logical and emotional appeal speeches were equally effective in producing changes in attitude.

> The mean change of attitude occurring in both dry and wet groups as a result of the argumentative appeals presented was statistically significant. The total amount of change occurring in the two groups was almost identical. These data indicate that it is possible to produce a statistically significant change of attitude in a group by presentation of an argumentative appeal.[3]

[2]F. H. Knower, "Experimental Studies of Changes in Attitudes: I. A Study of the Effect of Oral Argument on Changes of Attitude," *The Journal of Social Psychology*, 6 (1935), 315–47.
[3]Ibid., p. 342.

Other conclusions of interest to us here are as follows: (3) Both logical and emotional approaches were more effective in face-to-face situations than in audience situations. (4) Changes in attitude were more frequent among women than men. (5) Men were more impressed by logical argument than women. (6) Men were more effective with audiences than women. (7) Women were slightly more effective in the face-to-face situations.

In Chapter 1 we discovered that the decoding part of the communication process gives us insight into how people attach meaning to symbols by reaching into their storehouse of knowledge and experience. In Chapter 9 we discussed the learning process to give us the necessary theoretical background for the speech to inform. In Part Four the learning process is also a factor. Learning is usually thought of as involving habitual behavior. Once a habitual form of behavior (including attitudes) is firmly entrenched in a listener, the persuader is hard-pressed to alter it because the listener finds it less necessary to have his sorting and selecting device interpret the message. When he is faced with a specific or attention-getting argument, his hostile attitude and habit patterns may simply cause him to rehearse arguments against your general position and not really perceive your argument. For these reasons a discussion of a wide array of dimensions of human motivation makes up Chapter 10. Man is affected by his biological needs and his social and psychological needs. Man's personality is thought to have a lot to do with the way he decodes persuasive messages. The various theories of persuasion from classical rhetoric to source credibility and cognitive consistency are discussed. The latter is considered especially pertinent and suggests that man alters his attitudes when he feels seriously out of step with himself, as it were. Man seeks a consistency, balance, or consonance among his perceptions and reasonings on a given proposition. Conflicting perceptions, inconsistent facts, and confusing logic on a proposition lead to a state of tension, imbalance, or dissonance. This suggests a theory of motivation or persuasion in which man alters his attitudes and behavior to reduce inconsistency, imbalance, and dissonance. The research dealing with the persuading of relatively antagonistic audiences which is fascinating and most instructive for would-be persuasive speakers, is discussed under "Source and the Psychological Order" (see pp. 265–269).

Part Four also draws heavily upon A. H. Maslow's classification of dynamic needs to help explain the psychology of persuasion.

The logical supports of persuasion are a large part of successful communication. Evidence, proof, reasoning, and the four basic fallacies are explained in Chapter 11.

A general review of the hoped-for learning outcomes that will result from a close reading of Part IV, particularly when related to class projects and performances, follows. A more specific set of learning outcomes or lesson objectives and communication competencies, along with creative, relevant projects and tasks, is appended to each chapter.

We should learn of the importance of man's biology and the meaning of homeostasis as it relates to human needs.

We should learn the prescientific and philosophical explanations of man's social-psychological nature.

We should learn and be able to discuss the motivation theory of A. H. Maslow in terms of human needs.

We should have a working knowledge of the canons of rhetoric, cognitive consistency theory, source credibility, and the natural order.

We should learn to apply the characteristics of both-sides rationalistic persuasion.

We should learn how to relate the psychological order discussion and sequences to preparing persuasive messages.

We should learn of the persuasive importance of evidence and proof through reasoning.

We should learn to be a more critical and objective receiver of persuasive messages through knowledge of the basic types of fallacious reasoning and argument.

Chapter Ten

Dimensions of Human Motivation

SPRINGBOARDS OF MOTIVATION

The basic springboards of human motivation will be considered here in terms of man's biological nature, social-psychological nature, personality, and human needs.

The Biological Nature of Man

To some philosophers the proper study of man begins with man himself. The most remarkable thing about biological man is the striking similarity of all people. All doctors use the same anatomy chart and all search for your heart in about the same place.

The human apparatus appears to have a master biological plan that governs survival activity. There are an estimated 21 trillion cells organized into body systems, tissues, and bones. Biological man is a tough, adaptable, survival-oriented organism—within his limitations. But man cannot survive without oxygen (for ten minutes), heat (no more than ten degrees variance in body temperature), food (for thirty days), water (for six days), rest, and even love. The systems of the body and the maintenance of a constant, internal environment (homeostasis) provide some of our most basic motivations.

The principal system of the body is the nervous system, which has the function of coordinating all the parts and functions of the body. It includes the brain, spinal cord, nerves, ganglia, and our sensory organs. It provides the mechanism through which our human machinery responds to the outside world in avoiding injury, obtaining food, and performing all other activities.

One system that includes the heart, blood vessels, and lymphatics circulates fluids that transport fuel, gases, and other substances to the tissues and cells and then on the return trip, in a marvelously efficient way, transports waste products from these same cells for expulsion.

The respiratory system provides the body with oxygen and removes carbon dioxide. It includes the nose, pharynx, larynx, trachea, bronchi, and lungs. External respiration is breathing; internal respiration involves exchanges between the cells and body fluids. To physiologists, talking, along with sneezing and coughing, is an accessory function of this system.[1]

The digestive system prepares fuel for the metabolic functions carried out by the cells. Metabolism includes the complex functions involved in the release and utilization of chemical energy by the body. The digestive system includes the mouth, pharynx, esophagus, stomach, and intestines.

Elaborate systems of elimination and reproduction, together with muscles, bones, and glands, complete the critical machinery of the body. Everything a man does is dependent or made possible through the functions of these biological systems and equipment. These systems are involved in all human behavior and have much to do with persuasion and motivation.

Homeostasis refers to the body's unceasing, automatic, self-regulatory efforts designed to maintain its internal environment in balance and at a constant level. Temperature regulation is a good example of homeostasis. When overheated, the body automatically attacks the problem through dilation of superficial blood vessels, increased blood flow in the skin, and, of course, perspiration, Sweating provides moisture complete with salt, which hastens evaporation, thus expediting the cooling process. When the body is extremely cold, its response is equally automatic and selective. Additional heat is produced through a speeded-up metabolic rate, oxidation in the tissues, hormonal effects, and shivering. At some temperatures shivering and "gooseflesh" amount to the addition of a business suit in terms of insulation!

[1]Barry G. King and Mary J. Showers, *Human Anatomy and Physiology*, 6th ed. (Philadelphia: W. B. Saunders Co., 1969), p. 13.

This self-regulating tendency when threatened responds swiftly never losing account of side effects. The water level of the blood does not get out of balance during heavy perspiration. Body heat normally is not generated at the expense of our blood sugar level.

Despite unusual external conditions the body works incessantly to balance its internal environment. Man has little control over these homeostatic functions. Man's role is to replenish this internal environment with supplies. When the internal resources are low, homeostasis becomes a powerful biological motivation.

Biological needs. It is essential for survival that man have *oxygen, food, water, rest, elimination of wastes,* and *exercise.* While these needs originate within the body, it becomes obvious that once the body's reserves are in jeopardy the requirements must be met from outside the body. Needs, even at the basic level of food and water, offer us choices and behavior over which we have some control; however, we must satisfy our basic needs for fluids, whether we choose water, milk, or beer.

In our culture it is only in great stress situations, ill health, or drug abuse that a biological imbalance may cause serious conflicts. Nevertheless, these biological motivations are constantly with us, affecting our behavior and the intensity with which we search out related goals.

Deprivation studies suggest that a man becomes increasingly less interested in the niceties of culture as he is systematically starved. There is a priority or hierarchy implicit in all this. When these biological needs of *oxygen, food, water, rest, elimination,* and *exercise* are not being adequately met, even man's complex and serious social needs may be downgraded.

The Social-Psychological Nature of Man

Our biological nature, however important in a primary sense, is overlayed by many varieties of social-psychological motives usually involving learned needs and goals. Man learns to seek these social satisfactions with almost the same intensity that he seeks survival itself.

Prescientific explanations of personality attempted to predict human behavior and man's reactions to patterns of persuasion. Personality may be thought of as the totality of man's motives whatever their source.

One of the earliest *typological theories* is credited to Hippocrates, the father of medicine, in 460 B.C. It was the medical philosopher Galen who some six hundred years later related the earlier classification system of "humors" and biles to temperaments and personality.[2] There

2Galen, "On the Natural Faculties," Trans. A. J. Brock, in *Great Books of the Western World,* ed. R. M. Hutchins (Chicago: Encyclopedia Britannica, 1952), Vol. 10, pp. 163–215.

were four basic biles. According to Galen if the *blood* bile predominated, your personality was sanguine, that is, cheery, gay, optimistic, and warmhearted. If the *black* bile predominated, your temperament was melancholy, gloomy, or sad. If the *yellow* bile was foremost, you were choleric or hot-tempered. If *phlegm* predominated, your temperament was phlegmatic or slow and sluggish.

More recently Ernest Kretschmer in 1921 theorized about personality and three basic body shapes or morphological types.[3] First is the short-round or *pyknic* type, which is characterized as a fat figure with a deep chest and rounded shoulders. According to Kretschmer, who was a clinical psychologist, the pyknic tends to be extrovertive, and when mentally ill he becomes a manic-depressive characterized by alternating periods of intense excitement and depression. The second is the thin-long or *asthenic* type, characterized by an angular face, long, thin arms and hands, narrow shoulders, but a thick stomach. The asthenic tends to be introverted, a poor mixer and, when mentally ill, develops schizophrenia characterized by indifference to all that goes on about him. Third is an intermediate type called *athletic*, typified by broad shoulders, muscularity, a firm jaw, a short nose, and firm skin. His personality traits are similar to those of the asthenic.

Another approach to predicting personality based on body shape was offered in the 1940s by Sheldon, Stevens, and Tucker.[4] They presented a three-dimensional system of physique: *endomorphy, mesomorphy,* and *ectomorphy.* The endomorph, like the pyknic, is soft and round, the mesomorph is heavy, muscular, and firm, and the ectomorph, like the asthenic, is linear and weak. Sheldon and Stevens also presented us with three temperament dimensions, *viscerotonia, somatotonia,* and *cerebrotonia,* thought to be related to physique.[5] The extreme viscerotonic is extrovertive, sociable, and communicative; the somatotonic is aggressive and energetic; the cerebrotonic is introverted and inhibited. Most people were thought to be combinations of all three dimensions.

There have been many other theories for classifying people, including ones utilizing morphological and sociological determinants. Perhaps among psychological types you are most familiar with Jung's *introvert* and *extrovert* classification.[6] Even this useful system evidences the danger of typing people too hastily. Jung himself deplored the either/or system

[3]E. Kretschmer, *Physique and Character* (New York: Harcourt, Brace and Company, 1925).

[4]W. H. Sheldon et al., *The Varieties of Human Physique* (New York: Harper and Brothers, 1940).

[5]W. H. Sheldon and S. S. Stevens, *The Varieties of Temperament* (New York: Harper and Brothers, 1942).

[6]C. G. Jung, *Psychological Types* (New York: Harcourt, Brace and Company, 1922).

that seems inevitably to follow. He thought rather of all people having introversion-extroversion tendencies, with one or the other tending to predominate on a given continuum. The introvert in a speech class may be a tigerlike extrovert on the football field.

A recent, more eclectic theory of general personality determinants will be discussed shortly. Even for pathological cases physique should probably be suggestive rather than diagnostic.

In a very real sense the sources of persuasion are found in an understanding of human nature and behavior. Since ancient times man has tried to find simple explanations of what motivates people to do what they do. If one could find universal answers and systems, it was thought that one could theoretically control the behavior of others in ever so many specific ways. To some philosophers, most notably Aristotle, the proper study of man is man himself. The assumption is that all men, at least in a general sense, are much alike.

At the physiological level this presents few problems, for despite obvious individual differences in height, weight, color, and other physical attributes, the most amazing thing is the striking similarity of all people. We could hardly have a science of medicine were this not true.

In the nonphysiological realm the problem is more complicated. Plato argued that to study man one must investigate his environment, for to Plato man was a reflection of his society. In our modern-day thinking, we tend to say that both points of view are necessary to understand man's behavior.

Instinct theory is still with us and like other theories it has utility so long as we recognize its proper safeguards and qualifications. It is to some extent a perversion of Aristotle's innate human nature theory. If we could locate a long list of urges and drives that were in no way learned and that were universal among men, we could select our persuasion systems much more scientifically than we do now.

From psychology William McDougall gave us a durable list thought to have utility today, even though the instinct theory has been rather thoroughly discredited. McDougall called his list "Native Propensities," and these included:

1. To desire food periodically (hunger).
2. To reject certain substances (disgust).
3. To explore new places and things (curiosity).
4. To try to escape from danger (fear).
5. To fight when frustrated (anger).
6. To have sex desire (mating).
7. To care tenderly for the young (mothering).
8. To seek company (gregariousness).
9. To seek to dominate (self-assertiveness).

    10. To accept obvious inferiority (submissiveness).
    11. To make things (construction).
    12. To collect things (acquisitiveness)[7]

That many people in a given culture react similarly to similar stimulations seems obvious; however, to suggest that learning plays only a minor role or that man has absolutely no choice, which the word *instinct* implies, seems unrealistic and unobjective. As a matter of record so many so-called instincts were "discovered" that a social psychologist in 1924 recorded 6,000 different kinds.[8]

Among behaviorists J. B. Watson typified the belief that learning and conditioning were satisfactory explanations for complex emotional patterns. However, Watson did argue that there were three innate emotional patterns—fear, love, and rage.[9] In experiments with children it was discovered that all youngsters expressed *fear* when exposed to loud noises or sudden loss of support. It was also found that youngsters responded with *love* in the form of gurgling and cooing when stroked gently and, finally, that they expressed *rage* when their movement was seriously restricted. If these are reasonably universal behavior patterns, whether innate or learned, they may represent some basis for theorizing about persuasion.

Hedonism as an explanation of human motivation hearkens back to antiquity and represents a kind of ethical good-evil proposition. The brand of psychological hedonism credited to Jeremy Bentham postulates that man seeks that which is pleasurable and avoids the painful. Hedonism today is considered more an emotional attribute or adjunct of motivated behavior than a source or goal. A pleasurable hedonic set or mood probably does tend to facilitate approachability and acceptance; a painful or unpleasant set suggests rejection and withdrawal.

These classification systems have an obvious utility, if only in terms of creating more detailed descriptions of the receivers who must decode our communications. Their danger to human communication lies in the tyranny of quick and often permanent labeling of people or groups of people. When labels are extended to ethnic groups, national origins, and religions, the problem of overgeneralization overwhelms us, and any practical utility to be derived from these schema may be completely lost in the morass of misinformation.

---

[7]William McDougall, *An Introduction to Social Psychology* (London: Methuen & Co., Ltd., 1908), p. 106.

[8]L. L. Bernard, *Instinct: A Study in Social Psychology* (New York: Holt, Rinehart & Winston, Inc., 1924).

[9]J. B. Watson, *Psychology from the Standpoint of a Behaviorist* (Philadelphia: J. B. Lippincott Co., 1924).

Personality determinants

Our behavior as adults is oriented primarily in terms of what we have learned (i.e., experienced). Man acquires his needs, goals, and motives in response to the social world in which he lives as well as his biological necessities. Kardiner[10] suggests that personality is determined by cultural tradition, cultural lessons, and teaching methods; similar experiences, he suggests, will produce similar personalities.

What we call *personality* is the totality of a man's knowledge, motives, values, beliefs, and goal-seeking patterns. More academically, personality may be thought of as "the entire sequence of organized governmental processes in the brain from birth to death."[11] The major determinants of personality become of primary importance to the persuader and leader who must seek out those influences that may in part determine goals and motivations.

Kluckhohn and Murray provide us with a practical and intelligent classification of personality determinants or influences: constitution, group membership, role, and situation.[12]

Constitution. In one sense the most amazing aspect of man is his constitutional or biological similarity. Yet to overlook individual differences is to overlook an aspect of personality influence and motivation. Constitution refers to the total physiological makeup of an individual. This includes environmental factors of diet, drugs, and climate, as well as the hereditary factors. Geneticists are agreed that traits are not inherited as such, but we do have reason for believing that man varies, at least potentially, in his reaction time, energy level, and rate of learning. Man also varies constitutionally in terms of hearing, sight, and the like. A visual impairment or a severe hearing loss offers implications for personality development, even though there are no set patterns. These constitutional factors determine personality, even though the patterns are not completely predictable. Age, sex, characteristics of appearance, strength, and size influence a man's needs and motivations. The feedback he decodes from his society in terms of these constitutional factors may have a profound effect upon his personality and his needs system.

10A. Kardiner, *The Psychological Frontiers of Society* (New York: Columbia University Press, 1945), pp. vi–viii.

11C. Kluckhohn and H. A. Murray, *Personality in Nature, Society, and Culture* (New York: Alfred A. Knopf, Inc., 1956), p. 57.

12Ibid., pp. 53–72.

Group Membership. In this personality influence we hearken back to Plato. Man in part will reflect the society in which he lives. His family, his school, and his church are all thought to influence profoundly a man's life and personality. This is not to suggest that we are all carbon copies of those of similar exposure. Even the strong aspect of the culture in which we live determines only what we learn as a member of a group, not what we learn as a specific individual. This in part explains why man alters his behavior and motivations in what seems to be most inconsistent ways.

Our subcultures in America become predictable in a general sense. For example, Texans often have distinctive mannerisms, and the "eyes of Texas" may indeed influence their selection of needs and actions. New Yorkers also exercise strong group influences upon one another; their refusal to show surprise, awe, or even amazement is a constant and delightful mystery to the Midwesterner. Newcomers to the California climate quickly assume a California personality, and the influence of the resultant life style is rapidly affecting the personality of our entire nation; summer dress in Michigan has become more casual, and even the East Coast partially appears to have accepted a more leisurely and comfortable West Coast way of living.

Living in a special society requires certain standards or patterns roughly agreed upon by the members of that group. Much random and impulsive individual behavior is sublimated in deference to these group codes. This feeling of unity, purpose, and value gives us and the group members a rough pattern of prediction and understanding. The *conceptions* a person has of his total group mold personality more than the group itself.

Role. Role in part pertains to a more specific aspect of group membership. Some roles are cast upon us by society because of our age or sex, some we assign to ourselves on the basis of our life goals, and some are really disguises of our private personalities for the purpose of being accepted by certain groups. In its most important sense a *role* is the part we cast for ourself on the stage of life. We may portray many roles to the world, but each man determines, with the aid of society, what his particular role will be, and his personality is influenced by that decision. The professional person is often stereotyped, and we learn to expect certain roles from professors, lawyers, and doctors. Professors who do not act like professors are often real enigmas to society. The doctor who does not play the role patients expect had better develop an interest in research.

Role is determined both by the way in which man views or evaluates *himself* and by the way in which society and its subgroups expect him to behave. Personality tends to develop according to this role. Man is surely motivated by appeals to his specific role in life.

Situation. The situational determinants of personality refer to those exceptional, nonpredictable, and often accidental events that happen to all men. These are events that can seriously alter our lives and cast us into roles that may profoundly affect our emerging personality—a draft notice, a "Dear John" letter, a scholarship, a riot, an insight or perspective suddenly and never before achieved. A stimulating teacher probably alters the lives and careers of many unsuspecting students. An unexpected failing grade or a hard-won "A" can be a personality shaker.

The events of everyone's specific situation are not always as potent as those indicated above. Often we perceive only a minor event—a chance remark by a respected person, a brief exposure to danger, a book with a message—but it sets in motion, however slowly or rapidly, actions that make a man different than he was before. To that extent, they mold his personality. These random events do not always initiate personality changes in societally approved directions. An accidental opportunity to steal in a moment of great need and weakness might provide a person with an experience that could nurture a severe guilt complex, a new career, or a renewed faith and courage in his moral stature. In any event, the situational factors in our lives have the potential to importantly affect personality.

Classification of Human Needs

The needs system and personality determinants give us a basis for understanding the specific stimulants and conditions that are thought to trigger or set in motion these powerful forces. Though modern social scientists are dubious of the universality of any of these so-called wants, appeals, or propensities, such lists of motive appeals are thought to have utility to advertisers specifically and to persuaders in general. When properly related and evaluated in terms of the dynamic needs, personality factors, and communication processes of a specific listener or audience, they can be most helpful.

One of the older and more durable of these lists in speech education includes self-preservation, property, power, reputation, affections, sentiments, and tastes.[13] With all the dangers of overgeneralization in terms of nonspecific audiences as qualifiers, let us look at the explanation of two of these factors.[14]

13A. E. Phillips, *Effective Speaking* (Chicago: The Newton Co., 1931), p. 48.
14Ibid., pp. 53–54.

Affections: "Affections as an Impelling Motive" means the desire for the welfare of others—kindly concern for the interests of mother, father, wife, son, daughter, sweetheart, friends, any being, human or divine. Also it includes desire for the welfare of our town, country, state, and nation, in so far as this desire is altruistic and not selfish.

Sentiments: "The Impelling Motive of Sentiments" includes the desire to be and to do what is right, fair, honorable, noble, true—desires associated with intellectual and moral culture. It embraces duty, liberty, independence, and also patriotism considered as a moral obligation.

A clinical study reported by H. A. Murray lists twenty-eight social needs. In his book *Explorations in Personality* he reports fifteen as follows:

Abasement	To feel guilty when one does something wrong, to accept blame when things do not go right, to feel that personal pain and misery do more good than harm, to feel timid and inferior.
Achievement	To do one's best, to be successful, to accomplish tasks requiring skill and effort, to be a recognized authority, to accomplish something important, to do a difficult job well.
Affiliation	To be loyal to friends, to participate in friendly groups, to form strong attachments, to share things with friends, to write letters to friends, to make as many friends as possible.
Aggression	To attack contrary points of view, to tell others off, to get revenge for insults, to blame others when things go wrong, to criticize others publicly, to read accounts of violence.
Autonomy	To be able to come and go as desired, to say what one thinks about things, to be independent of others in making decisions, to do things without regard to what others may think.
Change	To do new and different things, to travel, to meet new people, to have novelty and change in daily routine, to try new and different jobs, to participate in new fads and fashions.
Deference	To get suggestions from others, to find out what others think, to follow instructions and do what is expected, to praise others, to accept leadership of others, to conform to custom.

Dominance	To argue for one's point of view, to be a leader in groups to which one belongs, to persuade and influence others, to supervise and direct the actions of others.
Endurance	To keep at a job until it is finished, to work hard at a task, to work at a single job before taking on others, to stick with a problem even though no apparent progress is being made.
Exhibition	To say clever and witty things, to have others notice and comment upon one's appearance, to say things just to see the effect upon others, to talk about personal achievements.
Heterosexuality	To engage in social activities with the opposite sex, to be in love with someone of the opposite sex, to be regarded as physically attractive by those of the opposite sex.
Intraception	To analyze one's motives and feelings, to understand how others feel about problems, to judge people by why they do things rather than by *what* they do, to predict others' behavior.
Nurturance	To help friends when they are in trouble, to treat others with kindness and sympathy, to forgive others and do favors for them, to show affection, and to have others confide in one.
Order	To keep things neat and orderly, to make advance plans, to organize details of work, to have things arranged so they run smoothly without change.
Succorance	To have others provide help when in trouble, to seek encouragement from others, to have others be kindly and sympathetic, to receive a great deal of affection from others.[15]

More modern lists of appeals are quite similar to those indicated above. Advertising studies supply us with a variety of terms that, like those of an earlier day, have utility for the persuader who is careful to relate them first to his specific audience. A random collection of these terms follows:

[15]Adapted from *Explorations in Personality* edited by Henry A. Murray. Copyright 1938 by Oxford University Press, Inc. Renewed 1966 by Henry Murray. Reprinted by permission of the publisher.

MOTIVE TERMS

Cleanliness	Power	Quality
Sanitary	Activity	Reputation
Hunger	Mating	Competition
Pleasure	Comfort	Ambition
Rest—sleep	Fighting	Curiosity
Health	Safety	Creating
Protection	Conformity	Enjoyment
Group Spirit	Anger	Devotion
Fear	Gregariousness	Social Distinction
Cooperation	Acquisition	Wealth
Conflict	Companionship	Adventure
Value	Sympathy	Independence
Mothering	Sex	Property
Approval	Deity	Achievement
Domesticity		

In any attempt to classify needs one must begin with biological or physiological needs. A system that starts with this kind of survival motivation as a cornerstone is supplied by A. H. Maslow and is particularly useful to the psychology of persuasion.[16] His five general categories of needs, in the order of their importance, are *physiological, safety, love, esteem,* and *self-actualization.*

Maslow takes a position quite opposite to the trait-psychologists and believes that most behavior is multimotivated. One act could engage all the needs. The theory is a general-dynamic one involving the integrated wholeness of the organism that is man.

Physiological Needs. These are the biological needs referred to previously. They are directly related to survival and self-preservation. Although they are generally rated first in importance, their importance diminishes if they are satisfied or in a state of equilibrium. A starving man may live in a world which to him is dominated by thoughts and visions of food, but for most of us these physiological needs do not completely dominate our behavior. The primary or survival needs may be indicated as follows: (1) oxygen, (2) food, (3) water, (4) rest, (5) exercise, (6) avoidance of bodily damage, and (7) excretion.

Safety Needs. These refer to our desire for a sense of security and to our aversion to personal violence, harm, or disease. We most often prefer a safe, predictable environment or world to one plagued with unknown and unpredictable events. It is this protective desire that may prompt us to be concerned with insurance and jobs that offer security first and

[16]A. H. Maslow, "A Theory of Human Motivation," *Psychological Review,* 50 (1943), 370–96.

high wages second. We are here primarily concerned with psychological safety rather than the physiological safety discussed previously.

Like physiological needs, our safety needs are not all-consuming in our lives except in times of emergency or danger. However, many people are seriously concerned with threats to their security and safety. A change in a work routine, even when carefully explained, often causes visible anxiety. A change in environment, such as a college freshman experiences, is often an extreme threat to his safety needs, and he may be quite amenable to persuasion that promises more security in groups, housing, trips home, and friends. The first year of military service represents a similar constellation of events. The desire for psychological safety is a strong need for all of us.

Love Needs. Some social scientists use the term *belonging* to designate this group of needs. Man must be loved and in turn must express his love. The sharing of life with others is important to man, and he will often react quickly to even the suggestion of a denial of this desire. Man finds satisfaction for this need most generally through his family and close friends, but the category extends beyond this area. We desire the approval and acceptance of our classmates, our fellow workers, and the many groups of people with whom we associate and with whom we tend to identify ourselves. We quite obviously alter our behavior and perhaps even our standards to be accepted, to belong, to be loved by our chosen friends and groups.

The most significant aspect of this set of dynamic needs is the realization that its satisfaction involves both giving and receiving. Man, to be well adjusted, must also give of his love. Our lonely-hearts clubs owe their very existence to this powerful need to give and share love. Unscrupulous persuaders have often taken advantage of this need through fraudulent campaigns to help suffering people.

Esteem Needs. When our physiological, safety, and love needs are satisfied, then theoretically our esteem needs become most important. These needs go beyond the more passive belonging or love needs into a more active desire for recognition and self-respect. It involves evaluation of self and, according to A. H. Maslow, is of two slightly different types or *sets:*

> . . . the desire for strength, for achievement, for adequacy, for confidence in the face of the world and for independence and freedom. Secondly, we have what we may call the desire for reputation or prestige (defining it as respect or esteem from other people), recognition, attention, importance, or appreciation.[17]

[17]Maslow, "A Theory of Human Motivation," p. 382.

In our culture this becomes a very important need. We are often accused as a people of being egocentric. A threat to our ego or self-esteem, real or fancied, often prompts swift reaction. Our radio and television commercials appeal to our esteem needs in selling the more expensive, prestige cars or in suggested threats to our station in a group should we be offensive or only "half-safe."

The satisfaction or partial satisfaction of esteem needs leads to self-confidence and a feeling of personal worth. Esteem needs are often fraught with many frustrations and personal conflicts, for man desires not only the recognition and attention of his chosen groups but also the self-respect and status that his moral, social, and religious standards call for. It is when the former groups call for behavior that is in conflict with the latter that man must often make heroic choices to remain an integrated, whole organism.

Man plays many roles to satisfy some of these different groups, and the problem of explaining the precise extent of his motivation is wrapped up in the complex dynamics of his entire system of needs. For some poorly adjusted people, esteem needs are so great that they will strive for achievement (or what they consider achievement) at the great price of their own self-respect, morals, and ideals. This is not to say that the so-called achievement motive is abnormal. Much has been written about the need for achievement as a motivating force.[18]

Self-Actualization Needs. This term, first used by Kurt Goldstein, pertains to what might be called *self-fulfillment*—or *self-realization*—the desire by man to reach the acme of his own personal abilities and talents. In Maslow's words, "What a man *can* be, he *must* be." Because this need becomes increasingly important as the previous four needs are satisfied, it becomes apparent that in our culture self-actualization becomes a very important aspect of human behavior and motivation. The large number of retired or established people who return to college or take adult courses in art, writing, or drama to satisfy creative urges is indicative of the role of self-actualization needs. At Wayne State University in Detroit (a large metropolitan institution), the *average* age of the student body is twenty-six years, and many students have full-time jobs. One part-time student is eighty-seven years old; the oldest full-time student is only 82.

In his 1968 and 1970 works Maslow talked of "trends to self-actualization . . . , an unceasing trend toward unity, integration or synergy within the person."[19] He spoke of growth needs when referring to young

---

18See D. C. McClelland, *The Achieving Society* (Princeton, N.J.: D. Van Nostrand Co., Inc., 1961), and S. W. Gellerman, *Motivation and Productivity* (American Management Association, Vail Ballou Press, 1963), Ch. 12.

19A. H. Maslow, *Toward a Psychology of Being* (New York: Van Nostrand Reinhold Company, 1968), p. 25.

people "growing well" on their way toward self-actualization. Just before his death Maslow implied a kind of extra or half-step up the needs ladder between esteem and self-actualization. What Frank Goble diagrams as *growth needs*, Maslow refers to as *being-values* or *metaneeds*.

The following diagram by Ross is an attempt to relate the psychoenvironmental prerequisites, and the transcendent nature of self-actualization to the basic needs system of Goldstein and Maslow.[20]

.The rank order and practical importance of these dynamic needs are subject to the degree of satisfaction attendant upon each need. Because the degree of satisfaction is constantly changing, even among our phys-

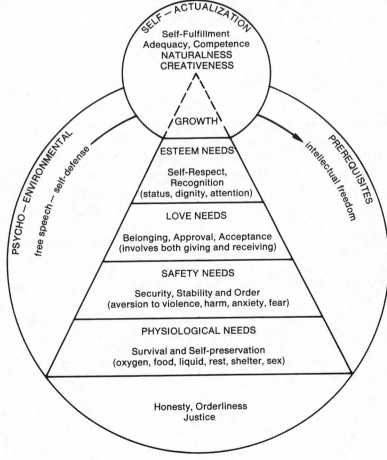

FIGURE 10–1.

[20]For another attempt see F. Goble, *The Third Force* (New York: Grossman Publishers, 1970), p. 50.

Self-Esteem	*Self-Actualization*
1. Pride	1. Creativeness
2. Reputation	2. Curiosity
3. Power	3. Constructiveness
4. Achievement	4. Ambition
5. Social distinction	5. Independence
6. Appearance	6. Freedom from restraint

The motive appeals must be filtered, evaluated, and decoded by layers of resistance such as dynamic needs, personality determinants, and finally the momentary "set" or disposition of the man underneath it all. Human motivation is terribly complex; one should be wary of sure-fire persuasive appeals. With man in the center of a maze of thinking, learning, persuasion, communication barriers, the situation theoretically appears as illustrated in Figure 10–2.

THEORIES OF PERSUASION

The dynamic, holistic theory of classifying human needs discussed in the previous section is a powerful and useful modern theory of persuasion and was featured for that reason. In this section we will briefly discuss classical rhetorical theory and the modern theories built around what is called cognitive consistency.

Classical rhetoric

Rhetoric is primarily a strategy and art of persuasion. Aristotle defined rhetoric as "the faculty of observing in any given case the available means of persuasion."[22] Aristotle's rhetoric is based on four fundamental assumptions: (1) Rhetoric is a useful art—it is an instrument of social adaptation. (2) Rhetoric can be taught. (3) Rhetorical theory is based on the doctrine of the mean—that is, it is free from extremes. (4) It is the method of giving effect to truth.[23]

The five basic tasks in preparing and sending persuasive messages are referred to as *canons* in classical rhetoric. They are described below.

Invention. This is the task of investigating the message and the audience to discover the available means of persuasion. It includes

---

[22]Aristotle, *Rhetoric and Poetics*, trans. W. Rhys Roberts (New York: The Modern Library, 1954), p. 24.
[23]Lester Thonssen and A. Craig Baird, *Speech Criticism* (New York: The Ronald Press, 1948), pp. 70–71.

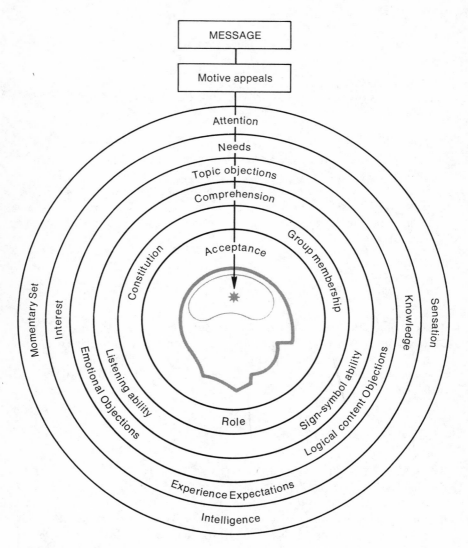

FIGURE 10–2. Persuasion Filters and Barriers.

narrowing the purpose and gathering and analyzing facts and evidence on the issues that are found, particularly as they relate to the receiver's needs. Goods considered to be desired by all beings are happiness, justice, courage, temperance, health, wealth, friendship, reputation, and life itself, among others. Aristotle defined three modes or means of persuasion that, when used to investigate a specific message and audience, become sources of persuasion.

Of the modes of persuasion furnished by the spoken word there are three kinds. The first kind depends on the personal characteristics of the speaker, ETHOS; the second on putting the audience into a certain frame of mind, PATHOS; the third on the proof or apparent proof provided by the words of the speech itself, LOGOS.[24]

Other tools provided by Aristotle in the *Rhetoric* to assist in the invention process include: (1) the *enthyme*, "a kind of imperfect syllogism which produces, not the conclusive demonstration that we get in science and logic, but belief or persuasion"; and (2) the *example*, which is a specific verifiable phenomena used as the basis for inductive reasoning.[25] More will be said of the enthyme and logos in the next chapter, "The Logical Supports of Persuasion." Ethos will be discussed later in this chapter under source credibility.

Arrangement. This canon is concerned with the process of organizing the speech or message. Aristotle used the Greek word *taxis*, denoting division or arrangement, to explain what he thought was the most obvious and logical arrangement of parts of a speech. He felt that the following elements were most closely related to the thinking habits of man: proem (introduction), statement, argument, and epilogue (conclusion).[26] Much has already been said of this canon in Part III, "Message Preparation"; more will be said of special persuasion sequences later in this chapter.

Style. This canon refers to the kinds of words and language in which one clothes his message. One is advised to use acceptable, correct, appropriate language; make your language clear and direct; make it polished, noble, and vivid; adjust it to the message, audience, and speaker. Style involves selecting words that arouse the appropriate emotional response in the audience and help establish the proper ethical image.[27] Much was said of style in Chapter 3, "Language Habits and Semantics."

Memory. This canon refers to a speaker's retention and grasp of his content in some kind of sequential order. Of the five canons Aristotle had the least to say about memory. There are two pages of good advice under "Protect Your Memory" (pp. 102–103) in Chapter 4, "Emotion and Confidence."

Delivery. This canon refers to the art of sending the oral message. Its main elements are voice and bodily action. The ancients warned of

[24] Aristotle, *Rhetoric and Poetics*, pp. 24–25.
[25] Edward P. J. Corbett, *Classical Rhetoric for the Modern Student* (New York: Oxford University Press, 1965), p. 68.
[26] Lane Cooper, *The Rhetoric of Aristotle* (New York: Appleton-Century-Crofts, 1932), p. 220.
[27] Corbett, *Classical Rhetoric for the Modern Student*, p. 375.

World War II our ship-building production rate was so fantastic that American propagandists reduced the actual figures for fear the enemy would be incredulous and therefore less likely to surrender.

Balance theory. According to balance theory, when two people interact with an event or object of mutual concern, the intrapersonal and interpersonal situation is cognitively either balanced or unbalanced. When it is balanced, no persuasion is really possible. When it is unbalanced, tension is produced, which generates a motivation to restore balance.

Old adages notwithstanding, the theory suggests that comparable personalities attract and that familiarity, other things being equal, breeds attraction, not contempt. According to Heider, "With similar attitudes proximity will increase the degree of positive sentiment; with slight dissimilarity of attitudes a mutual assimilation might be produced, and with it an increase in friendliness; with strong dissimilarities the hostility will be increased."[29]

A more interpersonal orientation to balance theory is provided by Newcomb's[30] *strain toward symmetry*, a tendency toward communication that reduces tension or imbalance. The individual respect and trust people have for one another in their interpersonal relations have much to do with the success of communication in reducing strain.

Rosenberg and Abelson[31] build on the balance model in their affective-cognitive consistency theory. Attitude consists of two elements, feelings and beliefs. People seek balance between them. Persuasion is then possible by modifying either the affective or cognitive element.

Congitive dissonance. Cognitive in this theory means "any knowledge, opinion, or belief about the environment, about oneself, or about one's behavior."[32] The word *dissonance* replaces the word *inconsistency* used previously; consonance refers to consistency. The basic hypotheses, according to Leon Festinger, chief architect of this highly regarded theory, are:

1. The existence of dissonance, being psychologically uncomfortable, will motivate the person to try to reduce the dissonance and achieve consonance.

[29]F. Heider, *Psychology of Interpersonal Relations* (New York: John Wiley and Sons, Inc., 1958), p. 190.

[30]T. M. Newcomb, "An Approach to the Study of Communication Acts," *Psychological Review*, 60 (1953), 393–404; see also T. Newcomb, "Individual Systems of Orientation," in *Psychology: A Study of a Science*, ed. S. Koch (New York: McGraw-Hill Book Company, 1959), Vol. 3, 384–422.

[31]M. Rosenberg and R. Ableson, "An Analysis of Cognitive Balancing," in *Attitude Organization and Change*, eds. C. Hovland and M. Rosenberg (New Haven: Yale University Press, 1960), pp. 112–63; also see M. Rosenberg, "An Analysis of Affective-cognitive Consistency," *Attitude Organization and Change*, 1960, pp. 15–64.

[32]Leon Festinger, *A Theory of Cognitive Dissonance* (Stanford, California: Stanford University Press, 1957), p. 3.

2. When dissonance is present, in addition to trying to reduce it, the person will actively avoid situations and information which would likely increase the dissonance.[33]

Festinger points out that one could substitute the notions of frustration, disequilibrium, and others for the word *dissonance*. It is the existence of nonfitting relations among cognitions, a practically unavoidable condition in a wide variety of situations.

Festinger suggests as typical sources of dissonance between two cognitions: *logical inconsistency, cultural mores, past experience,* and when *one specific opinion is included by definition in a more general opinion* (e.g., Democrats aren't supposed to favor a Republican candidate for office).[34]

The theory clearly postulates that behavior can cause persuasion. Many very creative research projects support this point and provide implications for involvement and self-persuasion.

In a study of *oral* counterattitudinal advocacy, that is, arguing against one's own point of view as college debaters must often do, Janis and King found that the speakers changed their attitudes more than did the listeners. This kind of behavior apparently creates dissonance and consequent self-persuasion. It also indicates the possible influence of role playing on opinion change.[35]

Literally hundreds of pieces of evidence confirm that our cognitive systems seek a harmonious, agreeable, balanced, consistent set of relationships between our notions of the world and our latest perceptions of it. These theories might better be called inconsistency theories since it is the inconsistency that causes the tension that may motivate to a change in attitude or behavior. These theories posit a kind of psychological homeostasis.

SOURCE AND THE PSYCHOLOGICAL ORDER

It may be more fact than fiction that "what you are speaks so loudly I cannot hear what you're saying."

Credibility and Ethical Proof

Credibility refers to the receiver's or audience's acceptance or disposition toward the source. Aristotle used the term *ethos* to designate the audi-

[33]Ibid., p. 3.
[34]Ibid., p. 14.
[35]I. Janis and B. King, "The Influence of Role-playing on Opinion Change," *Journal of Abnormal Social Psychology*, 49 (1954), 211–18.

ence's perception of the speaker. In terms of ethical proof Aristotle set forth the general rule that "there is no proof so effective as that of the character."[36]

Source credibility is related to Aristotle's *goodwill, good moral character,* and *good sense,* as perceived by the receivers. This has been discussed in modern times as good *intentions, trustworthiness,* and *competence* or *expertness.* Source credibility is related to perceptions and attitudes of trust and confidence based in part on beliefs about intent, position in society, knowledge, and sincerity. High credibility generally produces more attitude change. An audience's perception of a source's intent, trust, and competence are related to perceptions of credibility.

Pragmatic ethical proof refers to credibility as it is established or reinforced through ethical attributions and behavior during the message sending. In its most general sense it refers to impressions of the honesty of the speaker, his character, his sagacity, and his good will.[37]

Other dimensions of ethical proof include perceived attitude similarity (source-receiver), voice and language utilization, use of humor, and use of evidence. Other things being equal, a persuader may have influence when he is perceived as *attitudinally* similar by the receiver. Social status may be detected from language segments used and from cues in the voice. In studies of excess verbalizations and disorganization cues, it was found that an absence of these evidences enhanced a speaker's credibility.[38] The use of humor may enhance one's pragmatic ethical proof if not his persuasion, as measured by attitude shift. Humor and satire, when used with a professional touch, can affect interest and attention and thereby retention. That it can boomerang when not so used is abundantly clear from research and common experience.[39] Even a high-credibility source loses some of this ethical proof over time. Using evidence may help reinstate credibility. The variable of perceived source credibility by an audience is critical in any research design or communication episode. Including evidence may significantly increase immediate attitude change and source credibility when the message is delivered well, particularly when the audience has little or no prior familiarity with the evidence.[40] The medium of communication does not appear to affect the impact of evidence. Evidence appears to serve as an inhibitor to

[36]Aristotle, *Rhetoric,* 1377b21–1378a19.

[37]Lester Thonssen and A. Craig Baird, *Speech Criticism.* (New York: The Ronald Press Co., 1948), p. 387.

[38]Eldon E. Baker, "The Immediate Effects of Perceived Speaker Disorganization on Speaker Credibility and Audience-Attitude Change in Persuasive Speaking," *Western Speech,* 29 (1965), 148–61.

[39]D. K. Berlo and H. Kumata, "The Investigator; the Impact of a Satirical Radio Drama," *Journalism Quarterly,* 33 (1956), 287–98.

[40]J. C. McCroskey, "The Effects of Evidence as an Inhibitor of Counterpersuasion," *Speech Monographs,* 37 (1970), 188–94.

FIGURE 10–3.   The Closed Mind and Source Credibility.[41]

counterpersuasion. Assuming a message of some intrinsic worth, the delivery or oral communication and its concomitant ethical proof are pragmatically an important part of how we perceive the source (see Figure 10–3).

Antagonistic Receivers

Apart from the question of antagonism or hostility, the question of where to put or order your best argument is an old one. Answers from research are confusing and need interpretation. The elusive variable of initial attitude is of overriding concern. With unstructured initial attitudes it may be that subsequent attitude is most affected by first-position arguments.[42] Perhaps it is also true of retention, but until we do more re-

[41] © 1970 United Feature Syndicate, Inc.
[42] Irving L. Janis and Rosalind L. Feierabend, "Effects of Alternative Ways of Ordering Pro and Con Arguments in Persuasive Communications" in Hovland, *The Order of Presentation in Persuasion*, 115–28; and Norman Miller and D. T. Campbell, "Recency and Primacy in Persuasion as a Function of the Timing of Speeches and Measurements," *Journal of Abnormal and Social Psychology*, 59 (1959), 1–9; see also N. H. Anderson and A. A. Barrios, "Primacy Effects in Personality Impression Formation," *Journal of Abnormal and Social Psychology*, 63 (1963), 346–50.

search where the initial attitude variable is better accounted for it's still conjecture. The arrangement effects, in terms of organization for antagonistic receivers particularly when initial attitudes are known, are, however, quite generalizable.

In a classic study done for the War Department by Hovland, Lumsdaine, and Sheffield,[43] we can find many insights and suggestions for the psychology of persuasion, particularly where antagonism is involved. The experiment involved the issue of a long war (WWII) and overoptimism. The subjects were 625 army personnel. The War Department felt that the weight of evidence indicated at least two more years of war in the Pacific. The specific knowledge sought by the experimenter was: when the weight of evidence supports the main thesis being presented, is it more effective to present only the arguments supporting the point being made or to introduce also the arguments of those opposed to the point being made?

The persuasion was transmitted with the aid of two radio transcriptions. Both speeches were in the form of a commentator's analysis of the Pacific war. The commentator's conclusion was that the job of finishing the war would be tough and that it would take at least two years after V-E (Victory in Europe) Day. The first program (A—one side) presented only those arguments indicating the war would be a long one, arguments relating mainly to distance problems and logistical difficulties. The second program (B—both sides) presented all the same difficulties, except that time was also devoted to a brief consideration of arguments for a short war. Two of these arguments were our naval victories and superiority and our previous progress despite a two-front war.

A preliminary survey of estimates of war duration was used to determine initial opinions. To register a change in attitude a man had to revise his estimate of how long the war would continue at least six months or more. An added analysis involved the sorting out of scores for the high-school graduates and comparing them with men who did not graduate from high school.

Following are the researchers' conclusions:

1. Presenting the arguments on both sides of an issue was found to be more effective than giving only the arguments supporting the point being made in the case of individuals who were initially opposed to the point of view being presented.
2. For men who were already convinced of the point of view being presented,

43I & E Division, U.S. War Department, "The Effects of Presenting 'One Side' Versus 'Both Sides' in Changing Opinions on a Controversial Subject" in T. M. Newcomb et al., *Readings in Social Psychology* (New York: Holt, Rinehart and Winston, Inc., 1947), 566–77; see also C. I. Hovland, A. A. Lumsdaine, and F. D. Sheffield, *Experiments on Mass Communication* (Princeton: University Press, 1949), pp. 201–27.

however, the inclusion of arguments on both sides was less effective for the group as a whole than presenting only the arguments favoring the general position being advocated.

3. Better educated men were more favorably affected by presentation of both sides; poorly educated men were more affected by the communication that used only supporting arguments.

4. The group for which the presentation giving both sides was least effective was the group of poorly educated men who were already convinced of the point of view being advocated.

5. An important incidental finding was that omission of a relevant argument was more noticeable and detracted more from effectiveness in the presentation using arguments on both sides than in the presentation in which only one side was discussed.

The most important finding for our purposes was that the both-sides persuasion was significantly better than one-side persuasion when the audience was opposed to the point of view being presented. Though of less import to the very real issue involved in this study, it is interesting to note that the one-sided arguments were more effective when the audience was already convinced of the point being presented. However, if we knew that the latter group would be exposed to counterpropaganda at a later date, then what kind of a communication decision should we make?

Fortunately we have another similar study that throws light specifically on the issue of counterpropaganda. Lumsdaine and Janis[44] compared resistance to counterpropaganda produced by a one-sided versus a two-sided propaganda presentation. Once again the experimental design involved transcribed radio programs. A one-sided (Program A) and a two-sided (Program B) speech were put together, directed once more at a kind of overoptimism. The main difference between this study and the one previously described is that one week after the speeches half of the subjects were exposed to counterpropaganda (half who heard Program A and half who heard Program B).

The researchers found that the groups previously persuaded with both-sides argumentation were more resistant to counterpropaganda than those persuaded with one-sided argumentation. Only 2 percent of the later group maintained the desired attitudes when subjected to counterpropaganda, whereas 61 percent of the group previously exposed to both-sides persuasion resisted and maintained the desired opinion. The researchers concluded: "A two-sided presentation is *more* effective in the long run than a one-sided one (a) when, regardless of initial opinion, the audience is *exposed* to subsequent counterpropaganda, or (b) when, re-

44Arthur A. Lumsdaine and Irving L. Janis, "Resistance to Counter-Propaganda Produced by a One-Sided Versus a Two-Sided Propaganda Presentation," *Public Opinion Quarterly*, 17 (1953), 311–18.

gardless of subsequent exposure to counterpropaganda, the audience initially disagrees with the commentator's position."

It is readily apparent that this study supports the War Department study. It shows that we must consider the approach of both-sides persuasion because of the possibility that an audience may be exposed to counterargument.

There are many speech studies that have in part measured the effects of both-sides persuasion. They often indicate that "other" factors are so important as to make generalizations dangerous. For example, the role of a speaker's prestige or ethos[45] may seriously offset any predicted advantage. There is evidence that in full-blown, emotional, political oratory, a straightforward, argumentative approach may be more effective.[46]

Both-sides persuasion nevertheless has the appeal of objective, rational evaluation. It is a subtle and honest appeal to fair play. An opposed listener is not antagonized by omission of arguments on his side of the issue. Listening should be more favorably oriented because the listener will not be involved in rehearsing counterarguments during your positive (pro-side) persuasion. Both-sides persuasion not only helps insulate the audience against counterargument but also forces the speaker to be more audience-oriented. A speaker is forced to be more sensitive to the audience's attitudes and to the totality of arguments and issues involved in his subject. One student speaker, after much research on both sides of his speech, reported that he had now convinced himself of the "other" side of the subject. Both-sides persuasion is then (1) a most effective form of motivation and (2) a most scientific and rational form of preparation—a new rationalistic persuasion!

Some specific characteristics to be noted in this kind of persuasion are as follows:

1. *Objectivity*—fairness, honesty, bias based on evidence.
2. *Suspended judgment*—avoids superpositive statements, creates doubt, makes frequent use of the hypothesis form.
3. *Nonspecific opponents*—does not identify audience as the opposition, suggests audience is undecided, creates a common ground.
4. *Critical willingness*—arouses audience reevaluation, motivation to reconsider the "other" side.
5. *Qualified language*—does not overstate the position and evidence, is careful of overgeneralized statements.

[45]Stanley F. Paulson, "The Effects of the Prestige of the Speaker and Acknowledgment of Opposing Arguments on Audience Retention and Shift of Opinion," *Speech Monographs*, 21 (November 1954), 267–71.

[46]Thomas Ludlum, "Effects of Certain Techniques of Credibility Upon Audience Attitudes," *Speech Monographs*, 25 (November 1958), 278–84.

6. *Audience-sensitive*—adapts and adjusts the presentation to the feedback signs, considers alternative actions in advance of the speech.
7. *Ethical*—above all, honest; presents significant opposing arguments in an objective manner; honesty is also pragmatically the best policy.

The Natural Order

The apparent similarities between human motivation and thinking patterns, and learning patterns offer many suggestions for organizing persuasive material.

Probably the most famous natural-order system is the "reflective thinking" pattern of John Dewey. This same system is used frequently in problem-solving and group-discussion courses and is further discussed in Chapter 12. It involves:

(1) suggestions, in which the mind leaps forward to a possible solution; (2) an intellectualization of the difficulty or perplexity that has been felt into a problem to be solved, question for which the answer must be sought; (3) the use of one suggestion after another as a leading idea, or hypothesis, to initiate and guide observation and other operations in collection of factual material; (4) the mental elaboration of the idea . . . ; and (5) testing of the hypothesis by overt or imaginative action.[47]

Translating this to the organization of material from the viewpoint of a speaker trying to persuade, you are advised to arrange your material and strategy so that your audience will receive and decode it in the following natural thinking order:

1. Attention and awareness of felt difficulty.

2. A recognition of a problem or need.

3. The sorting of objections and counterplans in search of the best solution.

4. An elaborating and visualizing of the proposed solution.

5. An evaluation of the plan leading to acceptance or rejection of the solution.

Persuaders and speech scholars have made many adaptations similar to the one indicated above. Hollingworth suggests that the fundamental tasks of a speaker are attention, interest, impression, conviction,

[47]John Dewey, *How We Think* (Boston: D. C. Heath & Company, 1933), p. 107.

and direction.[48] Alan H. Monroe calls his system the motivated sequence, *"the sequence of ideas which by following the normal process of thinking, motivates the audience to respond to the speaker's purpose."*[49] The key steps in this natural order are (1) attention, (2) need, (3) satisfaction, (4) visualization, and (5) action. This system argues plausibly that first a man's attention must be caught; second, he must be made to feel a definite need; third, he must be shown a way to satisfy this need; fourth, he must be made to visualize the application of the proposal to him personally; finally, a definite suggestion must be made to indicate how he should act. It is really a need-plan or need-solution emphasis, as explained in Part III, "Message Preparation." In generalizing from empirical evidence, Carl Hovland supports this kind of natural order: "Presentation of information relevant to the satisfaction of needs after these needs have been aroused brings about greater acceptance than an order which presents the information first and the need-arousal second."[50]

Thinking patterns and learning patterns have a great deal in common. For theories on how we learn we consult the educational psychologist. Many learning theories revolve around stimulus-response bonds (sr) and experiences that tend to stamp in or reinforce the response (reinforcement). Habit or past experience plays a large part, as does frequency of occurrence of the response either intellectually or physically (shr or sor).[51]

The theory of Miller and Dollard[52] is typical. Their categories in the learning process are drive, stimulus, response, and reward.

Other variations or translations of speech organization might include attention, motivation (for drive), stimulus, reaction, and reinforcement. In very general terms, the srx bond or stimulus-response-reinforcement theory has usefulness to would-be persuaders.

It is evident that natural-order systems for organizing persuasion all make much of the attention concept. The famous psychologist William James said, "What holds attention determines action. . . . The impelling idea is simply the one which possesses the attention. . . . What checks our impulses is the mere thinking of reasons to the contrary."[53]

[48]H. L. Hollingworth, *The Psychology of the Audience* (New York: American Book Company, 1935), pp. 19–32.

[49]Alan H. Monroe, *Principles and Types of Speech* (Chicago: Scott, Foresman and Company, 1949), pp. 308–9; see also Alan H. Monroe and Douglas Ehninger, *Principles of Speech Communication* (Glenview, Ill.: Scott, Foresman and Company, 1969), p. 261.

[50]Carl I. Hovland, *The Order of Presentation in Persuasion* (New Haven: Yale University Press, 1957), p. 135.

[51](shr)—Stimulus (Habit Strength) Response (C. L. Hull).

(sor)—Stimulus Oscillation Response (C. L. Hull).

[52]N. E. Miller and J. Dollard in J. A. McGeoch and A. L. Irion, *The Psychology of Human Learning* (New York: David McKay Co., Inc., 1952), p. 54.

[53]William James, *Psychology: Briefer Course* (New York: Holt, Rinehart and Winston, Inc., 1892), p. 448.

Attention may be thought of as a focus of perception leading to a readiness to respond.[54] To think of attention as being literally capable of controlling behavior is a little frightening. This, of course, goes beyond James's meaning, but it does serve to point out the importance of attention in persuasion. If one thinks of hypnosis as a state involving complete, undivided attention,[55] it does appear that "that which holds attention determines action."

In Chapter 9 we found the forms of emphasis useful in terms of transferring information to the audience.[56] The audience was better able to recall and remember things they had been told with emphasis. This is an example of how a speaker can use this attention phenomenon in informative speeches. Although an enhancement of an audience's remembering or interest faculty does not necessarily prove that their attitudes have been changed or even that they are more susceptible to change—*if* attention and interest help determine action and a readiness to respond—then the suggestions for presenting information fit here also.

Our attention, like all perception, is selective. Because of this factor the persuasive speaker must concentrate on keeping the audience involved in his subject. Other factors are constantly vying for the listener's attention—sounds, sights, people, conflicting ideas, and so on.

The Gestalt-oriented psychologists remind us that learning is a dynamic interaction of the entire perceptual field rather than simple bonds or associations. Therefore, this is not meant to be a stereotype for organizing persuasive speeches. You are still better advised to use introduction-body-conclusion as a general outline format and to use these other systems of arrangement for further detailing and better understanding. This was explained in Part Three, *Message Preparation*.

A chart showing some of these persuasion systems in terms of introduction-body-conclusion is useful (see page 273).

Whatever specific organization adaptation you decide upon, the following psychological concepts are at least theoretically involved in all persuasion speeches:

1. Creation of an attention-need and feeling of difficulty in order to communicate in the acceptable code.
2. Arousal of interest and problem awareness by relating need to the specific audience through their dynamic needs and motive appeals.
3. Explanation and relation of the solution in terms of the problem, need, previous experience, knowledge, and personality of the audience.

[54]F. L. Ruch, *Psychology and Life*, 3d ed. (Chicago: Scott, Foresman & Company, 1948).

[55]Hypnosis is probably more closely allied to normal sleep.

[56]R. Ehrensberger, "An Experimental Study of the Relative Effectiveness of Certain Forms of Emphasis in Public Speaking," *Speech Monographs*, 12 (1945), 94–111.

SOME PERSUASION ARRANGEMENT SYSTEMS

	Hollingworth	Monroe	Miller & Dollard	Ross	Aristotle
Introduction	Attention	Attention	Drive	Attention	Proem
Body	Interest Impression Conviction	Need Satisfaction Visualization	Stimulus Response	Need Plan Objections	Statement Argument
Conclusion	Direction	Action	Reward	Reinforcement Action	Epilogue

4. Evaluation, when necessary, of all important objections, counterarguments, or alternative solutions.
5. Reinforcement of your message throughout your speech, particularly toward the close, through verbal reminders, reviews, summaries, and visualizations.

Model outlines illustrating various organizational patterns follow. Additional persuasive outlines may be found in Appendix C ("Rock Music" and "A Rampant Killer").

BUCKLE UP AND STAY ALIVE[57]

General End: To persuade.
Specific Purpose: To persuade the audience always to use the seat belts in their cars.

Introduction

(Attention)

I. A cure for cancer or heart disease! What excitement would be generated if medical authorities made this announcement. Mortality would be reduced to less than one-fifth.
II. For the third leading cause of death, namely, auto accidents, there already exists a lifesaving device that relatively few people use.
   A. An investigation of the July 4th accidents.
     1. 442 victims, with no belts at all.
     2. Belts would have prevented exactly one-half the deaths.

(Physiological and Safety Needs)

   B. These statistics are very meaningful to me because last summer I was involved in an accident in which a person without a belt was killed.

[57]From a student speech by Darlene Uten, Wayne State University.

Body

I. No medical miracle short of a cure for cancer or heart disease can save so many lives.

(Safety Need)

 A. Auto ·accidents are the leading cause of death between the ages of fifteen to twenty-four.

 B. The risk of death is cut by 80 percent when safety belts are used.

II. Most drivers don't know the facts.

 A. Ejection of an occupant is the most frequent factor in serious injury. Investigation of twenty-two states indicates that you are five times more likely to be killed if ejected.

 B. The typical victim is not a speed demon on a strange road.

  1. The National Safety Council found that three out of five fatal crashes occur on roads familiar to the driver.

  2. My accident was on a road I've been traveling all my life.

(Interest)

  3. He is more typically a young homeowner, a wife picking up her husband, or a teenager backing out of a driveway.

  4. Fifty percent of all fatalities occur at less than 40 mph.

  5. There is no guarantee against getting struck from behind or sideswiped.

 C. Common misconceptions set straight.

  1. You are not safer if thrown out of your car.

  2. Careful drivers are not immune to accidents.

  3. Local drivers are not immune to accidents.

  4. Driving slowly is no protection.

 D. Some objections set straight.

  1. Don't seat belts often cause injuries?

(Meeting Objections)

   a. Hip bruises—my friend would have traded her fractured skull for a dozen hip bruises.

   b. Submerged in water or on fire.

(Visualization)

    (1) With a seat belt you are more apt to remain conscious.

    (2) Seat belts can be released with one hand in two seconds.

  2. I don't drive often, far, or fast; why bother?

   a. Three of five fatal crashes are on local and familiar roads, within 25 miles of home.

(Reinforcement)

   b. Fifty percent of all fatalities are under 40 mph.

   c. It takes *two* to tango.

Conclusion

I. Safety belts have been publicized and made manda-
tory.
   A. All car manufacturers.
   B. United States Health Service.
   C. American Medical Association.
   D. Insurance companies.
II. Always buckle up for safety to save lives and prevent
serious accidents.
   A. Have everyone buckle up no matter how short
   the ride.
   B. It takes only six seconds to cut the risk of death
   by 80 percent.

OVER SIXTY-FIVE[58]

General End: To persuade.
Specific Purpose: To persuade people to change their attitudes and/or behavior toward senior citizens.

Introduction

(Attention)

I. The Los Angeles Times recently received a letter
from an eighty-four-year-old widow. Mrs. Brown's
letter began, "I'm so lonely I could die. I see no
human beings. My phone never rings. The people
here say, 'Pay your rent and go back to your room.' "
She enclosed one dollar and six stamps. "Will
someone please call or write?" she asked. In a city
of almost three million people, Mrs. Brown didn't
have *one* person with whom she could talk.

II. Now I'm going to tell you another true story. Every
single one of us is going to grow old someday! There
is no fountain of youth! You may end up like Mrs.
Brown, unless you help change society's attitudes
and behavior toward our senior citizens. I am going
(Overview)   to tell you what it means to be over sixty-five in
America: it typically means inadequate income,
poor health care, and near isolation.

Body

I. People over sixty-five are inordinately poor.
   A. One out of every four of the 20 million Amer-
   icans over sixty-five lives below the poverty
   level.
   B. One-third are forced to go on welfare for the
(Love Needs)   first time.
   C. The majority of older citizens are hit by in-
   flation and fixed income.

[58]From a student speech by Darlene Glowgower, Wayne State University.

D. Pension plans are deceptive.
   1. U.S. Senate study revealed only 5 to 15 percent of workers covered since 1950 have ever received any pension money.
   2. Layoffs, plant shutdowns, company mergers, and employer bankruptcies have altered originally sound pension plans.
   3. The average U.S. American couple gets only $3,252 in social security a year; the poverty level is approximately $3,000 a year.

II. People over sixty-five are inordinately ill.
  A. 86% of men and women over 65 have serious chronic illnesses.

(Physiological Needs)

  B. Medical bills of average elderly couple are $1,700 a year, three times those of younger people.
  C. Medicare does not alleviate the medical bill problem.
   1. Astonishingly, the elderly pay the same with Medicare as they did without it. One-third can't pay their bills.
   2. Medicaid doesn't pay for drugs, eyeglasses, or dentures.
  D. It is estimated that one-third to one-half of all health problems of the elderly are related to malnutrition.

III. People over sixty-five are inordinately isolated.
  A. The elderly are troubled by a sense of alienation from human companionship.

(Love Needs)

  B. Nursing homes are impersonal. People are sent there simply because they have nowhere else to go.
  C. Men and women over sixty-five commit suicide at a rate 20 percent higher than the national average.

Conclusion

(Reinforcement)

I. How ironic it seems that a nation that has advanced so far in one century to stretch the life expectancy of its citizens from forty-seven to seventy cannot make these additional years worthwhile.

(Review)

II. This is the terrible plight of those citizens over 65. They are victims of inadequate income, poor health care, and isolation. Everyone should try to help improve these conditions. Let's change our attitude toward older people. How much can we tolerate the abuse and neglect of older, vulnerable people for the sake of avoiding the inconvenience and cost of properly caring for them. Let's make the "golden years" the best years.

SUMMARY

The psychology of persuasion is concerned with the alteration of attitudes. We have reliable evidence that oral speech does affect attitudes. In this chapter the basic springboards of human motivation are discussed in terms of one's biological nature, social-psychological nature, personality, and human needs.

The systems of the body (nervous, circulatory, digestive, respiratory) and the maintenance of a constant internal environment provide some of our most basic motivations. Homeostasis refers to the body's unceasing self-regulatory efforts designed to maintain this internal environment. Man's role is to replenish this internal environment with supplies. When the internal resources are low, homeostasis becomes a powerful biological motivation. It is essential for survival that man have *oxygen, food, water, rest, elimination of wastes,* and *exercise.* In our culture it is only in great stress situations, ill health, or drug abuse that a biological imbalance may cause serious conflicts. Nevertheless, these biological motivations are constantly with us, affecting our behavior and the intensity with which we search out related goals.

Our biological nature, however important in a primary sense, is overlayed by many varieties of social-psychological motives. Prescientific explanations of personality attempted to predict human behavior and man's reactions to patterns of persuasion. Personality may be thought of as the totality of man's motives whatever their source. Early typological theories considered humors and body biles to be related to personality. These were followed by theories of body shapes or morphological types. Among psychological theories Jung's introvert-extrovert classification is best known. In a very real sense, the sources of persuasion are found in an understanding of human nature and behavior. Instinct theory has given us many useful concepts (whether innate or not) for theorizing about persuasion. Such "native propensities" as hunger, disgust, curiosity, fear, anger, and gregariousness from the works of McDougall are still popular. Hedonism as an explanation of human motivation hearkens back to antiquity and to a kind of ethical good-evil proposition. It postulates that man seeks that which is pleasurable and avoids the painful. A pleasurable hedonic set or mood probably does tend to facilitate approachability and acceptance; a painful or unpleasant set suggests rejection and withdrawal. Historic points of view about man's behavior and motivation patterns have utility for us if we are careful to evaluate and qualify them in terms of the more scientific modern theories.

Kluckhohn and Murray provide us with a modern, practical, and intelligent classification of personality determinants or influences: constitution (total physiological makeup), group membership, role (the part we cast for ourselves), and situation. Man, the great learner, sees the world and is motivated to a large extent through his personality.

Maslow provides us with a useful classification of human dynamic needs. In the order of their importance the needs are physiological, safety, love, esteem, and self-actualization (a kind of self-realization). A satisfied need is no longer a motivator in this theory. Motive appeals are useful triggers of human needs. They must be evaluated in terms of the layers of resistance indicated as dynamic needs, personality determinants, and the momentary "sets" or dispositions of the listener.

In classical rhetoric the five basic tasks in preparing and sending persuasive messages are referred to as *canons*. They are *invention* (investigating the message and audience), *arrangement* (message organization), *style* (selecting language that arouses the appropriate emotional response), *memory*, and *delivery*. In classical theory a persuasive orator is a *good man* skilled in speaking.

Cognitive consistency theories provide us with many practical and reasonable principles of persuasion. They refer to a kind of mental agreement between a person's notions about some object or event and some new information about those same objects or events. Three major theories are congruity, balance, and cognitive dissonance. The assumption of these theories is that when the new information is contradictory or inconsistent with a person's notions and attitudes, some psychological confusion and tension will result. This tension motivates a person to alter or adjust his attitudes or behavior in order to reduce this inconsistency. These theories posit a kind of psychological homeostasis. Persuasive communications tend to be effective when they reduce dissonance and inconsistency and ineffective when they increase dissonance.

Credibility, or *ethos*, refers to the receiver's or audience's acceptance of disposition toward the source. It is related to Aristotle's *good will, good moral character*, and *good sense*. In modern times it is called *good intentions, trustworthiness*, and *competence* or *expertness*. High credibility generally produces more attitude change.

The use of both-sides persuasion has been shown by experiments to be superior to one-sided persuasion when the audience is opposed to the point of view being presented or when, regardless of initial attitude, the audience is exposed to counterargument. This rational form of persuasion is characterized by objectivity, suspended judgment, nonspecific opponents, critical willingness, qualified language, audience sensitivity, and ethical conduct.

The role of attention is vital to persuasion because so many other factors may distract the listener.

Thinking and learning theories offer many suggestions for the arrangement of persuasive speech material. One such theoretical persuasion progression involves attention, need, plan, objections, reinforcement, and action. Human motivation is a highly complex phenomenon involving dynamic interaction of the totality of our previous experiences in the perceptual field. The dangers of oversimplified, overstructuralized, or other sure-fire systems of persuasion are considerable.

Speech Communication Principles

1. Oral communication and argument affect attitudes.

2. Reasonably constant laws about our internal biological environment affect human motivation.

3. The maintenance of a constantly balanced internal environment (homeostasis) is a basic springboard of human motivation.

4. Man's basic biological needs are oxygen, food, water, rest, elimination of wastes, and exercise. When these are not being met, his social needs may have to stand in abeyance.

5. Persuasion, biological or otherwise, involves motivated behavior prompted by a need to reach a goal thought to satisfy the need.

6. In our culture man seeks psychological-social satisfactions with almost the same intensity that he seeks survival at the biological level.

7. Understanding a receiver's personality (the totality of man's motives), especially his self-image, value system, assumed role, and life experience, is critical to a meaningful theory of persuasion.

8. Hedonism is more an emotional attribute or adjunct of motivated behavior than a source or goal.

9. Motivation is tensional, persistent, often instinctual, and often unconscious.

10. The concept of instinct is more descriptive than explanatory, but still provides valuable insight into human motivation.

11. Major determinants of personality are constitution, group membership, role, and situation.

12. The basic needs of all men are essentially the same: physiological wants, safety, love and belongingness, esteem, and self-actualization.

13. The order and practical importance of man's dynamic needs are subject to the degree of satisfaction attendant upon each need.

14. Multiple motivation is possible and probable.

15. When new information is contradictory or inconsistent with a person's notions and attitudes, it leads to psychological confusion and tension. Persuasion is the result of pressure to reduce incongruity.

16. When incongruence is so gross as to be unbelievable, it inhibits persuasion and attitude change.

17. Cognitive dissonance, being psychologically uncomfortable, will motivate a person to reduce the dissonance and achieve consonance.

18. Man will actively avoid situations and information that increase dissonance.

19. Behavior can cause attitude change.

20. High credibility generally produces more attitude change.

21. Source credibility is related to perceptions and attitudes of trust and confidence based in part on beliefs about intent, position in society, knowledge, and sincerity.

22. The most persuasive arrangement in terms of general psychological order is closely attuned to the normal thinking habits of man.

23. Both-sides persuasion is superior to one-sided persuasion when the audience is opposed to the point of view being presented; one-sided persuasion is more effective when an audience is already convinced of the view being presented.

24. People persuaded with both-sides argument, regardless of their initial attitudes, are more resistant to counterpropaganda than those persuaded with one-sided argumentation.

25. A hostile or antagonistic audience is more readily persuaded by a con-pro, both-sides order than a pro-con order. When an audience initally agrees with the position taken by a credible source, the pro-con order is superior.

A. *General Learning Outcomes*

   1. We should learn the importance of man's biology and the meaning of homeostasis as it relates to human needs.

2. We should learn the prescientific and philosophical explanations of man's social-psychological nature as they relate to his motivations.

3. We should learn A. H. Maslow's theory of dynamic human needs and how it relates to the psychology of persuasion.

4. We should learn about such basic dimensions of human motivation as rhetoric, cognitive consistency, source credibility, and natural order.

5. We should learn of the nature and applicability of rationalistic both-sides persuasion.

6. We should learn how to relate the psychological order and psychological sequences to persuasive messages.

7. As receivers of persuasion we should be able to detect at least some of the strategies, theories, and devices being directed at us and learn to sort out the rational from the emotional.

B. *Specific Learning Outcomes*

1. We should learn about man's essential biological needs: oxygen, food, water, rest, elimination of wastes, and exercise.

2. We should learn about the functions and similarities of psychological homeostasis.

3. We should be aware of the persuasion role of typological theories, instinct theories, hedonism, and the personality determinants of Kluckhohn and Murray.

4. We should learn the systems for classifying human needs, especially Maslow's scheme (physiological, safety, love, esteem, and self-actualization).

5. We should learn about the canons of classical rhetoric: invention, arrangement, style, memory, and delivery.

6. We should learn about cognitive consistency, especially congruity theory, balance theory, and cognitive dissonance.

7. We should learn the basic dimensions of source credibility: intention, trustworthiness, and expertness.

8. We should learn the meaning of ethical proof as it relates to persuasion.

9. We should learn the specific characteristics associated with rationalistic both-sides persuasion.

10. We should learn the specific persuasion arrangement systems of Hollingworth, Monroe, and Ross.

11. We should be able to relate the foregoing general and specific learning outcomes to the speech communication principles above.

C. *Communication Competencies*

1. We should be able to prepare an intelligent two- to three-page outline for a five- to eight-minute speech to persuade that applies the psychology of arrangement and follows one of the outline formats suggested by the models in this chapter.

2. We should learn to apply the basic physiological and psychological needs posited by A. H. Maslow to a persuasion strategy.

3. We should learn to apply the psychology of cognitive inconsistency to a persuasion strategy.

4. We should learn how to select a high-credibility source as a form of support for persuasion.

5. We should be able to apply both-sides or rationalistic persuasion in a persuasive speech or strategy directed at antagonistic receivers.

6. We should be able to apply a natural, motivated sequence in a persuasive message (e.g., attention, need, satisfaction, visualization, action).

7. We should become more critical, more objective receivers of persuasive messages.

D. *Study Projects and Tasks*

1. Prepare a three- to five-minute talk in which you attempt to persuade the audience to belief or action on any subject. You must effectively use the primary needs, motives, and motive appeals previously discussed. This is an exercise and therefore you need not use the both-sides approach nor have an elaborate outline. Simply demonstrate that you know how to apply the

theory in a speaking situation. Indicate on your outline the primary theories, appeals, and other devices you, are using.

2. Prepare a detailed two- to three-page outline for a four- to six-minute persuasive speech that follows any of the formats found in the model outlines in this chapter. Indicate in the margins of your outline those needs, theories, or appeals etc. that you are stressing (e.g., safety, love, esteem, self-actualization, dissonance, and so forth).

3. Prepare a detailed outline for a five- to seven-minute persuasive speech that is based on a motivated sequence (see pp. 269–272). The five major divisions of the outline could be labeled:

I. Attention		I. Attention
II. Need		II. Problem
III. Satisfaction	or	III. Solution
IV. Visualization		IV. Visualization
V. Action		V. Action

Indicate the primary motives, appeals, and other devices you are relying on in your outline (e.g., safety, esteem, self-preservation, etc.).

4. Clip three newspaper or magazine advertisements and evaluate them in terms of the sequence shown above. Create one of your own.

5. Report and illustrate a radio or television commerical or other appeal that made use of both-sides persuasion (whether for antagonistic groups or not). Create one of your own.

6. Prepare an eight-to ten-minute persuasive speech on a topic to which your class audience is relatively hostile or antagonistic (e.g., pick the more unpopular side of a social issue). Meet the significant opposition arguments first and make concessions where you must before turning to the other side of the question. Make use of the best of both-sides persuasion utilizing specific characteristics noted on page 268. See project 7 below for further assistance.

7. Use the following criteria in building your own both-sides persuasive speech; use them also in judging and critiquing the speeches of your classmates.

    a. Did the speaker impress his audience with his objectivity, openmindedness, and bias based only on evidence? Could any of the following methods be identified?
      (1) Presented the significant opposing arguments.

(2) Did not try to hide his own stand on the issue.

(3) Did not begrudgingly grant opposing arguments.

b. Did the speaker develop a oneness with the audience and prevent the audience from identifying itself as his opposition? Could any of the following methods be identified?

(1) Avoided "I"; used "we" and "you and I."

(2) Was nonspecific about opposition; identified others than audience as opponents.

(3) Suggested audience was an undecided group; created a common ground.

c. Did the speaker develop suspended judgment in the audience and arouse a critical willingness to consider both sides? Could any of the following methods be identified?

(1) Avoided superpositive statements, created doubt, made frequent use of hypothesis form.

(2) Created doubt rather than certainty, did not overstate the position and evidence, was careful of overgeneralized statements.

(3) Was above all ethical; presented significant opposing arguments in an objective, honest manner.

8. The following topics were found to have an antagonism or controversy rate (attitude disagreement) of 25 percent or more for 348 college students.[59] They might suggest topics for study projects 6 and 7 above.

a. Capital punishment should be the mandatory penalty for aircraft hijacking.

b. The NAACP is relevant to all black Americans.

c. Automobile gasoline engines should be banned in the U.S.

d. U.S. Olympic athletes should be subsidized by the federal government.

e. Sex education should be required in all public schools.

f. Black mayors are more beneficial to large cities than white mayors.

g. College students should hold a part-time job while in school.

h. America should train women astronauts for future space flights.

i. High school dropouts should be drafted into the armed forces.

j. The federal government should enact a law to require the sterilization of the feebleminded and the insane.

k. College social fraternities and sororities should be banned.

l. Most college students drink too much.

m. The population explosion should be curbed by a federal law limiting families to two children.

n. Movies should be taxed according to their movie code ratings.

o. Gambling should be legalized in our state.

p. Black college students receive undue advantages.

[59]S. A. Ratliffe and L. K. Steil, "Attitudinal Differences Between Black and White College Students," *Speech Teacher*, 19, No. 3 (1970), 191–97.

    q. The honors system for taking exams should be adopted at this school.

    r. Marijuana should be legalized.

    s. Cigarettes should be taxed more heavily.

    t. A conviction for drunk driving should be automatically penalized by loss of license.

    u. Men are unduly discriminated against in divorce proceedings.

    v. Further manned exploration of the moon is worth the expense.

    w. The choice of abortion should rest solely with the pregnant female.

    x. Men are better suited for high political office than women.

    y. Aid to Dependent Children should be eliminated.

    z. Premarital sexual relations should be encouraged.

9. Prepare an oral report or essay attempting to prove or disprove any of the speech communication principles listed earlier.

10. Analyze the speech in the appendix, "Communication and the Survival of Democracy," and locate by line numbers the following "natural-order" steps: attention, need, satisfaction, visualization, and action.

11. In the speech in the appendix locate by line numbers where the speaker is appealing to any of the following human needs: physiological, safety, love, esteem, self-actualization. Take the specific audience into account.

12. In what ways does the speech in the appendix use the cognitive consistency theories?

13. What evidence do you find in the appendix speech that the speaker attempted to use both-sides persuasion when he expected some disagreement, if not outright antagonism (e.g., lines 182–194).

14. Locate examples by line numbers of where the speaker in the appendix speech employed ethical attributions in the message (e.g., lines 1–6).

Chapter Eleven

The Logical Supports of Persuasion

PATHOS vs. LOGOS

In the previous chapter we were concerned with the human dimensions of persuasion or the psychological supports of persuasion. In this chapter we shall be primarily concerned with evidence, formal reasoning, and argument—the logical supports of persuasion. The ancient Greek rhetoricians used the words *pathos* and *logos* to make this kind of a distinction, and debates about the nature and advisability of using each approach continue to this day. For our purposes as communication-conscious individuals, we have need of knowledge about both *pathos* and *logos*; we cannot exclude either.

EVIDENCE

Aristotle was one of the first to make the distinction between "extrinsic" and "intrinsic" proof.[1] *Extrinsic* proof deals with facts in the world about

[1] *Intrinsic* and *extrinsic* are also frequently referred to as *artistic* and *nonartistic*. See L. Cooper, *The Rhetoric of Aristotle*. (New York: Appleton-Century-Crofts, 1932), p. 8.

us or statements based upon such facts—that is, self-evident, observable phenomena. If you were to go to Baldwin school and count 525 students, it would be a fact that you had observed. It would still be a fact if a document written by the principal said there were 525 students in Baldwin school. *Intrinsic* proof depends upon reasoned effort on our part, that is, the application of rhetoric and logic without which the proof would not emerge.

Essentially, the sources of evidence involve objects or things that are observable or reports about things that are observable. The most useful sources of evidence for our purposes are statements by authorities, examples, and statistics.

AUTHORITY

This evidence or proof is typically in the form of quoted testimony from a person better qualified to give a studied opinion about something than is the speaker. However, the value of an authority depends on how expert he is. Perhaps the testimony simply corroborates the observations of the speaker. In the last chapter this was discussed in part under "Source Credibility" and was translated into intent, trustworthiness, and competence.

The nature of the idea or statement being supported determines in part who the experts are. If you are trying to prove that the man who crashed into your car ran a red light, the expert is the lone man who was standing on the corner and saw the whole thing. With this kind of nonprofessional testimony you often need more than one witness. If you are trying to prove that you have observed a bird considered extinct, such as the passenger pigeon, you will need the testimony of a qualified ornithologist. He will insist on firsthand observation of a captured bird in this exceptional case.

Your authority is qualified to give expert testimony by virtue of his proximity or closeness to a firsthand observation or experience and by virtue of his training to observe the particular phenomenon in question. He should be an expert *on the topic under discussion.* You would not ask a doctor of medicine to diagnose a problem in an airplane engine.

Other problems of authority involve your audience's knowledge and opinion of the person quoted. The personal interest or bias assigned your expert may be a very real problem. When the audience simply does not know who John Doe is, then you must explain why his testimony is authoritative (for example, John Doe is a Professor of Economics at Cornell University and a member of the U.S. Tax Commission).

EXAMPLES

An example is a specific illustration, incident, or instance that supports or brings out a point you are trying to make. A contrived or hypothetical example (as discussed in Chapter 9) may be a real aid to clarity and is often very persuasive, but it is *not* proof as we are discussing it in this chapter. We are here concerned with real or factual examples.

To prove that man can operate normally in a state of weightlessness, we can cite one example of an astronaut who has successfully done so. However, in some situations *one* factual example, though proving its own case, may be so unique or exceptional that it does not truly support a generalization. If you were arguing that Volkswagens were poorly and carelessly assembled and you supported this statement with only *one* example of a car that was indeed poorly assembled, then your proof would become suspect. The question in the latter case becomes, "How many specific examples do I need?" This involves the whole question of inductive proof, which will be discussed in the next section.

STATISTICS

A wag once said, "First come lies, then big lies, then statistics." (Or was it, "Figures don't lie, but liars figure!") Despite the jokes and despite fraudulent uses of statistics, the truth is that we live by statistics. We accept actuarial data on births, deaths, and accidents as facts. However, the very complexity of statistics as a method is what bewilders many people. You do not have to be a statistician to realize that an average (mean) is not always the most representative measure. Let us hypothetically take 11 educators and their yearly incomes as follows:

	Salary		*Salary*
Educator A (Administrator)	$26,000	Educator G	$10,000
Educator B (Administrator)	25,400	Educator H	8,950
Educator C	15,000	Educator I	8,600
Educator D	14,200	Educator J	8,300
Educator E	12,000	Educator K	8,000
Educator F	10,500		

The average (mean) income of these eleven educators is $13,359. The problem is obvious. Two educators (the administrators) make the figure unrepresentative, particularly if you are talking about "teachers." Counting down halfway, we find $10,500. This is the median, and is much more meaningful and representative. The average of the teachers less the two administrators is $10,617, and the median is then $10,000. You could further figure the amount each income deviates from the average and indicate a figure called the *average deviation*. If you were to translate these deviations from the average onto a so-called normal, bell-shaped curve or distribution, you could then determine a figure called a *standard deviation* or *sigma*.

It should now be evident that statistics can very quickly become complicated, capable of many applications, and (if we are not careful) meaningless. The lessons are (1) to select the most appropriate statistics for your point or proposition and (2) to make sure they are made understandable to your audience. Statistics (figures) do not lie, but liars *do* have the opportunity to "figure"!

INDUCTIVE AND DEDUCTIVE PROOF

Induction is that process of reasoning by which we arrive at a conclusion or generalization through observing specific cases or instances. If you were to observe 500,000 spiders, and if each and every one had eight legs, it would be a reasonable conclusion that spiders have eight legs. The induction is perfect for the 500,000 cases, since there were no exceptions; to be intolerably scientific, however, it is a prediction when applied to all the spiders in the world, albeit a highly probable one. Assuming one is happy with the generalization "All spiders have eight legs," we can then conclude *deductively* that this eight-legged thing in our garden is a spider. In sum, inductive proof starts with the particular cases and proceeds to a generalization, whereas deductive proof starts with a generally accepted law or principle and applies it to a particular case. Formal deduction involves the use of syllogistic reasoning (see page 290. Requirements for safe inductive reasoning are as follows:

1. Is the example relevant?
2. Are there a reasonable number of examples?
3. Do the examples cover a critical period of time?
4. Are the examples typical?
5. Are the negative examples noncritical?[2]

[2]Austin J. Freeley, *Argumentation and Debate* (Belmont, Calif.: Wadsworth Publishing Co., 1971), pp. 118–19.

Causal Relations

If we were to see a man accidentally shoot a live man and then see the victim fall dead with a bullet in his heart, we could say the *effect* was death and the *cause* the bullet or the man with the gun. Even this simple, observed, cause-to-effect relationship is full of problems. If the shooting were deliberate, would it in any way change the relationship? Let us suppose you found a dead man (effect of something) with a bullet in his heart. Can we conclude absolutely that the bullet is the cause? This is reasoning from effect to cause, or *a posteriori*. The bullet is certainly a possible cause, but, as any Perry Mason fan knows, the man might have been killed by arsenic poisoning and then shot after his death to hide the real cause!

One more—suppose a man dashes into your classroom, shoots a gun at your professor, and dashes out. Your professor falls to the floor and everyone runs out screaming. You observed the cause and concluded that the effect was murder or attempted murder. (A role-play?)

Your car battery is weak, you observe that it is 10° below zero, and you come to the conclusion that your car is not going to start. This is before-the-fact, or *a priori*, reasoning; the conclusion is based upon circumstances observed before the disputed fact (*cause to effect*).

If when you get up tomorrow morning you say, "It's 10° below zero; my car won't start; I'll be late for school," you are reasoning from *effect to effect*. Both your faltering battery and your tardiness (the thermometer reading too) are the effects of a common cause, low temperature.

In argument from effect to effect, you must first sort out the effect-to-cause and cause-to-effect elements and then apply the general requirements for arguments from causal relations. These requirements are as follows:

EFFECT TO CAUSE

1. Is the attributed cause able to generate the particular effect?
2. Is the claimed cause the only possible cause of the effect?
3. Has coincidence been mistaken for cause?[3]
4. The alleged cause must not have been prevented from operating.

CAUSE TO EFFECT

1. Is the alleged cause relevant to the effect described?
2. Is this the sole or distinguishing causal factor?

[3]Craig R. Smith and David M. Hunsaker, *The Bases of Argument* (Indianapolis and New York: The Bobbs-Merrill Co., Inc., 1972), pp 88–89.

3. Is there reasonable probability that no undesirable effect may result from this particular cause?
4. Is there a counteracting cause?
5. Is the cause capable of producing the effect?[4]

Syllogistic Reasoning

A brief discussion of the forms and tests of syllogistic argument should help you evaluate your logical supports of persuasion before you present them. Most student audiences, if not all audiences, contain a person who will argue that you are using only "negative premises," that neither of your premises is a "universal," that you have too many "terms," that you have an "undistributed middle term" and so on. Your listener may not use these terms or even have been exposed to training in formal logic, but this is technically what he is asking. Your answer to him or, better, your logical preparation should be consistent with the discussion of reasoning and argument that follows. Your role as a listener can also be sharpened by a careful reading of the following material.

The syllogism is a formal pattern of logic by which from two known or accepted statements (propositions) we can arrive at a third statement (conclusion) that must follow.

> In a syllogism, we so unite in thought two premises or propositions that we are enabled to draw from them or infer by means of the middle term they contain, a third proposition called the "conclusion."[5]

The Categorical Syllogism. When a syllogism involves two statements or premises that are accepted as absolute or universal, that is, needing no qualification, it is called a categorical syllogism. It begins typically with the word "all."

> *Premise* 1: All birds have wings.
> *Premise* 2: All ostriches are birds.
> *Conclusion*: Therefore all ostriches have wings.

You can check your conclusion with simple geometry. Let one circle be "all birds," another be "wings." Because all birds have wings, but not all winged things are birds (e.g., insects, airplanes), let the first circle "all birds" be included completely within the circle "wings."

---

[4]Freely, *Argumentation and Debate*, pp. 123–27.
[5]Lionel Crocker, *Argumentation and Debate* (New York: American Book Company, 1944), p. 114.

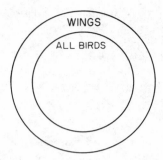

FIGURE 11–1.

The third term, "ostrich," should be conceived as a still smaller circle, for while "all ostriches are birds," not all birds (e.g., robins, sparrows) are ostriches.

FIGURE 11–2.

Because the circle "ostriches" is a part of and completely within the circle "wings," it follows that *all ostriches have wings.* In this example, "wings" is the major term, "birds" the middle term, and "ostriches" the minor term.

The formal science of logic involves eight general rules that govern every type of categorical syllogism. They are as follows:

1. Only three terms may appear in the syllogism (e.g., "birds," "wings," and "ostriches").
2. Neither the major nor the minor term may be a universal in the conclusion if it was only a particular term in the premises. ("Ostriches" was universal [all].)
3. The middle term may not occur in the conclusion.
4. The middle term must be used at least once distributively in the premises. ("Birds" is in both premises.)

5. If both premises are affirmative, the conclusion must also be affirmative. (This is our case—affirmative.)
6. Both premises may not be negative; one at least must be affirmative. (Both of ours were affirmative.)
7. If one of the premises is negative, the conclusion must be negative. If one of the premises is a particular proposition, the conclusion must be a particular proposition. (Ours were both positive and both universal.)
8. No conclusion can be drawn from two particular premises; one at least must be a universal proposition. (Both of ours were universal—"all.")[6]

The Hypothetical Syllogism. A hypothetical syllogism has a hypothetical statement as a major premise. There are three types: "if" (conditional), "either-or" (disjunctive), and "be and not be" (conjunctive).

The first type may be illustrated as follows:

> If an ostrich has wings, it is a bird.
> An ostrich has wings.
> Therefore, an ostrich is a bird.

> If it is A, then it is B.
> It is A.
> Therefore, it is B.

> If it is A, then it is B.
> It is not B.
> Therefore, it is not A.

The "either-or," or disjunctive, type of syllogism appears as follows:

> This organism is either animal or vegetable.
> It is vegetable.
> Therefore, it is not animal.

> It is either A or B.
> It is A.
> Therefore, it is not B.

> It is either A or B.
> It is not A.
> Therefore, it is B.

The "be and not be," or conjunctive, type of hypothetical syllogism appears as follows:

> A man cannot be living and dead at the same time.
> This man is living.

[6]Reprinted with permission of the Bruce Publishing Company from *The Science of Correct Thinking* by C. N. Bittle, O.F.M. Cap. © Copyright 1950 by The Bruce Publishing Company, pp. 187–88.

Therefore, he is not dead.

He cannot have been in Detroit and Los Angeles at the same time.
He was in Los Angeles.
Therefore, he was not in Detroit.

The Enthymeme. The enthymeme is a syllogism that is not presented in the formal patterns illustrated above. The enthymeme may omit one or more formally stated premises because: (1) the format would appear artificial to the audience; (2) the premise is obvious; or (3) it is deemed more persuasive to let the audience supply the missing premises. Many times the use of an enthymeme will involve more than one formal syllogism (that is, it is polysyllogistic), For example, take the following syllogisms:

Actions that cause cancer are evil.
Smoking is an action that causes cancer.
Therefore, smoking is evil.

That which is evil should be made illegal.
Smoking is evil.
Therefore, smoking should be made illegal.

The speaker might find it more expedient and more persuasive to use an enthymeme and say, "Any action that causes cancer is evil, and therefore smoking should be made illegal." He might also have used a more formal, abridged polysyllogism called *sorites*.

1. Smoking is an action that causes cancer.
2. Actions that cause cancer are evil.
3. Smoking is evil.
4. That which is evil should be made illegal.
5. Therefore, smoking should be made illegal.

It is useful for the listener to try to put enthymemes into a more formal arrangement if he feels the speaker is either in error or in some other way suspect. Some enthymemes fall in place very easily. For example:

Smoking causes cancer and should be outlawed.

Any action that causes cancer should be outlawed. ⎫
Smoking is an action that causes cancer.   ⎬ *not*
Therefore, smoking should be outlawed.   ⎭ *stated*

Rhetoric experts even to this day argue about the exact definition and intended use of enthymemes that Aristotle had in mind. For our purposes we can say that most enthymemes involve unstated premises. These premises may be unstated because of the conventions of our language, because they are considered self-evident, because they would appear artificial, or because the speaker deems it more persuasive to let the audience supply the missing or weakly supported premises. The last statement is of great rhetorical importance, for it suggests the necessity of adapting your logical support or proof to your audience. Particularly when the suppressed premises involve probability rather than universality, a speaker might find it more expedient to use an enthymeme. An enthymeme in the rhetorical sense, then, is effective only when the audience and speaker agree logically, for the audience must supply the predicted and hoped-for missing premises.

A searching and definitive article by Professor Bitzer concluded that an enthymeme is an incomplete syllogism, but in a very special sense:

> The enthylmeme is a syllogism based on probabilities, signs, and examples, whose function is rhetorical persuasion. Its successful construction is accomplished through the joint efforts of speaker and audience, and this is its essential character.[7]

The Toulmin System

The system of logic devised by Stephen Toulmin[8] gets one from evidence to inference without use of the relationships seen in the syllogistic models. For some, it may be easier to relate to everyday argument, and most importantly it tries to avoid the "allness" problem often associated with formal syllogisms. Its limitation for persuasion is that it is based on the logical rather than the rhetorical tradition.

According to this model, we reason from a presumed, or at least stated, piece of evidence or fact (the *data*) to a statement of an inferential nature (the *claim*). The two are connected or made reasonable by a more general bridging statement. Toulmin calls these bridges *warrants*. The last element is the *qualifier*, which allows for exceptions, qualifications, or reservations. Toulmin symbolizes the relationship between the data and the claim in support of which they are produced by an arrow, and indicates the authority for taking the step from one to the other by writing the warrant below the arrow.

---

[7]L. F. Bitzer, "Aristotle's Enthymeme Revisited," *Quarterly Journal of Speech*, 45, No. 4 (December 1959), 408.

[8]S. Toulmin, *The Uses of Argument* (Cambridge, Eng.: Cambridge University Press, 1964); for a more complete application to substantive proof, see also Douglas Ehninger and Wayne Brockriede, *Decision by Debate* (New York: Dodd, Mead & Co., 1963), pp. 125–57.

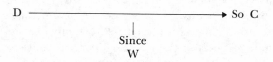

To allow for exceptions, special conditions, or qualifications Toulmin uses the symbol "Q" for such qualifiers. "R" stands for rebuttal.

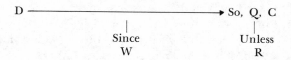

For example:

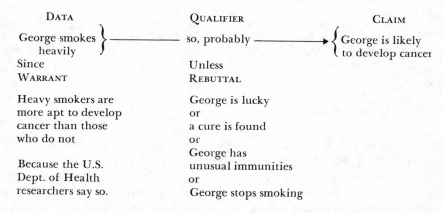

This system stresses the reservations (qualifiers) and should suggest caution to both speakers and listeners in making claims. It also puts a priority on *warrants*, the explicit justification of the reasoning between data and claim. It puts new emphasis on the importance of material validity. It should be considered a supplement for syllogistic argument[9] and is particularly valuable in the analysis of legal argumentation.[10]

FALLACIES

Aristotle, in an appendix to his book *Topics* that he titled *Sophistic Elenchi*, devised a classification of fallacies that has been the springboard

[9] Jimmie D. Trent, "Toulmin Model of an Argument: An Examination and Extension," *Quarterly Journal of Speech*, 54, No. 3 (October 1968) , 252.
[10] Jerie M. Pratt, "The Appropriateness of a Toulmin Analysis of Legal Argumentation," *Speaker and Gavel*, 7, No. 4 (May 1970) , 133–37.

for all classification systems to this day. He divided fallacies into two principal types: those in the language of the argument and those in the content or matter of the argument. Fallacies of language were discussed in Chapter 3. The fallacies of matter, or *extra dictionem*—beyond the language—are seven in number. Aristotle himself admitted problems in his own system, so we may presume to rearrange his list and translate it in terms of the twentieth century. For our purposes we shall examine four major types of fallacies together with their respective subtypes. The four are *secundum quid* (overgeneralization), *non sequitur* (false cause), *petitio principii* (begging the question), and *ignoratio elenchi* (ignoring or ducking the issue). A *sophism* is a deliberate use of a fallacy for some expected argumentative gain. The intentional use of these devices is called *sophistical reasoning*.

1. Secundum Quid (overgeneralization)

Snap judgments or generalizations based on insufficient evidence or experience belong in the category of overgeneralization. We are not talking about language and the dangers of the word *all* but rather the concept of *allness* itself. This fallacy results in going from the general case to a specific case, or vice versa. It is similar to the problems of induction and deduction.

It is in the exceptions to generally accepted rules that we often have the most trouble. We would all agree that it is wrong to kill a person. However, a specific application of the rule to a case of killing in self-defense is for most of us an exception. The same could be true of "alcohol is harmful" in many instances.

Sampling. A group of star high-school football players was being oriented to a certain Big Ten university campus when they observed a dozen devastatingly chic females coming out of a campus building. To a man, the generalization was "Wow! What coeds this place has!" The coach did not bother to tell them that these girls were all professional fashion models who had just come from a faculty wives' program. The size and representativeness of your sample should give you pause before generalizing. A rash of teenage delinquencies may cause some to conclude that all teenagers are juvenile delinquents, but this would be an unfair generalization.

The most insidious part of this fallacy is that it does start with facts. There *were* twelve stylish females on a given campus; teenage delinquency *has been* recorded. It is our lack of objective analysis of our sample of experiences or subjects that gets us into trouble.

Extrapolation. Stuart Chase refers to this fallacy as the "thin entering wedge."[11] It is also known as the "camel's nose in the tent." It is a form of sampling trouble (as are all overgeneralizations), except that this one is keyed to prediction and probability. The space scientist extrapolates or he does not predict at all. This is also true of the economist and the weatherman. The scientist typically knows the dangers of extrapolation, even to the point of couching his predictions in terms of statistical confidence. Chase put it well: "You chart two or three points, draw a curve through them, and then extend it indefinitely!"[12] The scientist draws predictive curves only when he has located enough points to warrant qualified prediction. We are well advised to do the same.

2. Non Sequitur (false cause)

This is the fallacy of assigning a wrong or false cause to a certain happening or effect. It also involves refutation with irrelevant arguments. Superstitions belong here. If you blow on the dice and win, was it the blowing that brought you luck? We still sell rabbits' feet, and most hotels still have no floor labeled "13th."

Post Hoc Ergo Propter Hoc. This translates "after this, therefore because of this." The list of superstitions fits here, too, except that in our saner moments we are not really unaware of the fallacy. It is the more subtle type of chronology that hurts us. If a new city government comes into power after a particularly rough winter and is faced with badly damaged roads, it may indeed be easier than not to hold them responsible as you survey one ruined $50 tire. "We didn't have roads like this until after their election." After this, therefore because of this. The great Roman Empire fell after the introduction of Christianity—care to try that one?

Tu Quoque. This fallacy translates "thou also" and consists of making a similar, but essentially irrelevant, attack upon one's accuser. A discussion between a Brazilian student and several Americans about communist infiltration in Latin America became quite heated when suddenly the Brazilian said, "Communists? How about segregation in your country? The retort was equally brilliant: "How about Nazis in Argentina?" A classic instance of this fallacy occurred in an army basic-training mess line a few years ago. The mess steward put a perfectly good salad right in the middle of a soldier's mashed potatoes. When told what an ignoramus he was, the steward retorted in a most effective (if illogical) way, "Yeah, what about those poor guys in Vietnam?"

---

[11]Stuart Chase, *Guides to Straight Thinking* (New York: Harper & Row, Publishers, 1956), p. 6. This is an excellent book to augment your reading on fallacies.
[12]Ibid., p. 6.

Consequent. This fallacy simply involves the corruption of the inferential process as applied to conditional syllogisms. The problem once again is with possible, partial, or even probable truths. If he lies, he will be expelled from school; he was expelled; therefore he lied. (In actuality, he may have been expelled for poor grades.)

When we use a conditional syllogism and argue from the falsity of the antecedent to the falsity of the consequent or from the truth of the consequent to the truth of the antecedent, we are committing the fallacy of the consequent.

Either-Or. Certainly there are things that are either one way or another in this world. You are either living or dead; the lake is frozen or it is not. There is no such thing as being a little bit pregnant. However, when a statement or problem with more than two possible solutions is put in a dichotomous either-or context, we have a fallacy. "The fight is either Jan's or Jim's fault." It may be neither's fault, or it may be the fault of both. There are shades of gray in most things. All too often we hear either-or arguments that only slow real solutions: science vs. religion, capitalism vs. socialism, suburban vs. city living, and so forth.

Loaded Questions. The vernacular is probably more clear than *plurium interrogationum*, or "many questions." This device usually involves asking two questions as if they were one. It typically puts you in an awkward position no matter how you answer. In a speech it may take the form of a great many questions, the combination of answers leading to fallacious reasoning. The answers typically sought are yes or no. The classic loaded question is, "Have you stopped beating your wife?" Yes or no? If you answer "no," you are an admitted wife-beater. If you answer "yes," you are an admitted former wife beater. Either way, the loaded question stacks the deck against you!

3. *Petitio Principii (begging the question)*

This fallacy is commonly called "begging the question," that is, assuming the truth or falsity of a statement without proof. A common form involves using two or more unproved propositions to establish the validity of one another. Other forms involve simple, unwarranted assumption or assertion.

Circulus in Probando. This form of question begging is called "arguing in a circle." This is the classic example of using two or more unproved propositions to prove one another. Professional boxing should be outlawed for it is inhumane; we know it is inhumane because it is a practice that should be outlawed. Take the course in Speech and Communication Theory at Northwestern University because it is the best in the country. Why is it the best in the country? Because it is taught at Northwestern University.

Direct Assumption. In this form of *petitio principii* language is carefully selected to help conceal bald assertions. Many statements may be used or just a word or two subtly inserted. In a discussion of big-time college football, an opposition speaker started with the words "It is my purpose to show that buying professional players is not in the best interest of college football." This statement begged the whole proposition by assuming at the outset that colleges buy professional players. Unless the statement is proven, it remains an assertion.

4. *Ignoratio Elenchi (ignoring or ducking the issue)*

This is ignoring the issue, or, in the vernacular, ducking the issue. It can be a subtle, insidious, and often vicious process. It almost always involves using apparently pertinent but objectively irrelevant arguments to cloud or duck the real issue or argument. There are several types of this fallacy, and each is worthy of a word of warning to the listener and to the naive or unsophisticated speaker.

Ad Hominem. When a speaker attacks the personal character of an opponent rather than the issue at hand, he is guilty of *ad hominem* argument. If intended, the purpose is to change the issue from an argument on the proposition (*ad rem*) to one of personalities. To argue the stage and screen abilities of Frank Sinatra by referring to him as "that self-centered, woman-chasing louse" is a good example of *ad hominem*. His alleged stage and screen *abilities* have no direct logical connection to his off-stage pursuits. This is not to say that every personal attack is unfair or illogical. If Mr. Sinatra were being evaluated on his public relations abilities, it might be a different matter.

Ad Populum. This is an appeal to the people in terms of their prejudices and passions. The symbols of motherhood, the flag, race, and sin are typical themes. Vicious and often unsupported attacks have been carried on against liberal-minded Americans in the name of "un-Americanism." "Romanism" was tried again in the presidental campaign of 1960. Hopefully, bald-faced *ad populum* appeals will become less successful as the general population becomes better educated and more sophisticated.

Ad Verecundiam. This type of fallacy involves an appeal to authority and dignity. When the authority is legitimately connected to the subject, as Aristotle is to logic, we have no problem. However, if in our reverence of Aristotle we use him to oppose modern probability theory, we are guilty of *ad verecundiam.* Joe Namath and Johnny Bench are well-paid experts in their highly specialized fields. They are probably not authorities on laser theory or even shoes or shaving cream. If you are impressed because Dr. Whosis says that alcohol causes cancer, find out if Whosis is an M.D. or an English professor!

Ad Ignorantiam. This term refers to appeals to ignorance—hiding one's weak arguments by overwhelming an audience with impressive materials or oratory in which they are untrained. A twelve-cylinder vocabulary can screen many a specious argument. An improper use of statistics (or even a proper one) for people ignorant of the theory or the numbers involved is a good example of *ad ignorantiam.* This is not to say that vocabulary and statistics are the problem. It is the adaptation to the audience in terms of the speaker's intent.

SUMMARY

In this chapter we were most concerned with the nature, source, and types of evidence and logical support.

Extrinsic proof deals with facts in the world about us or statements based upon facts, that is, self-evident, observable phenomena. *Intrinsic* proof depends upon reasoned effort on our part, that is, the application of rhetoric and logic without which the proof would not emerge.

The types of most useful evidence were those based on authority, examples, and statistics.

Inductive and deductive proof are differentiated as follows. *Induction* is that process of reasoning by which we arrive at a conclusion or generalization through observing specific cases or instances. *Deduction* starts with a generally accepted law or principle and applies it to a particular case.

Causal reasoning involves cause to effect, effect to cause, and effect to effect. The requirements for legitimate argument from effect to cause and cause to effect follow. In arguing from *effect to cause:*

(1) Is the attributed cause able to generate the particular effect?
(2) Is the claimed cause the only possible cause of the effect?
(3) Has coincidence been mistaken for cause?
(4) The alleged cause must not have been prevented from operating.

In arguing from *cause to effect:*

(1) Is the alleged cause relevant to the effect described?
(2) Is this the sole or distinguishing causal factor?

(3) Is there reasonable probability that no undesirable effect may result from this particular cause?
(4) Is there a counteracting cause?
(5) Is the cause capable of producing the effect?

The syllogism is a formal pattern of logic by which from two known or accepted statements we can arrive at a third statement that must follow. When a syllogism involves two statements or premises that are accepted as absolute or universal (needing no qualification), it is called categorical. A hypothetical syllogism has a hypothetical statement as a major premise; three types of hypothetical syllogism are "if" (conditional), "either-or" (disjunctive), and "be and not be" (conjunctive).

The enthymeme is a syllogism that typically is not presented in a formal pattern; it may have one or more premises left unstated. These premises may be unstated because of the conventions of our language, because they are considered self-evident, because they would appear artificial, or, most importantly, because the speaker deems it more persuasive to let the audience supply the missing or weakly supported premises. The last statement is of great rhetorical importance, for it suggests the necessity of adapting your logical support or proof to your audience. An enthymeme in the rhetorical sense, then, is effective only when the audience and speaker agree logically, for the audience must apply the predicted and hoped-for missing premises.

According to the Toulmin model we reason from evidence or facts called *data*, to a statement of an inferential nature, or *claim*. The two are bridged or related by a *warrant*, which justifies the reasoning between them. The *qualifier* allows for exceptions or reservations. The system attempts to avoid the "allness" problem associated with more formal syllogistic models.

There are four major types of fallacies: (1) *secundum quid*, or overgeneralization; (2) *non sequitur*, or false cause; (3) *petitio principii*, or begging the question; and (4) *ignoratio elenchi*, or ducking the issue. Specific cases of the last type are: *ad hominem*, attacking the personal character of an opponent rather than the issue; *ad populum*, appealing to popular prejudices and passions; *ad verecundiam*, appealing to authority and dignity on inappropriate subjects; and *ad ignorantiam*, appealing to or misusing audience ignorance.

Speech Communication Principles

1. Evidence enhances persuasion and source credibility when the message is delivered well and the evidence is relatively new to the audience. (A highly credible source has less need of evidence).

2. *Sources* of evidence (e.g., authority, examples, statistics) involve objects or things that are observable or reports about things that are observable.

3. *Extrinsic* proof supports persuasive efforts and deals with facts in the world about us or statements based on such facts, that is, self-evident, observable phenomena.

4. *Intrinsic* proof supports persuasive efforts and depends upon reasoned effort, that is, the application of rhetoric and logic without which the proof would not emerge.

5. Authority as evidence depends upon the intent, trustworthiness, and competence of the source.

6. *Induction* supports persuasive effort and is that process of reasoning by which we arrive at a conclusion or generalization through observing specific cases or instances.

7. *Deduction* supports persuasive effort and is that process of reasoning that starts with a generally accepted law or principle and applies it to a particular case.

8. *Causal reasoning* is a logical support of persuasion and involves generally agreed upon requirements for legitimate argument from effect to cause and cause to effect.

9. The *syllogism* is a formal pattern of logical support in which from two known or accepted statements we can arrive at a third statement that must follow.

10. The *enthymeme* is an informal syllogism that, when used rhetorically, allows the audience to supply the missing or weakly supported premises.

11. The Toulmin system of logic supplements syllogistic argument, its virtue being that it attempts to avoid the "allness" problem often associated with formal syllogisms.

12. The intelligent receiver of persuasive messages needs to know and recognize the major types of fallacious reasoning (e.g., overgeneralization, false causability, begging the question, and ducking the issue).

A. *General Learning Outcomes*

1. We should learn about the importance to persuasion of evidence and proof through reasoning.

2. We should learn to be more critical and objective receivers of persuasive messages through a knowledge of the major types of fallacious reasoning and argument.

B. *Specific Learning Outcomes*

1. We should learn the differences between extrinsic and intrinsic proof.

2. We should learn the characteristics of evidence derived from authority, examples, and statistical data.

3. We should learn the differences between inductive and deductive proof.

4. We should learn the requirements of the several types of causal reasoning (e.g., cause to effect, effect to cause, and effect to effect).

5. We should learn the characteristics of the categorical and hypothetical syllogisms.

6. We should learn how to relate the enthymeme rhetorically to a persuasive message.

7. We should learn the characteristics of the Toulmin system of logic.

8. We should learn the four major types of fallacies and their respective subtypes.

9. We should be able to relate the foregoing general and specific learning outcomes to the speech communication principles above.

C. *Communication Competencies*

1. We should be able to prepare an intelligent outline for a two- to three-minute persuasive one-point speech that primarily uses the logical supports of persuasion.

2. We should learn to apply the principal tests of evidence to the one-point speeches of others, thus becoming a more able critic.

3. We should be able to locate and define examples of fallacious reasoning from daily print media (or oral-video media).

D. *Study Projects and Tasks*

1. Prepare a detailed two- to three-page outline for a two- to three-minute persuasive one-point speech using primarily the logical supports of persuasion (e.g., authority examples, statistics, causal reasoning, syllogistic reasoning, and so forth).

2. Critically evaluate the logical support of your classmates' speeches; be especially watchful for fallacious reasoning. Write out your critique and be prepared to cross-examine the speaker.

3. Search the daily print media and locate two examples of fallacious reasoning; define and explain the fallacies in terms of the material in this chapter.

4. Prepare a two- to three-minute oral exercise in which you attempt to use as many fallacies as possible. See if you can fool your classmates, but be prepared to explain your sophistry should you prove too successful at deceiving them.

5. Check your thinking habits on the following items:
   a. An archeologist found a coin marked 45 B.C. How old was it?
   b. If you divided 30 by ½ plus 10, how much would you have?
   c. Which side of a horse has more hair?
   d. How far can a dog walk into the woods?
   e. If you went to bed at 8:00 and set the alarm to ring at 9:00 in the morning, how many hours of sleep would you get?
   f. Does England have a Fourth of July?

6. Of what fallacy is the Wizard of Id guilty in Figure 11–3?

7. Apply the various tests of reasoning to the following thought by R. L. Evans, and be prepared to discuss your observations and conclusions in class.

"CHANCE COULD NOT HAVE DONE IT . . ."[13]

As men move farther out from the magnificent earth and look back on its awesome beauty, its movement, its precision and proportion, upon the wondrous working, and magnificent majesty of it all, we come to the quiet conviction of these simple words: "In the beginning God created heaven and

[13]Copyright 1969 by Atesons. Used by permission.

THE WIZARD OF ID
by parker and hart

FIGURE 11–3. The Wizard of Id by Parker and Hart.[14]

the earth. . . . " Chance could not have done it. "And God saw everything that he had made, and, behold it was very good."*

Well, man has done much with his marvelous God-given mind, in the discovery and use of natural law. But much as man has done, he has scarcely touched the surface of all this majesty of meaning, and of infinite understanding.

Think a moment of the organizing and engineering and operation of it

[14]By permission of John Hart and Field Enterprises, Inc.
*Genesis 1:1.

all—of keeping a world within a livable range of temperature; of air and water renewing themselves; of insect, animal and bacterial balance in infinite variety. And the creation is evidence of a Creator, design is evidence of the Designer, and law is evidence of its Maker and Administrator.

"When a load of bricks, dumped on a corner lot, can arrange themselves into a house;" wrote Bruce Barton, "when a handful of springs and screws and wheels, emptied onto a desk, can gather themselves into a watch, then and not until then will it seem sensible, to some of us at least, to believe that all . . . [this] could have been created . . . without any directing intelligence at all."** Then and only then will I believe that this was done by chance—or without eternal plan and purpose.

"Behind everything stands God. . . . " said Phillips Brooks. "Do not avoid, but seek the great, deep, simple things of faith."†

"And God saw everything that he had made, and, behold, it was very good."

8. Prepare an oral report or essay attempting to prove or disprove any of the speech communication principles listed earlier.

9. In the speech in the appendix, "Communication and the Survival of Democracy," locate by line number examples of evidence used by the speaker to show that (1) "Western democracy stands today on the brink of disaster" and (2) that his solution is a practicable one. Evaluate the evidence and its use.

10. Evaluate the arguments in lines 82–108 and 132–146 of the appendix speech.

11. See if you can find a fallacy or near fallacy in the appendix speech.

** Bruce Barton, *If a Man Dies, Shall He Live Again?*
†Phillips Brooks, *The light of the World and Other Sermons: The Seriousness of Life.*

PART FIVE

SMALL-GROUP AND SPECIAL OCCASION COMMUNICATION

More and more man finds himself communicating in small groups. It's a sign of the times to be involved in study groups, workshops, committees, boards, councils, buzz groups, case conferences, and many other such groupings. Our modern teaching methods call for subgroups of larger groupings, such as task forces, research groups, and role-playing groups. Our jobs often put us into very specialized work groups. Then, of course, there are the innumerable social and recreational groups that help divide the time and efforts of us all. We are asked to interact, to discuss cooperatively, sometimes quite systematically and sometimes for the vaguest of reasons.

We discuss and interact for social and emotional reasons as well as to direct the logical work of society. Man is a social animal and may on occasion seek out others for the sheer joy of their presence or may affiliate himself with others to overcome his loneliness or misery. While our interest in Part V is directed primarily at groups with some kind of purpose or goal, we should be reminded that the casual group is a potent communication force capable of releasing the same tensions and emotions that often emanate from the more structured goal-seeking group.

The discussion groups with their procedures described in Part V are to be viewed as engaging in a democratic process—in point of fact, it could hardly be otherwise. Assigned or emergent leaders may vary in style, but the decision process is essentially democratic. "To discuss means to behave democratically."[1] In the broadest sense we can say that small-group discussion is essential to the success of a democratic society.

We will learn of the contemporary forms of discussion, agenda systems, problem solving, leadership, climate setting, and participant responsibilities primarily in Chapter 12. To better relate the previous chapters, it is useful to think of the small group as a type of audience. It will be shown that in many respects it is a more threatening audience since the feedback is typically so immediate and differences of opinion cannot be so easily generalized as with a larger audience.

When the group enlarges past six or seven members or approaches a class size of eighteen or twenty, our participation as a leader becomes of special concern. If questions and interruptions are commonplace or even solicited within the group, the suggestions in Chapter 13, "Audience Participation," will enable us to participate more actively both as participant and group leader. The chapter contains six principles of preparation and four rules for handling questions, with suggestions for stimulating participation by other members.

Some communication occasions are so special that they have developed almost a ritual or protocol about them. In such situations intelligent prescription to a point makes some sense. The eulogy is not a place for jokes; the tribute speech is not typically given in a "ha-ha" manner; a speech of introduction should say something informative about the speaker. These special occasion speeches occur so often and involve routinely the same principles that a special chapter has been devoted to them. In Chapter 14 we will describe and discuss speeches of introduction, speeches of presentation and acceptance, tribute and commemorative speeches, after-dinner speeches, and the adaptation of speech material for presentation on radio and television. We're not only involved in more small groups; we're involved in more speech communication of the special occasion variety. It is estimated that in New York City alone approximately 11,000 speeches, mostly of this special variety, are given in one week.

A general review of the hoped-for learning outcomes that will result from a close reading of Part V, particularly when related to class projects and performances, follows. A more specific set of learning outcomes and communication competencies, along with relevant projects and tasks, is appended to each chapter.

We should learn the nature of dynamic small-group discussion.

We should learn that cooperative communication is a real and vital act essential to success in a democratic society.

We should learn about the contemporary forms of discussion and their applicability to given situations.

We should learn about the reflective thinking process and its relationship to agendas.

[1]Dean C. Barnlund and Franklyn S. Haiman, *Dynamics of Discussion* (Boston: Houghton Mifflin Co., 1960), p. 5.

We should learn the definitions of and distinctions among the various types and functions of leadership.

We should develop our abilities as critics of communication in small groups.

We should learn that every speech communication situation represents a potential open forum or setting for audience-involved participation.

We should learn the basic principles that apply to four standard special occasion speeches.

We should learn the special preparation and speech adaptation necessary when dealing with the mass media.

Chapter Twelve

Discussion: Cooperative Communication

THE NATURE OF DISCUSSION

This chapter is primarily concerned with systematic, cooperative decision making in small-group discussions. The term *discussion* is derived from the Latin *discussus*, to strike asunder, that is, to pull apart, to separate and subordinate the elements and ideas that make up a question or topic. Discussion is not to be confused with debate. Debate is two-sided, discussion many-sided. Debate is competitive, discussion cooperative. If decision is impossible through discussion, it may very well lead to debate. Debate may then lead to resolution. If not, one might very possibly return to discussion. Premature or unnecessary debate has hung up many group discussions. The nature of a discussion-debate continuum is illustrated by Gulley in Figure 12–1.[1]

In terms of the communication theory discussed in Chapter 1, the unique aspect of discussion is that a participant is both sender-receiver and encoder-decoder at the same time—producing a truly dynamic, interactive, interpersonal communication situation. Feedback and perception take on even greater significance under these circumstances.

[1] Halbert Gulley, *Discussion, Conference, and Group Process*, 2d. ed. (New York: Holt, Rinehart and Winston, Inc., 1968), p. 139.

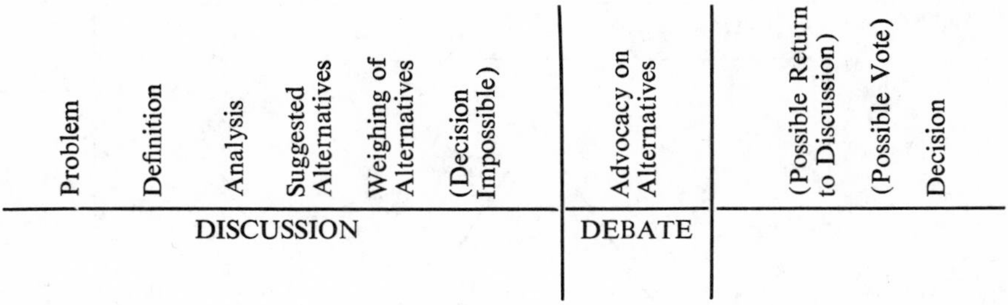

Problem	Definition	Analysis	Suggested Alternatives	Weighing of Alternatives	(Decision Impossible)	Advocacy on Alternatives	(Possible Return to Discussion)	(Possible Vote)	Decision
		DISCUSSION				DEBATE			

FIGURE 12-1.

The Nature of Small Groups

Most of our social interaction takes place in small groups. We are interested in groups of people that are more than just small, casual collectivities. There must be some connecting link, common purpose, intent, or problem that requires some modest interaction to make what Floyd Allport calls a "co-acting" group. One might say there is a kind of mutual identification. The small group is a dynamic collectivity so long as it has *cohesiveness. Cohesion* refers to the forces that bind members of a group together. One's own sense of interpersonal responsibilities and behavior greatly affects his successful interaction. One must be sensitive to his own behavior as well as the behavior of others. The feedback is often swift and pointed in small groups; audiences are typically slower to respond and more formal in their response patterns.

The small group differs from the larger audience in still other psychological ways. The audience is passive, the group typically active and dynamic. Its small size permits active verbal involvement and instant participation. Some members have a greater desire to take charge than others. The interacting group often develops an esprit or cohesiveness that resembles the "collective mind" of the mob. This phenomenon, called *social facilitation,* is usually thought of in positive terms, but small groups have been known to run wild, something that audiences rarely do (except in panics).

The dyadic communication model of Chapter 1 (Figure 1-7) can be adapted here to show the complexity of the small, co-acting group process. If one considers interpersonal communication in terms of feedback or *transactional loops,* with every dyad within a larger group having its own loop, then one quickly sees why three people constitute something quite different interpersonally and transactionally than two alone.

We suddenly have three times as many dyadic transactional loops to follow. If one wishes to consider all possible subgroups and relationships,

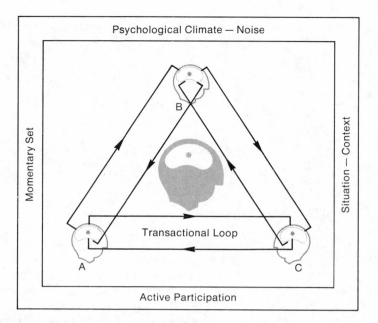

FIGURE 12-2.   Transactional Model for a Co-Acting Group of Three.

the number of relationships grows to seven. For example, in a group of three (ABC) we can chart the following:

A–B–C   AB–C
A–B   AC–B
A–C   BC–A
B–C

Two's company, three's a crowd!

The reason most small-group experts limit their research to groups of six or seven is clear if we look at a group of eight in terms of transactional loops and subgroup relationships (see Figure 12–3). Single lines with arrows are substituted for loops.

We now find ourselves with twenty-eight dyadic transactional loops. Time is part of the equation. Perhaps over a period of days or weeks one could master part of the problem. However, the total number of relationships and subgroups is something else! Would you believe 1009!?[2]

[2]The formula for predicting the total number of subgroup relationships may be expressed: $R = \Sigma d \dfrac{n!}{d!(n-d!)+1}$ where $d = s (n-1), (n-2)(n-3) \ldots$ (2)

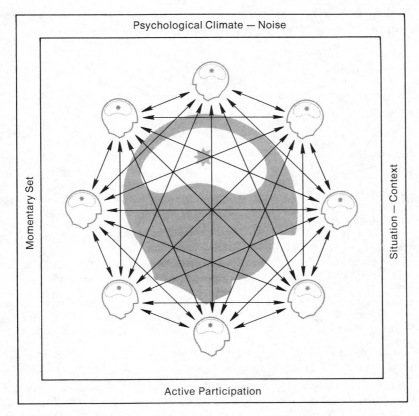

FIGURE 12–3. Transactional Model for a Co-Acting Group of Eight.

Certain generalizations regarding the co-acting small group are war-
ranted from the research.[3]

1. Attitudes and behavior can be changed through group discussion.
2. Small-group judgment on the average tends to be better than individual
   judgment.
3. Small, agreeing groups, more than audiences, develop a feeling of personal
   involvement and responsibility.
4. Cooperative group communication can be improved through training.

[3]See Jon Eisenson, J. Jeffrey Auer, John V. Irwin, *The Psychology of Communication*
(New York: Appleton-Century-Crofts, 1963), pp. 253–70; B. M. Bass, *Leadership, Psy-
chology and Organizational Behavior* (New York: Harper & Row, Publishers, 1960) ;
A. P. Hare, *Handbook of Small Group Research* (New York: Free Press, 1962); J. W.
Thibaut and H. H. Kelley, *The Social Psychology of Groups* (New York: John Wiley
& Sons, 1959); and Joseph E. McGrath and Irwin Altman, *Small Group Research*
(New York: Holt, Rinehart and Winston, Inc., 1966).

In a broader sense we might conclude that cooperative communication in small groups is an act essential to success in our society.[4]

Discussion Defined

The experts are in basic agreement about what we mean by group discussion.

> Discussion is the process whereby two or more people exchange information or ideas in a face-to-face situation.[5]
> They [discussion groups] consist of a number of persons who perceive each other as participants in a common activity, who interact dynamically with one another, and who communicate their responses chiefly through words.[6]
> Discussion occurs when a group of persons assemble in a face-to-face situation and through oral interaction exchange information or attempt to reach a decision on shared problems.[7]
> . . . an orderly process of cooperative deliberation designed to exchange, evaluate, and/or integrate knowledge and opinion on a given subject or to work toward solution of a common problem.[8]
> . . . a number of persons who communicate with one another over a span of time, and who are few enough so that each person is able to communicate with all others, not at secondhand, through other people, but face-to-face.[9]

Hedde and Brigance put it well years ago when they said, "Discussion, then, is a means of thinking together through purposeful conversation."[10]

Assuming then that we have a real, interacting, face-to-face group—that is, persons with some common goal, not just a loose collection of individuals—we might synthesize the above descriptions by saying that at its best *group discussion is systematic, cooperative, reflective thinking and communication.*

Contemporary Forms of Discussion

The word *form* refers to the type or format of discussion. In its most general sense group discussion refers to a cooperative thinking endeavor

[4]See Gerald M. Phillips and Eugene C. Erickson, *Interpersonal Dynamics in the Small Group* (New York: Random House, 1970).

[5]R. Victor Harnack and Thorrel B. Fest, *Group Discussion Theory and Technique* (New York: Appleton-Century-Crofts, 1964), p. 21.

[6]Dean C. Barnlund and Franklyn S. Haiman, *The Dynamics of Discussion* (Boston: Houghton Mifflin Company, 1960), p. 20.

[7]Gulley, *Discussion, Conference and Group Process*, p. 5.

[8]Horace Rahskopf, *Basic Speech Improvement* (New York: Harper & Row, Publishers, 1965), p. 348.

[9]G. C. Homans, *The Human Group* (New York: Harcourt, Brace & World, 1950), p. 1.

[10]Wilhelmina G. Hedde and William N. Brigance, *American Speech* (Philadelphia: J. B. Lippincott Co., 1942), p. 40.

typically among twenty people or less. The basic forms are *dialogue, panel,* and *symposium.* Three techniques that may be used in combination with any of the forms include the *buzz group, role playing,* and *brainstorming.* A *forum* is simply that part of a discussion in which the audience may speak. It could be and often is applied to any of the discussion forms.[11]

A *dialogue* is a two-person interaction that may involve simple conversation, an interview, or counseling. If a dialogue is held before an audience and the audience is invited to participate, it becomes a dialogue-forum.

The *panel* discussion is typically composed of three to seven people pursuing a common goal in an informal climate that facilitates spontaneous interaction. An audience may or may not be present. It typically calls for a procedural leader and some agenda.

A *symposium* is a small group (typically three to five) with special knowledge about differing aspects of a broad topic who make individual, uninterrupted speeches before an audience. A procedural leader controls speaker order and time limitations. A forum usually follows except when an audience is not physically present (radio-TV). Frequently the symposium speakers then relate to one another more informally in a panel discussion.

Discussion forms may be used for information sharing, problem solving, or decision making, as well as for instructional purposes.

Examples of information-sharing groups might include *staff meetings, study groups,* and *workshops.* Overlap is evident and probably unavoidable. A workshop, for example, may be thought of as a study group that has consolidated its work into a couple of days or even a few concentrated hours.

Examples of problem-solving groups include *committees, conferences,* and governing *boards* or *councils.* These are discussion groups that have the power of decision or at least the power to strongly recommend action based on their collective problem solving. Their group discussions are typically closed.

A *case conference* is simply a discussion about a real or contrived critical incident that hopefully leads to a learning outcome for the participants. It may or may not be conducted with an audience present. It can be evaluated in terms of participant interaction, leadership, agenda setting, and the solution itself.

In large groups where wider forum participation may be desired, the audience may be divided into subgroups of four to six people to allow

---

[11]See especially Kenneth G. Hance, ed., *Michigan Speech Association Curriculum Guide 3, Discussion and Argumentation-Debate in the Secondary School* (Skokie, Ill.: National Textbook Corporation), 1968.

more intimate, informal discussion. This technique is known as *buzz,* "Phillips 66," or "Discussion 66." It refers typically to subgroups of six, which discuss a carefully worded question.[12] The results of these individual buzz sessions are reported to the larger group by a spokesman. The anonymity of the people in the subgroups seems to be an important factor. A person is more apt to speak up in a group of 6 than 600.

If in a group, typically a case conference, roles or dramatic parts are assigned and acted out extemporaneously, it becomes the technique of *role playing* or what Hirschfeld has described as *extemporaction,* "a technique that adds experiential kinesthetic and emotional factors to the intellectual learning process."[13] In the Hirschfeld technique considerably more instructor planning and participation are involved. As a technique, role playing is often a good prelude to the other forms of discussion.

A unique technique that some speech communication instructors use to show the effect of eliminating premature and discussion-inhibiting comments of an arbitrary or critical nature is *brainstorming.* In this technique an arbitrary psychological climate complete with penalties is prescribed, which in effect prohibits immediate criticism of ideas. This typically permits more creative ideas to come to light in a short period of time than in the more traditional climate.[14] This technique can also be combined with other forms and used for various purposes other than instruction. It can be particularly useful when a great many ideas are wanted from a group in a short period of time. It is a good technique for screening attitudes and opinions. For example: "What should this class use as a topic for a project discussion?" This question under brainstorming rules regularly produces sixty or seventy topics in ten minutes. No evaluative discussion of the topics is allowed until later. Buzz groups are a good follow-up to screen the list more systematically.

AGENDAS

If group discussion is *systematic, cooperative, reflective thinking and communication,* then we had better explore reflective thinking in detail to see what kind of system or scheme it suggests for orderly agendas or discussion outlines. That orderliness pays off in terms of consensus or

[12]J. Donald Phillips, "Report on Discussion," *Adult Education Journal,* 7 (October 1948), 181–82.

[13]From material supplied by Adeline Hirschfeld, director of P.A.C.E. project, "Creative and Sociodramatic Supplementary Educational and Cultural Enrichment Service," Title III, E.S.E.A., Oakland University, Rochester, Michigan, 1967.

[14]Alex F. Osborn, *Applied Imagination: Principles and Procedures of Creative Thinking* (New York: Charles Scribner's Sons, 1953).

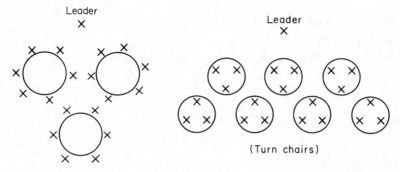

BUZZ GROUPS

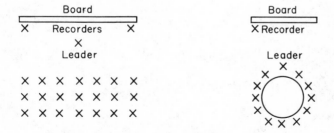

ROLE PLAYING

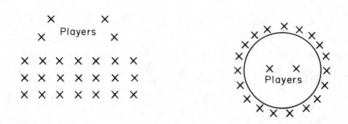

BRAINSTORMING

FIGURE 12–4. Participant Configurations.[15]

[15]For an interesting discussion of physical arrangements, see Paul Bergevin, Dwight Morris, and Robert M. Smith, *Adult Education Procedures* (Greenwich, Conn.: The Seabury Press, 1963); see also Robert Sommer, *Personal Space* (Englewood Cliffs, N.J.: Prentice-Hall, Inc., 1969), pp. 58–73.

DIALOGUE FORUMS

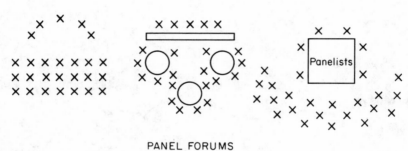

PANEL FORUMS

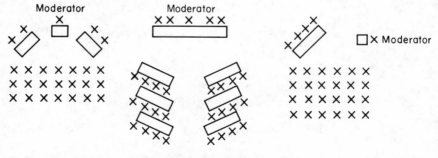

SYMPOSIUM FORUMS

FIGURE 12–4. Participant Configurations (Cont'd.).

agreement is shown in a study of seventy-two conferences by Collins and Guetzkow. They report: "Those meetings in which discussion is orderly in its treatment of topics, and without backward references to previously discussed issues, tended to end in more consensus. . . . When participants discussed but one issue at a time, instead of simultaneously dabbling in two or three, it was more possible for the group to reach consensus."[16]

Reflective Thinking Process

Reflective thinking was defined by John Dewey as "active, persistent and careful consideration of any belief or supposed form of knowledge in the light of the grounds that support it, and further conclusions to which it tends," as opposed to nondeliberate, everyday thinking. Dewey thought of reflective thinking as scientific habit, which consisted of acquiring the attitude of *suspended judgment,* and a mastery of the various methods of searching for materials. Maintaining an intelligent state of doubt and systematic inquiry are the essentials of reflective thinking.

Dewey's point of view about general education is also pertinent to group discussion, both in terms of agendas and the way you conduct yourself. He thought of the aim of education as the establishment of a kind of *self-discipline* in students. This self-discipline was thought of in terms of *systematic observation, thorough examining,* and, most importantly for us, agendas, or the *methodical arrangement of thought.* There are five steps in the Dewey system, which are interpreted below.[17]

1. The occurrence or awareness of a *felt difficulty.* You know something is wrong, unexpected, or unidentified. You experience a state of disequilibrium.

2. The *definition* of the felt difficulty to see what kind or nature of problem you have and how serious it is. Look carefully, don't misdefine. Suspend your judgment regarding solutions.

3. The formulation of alternative suggestions, explanations, and hypotheses as *possible solutions.* Inference and analysis take place here. (Review Chapters 1 and 11).

4. The rational elaboration of the possible solutions by gathering facts, evidence, and inferences. Further analysis of the consequences of alternative solutions.

5. Further testing, rejecting, or corroborating of the solution chosen in step 4—by observation, measurement, hypothetical case or model building, or actual experiment if applicable. You now have a reasoned solution in your thoughts

16Barry E. Collins and Harold Guetzkow, *A Social Psychology of Group Processes for Decision-Making* (New York: John Wiley & Sons, 1964), p. 111.

17John Dewey, *How We Think* (Boston: D. C. Heath & Company, 1910), pp. 68–78.

Agenda Systems

It is obvious that the reflective thinking system just discussed, while addressed to an individual, would make just as much sense for a group of individuals solving a problem or making decisions. More recent research tends to support the Dewey stages or phases. Bales and Strodtbeck divided problem-solving discussions into three periods according to the number of interactions. They found that in the first period or phase the communications pertained primarily to *orientation, information, repetition,* and *confirmation.* In the second phase the interactions involved primarily *analysis, evaluation,* and *communications* seeking or giving *opinions* and *feelings.* In phase three they found that acts of *control,* that is, communications involving possible directions and ways of action, predominated.[18]

The researchers also indicate that as a group approaches the third phase it experiences increasing strains on members' solidarity and social-emotional relationships. Both positive and negative reactions tend to increase. Tension reduction is apparent as differences are resolved and agreement is reached.

The danger of oversimplifying so complicated a process is made clear by the research of Scheidel and Crowell, who suggest that the reflective thinking process as an agenda system is not a simple linear progression after all, but rather a circular or spiraling course.[19] After studying idea development in ten discussions, they concluded that members devoted one-fourth of their comments to confirming statements and another fourth to clarifying and substantiating them. The latter function is represented by the outward movement of this spiral model. The progress toward decision is represented as the onward movement.

The best agenda systems found in the literature are those derived from research findings coupled with creative insight. Some excellent examples follow.

TWO-PHASE AGENDA

I. The Analysis Phase
    A. Definitions: What does the question mean?
    B. Limitations, if any: What part of the problem do we intend to concentrate on if we cannot discuss the whole problem now?

---

[18]Robert F. Bales and Fred L. Strodtbeck, "Phases in Group Problem-Solving," in *Group Dynamics: Research and Theory,* eds. Darwin Cortwright and Alvin Zander (New York: Harper & Row, Publishers, 1960), pp. 624–38.

[19]Thomas M. Scheidel and Laura Crowell, "Idea Development in Small Discussion Groups," *Quarterly Journal of Speech,* 50 (1964), 140–45.

C. What are the important facts about this problem?
  1. What is its history?
  2. What are its causes?
  3. What has happened or is happening?
  4. What has happened elsewhere that illuminates the problem under discussion?
II. The Solution Phase
  A. What are the advantages and disadvantages of each alternative course of action?
  B. By what or whose standards must any decision be evaluated?
  C. What decision should we reach?[20]

SIX-STEP AGENDA

  I. Ventilation (general establishment of rapport)
 II. Clarification (phrasing the question)
III. Fact Finding
 IV. Discovery (finding hypotheses or solutions)
  V. Evaluation (of proposed solution)
 VI. Decision Making (verbal formulation of conclusion)[21]

SIX-STEP AGENDA

Problem Description Phase	1. Problem Formulation
	2. Problem Analysis
	3. Problem Reformation (if necessary)
Problem Solution Phase	4. Solution Proposal
	5. Solution Testing
	6. Action Testing[22]

ROSS FOUR-STEP AGENDA

  I. *Definition and limitation*—a concise but qualified statement of the felt difficulty, problem, or goal
 II. *Analysis*—the determination of the type or nature of the problem and its causes
   a. Puzzles—questions of fact
   b. Probabilities—reasonable predictions—chance
   c. Values—beliefs, attitudes
III. *Establish Criteria*—a group consensus on the standards to be used in judging solutions
   a. Minimum and/or maximum limits
   b. A rating of hierarchical importance
 IV. *Solutions*
   a. Evaluation in terms of the criteria
   b. Decision and suggested implementation or action

[20]Gulley, *Discussion, Conference, and Group Process*, pp. 215–16.
[21]Barnlund and Haiman, *The Dynamics of Discussion*, pp. 86–97 (material in parenthesis added).
[22]Harnack and Fest, *Group Discussion Theory and Technique*, pp. 64–68.

A visual aid or chart depicting the agenda may prove helpful to participants.[23]

Agenda System Elaborations

Using the Ross four-step system as a point of reference, but with the understanding that what is said here will apply for the most part to all the possible agenda systems shown, let us look at some of the finer points.

1. The Definition Step. In most problem-solving discussions the suggestion to take stock of the felt difficulty, to ventilate it fully, is pertinent. It helps take emotional heat, if any, off the topic; it gives a quick audit of feelings (for example, there may be more than one felt difficulty in the group). It helps the group formulate the problem and determine goals.

The first major content aspect is *definition* of the problem and, where pertinent, *limitation* of the problem in terms of agenda. (For example, are we talking about unemployment in Chicago, in Illinois, or in the United States as a whole?) If a group has several different definitions of a problem and, worse yet, isn't aware of the differences, confusion and irritation can be assured. Discussion time is well spent on the definition aspect. Agree on the problem and/or goal *before* you move on.

In some cases a thorough discussion of the problem may make the solution obvious or known from previous identical situations (for example, medical diagnosis). Most often, however, a group is now ready to *analyze* systematically its agreed-upon problem. Agenda suggestions range from fact finding and problem restatement to a systematic determination of the essential *nature* of the problem. *Nature* is typically divided into problems of *fact, policy*, and *value* or, in the Ross system, *puzzle, probability*, and *value*. In the first division the term *fact* appears obvious. Can the phenomenon be empirically verified to the satisfaction of group members? One cantankerous professor claims he never has heard a good definition of a fact. For the most part, facts are actions, events, or conditions that have been properly observed, described, classified, and reported. *Policy* is concerned with the feasibility or desirability of a future course of action. Of course, facts will probably be a part of this kind of deliberation also. Questions of *value* are primarily concerned with judgments about attitudes, beliefs, and feelings—very often those things most difficult to quantify. More will be said about value later.

23John K. Brilhart, "An Experimental Comparison of Three Techniques for Communicating a Problem-Solving Pattern to Members of a Discussion Group," *Speech Monographs*, 33, No. 2 (June 1966) , 176.

POSSIBLE AGENDA SYSTEMS

Dewey	Gulley	Barnlund-Haiman	Harnack-Fest	Ross
1. Felt Difficulty	*ANALYSIS*: Definition	Ventilation	*DESCRIPTION*: Problem Formulation	Definition & Limitation / Felt difficulty / Problem / Goal
2. Definition	Limitation	Clarification	Problem Analysis	
	Important Facts	Fact Finding	Problem Reformation	Analysis—Nature of Problem / Puzzle / Probability / Value
3. Possible Solutions	*SOLUTION*: Alternate Courses of Action	Discovery	*SOLUTION*: Solution Proposal	Establish Criteria / Limits / Hierarchical importance
4. Rational Elaboration	Standards	Evaluation	Solution Testing	
5. Further Testing	Decision	Decision	Action Testing	Solutions / Evaluation against criteria / Decision

FIGURE 12–5. Possible Agenda Systems.

2. *The Analysis Step.*

a. *Puzzles.* In the division under nature of the problem, the *puzzle* dimension refers to questions of *fact* previously discussed, but more than that, it is easier to apply, though it may be less comprehensive. As an illustration, consider a common jigsaw puzzle. No one would argue that a jigsaw puzzle cannot be difficult or frustrating (or amenable to group effort). Yet there is definitely a solution—there is really only one best solution—and, better yet, the solution is recognizable when you achieve it. It *is* the *canals* of Venice! Early detection and agreement on a problem, as on a puzzle, can save much time and aggravation. If someone were to view the jigsaw puzzle as a question of value—perhaps a threat to his intelligence—then the problem would be compounded, the solution probably delayed (getting the puzzle together).

Some puzzles are complicated. Thus, we use computers to solve engineering problems and adding machines and cash registers in supermarkets. But they are still puzzles and one is well advised not to get his emotions, morals, or value system involved too quickly.

b. *Probability.* The *probability* dimension refers to common sense reduced to calculation. The suggestion here is that certain problems are of the nature of a probability calculation. They are then theoretically amenable to probability theory or the laws of chance. While the very nature of the word *probability* indicates that such a problem may never be known with certainty, the mathematical chance or probability itself may often be treated as an operational fact. A gambler can predict his odds with relative certainty. He knows that he has a 50 percent chance of getting a head in flipping a coin. However, even in simple games, determining probability figures can quickly become complicated. If your winning point is 5 in a dice game involving two dice, you have only four possible combinations: 1–4, 4–1, 3–2, and 2–3. Since theoretical probabilities are multiplied (two 6-sided dice give 6×6 or 36 possible combinations) the odds are 4/36 or 1/9. The six combinations yielding the number 7 have a probability of 6/36 or 1/6. The number of rolls is of course a significant variable. The larger the number of rolls, in general, the greater the likelihood of the theoretical probability occurring. All probability and prediction problems are not as theoretically absolute. An insurance company never knows exactly how many accidents, deaths, fires, and so on will occur among its policy holders, but can make quite accurate predictions on the basis of past experiences. This science of probability prediction is called statistics. From statistics we learn not only to ask "what caused the difference" but also how to test whether a change or difference is merely a random variation or indicates some known or unknown factor at work. There are significance tests that make it possible to express the difference on variations mathematically. This expression or number may be interpreted as an indicator of the "level of confidence" we may justifiably have in the data, or our chances of being wrong. Every discussant need not be a statistician, but he should be aware of the nature of probability-type problems and also the role that theory can play in making decisions about problems involving large masses of data.

c. *Values.* The *value* dimension concerns desirability rather than probability or inevitability.

Ethical value structures held by group members are commonly considered as deriving from their past experiences. It is in this light that questions of *ethical* value must, in part, be evaluated.

A person's general value system is determined by his past experiences, by his understanding and acceptance of the concept of law as natural, universal, and/or pragmatic, and by his personal idea of the various continua from good to bad, pleasure to pain, noble to ignoble, loyal to disloyal, as well as by a multitude of minor preferences that often defy any search for principle (for example, food, color, architecture, and so on). With knowledge of the categories indicated above, it is often possible to make fairly reliable nonnumerical predictions and analyses regarding questions of value.

To the extent that preferences and attitudes may be referred to as values, the problem is slightly less ambiguous. It is possible to determine attitudes (a form of preference) in a quantified way about many things, from the size of next year's cars to the latest high fashion innovations. Differences in attitudes toward a given subject can, in fact, be measured fairly accurately through the use of standard statistical techniques described previously.

Knowledge of preferences (of others) pertinent to the group decision in which you are involved affords you predictive insight of a relatively uncomplicated nature. Some value theorists speak of a "rational-preference-ranking,"[24] which is a way of selecting the preferred or most valued alternative. Comparative preferences on like or similar things have been found to be measurable and meaningful. However, the measurement of comparative and/or cumulative preferences for dissimilar things is less amenable to reliable measurement. An "other things being equal" preference for the color red and another similar preference for Cadillacs does not necessarily add up to a preference for red Cadillacs. The further question of whether a person likes the color red better than he likes

[24]Donald Davidson, J. C. C. McKinsey, and Patrick Suppes, "Outlines of a Formal Theory of Value," *Philosophy of Science*, 22 (1955), 140.

Cadillacs, and to what extent, points up a quantification problem that has been a long time bone of contention among social science philosophers.

While the *value* dimension of analysis is the part most resistant to numerical quantification and measurement, this does not mean we should not try to quantify, objectify, and search for systematic analysis. It does mean that we must know our own intelligently derived values and how they may be applied to the group's analysis of a specific problem. It also means that we must make every effort to ascertain differences in preferences and values among the people in our group and also those who may be affected by this group's decision. This kind of analysis should lead to better and more prudent group decisions regarding questions of *value*.

3. The Criteria Step. Whether one thinks of this step as really a continuation of analysis or the beginning of the solution phase is of no great import. It is, however, an important enough agenda item to warrant your close attention. *A criterion is a standard or yardstick by which we may measure or evaluate something.* In the case of group discussion, it refers to an *agreed-upon* standard. If a group has reasonably clear and agreed-upon criteria in mind, the evaluation or testing of suggested solutions is a lot easier or at least more systematic. If a group were discussing the problem of a clubhouse for their organization, they would want to clearly establish such criteria as *cost, size, location, new or old,* and so on. The concept of *limits* can help a group at this point. If we are talking about cost in terms of $100,000, what do we really mean? Is that the top *limit* or the bottom? If the group really meant $75,000 to $110,000, it should so state it, at least to itself. The same could be said for size and location. Criteria can also be negative. The group could, for example, name locations that it would not consider under any conditions.

The concept of *weighting* your criteria in terms of importance should also be considered. If size is the single most important criterion, then get group agreement on that point. Say, for example, that the old clubhouse is crowded; unless the next place is X amount larger, however beautiful a bargain, it won't solve the problem. If location is next most important (that is, say the facilities must be close to where the members live), and then cost, parking, architecture, and so on, you have the beginnings of a sub-agenda for evaluating solutions. Your list of criteria then should appear in some kind of rank or weighted order in terms of importance. *Weighting* may be profitably considered by a group if some of the criteria are close together in importance. Assuming a 100-point weighting scale and the determination that both size and location are very important, the group might assign size 90 points, location 80 points, cost 50 points, architecture 20 points, and so on, along with specific upper and lower limits for each. Such a scale gives the group considerably more insight into the distances between its ranked criteria. Further it gives the group a more logical, systematic approach to the solution step.

4. The Solution Step. To continue the illustration of the clubhouse under the criteria step, the group may now consider solutions that individuals may offer. If David W. offers pictures and real estate data on a building he's found, but an assessment against the criterion of size indicates it does not meet the lower criterion (and no plan for enlargement is provided by the contributor), then the group is quickly and systematically ready to go on to the next possible solution. It is possible that a group may come up with several solutions that meet the major criteria, and the discussion may then focus on the less heavily weighted criteria. This is progress and the group is aware of it. Without stated criteria to go by, the group might engage in lengthy argument over minor aspects of a problem while virtually ignoring the major aspects.

You may wish to discuss and evaluate your alternative solutions further in terms of the puzzle-probability-value analysis suggested. You may wish some additional firsthand observation or action testing, but the group is ready for *decision*.

5. Agenda and Process. The problem-solving, normal thinking, or decision process being recommended as a basis for agenda building should not be construed as a totally linear function in which each step is equally long and/or independent. Groups often find it necessary to overlap or back up as new insight or information comes to light. A spiral model was discussed previously that indicates that while a group is moving toward a solution, it is following a circular course in which members devote one-fourth of their comments to confirming statements already made and another fourth to clarifying and substantiating them.

It is then the nature of process as explained in Chapter 1 not to suddenly freeze or hold still, but rather to be a moving, dynamic phenomenon. Stated agendas have a way of becoming much more static and should be worked out carefully with full consideration of the nature of process.

The same qualifications should be applied to your consideration of the nature of problems as puzzle, probability, and value. No problem is typically 100 percent puzzle; most problems have all three dimensions present. For most cases, after a group has determined the nature of a problem, it is well advised to take up the less controversial puzzle dimension first and the value dimension last. There are exceptions, and this in no way suggests that values are less important than puzzles or probabilities. A person's communication behavior in a group is often qualitatively as well as quantitatively different when he feels his value system is in constant jeopardy.

DISCUSSION LEADERSHIP

In general, *leadership* should be thought of as any significant action by any discussant that has influence on group achievement.[25] We may have an assigned or appointed group *leader* whose duties or behavior may range from a modest regulation of participation to near domination and control. It is possible to be in a *leaderless* group (i.e., one with no appointed leader) and still have considerable *leadership*, should it emerge from the group. By the same token, one could be in a group with a poor assigned *leader*, and, none emerging, have really no *leadership*. The distinction, therefore, between *leader* and *leadership* and *leaderless* and *leadershipless* is a critical one. All group members have a stake and often a role in *leadership*. Thus, what follows applies to all group discussants whether they happen to be assigned group leader, chairman, moderator, or whatever.

Sources of Leadership

Leadership may accrue to a person in a group because he was appointed the moderator. It may accrue to a person if only on given issues because he happens to be the best informed. It may befall a person by reason of his role or status in the group (for example, he happens to be the boss, a full professor, and so on). It may also befall a person, particularly in leaderless groups, who happens to perform vital group functions and procedures exceptionally well: one who knows about agendas, reflective thinking, democratic leadership, the communication process, and interpersonal relations.

Functions of Leadership

Leadership, whatever its source (and all group members have responsibility here), should in general help a group move toward its goal or purpose, or help it locate its goals. Leadership should also promote a healthy, democratic communication climate within the group. The major functions of leadership then are related to *goal achievement* (content), *interpersonal relations* (communication climate), and *procedural functions*.

[25]See especially Barnlund and Haiman, *The Dynamics of Discussion*, ch. 13; and Gulley, *Discussion, Conference and Group Process*, ch. 10.

Goal Achievement. Dimensions of leadership related primarily to content include such things as contributing and evaluating ideas, locating issues and consensus, synthesizing and cross-relating the ideas of others, and generally seeking specific contributions leading to a goal.

Interpersonal Relations. Dimensions of leadership related to these peculiarly human problems include such things as controlling emotions, setting communication and psychological climates, resolving conflict, regulating the over- and undertalkative, and generally promoting those actions concerned with the social and human aspects.

Procedural Functions. Leaders, particularly when assigned or designated, must also attend to the more specifically *practical* functions such as starting the meeting, agenda making and/or following, clarifying, summarizing, and ending the meeting. Procedural functions may also include advanced planning and physical arrangements. The procedural leader must review the purposes of the meeting. He should consider the members individually and decide the degree of formality necessary and the specific way he wishes to open the discussion. He should consider group goals in terms of the time available.

The procedural leader is also responsible for participation, that is, for preserving order, seeing that only one person speaks at a time, and fairly distributing the right to speak. He may find it necessary to clarify what has been said on occasion as well as remind the group of the agreed-upon agenda. The agenda should be agreed upon by the members unless it is already prescribed.

Styles of Leadership

Style refers in part to method and in part to philosophy. Some styles of leadership are variously described as laissez-faire, nondirective, permissive, democratic, supervisory, authoritarian, and autocratic. The styles in Figure 12–6 are ordered on a control continuum from "none" to "much."[26]

As with most things, virtue is near the middle. Everything said so far about discussion advises that a *democratic* style is superior to a highly autocratic or near "abdication of responsibility" style. This is not to say, however, that in some group situations where *goal achievement* becomes unusually pressing, leadership should not go up the scale when it will help. Most union-management discussions are cooperative negotiations. On the other hand, to achieve sincerely healthy *interpersonal*

[26]See also Gulley, *Discussion, Conference and Group Process*, p. 179.

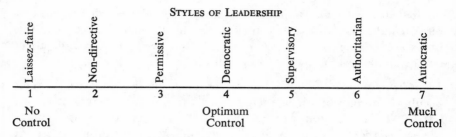

FIGURE 12-6.

relations, particularly when emotions are strained or personalities are in conflict, it may be advisable to go down the scale.

An interesting study by Simons indicates that the more participative patterns or styles of deliberation, even with relatively large groups (fifteen to twenty), were more productive in problem-solving discussion than the more formal patterns.[27]

Communication Climate

A healthy group communication climate might be described as a *cohesive* environment in which the discussants through *interaction* achieve a mental state of relative psychological safety and freedom. According to Shepherd[28] *cohesion* refers to the forces that bind members of a group, the degree of closeness and warmth they feel for one another, their pride as members, their willingness to be frank and honest in their expression of ideas and feelings, and their ability to meet emergencies and crises that may confront them as a group.

Interaction refers to the type and degree of communication behavior directed toward another person or persons when their reaction or reciprocal behavior is taken into account. It pertains directly to one's interpersonal responsibilities in group discussion.

For Carl Rogers[29] psychological safety involves being accepted as an individual of some worth, operating in a climate where one is not persistently evaluated as a person, and being able to understand (and be understood) empathically, that is, from the other person's point of view. Psychological freedom involves group facilitation of a person's symbolic expression, an openness to communicate concepts and meanings.

---

[27]Herbert W. Simons, "Representative Versus Participative Patterns of Deliberation in Large Groups," *Quarterly Journal of Speech*, 52, No. 2 (April 1966), 164–71.

[28]Clovis R. Shepherd, *Small Groups: Some Sociological Perspectives* (San Francisco: Chandler Publishing Company, 1964) p. 26.

[29]See Carl R. Rogers, *On Becoming a Person* (Boston: Houghton Mifflin Company, 1961) pp. 356–59.

This healthy communication climate should also include facilitating situations and facilitating people. It should be a climate where a person's status is not unreasonably threatened, where he feels accepted as a person, where he has the freedom to be wrong and the freedom to participate based on involvement. This is not a bad communication climate for all matters of learning and personal growth and development.

Congruence is a term by which Rogers meant a matching of experience, awareness, and communication.[30] Rogers's general law of interpersonal relationships is useful to us. While it describes a two-person relationship, the wisdom is equally pertinent to small groups. For Rogers it is the perception of the receiver of communication that is most crucial.

> The greater of the congruence of experience, awareness, and communication on the part of one individual, the more [his] ensuing relationship will involve: a tendency toward reciprocal communication with a quality of increasing congruence; a tendency toward more mutually accurate understanding of communications; improved psychological adjustment and functioning in both parties; mutual satisfaction in the relationship.
>
> Conversely the greater communicated incongruence of experience and awareness, the more ensuing relationship will involve: further communication with the same quality; disintegration of accurate understanding, less adequate psychological adjustment and functioning in both parties; and mutual dissatisfaction in the relationship.[31]

Participant Responsibilities

In addition to the general climate-setting responsibilities for which all participants are accountable, certain more specific participant responsibilities may be described.

Sattler and Miller suggest desirable role descriptions for participants who would help promote the group and its goals:[32]

Encourager	Standard Setter
Harmonizer	Group Observer
Compromiser	Follower
Gate Keeper (opens channels of communication)	

They also suggest roles that have a negative effect:

Aggressor (deflates status of others)	Playboy
Blocker (opposes beyond reason)	Dominator
Recognition Seeker	Help Seeker
Self-Confessor	Special Interest Pleader

30Ibid., p. 339.
31Ibid., pp. 344–45.
32William M. Sattler and N. Edd Miller, *Discussion and Conference* (Englewood Cliffs, N.J.: Prentice-Hall, Inc., 1968) pp. 330–46.

Participants as well as leaders have an interpersonal responsibility whenever these situations arise:

One or two members dominate
Some members will not talk
Some apparently lack interest
Discussion drifts to irrelevant matters
Conflict occurs between members
Discussion "techniques" backfire

Sattler and Miller conclude that the good participant should, in general, "(1) use tact, (2) be enthusiastic, (3) exhibit a sense of humor, (4) be cooperative, (5) minimize differences that exist between him and others, (6) be friendly, (7) identify with the group's goals, (8) consider the rewards of group membership, (9) interact, and (10) work to make the group successful."[33]

In this context Shepherd concludes, "The definition of a successful group is a group with high cohesion and high productivity, in which objectives, role differentiation, values and norms, and membership criteria are clear and agreed upon, and in which communication is open and full."[34]

OBSERVING AND EVALUATING DISCUSSION

One of the most popular observational schemes for small-group research was developed by Bales. The system involves a classification of communicative acts where act is defined as verbal and nonverbal behavior. It is called "Interaction Process Analysis." Bales divides an observer's duties into three areas, first the positive social-emotional acts, then the "task" acts, and thirdly, the negative social-emotional acts. A modified outline of the system follows (see Figure 12–7).

A tabulating of acts by observers in various research studies (typically college students) indicates an average group profile of 25 percent positive reactions (A), 56 percent attempted answers (B), 7 percent questions (C), and 12 percent negative reactions (D). As Shepherd stated, "The portrait is of a group in which most of the discussion involves expressing *opinions* and *information* and conveying *agreement,* with occasional expressions of disagreement and tension release (such as joking) and occasional requests for *information* and *opinion.*"[35] A relatively simple and

[33]Ibid., p. 312.
[34]Shepherd, *Small Groups,* p. 124.
[35]Shepherd, *Small Groups,* p. 32.

Major Categories	Subcategories	Illustrative Statements or Behavior
Social Emotional Area A. Positive (and Mixed) Reactions	1. Seems friendly	Jokes, gives help, rewards others, is friendly
	2. Dramatizes	Laughs, shows satisfaction, is relieved
	3. Agrees	Passively accepts, understands, concurs, complies
Task Area B. Attempted Answers	4. Gives suggestion	Directs, suggests, implies autonomy for others
	5. Gives opinion	Evaluates, analyzes, expresses feeling or wish
	6. Gives information	Orients, repeats, clarifies, confirms
C. Questions	7. Asks for information	Requests orientation, repetition, confirmation
	8. Asks for opinion	Requests evaluation, analysis, expression of feeling
	9. Asks for suggestion	Requests direction, possible ways of action
Social Emotional Area D. Negative (and Mixed) Reactions	10. Disagrees	Passively rejects, resorts to formality, withholds help
	11. Shows tension	Asks for help, withdraws, daydreams
	12. Seems unfriendly	Deflates other's status, defends or asserts self, hostile

Reciprocal or Opposite Pairs

a b c d e f

Key: a. Problems of Communication
b. Problems of Evaluation
c. Problems of Control
d. Problems of Decision
e. Problems of Tension Reduction
f. Problems of Reintegration

FIGURE 12-7. Categories for Interaction Process Analysis.[36]

[36]Based on Robert F. Bales, *Interaction Process Analysis* (Cambridge, Mass.: Addison-Wesley Press, 1950), p. 9; A. Paul Hare, *Handbook of Small Group Research* (New York: The Free Press of Glencoe, 1962), p. 66; and Robert F. Bales, *Personality and Interpersonal Behavior* (New York: Holt, Rinehart and Winston, Inc., 1970), pp. 91-97.

self-explanatory general discussion rating form for observing participants is shown in Figure 12–8.

Observing and evaluating discussion can also be approached in terms of diagraming the participation. These chartings are referred to as sociograms and may provide graphic insights into group behavior. One can simply tabulate the number and length of contributions or the contributions according to categories or types as Bales does, for example. One

---

DISCUSSION EVALUATION FORM—WSU

1-2-3	4-5-6	7-8-9
Weak	Average	Strong

Criteria for Evaluating Discussion Participation Include the Following:

A. Information about the problem. (Breadth, accuracy, and use of information.)
B. Analysis of the problem. (Sensing problem's importance; finding the issues; avoiding irrelevant matters.)
C. Ability to think cooperatively. (Open-mindedness; alertness; willingness to abandon weak arguments; ability to synthesize the contributions of others.)
D. Skill in speaking. (Adapting voice, action, and language to the occasion; ability to state ideas clearly and briefly.)
E. Good manners. (Listening attentively; quoting others accurately; giving others a chance to speak; general courtesy.)
F. General overall effectiveness.

	1	2	3	4	5	6	7	8	9	10	11
Project											
Class Hour											
Date											
A. Information											
B. Analysis											
C. Cooperative Thinking											
D. Speaking Skill											
E. Good Manners											
F. Overall Effect											
Total Scores											
Rank Order of Participants											

General Comments on the Group as a Whole (Use back of sheet as needed):

FIGURE 12–8.

can also draw circles on a piece of paper representing the discussants and then with lines and arrows diagram the flow and amount of interpersonal communication. One can often find graphic evidence to show to the overtalkative.

SUMMARY

The unique aspect of discussion is that a participant is both sender-receiver and encoder-decoder at the same time. It is a dynamic, interactive, interpersonal communication situation. If decision is impossible through discussion, it may very well lead to debate. Debate is competitive and two-sided, discussion cooperative and many-sided. A discussion-debate continuum is shown.

A small group is a dynamic grouping, while an audience is typically passive. If one considers small-group discussion in terms of subgroups and transactional loops, he quickly sees why "two's company, three's a crowd." Generalizations regarding coacting small groups include these: (1) groups can change attitudes and behavior; (2) a group's consensus judgment tends to be better than individual judgment; (3) consensus groups may develop a strong feeling of personal involvement; and (4) cooperative group communication can be taught.

Assuming a real group—that is, persons with a common goal, not just a loose collection of individuals—we can define group discussion as *systematic, cooperative, reflective thinking* and *communication*.

Group discussion involves a cooperative thinking endeavor among twenty people or less. The basic forms are *dialogue, panel,* and *symposium*. Three techniques that may be used in combination with any of the forms include the *buzz group, role playing,* and *brainstorming*. A *forum* is simply that part of a discussion in which the audience may speak.

Discussion forms may be used for information sharing, problem solving and instruction. Information-sharing groups include staff meetings, study groups, and workshops. Problem-solving groups include committees, conferences, and boards or councils. Instructional formats include case conferences, role playing, and to some extent all of the forms and techniques.

Systematic inquiry and maintaining an intelligent state of doubt are the essentials of reflective thinking. There are five steps in the Dewey system: (1) felt difficulty, (2) definition, (3) possible solutions, (4) rational elaboration, and (5) further testing or corroborating. One four-step adaptation involves (1) *definition*, (2) *analysis* as puzzle, probability, and value, (3) establishing *criteria*, and (4) the *solution* step. Discussion is a dynamic phenomenon that may be more circular than linear in function as a group moves. Modern research suggests three phases in problem-solving discussions. Phase one involves orientation, information, repetition, and confirmation. Phase two involves analysis, evaluation, and expressions, the seeking or giving of opinions and feelings. Phase three involves controlling possible directions and ways of action. Five agenda systems thought to creatively reflect and synthesize the literature are shown.

Leadership should be thought of as any significant action by any discussant that has significant influence on group achievement. It is possible to have no appointed leader and still have leadership; the reverse is also true. The distinction between *leader* and *leadership*, and *leaderless* and *leadershipless*, is a critical one. All group members have a stake and often a role in leadership.

Leadership may accrue to a person through designation, through his information, because of his status, or through his ability in performing vital group functions. The major functions of leadership are related to *goal achievement* and *interpersonal relations*. Leadership, particularly when designated, must also attend to the *procedural* functions.

Procedural functions may include planning, physical arrangements, purposes, degree of formality, goal setting, and considerations of agenda. The procedural leader is also responsible for general participation control and preserving order. Styles of leadership may be described as autocratic, authoritarian, supervisory, democratic, permissive, nondirective, and laissez-faire. The democratic style is recommended.

A healthy group communication climate is described as a cohesive environment in which discussants achieve a mental state of psychological safety and freedom. Interaction involves reciprocal communication between members and pertains to interpersonal responsibilities. Congruence means a matching of experience, awareness, and communication. Rogers's law of interpersonal relationships suggests that with congruence comes more mutually accurate understanding, improved psychological adjustment and functioning, and a more satisfying relationship. Other specific participant responsibilities are described.

Interaction process analysis is an observational system that classifies verbal and nonverbal behavior as communicative acts. An observer's duties are divided into three major areas: positive social-emotional acts, task acts, and negative social-emotional acts. Twelve subcategories for analysis are shown.

A successful group discussion is the product of an interacting, reflective group of people with goals, systematic leadership, high cohesion, high productivity, and cooperative interpersonal communication.

Speech Communication Principles

1. Small-group discussion is essential to the success of a democratic society.

2. We discuss and interact for social and emotional reasons as well as to divide up the logical work of society.

3. Some people find it more difficult to interact in small groups than in larger ones.

4. Discussion is systematic, cooperative thinking and communication.

5. A co-acting group involves some common purpose and some interaction between members.

6. Our own sense of interpersonal responsibilities and behavior, as it relates to our status in a small group, greatly affects our interaction.

7. Successful interaction involves the style, kind and amount of communication directed toward another person or persons when their reaction or reciprocal behavior is taken into account.

8. Three- to seven-member groups constitute something quite different interpersonally and transactionally from two alone.

9. Co-acting small groups have considerable impact upon individual behavior and attitude.

10. Once their members achieve consensus, small groups, more than larger audiences, develop a feeling of personal involvement and responsibility for the solution.

11. Group conclusions and attitudes tend to be held more persistently than similar conclusions arrived at individually.

12. Orderly discussion tends toward more consensus than that not guided by any system or agenda.

13. A healthy skepticism, a conviction to systematic inquiry, and an attitude of suspended judgment are essentials of cooperative communication (as well as scientific habit).

14. An agenda based on the reflective thinking steps represents more a spiraling progression than a simple linear progression.

15. Leadership is any significant action by any discussant that has influence on group achievement.

16. The major functions of leadership are related to goal achievement, interpersonal relations, and procedural matters.

17. For most small-group discussions a democratic style of leadership is superior to a highly autocratic or laissez-faire style.

18. A healthy group climate is a cohesive one in which discussants, through interaction, achieve a mental state of relative psychological safety and freedom.

A. *General Learning Outcomes*

   1. We should learn the nature of dynamic small-group discussion.

   2. We should learn that cooperative communication is an act essential to success in a democratic society.

   3. We should learn the contemporary forms of discussion and know when they are applicable.

   4. We should learn about the reflective thinking process and its relationship to discussion agendas.

   5. We should learn to distinguish among the various types and functions of leadership.

   6. We should learn to develop our powers as critics of communication in small groups.

B. *Specific Learning Outcomes*

   1. We should learn the nature of a discussion-debate continuum.

   2. We should be able to define the co-acting group and the related concepts of cohesion and interaction.

   3. We should learn of the complexity of interpersonal, cooperative group communication in terms of transactional loops and sub-group relationships.

   4. We should learn the classic definitions of discussion and its contemporary forms.

   5. We should learn the five steps in the reflective thinking process described by John Dewey and be able to relate them to problem solving and specific discussion agendas.

6. We should learn the essential differences between "goal," "interpersonal," and "procedural" leadership.

7. We should learn about the leadership control continuum in terms of styles of leadership.

8. We should learn the role of communication climate in fostering cohesion and useful interaction.

9. We should learn of participant responsibilities, recognizing those roles that promote group goals and those that do not.

10. We should learn the criteria to apply as an observer and critic of discussion.

11. We should be able to relate the foregoing general and specific learning outcomes to the speech communication principles above.

C. *Communication Competencies.*

1. We should be able to participate knowledgeably and responsibly in the major contemporary forms of group discussion.

2. We should be able to recognize the difference between a co-acting small group and a simple collection of people.

3. We should have and be able to apply a knowledge of procedural leadership in group discussion exercises.

4. We should develop a sensitivity to and an ability in interpersonal or social-emotional dimensions of group leadership.

5. We should be able to develop systematic agendas pertinent to the goals or tasks of a given discussion group.

6. We should learn to "play the scale" of leadership styles and still remain an essentially democratic leader during short discussion projects.

7. We should learn to evaluate group participation through the IPA and WSU systems shown in this chapter (see pp. 333 and 334).

8. We should be able to set up various participant configurations to accommodate the major contemporary forms of discussion.

D. *Study Projects and Tasks*

1. After being assigned to a group of three to six, pick one of the following problems and prepare for a ten to fifteen minute panel discussion in which you spend the first two to three minutes setting an agenda and the remaining time following it toward a problem solution. (See the suggestions of veteran teachers after problem *f*.)

a. You are in the freshman year of a medical school in which the lowest third of the class will be cut after final examinations. Before the exams you accidentally overhear a good friend of yours who is inferior to you academically and who you suspect has cheated before make plans to cheat on the finals. Your standing might be endangered and there isn't a formal honor system at the school. You also realize that it would be difficult to prove any accusations after the exams.

You should:

(1). Ignore it.

(2). Talk to him about your feelings.

(3). Report him formally to the proper authorities.

(4). Ask other students their opinions on the matter using fictitious names.

(5). Write an anonymous letter to your friend or to the proper authorities.

b. While shopping in a grocery store, a customer noticed one of the cashiers taking money from the cash register. Startled by the incident, the customer rushed to the manager and reported what he had seen. The manager could not decide how to approach the situation at that particular moment. Finally he decided that the best approach would be to:

(1). Go to the cashier and tell her she is fired.

(2). Investigate the matter to be certain the customer had reported accurately.

(3). Call the union to report the incident.

(4). Have someone stand and watch the girl to guard against a recurrence.

(5). Assure the customer and forget it.

c. One of your instructors, who has tenure, appears to be an alcoholic. He keeps coming to class somewhat drunk and because of his drinking misses 25 percent of all class meetings. Most of the students like him, and he is a qualified instructor. The material is taught if the students want it, but they end up getting most of it from the textbook. The instructor doesn't push his students and gives just one test during the semester.

Your success in future courses in this field depends on how well you grasp the material and basics in this course. Your course of action should be to:

(1). Go straight to the dean and ask that disciplinary action be taken against the professor.

(2). Drink with your professor in order to get a good grade in his class.

(3). Take some action in the form of boycotting his class and trying to get the other students to do the same. This way you would draw attention to the situation.

(4). Talk to the professor and explain your feelings and ask for an explanation.

(5). Inform the department chairman of your suspicions after checking with other students.

d. George Tuffguy is a student in Ms. Smith's tenth-grade classroom. It seems George is fairly intelligent but doesn't care about school and spends his time getting into trouble. Miss Smith has investigated his home situation and found two alcoholic, uncaring parents. She wants to establish George's trust and hopes he will do better.

Today when she was leaving school George backed her against the wall with a switchblade. There is a school regulation that prohibits the carrying of a switchblade in the school at any time. She feels he is testing her to see what she will do. What should Miss Smith do?

(1). Tell George that if he puts the knife away and doesn't bring it back to school she won't report him.

(2). Report George for breaking the school regulation.

(3). Ignore the situation, hoping that the evident lack of interest will induce him to get rid of the knife.

(4). Threaten to report him if he brings the knife back to school.

(5). Call the police.

e. Mrs. Smith is not a busybody, but she has herself in a pinch and does not want to be labeled "neighborhood busybody." One day as she was shopping she came across Johnny Barker, age sixteen, trying to sell pot to a group of his peers. She has known the Barkers for about five years and has great respect for them. She is undecided if she should take any action. She should:

(1). Forget having seen Johnny.

(2). Go to the Barker residence and tell Mrs. Barker what she saw.

(3). Persuade a neighbor to tell Mrs. Barker.

(4). Mail Mrs. Barker an anonymous note informing her of Johnny's activities.

(5). Tell Johnny she knows about it and attempt to persuade him to quit doing it.

f. Your daughter Mildred, a sixteen-year-old, announces that she has been asked to go to the high-school Junior Prom at the country club, with breakfast to follow at 6:00 A.M. at a classmate's house.

Assuming that Mildred asks your permission to go in a pleasant manner, what should be your response as a parent?

(1). Yes, but with a warning.

(2). A flat no.

(3). No, and describe the undesirable experiences she might get herself into.

(4). Let Mildred make her own decision.

(5). Get more information before helping Mildred decide.

After observing several hundred similar short panel discussions, veteran teachers advanced the following conclusions. These may alert you to potential problems or faults in your own sessions.

    a. Vocal subgroups often developed.

    b. Seating was often awkward and dysfunctional.

    c. Leaders were seldom appointed or voted upon.

    d. Time was not always well budgeted.

    e. Systematic discussion was infrequent.

    f. Some group members were allowed to dominate the discussions.

    g. Some members should have been drawn out more frequently.

    h. Initial agreement often was not challenged.

    i. Language was often too absolute and unqualified for the type of question involved.

    j. With a few exceptions, the group thinking was relatively nonrigid in character.

    k. The participants seemed to enjoy their work.

    l. The preferred answer was generally accepted as intelligent after discussion by the entire class.

    m. The groups were primarily interested in answers—not the problems.

    n. For some this appeared to be a new experience in nonrigid thinking.

2. Select a class discussion project on a social issue of some consequence that is suitable for two or three days of research. Word it as a question, prepare a one-hour agenda, select a procedural leader, do your research, and prepare for class discussion(s). You may use combinations of the various forms of discussion. Some topics of general interest are:

Abortion	Fraternities and sororities	Gambling
Narcotics	Changing morals	Population
Black power	Lotteries	Euthanasia
Welfare	Censorship	Prostitution
Sex education	Crime	Black studies
Medicare	Capital punishment	Quarter system
Birth control	Bussing	Communal living
Gun laws	Transportation	S.D.S.
Pollution	Prisons	Nudism
Advertising	Amnesty	Ecumenism
Pornography	Homosexuality	Big cities
Racism	Gerontology	

3. Study the content of the model speech in the appendix. Use it as a springboard and resource for a general discussion on the topic "What role should communication theory and technology play in a democracy (whether representative or participatory) by the beginning of the twenty-first century?"

4. Observe a discussion group and chart the flow of communica-

tion among the participants. Use arrows for direction, one for each substantive comment (i.e., other than a simple exclamation or "yes" or "no" answer). A sample model is shown in Figure 12–9. Discuss what it says about individual participants.

5. Observe the people very carefully in your next informal out-of-class co-acting group interaction and make note of those actions and communications typical of a person exercising social-emotional or interpersonal relations leadership (those things that help hold a group together apart from the procedures and the topic [task] itself).

6. Consider the differences between preparing for discussion and for a more formal speech. What is the same? What is different? Which is easier? Be prepared to discuss the issue in class.

7. Observe a radio or television discussion and attempt to classify the various leadership styles that emerge (e.g., goal achievement, interpersonal relations, procedural). Be alert for changing styles by the participants. Assess their effectiveness.

8. Prepare a two- to three-minute speech on a class-selected topic, and be ready to deliver it in a symposium format. Be further prepared for a panel discussion with the symposium members and for a possible open forum with the audience.

9. Write up a two- to three-page report of an out-of-class "contemporary form of discussion" you have observed or in which

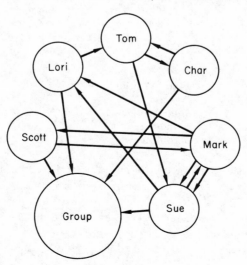

FIGURE 12–9. A Sample Sociogram.

you were involved, and evaluate it according to Bales's system, illustrated on page 333.

10. After the discussion unit is completed, write a three-page personal, introspective report about your own interpersonal communication attitudes and behaviors. What have you learned about yourself as a participant in cooperative communication?

11. Prepare an oral report or study attempting to prove or disprove any of the speech communication principles listed earlier.

Chapter Thirteen

Audience Participation Situations

QUESTIONS AND INTERRUPTIONS

One of the most elementary mistakes a speaker or panelist can make is to assume that everyone in his audience has heard and understood a question asked of him. To listen to answers without knowing the question is the epitome of frustration for most listeners. In this chapter you will learn about the principles and methods of dealing with questions and interruptions. The problem of generating and controlling audience participation will also be discussed.

In a sense every speech situation represents at least potential audience participation. Questions, comments, and objections from the audience may come at any time. You should always calculate the risk of being interrupted or even heckled. Some speakers seem to ask for trouble by pleading with the audience to interrupt for any reason whatsoever. A very large audience of perhaps hundreds can be a real nightmare if there is no prearranged system of handling questions. The Economic Club of Detroit has the audience (800–1,000) turn in written questions that are screened for duplication, relevance, pointedness, and so on while the speaker is still on the platform. Of course, there are situations when you do wish immediate audience participation, as with some discussion groups or small-group teaching situations. Although one should be

democratic and audience-centered, the formal speaker also has an obligation to cover his subject and stay within his allotted time. Unreasonable
questions and interruptions have ruined many an otherwise good speech
and have shaken many an experienced speaker. The solution to the
general problem is in the word *control*. The speaker has to stay in control
of the communication situation. He must control the audience participation so as not to do injustice to the *audience,* the *material* to be
covered, or the *time* restrictions placed upon his speech.

Most business communication and training programs involve a great
deal of audience participation. This is as it should be, for educational
psychology teaches us that people learn faster and better when they have
a feeling of participation and involvement. The audience, particularly
in training programs, is typically invited to interrupt the speaker or
teacher. If, however, the speaker chases after every question, relevant or
not, he will soon be in serious trouble.

A well-known businessman came to an Institute of Industrial Relations training program as a guest instructor. He was an expert in his
field, an above-average speaker, and a genuinely nice person. He was
given nearly two hours to cover his subject. After a ten-minute break,
he was to be followed by another expert whose subject matter demanded
that the class be exposed to the previous speaker's material. The situation was similar to an advanced course in algebra making more sense
if the teacher in the first course covered *all* the preliminary material and
did his job thoroughly. Our man pleaded sincerely for interruptions and
got them—some good, some bad, some ridiculous, but he tried to react,
answer, or comment on each equally. The result was that he was unfair
to his audience collectively. The audience's evaluation of him reflected
this fact. He covered only one-fourth of his material, and even this part
was confused because of the virtual free-for-all participation. Imagine
the problem faced by the next speaker!

Another situation in which you may find yourself is the more typical
open forum after a speech. The problems indicated previously all apply
here, but perhaps to a lesser degree. This is true because you have much
better control of your time and you have probably covered the points
you set out to cover. Whatever time is left is controlled by simply cutting
off the questions. Life can be miserable, however, when you are given
three hours and have only one hour's material. It is just as bad when you
have no time for a promised question period.

The third typical audience situation is the symposium forum. Any
discussion situation obviously involves participation with the *other*
members of the group. However, a symposium forum typically allows
one-third of the total time for questions from the general audience.
Many convention programs are run this way. The rules and problems

once again are similar to the two situations previously discussed, except that often a decision must be made as to which participant should respond. The respondent must now consider both the audience and his fellow panel members. The size of the audience is once again a key factor. If a larger audience than expected appears (say, 100 instead of 35), the moderator might have the panelists ask one another questions first, thereby assuring some intelligent questions. Audience size alone may intimidate members from asking questions.

GENERAL PRINCIPLES

The *first* principle obviously ought to be "Know your subject and audience." If you know your subject and audience, you are in a position to apply the *second* principle, "Second-guess the situation." Try to guess what areas of your subject are most vulnerable to questions and try to predict what questions this particular audience will ask. *Third,* "Sincerely try to answer or at least react to all questions." Consider and react courteously to even the irrelevant questions and attempt, if necessary, to clarify, delay, or postpone. The *fourth* principle, and one very easy to overlook in your eagerness to meet the question asked, is "Carefully consider the rest of the audience." You not only must try to satisfy the person asking the question, but the total audience as well. You might satisfy the statistician while thoroughly confusing everybody else. *Fifth,* "Do not feel or act as if you have to know everything or win every argument." Finally, *sixth,* "Attempt to encourage good questions and audience participation." It is very easy to discourage questions by even a slightly overbearing attitude (unless you are so overbearing that the audience decides to interrogate you).

People who assume leadership constantly have to be on guard not to intimidate others simply because of their position or rank. The colonel who follows the manual's advice and asks the cadets, "Are there any dumb questions?" is not apt to get many. But he knew that; that was why he said it! When such an attitude is *not* intended, it is even more tragic. A training director for a large corporation sincerely asked the trainees to comment on the meals during their three-week session. He had prefaced his request with some funny stories about the "idiot club" that had registered all kinds of silly complaints during the last session. Most of the complaints *were* silly and even funny. The training director did not mean to intimidate anyone, and the trainees did think the anecdotes were funny. Nevertheless, because of the prefatory remarks not a word was said about the meals, despite numerous private bitter complaints about the food and the preselected menus! The tragic part is that not only did the director fail to get accurate feedback information but the lack of response was in itself taken as an indication of satis-faction. This is how you can be 100 percent wrong, but, worse, this un-fortunate lack of communication can be reinforced and may become habitual.

RULES FOR ANSWERING QUESTIONS

Years ago at Purdue University, an audience of about four hundred stu-dents was listening to a famous philosopher speak. He did a creditable job for a person who came from a school where speech communication was not in the catalogue. At the close of the speech the chairman asked for questions from the audience. Most of the raised hands were in the first row, where the philosophy club had gathered. The speaker pointed to a hand in the first row, a mouth opened, and to those near the middle of the audience the question sounded like this: "I should zzum ug ask hrump zud Hegel?" The speaker moved to the lectern, stroked his chin, and said, "A very good question." He then proceeded to give what was probably a very good answer. The problem was that most of the audi-ence did not know the question because they had not *heard* it. The speaker handled three or four more questions in the same manner, the audience becoming frustrated, then restless, and finally in some cases rude as they started to leave.

Repeat the questions is the first rule. This is a good idea even with smaller audiences, for though the members are in a position to hear, they may not be listening. Another serious aspect of this all-too-common error is that people will attempt to reconstruct what the question must have been in terms of the answer. You can immediately see the invitation to confused communication that this represents. Counter-questions based on inaccurately reconstructed questions can really raise confusion to a high level.

You may hear a question that is asked in a loud, clear voice, but the wording is awkward or ambiguous. A famous army general was giving a speech at the Ohio State University during the time of the Suez crisis. In the large audience were foreign students from all of the countries involved, including the United Arab Republic, France, England, and Israel. One of these took the general to task in perfectly clear and audible English, except that the question was long, complicated, and included a short preamble and peroration. The general said, "I know what you're getting at," and proceeded to answer for about ten minutes. As the general completed his answer, the foreign student leaped to his feet and proceeded to give another short speech, which said in effect, "But that's not what I asked." The general tried again for five minutes this time, still with no success. After one more unsuccessful attempt, a desperate general finally held up his hand and said, "Let's see if we can agree on what the question is." Sometimes it is necessary not only to repeat but also to *rephrase the questions*. Along with rephrasing, one should always gain the approval of the inquisitor or questioner. Some ways of checking the adequacy of your restatement of the question are to ask the questioner if your phrasing is a fair statement of the question, to look at the person and see if he is shaking his head yes or no, or to pause a moment and see if he objects verbally. You do not always have to rephrase questions; only do so when it is necessary for clarity, and then always seek approval.

Some of the long, complicated questions discussed above deserve careful attention if they are pertinent to the issue and if you are capable of giving some kind of answer or reaction in the time available. When, however, you receive questions which, long or short, are irrelevant, demand a highly technical or complex answer, or would consume all the open-forum time, you have a different kind of problem. Though in principle you do not want to avoid questions, you also owe it to the rest of your audience to stay on the subject and to give more than one person a chance to ask a question. Such a question can ruin an otherwise good speech. Let us therefore formulate our third rule: *delay or postpone the irrelevant, overly technical, or time-consuming questions*. Postpone these questions until after the official open-forum period or until the end of the period if you have time remaining. In interruption situations this rule takes on even more complexity, for a person may ask a question that you had intended to cover later on in the speech. In this situation you should most often delay the answer until you get to that point (for example, "Could I hold the answer to that for a few minutes? I will cover the issue a little later.") The problem is trying to remember the questions you may have delayed or postponed. One solution is to suggest that he ask the question again, but after you've covered the point at issue.

The loaded question (see p. 298) is also a danger here. People will sometimes deliberately ask the "Are you still beating your wife?" kind of question, but far more difficult are the unintended, often naive questions that are loaded. These are difficult to detect because they are often subtle and naive at the same time and are frequently asked by people who are not troublemakers by reputation. "Why is it that textbook writers have such insatiable egos?" an author was once asked. If you are a writer, try to answer that without condemning yourself! Thus, rule four is, *label a loaded question*. There are several ways to do this if you are lucky enough to detect it in time. The most effective way is to pause long enough for the audience to label it for you. An audience is often quick to chuckle if they see the speaker faced with a "heads I win, tails you lose" situation. Or the speaker could forthrightly say, "That's a loaded question." A more tactful way might be, "It looks like I'm in trouble no matter how I answer this." Another method of labeling is to ask the questioner to please repeat his question. The audience will listen more closely and may label it for you, or the questioner may "unload" it. After you have successfully labeled or unloaded the question in as courteous a way as possible, you should then attempt to answer. With the proper labels applied, the audience is not apt to go too far astray in terms of your answer.

The surest way to get in trouble in an open-forum period is to try to bluff your way through a question for which you honestly do not have a good or satisfactory answer. Once an audience senses that you are bluffing, you can expect them to ask more questions specifically on this bluff point. The solution is to know your subject thoroughly—but if you do not have an answer, say so right away and save yourself the embarrassment of being trapped later on. No speaker is expected to have all the answers to all the questions in the world. This rule, then, might simply be called the *"I don't know"* rule.

A graduate student once learned the preceding advice the hard way. It was the occasion of his final oral examination. The committee of examining professors was seated in a circle, ready to fire questions for the next two hours. The very first question was a highly theoretical and complex one that not even the members of the committee could adequately answer (if indeed it was answerable at all). The candidate, under great emotional pressure, felt that he simply had to answer the first question. He stumbled and fumbled for ten minutes, and a narrow-eyed committee then proceeded to ask ever increasingly specific questions on the same point. After another twenty minutes of torture, the candidate finally blurted out, "I guess I just don't know the answer." The rejoinder from the chairman of the examining committee is worthy of a piece of marble: "We didn't expect you to answer the question, but we expected you to *know when you didn't know.* It is a wise man who knows when and what he doesn't know." The candidate was summarily failed.

However, you cannot escape the hard facts of life by simple saying, "I don't know." In some question-answer situations, you may wish to say, "I don't know, but I have an opinion," or "I don't know, but I can answer in terms of my specialty." The point is that you should answer any question you are capable of answering and yet be honest enough to admit it when you cannot supply an answer.

GENERATING PARTICIPATION

In the general principles discussed previously, the last suggestion was to encourage feedback and questions. The dangers of letting an audience run off with your speech were illustrated, as were the dangers of in-advertently intimidating an audience to the point of no participation.

Your general and total speech personality has much to do with the kind of communication climate in which you find yourself. In some cases audiences just seem to spring into action. In other cases, even for very adept and audience-sensitive speakers, they must be given the proper stimulus for participation. Here are several speaker-originated techniques that might be useful to you.

The Overhead Question

This is a question directly from the speaker or discussion leader to the entire audience. If no questions arise from the audience (or even if they do), you might say, "Let me ask this question to get a reaction from an intelligent Midwestern audience." The immediate problem is to make sure you choose a question that will cause a reaction, for if there is silence you may be worse off than before. Sometimes you can react to your own question in such a way as to promote participation. Carefully consider the wording of a few general overhead questions and expected reactions as a method of fostering participation.

The Direct Question

This technique involves choosing a specific member of the audience and directly asking him a question. This is often very effective if the in-dividual listener is known to the rest of the audience or is in some special way qualified to answer. The size of your audience presents a problem insofar as the audience may have difficulty seeing or otherwise deter-mining who has been singled out. Classroom-size audiences or larger groups, if they meet regularly, respond well to this technique. You probably know many good teachers who make excellent use of the direct-question technique. Social and civic groups such as the Lions, Elks, Kiwanis, Knights of Columbus, and Rotary, where the members know one another, often make good use of direct questions.

Try not to call on the same person all the time, but do pick those who are most apt to get participation started. Try to tailor the question directly to the individual chosen. The question should be relatively short and clear and should avoid a simple yes or no answer—but if the situation is really desperate, you may have to settle for yes or no.

The Redirected Question

This technique may also be referred to as the reverse or relay method. However, there are some simple differences. In the reverse technique you simply redirect the question to the person who asked it. "That's a very good question—how would you answer it?" In the relay method you redirect it to some other person. "A good question; let's see how Mr. Wright would answer it." You might, of course, overhead the question to the whole audience.

There are some guideposts that are useful. As a general rule, do not redirect a question unless you yourself know some partial answer to it, except a simple question of fact upon which you can freely admit ignorance. The story of the beginning teacher who redirected a tough question (to which she did not have the answer) to each individual of the class, only to find that it came right back to embarrass her, is not entirely contrived. A second suggestion is to not redirect so freely that you lose control of the situation.

Priming the Pump

This is the overriding technique of building questions into the speech. When preparing your speech, consider the problems of meeting questions and interruptions during the presentation, not just during an open-forum period. In the main, your questions or implied questions should seek to develop your point, to stimulate thinking, or generally to obtain interest and attention.

SUMMARY

One of the most elementary mistakes a speaker can make is to assume that everyone has heard and understood a question asked of him. To listen to answers without knowing the question is the epitome of frustration. Every speech represents potential audience participation, typically in the form of questions, comments, or objections. You should calculate this as part of the risk. Unreasonable questions and interruptions have ruined some speeches. The speaker has to control the audience participation so as not to do injustice to the audience, the material to be covered, or the time restrictions. The typical audience participation situations involve open forums, symposium forums, instructing situations, and group discussion before an audience.

Some general principles explained were: (1) know your subject and audience; (2) second-guess the situation; (3) do not begrudgingly grant opposing arguments; (4) answer the question; (5) consider the total audience; and (6) generally encourage questions.

Specific rules for answering questions are as follows: (1) repeat the questions; (2) when necessary, rephrase the questions; (3) delay or postpone irrelevant or overly complicated questions; (4) label loaded questions; and (5) don't bluff, say "I don't know."

To help generate participation you may use the *overhead technique*— a question from the speaker directed to the total audience. You may use the *direct question* by directly questioning a specific member of the audience. You may also use the *redirect* technique, which involves reversing or relaying the question. In the reverse technique, you redirect the question to the person who asked it; in the relay, you redirect it to some other person. You are also counseled to *prime the pump*, to build questions into the formal part of your speech.

In the participation part of your speech try not to call on the same person all the time; try to tailor the questions directly to the audience or individuals chosen; keep your overhead or direct questions short, clear, and free of yes-or-no answers. In the main, your questions or implied questions should develop your point, stimulate thinking, and generally obtain attention and interest.

Speech Communication Principles

1. Evaluating answers without knowing the question is the epitome of frustration for most listeners.

2. A speaker must control audience participation so as not to do injustice to the audience, the material to be covered, or the time restrictions.

3. Audience size alone may intimidate members from orally asking questions.

4. "Priming the pump" or building questions into your speech will help generate audience participation.

5. We are better equipped to generate and deal with questions and interruptions if we: know the subject and audience; second-guess the situation; try to react to all questions; consider the whole audience; concede points when readily necessary; and encourage participation.

6. We are apt to be more successful in audience participation situations if we will: repeat the questions; when necessary, rephrase the questions; delay or postpone irrelevant or overly complicated questions; label loaded questions; and say "I don't know," don't bluff.

A. *General Learning Outcomes*

1. We should learn that every speech communication situation represents a potential open forum or audience-involved participation.

2. We should learn of our overriding responsibilities to the audience, the material covered, and the time frame, despite interruptions.

3. We should learn how to deal with questions and interruptions in audience participation situations.

B. *Specific Learning Outcomes*

1. We should learn the general preparation principles for audience participation situations.

2. We should learn the specific rules for answering questions originating from the audience.

3. We should learn the general techniques for generating audience participation.

4. We should learn that special accommodations are necessary for audience participation with really large audiences (roughly 100 or more).

5. We should be able to relate the foregoing general and specific learning outcomes to the speech communication principles above.

C. *Communication Competencies*

1. We should learn to be able to stay in control of an audience participation situation when under fire as a speaker from a group of twenty or more during the course of a five- to eight-minute open-forum speech.

2. We should be able to stay in control and help generate audience participation in a five- to eight-minute interrupted speech situation.

3. We should be able to apply the five basic rules for handling questions in any audience participation situation.

4. We should be able to anticipate both obvious and subtle questions about our messages.

D. *Study Projects and Tasks*

1. Prepare a four- to five-minute persuasive speech that will be followed by a three- to four-minute open forum. Remember to stay in control by following the principles, rules, and suggestions in this chapter.

2. Prepare a six- to eight-minute persuasive speech in which you invite interruptions. Control your interruptions to the point that you cover the material in your outline and stay absolutely within your time frame (eight minutes).

3. Observe an open forum or interrupted speech episode in person or on radio or television. Critically evaluate how well the participants follow the principles and rules described in this chapter. Be especially alert to the five rules for answering questions.

4. Prepare an informative or instructional four- to six-minute speech in which you attempt to generate audience participation. Use the overhead, direct, and redirect question technique. Make sure you cover your material and stay within both the minimum and maximum time limits.

5. Assume you have just delivered the appendix speech, "Communication and the Survival of Democracy," to your classmates. Now prepare for a two- to three-minute open forum. Anticipate the key questions and give some thought to their answers. Remember to follow the five basic rules for answering questions.

6. Prepare an oral report or essay attempting to prove or disprove any of the speech communication principles listed earlier. Expect to be interrupted in your presentation.

Chapter Fourteen

Special Occasion Speaking

SCOPE OF THIS CHAPTER

All communication occasions are in a sense special, yet many occasions call for surprisingly similar speeches in form and style, if not content. Speeches of introduction, for example, occur often enough, involve routinely the same principles, and are so frequently unsuccessful that a further and more specific application of the speech and communication theory previously discussed is useful. In addition to speeches of introduction, the following special occasions will be discussed: speeches of presentation; tribute and commemorative speeches; after-dinner speeches; and adaptation of speech material to radio and television.

SPEECHES OF INTRODUCTION

"I just now met our speaker, who is a friend of our chairman and a speaker on human relations. He teaches speech communication and should be a good example for all of you to follow. It gives me great pleasure to introduce Mr. James E. Mason."

How would you like to speak to a strange audience after that introduction? Attention was called to the speaker's oratory instead of his subject. It sounded as if the speaker were foisted upon the group by a buddy in the organization. It was evident that the introducer in this case did not know anything about the speaker and was not particularly interested in "human relations." The only good point about the introduction was its briefness!

Even more devastating as a speech of introduction is a twenty-minute nightmare of poor jokes, trite language, and overly dramatic praise of the speaker's virtues. This is especially cruel when the speaker only intends to speak for thirty minutes. What makes the situation really impossible is that the introducer is typically a well-intentioned, sincere, and genuinely nice person who is simply socially inept at introducing people.

This last fact makes it most difficult for a speaker to recover his poise, because ordinarily he cannot lash back as he is wont to do. However, on one occasion a speaker evened the score. A young instructor was introducing a distinguished professor to a group of university personnel who knew the professor. He proceeded to give a speech that involved an explanation of every accomplishment and every entry on the professor's bibliography. It was embarrassing to everyone and almost began to sound like satire because of the sheer volume of detail. His final remark was, "Professor, have I overlooked anything?" The obviously irritated professor rose to his feet, glowered at the introducer, and said, "I caught a big fish once!"

What then are some principles and rules of introduction that you can apply to avoid making life intolerable for the speaker?

Remember that the major purpose of a speech of introduction is to create a rapport between the speaker and the audience, which in turn creates a desire for people to want to hear his subject. You want the audience to like him, to respect him, and to be predisposed to listen attentively. Remember that the research on credibility discussed in Chapter 10 indicated the importance of pragmatic ethical proof to the speaker's success. Toward this end:

1. *Make sure that you know something about the speaker and his subject.* Consult with him before the meeting if you can; see if there are some things he prefers said or not said.

2. *Be brief but adequate.* Make sure that enough is said about the speaker and his subject to achieve a rapport and enhance his ethos of credibility. Do not overplay *your role*, for you are not the main speaker. Remember that your job is to focus attention on the speaker and his subject.

The length of the speech of introduction is also related to how well the speaker is known to the audience. You might introduce Richard Nixon simply and adequately with "Ladies and Gentlemen: the President of the United States." Seldom should a speech of introduction run more than three or four minutes.

3. Stress the importance and appropriateness of the speaker's subject. However, take care not to give his speech for him. Do not explain the speaker's qualifications to the point of neglecting to create curiosity and attention for his subject.

4. Speak with sincerity and enthusiasm. If you are not familiar with the speaker or his subject or are simply not interested, get someone else to make the introduction. Do not become artificial in your enthusiasm; do not overpraise; do not stress the speaker's "oratorical" skill; do not use trite language. In general, speak about accomplishments rather than virtues.

5. Pay attention to the speaker. After you have finished your speech of introduction, making sure that the speaker's name and subject were announced clearly and correctly, be a model listener. This suggests that the audience also be good listeners. A gabby or hyperactive introducer can ruin the speaker's attention and rapport. Mark Twain lost his patience with inept introductions and for a while insisted that he not be introduced at all!

An excellent sample is a speech by Professor Glenn R. Capp introducing Dr. A. Q. Sartain to the Baylor University chapter of the American Association of University Professors:

"If a man be endowed with a generous mind, this is the best kind of nobility." This statement by Plato characterizes our speaker for tonight. During the more than twenty years that I have known Dr. Sartain, I have become increasingly impressed not only with his generous and penetrating mind, but with his kindly spirit.

A risk that one runs in introducing a cherished friend is that he may deal in extravagant statements. I find myself in somewhat of a paradoxical situation this evening because a simple factual recital of the training, accomplishment, and contributions of Dr. Sartain appears to be overstatement. I am tempted to dwell at length on such matters as these:

(1) His writings, which include co-authorship of a recent textbook, *Human Behavior in Industry*, his forthcoming textbook to be published by Prentice-Hall, and numerous articles in professional journals.

(2) His important positions, which he has held at Southern Methodist University, where he was first the Director of Forensics, later Professor of Psychology, and now is chairman of the Department of Personnel Administration. He also has more than a passing interest in Baylor University, having taught recently as visiting professor in our summer session.

(3) His membership in important organizations. For example, he served recently as president of the Southern Methodist University chapter of the American Association of University Professors. He is president of the Southwestern Psychological Association, a fellow of the American Psychological Association, and a member of the Association for the Advancement of Science.

Rather than dwelling on these matters, may I say simply that I congratulate you for securing Dr. Sartain for this occasion. I have been impressed with the excellence of his forensic terms, but even more with him as a man—

his pleasant disposition, his sense of fair play, his high ethical standards, and his ability as a scholar. I present to you my friend and the friend of all teachers—Dr. A. Q. Sartain.[1]

SPEECHES OF PRESENTATION AND ACCEPTANCE

"Thanks for holding down the other end of the log" was engraved on a simple brass plaque and signed by four outstanding graduate students. This award was presented by simply placing it on the center of a professor's desk before he retired from a major university. With this close little group a speech, a banquet, even a personal confrontation was unnecessary. The recipient was honored and felt that his efforts were appreciated and recognized. Most often, however, a speech is called for, and it should seek as its major purpose to show honor, appreciation, and recognition.

The same sense of good will and appreciation can be transmitted under considerably different circumstances. A five-minute formal speech was read from a manuscript before a banquet audience of 300 people. It concluded: "For these and his many other achievements, it was unanimously agreed by the Executive Faculty of the Marquette University School of Speech that Dr. James W. Cleary was richly deserving of our Distinguished Alumni Award in the field of Speech Education." The point is that presentations vary widely. The size of the group involved, the nature of the award, and the occasion are all critical factors in how much is said and how formally it is said.

Two general principles for most speeches of presentation are as follows:

1. *The speech should sincerely communicate honor, appreciation, and recognition.* It should not stray from the facts or else it becomes insincere. Do not overpraise, overstate, or overemotionalize. Honestly review the recipient's accomplishments and virtues.

2. *Adapt your speech to the occasion and the award.* For annual and routine service awards, only a short, forthright word of congratulations may be necessary, even on a formal occasion. When many similar awards are given, as with forensic contest winners, one short speech can often serve to show honor and recognition for the entire group, each of whom might then individually step forward to receive his medal. This is not to say that the speech should be any less sincere. Make sure the speaker selected to present such awards is thoroughly familiar with the kind of effort and achievement involved.

[1]Glenn R. Capp, *How to Communicate Orally*, 2d ed. (Englewood Cliffs, N.J.: Prentice-Hall, Inc., 1966), p. 351.

On some occasions the speaker may also have to consider the donor of the gift. A university giving an honorary degree or a distinguished alumni award deserves some recognition and reflected glory. This is also true of business and industrial concerns who honor longtime employees. In situations where the award may have a history or be otherwise unusual, a short description of these facts may be in order.

An acceptance speech should measure up to the total communication situation, including especially the expectations of those making the award. If you are representing a group or organization, make this clear and briefly explain why the award is appreciated by the others as well as yourself. If appropriate you may wish to mention individuals and their specific efforts or merits related to the award. If it is a personal gift or award, your response might vary from a simple but sincere "Thank you" to a short statement of gratitude. So much depends on the nature of the award, the expectations of those honoring you, the total communication climate—and, of course, your own feelings.

As a sample of a speech of presentation, let us turn to the presentation of a volume of tributes to Dr. J. W. Crabtree, Secretary Emeritus and founder of the National Education Association, by W. E. Givens.

> Dr. Crabtree's record speaks more eloquently than any speaker could. He came to Washington in 1917 and started the office of the National Education Association in one room of his house, with one secretary. On January 1, 1935, when he became Secretary Emeritus, he left a modern, seven-story building on the "Street of the Presidents" six squares from the White House in our nation's capital, and he left there a loyal office force of one hundred and forty-five people, all of whom love and respect him.
>
> He started in 1922 the life membership movement that put up that great building, and that has grown from that time until tonight our great national Association has some 5400 life members scattered throughout this great nation.
>
> Miss Hale read you a few of the letters that he has received. It is my pleasure on behalf of his friends throughout the nation to present to him from you a beautiful volume of some seven hundred letters from his friends, bound in a beautiful binding presented by the publishers of our *Journal* as a compliment to Mr. Crabtree. It is a great pleasure to present this volume to Mr. Crabtree tonight and to assure you all that it is a great honor to be the successor of such a man.[2]

TRIBUTE AND COMMEMORATIVE SPEECHES

This form of special occasion speaking includes such subclassifications as eulogies, anniversary addresses, dedicatory speeches, and some nominating speeches. The *eulogy* is typically a speech of tribute upon the

[2]W. Hayes Yeager, *Effective Speaking for Every Occasion* (Englewood Cliffs, N.J.: Prentice-Hall, Inc., 1940), p. 159.

death of a person or shortly thereafter. It may also apply to the anniversary of the birth or great moments in the life of a historical figure such as Lincoln or Washington. *Anniversary* speeches celebrate and commemorate an event, a man, or an institution. Dedicatory speeches are typically tributes; buildings, monuments, ships, libraries, and other things are generally dedicated in the honor of some outstanding personality, institution, or group of men. In some nominating speeches, it is the practice to pay tribute to the nominee as a way of proving his qualifications for office. Since most organizations now use nominating committees, nominations are made with less oral flourish.

All commemorative speeches involve tributes to men, their ideals, and their achievements. The purpose is to gain or increase respect, emulation, and appreciation of the men involved and their impact upon society or its institutions.

Organizationally, you can proceed chronologically according to the history of the man or institution being commemorated, or, when time is short and the chronology generally well known, you can proceed topically and concentrate on selective aspects of personality, achievement, or societal impact.

Three general rules for most tributes and commemorative speeches are as follows:

1. *Develop a sensitive understanding about the subject.* To deliver a funeral oration about a stranger would be awkward and embarrassing, if not sacrilegious. Make sure you have *more* than just the immediate facts about the man, the occasion, the memorial, or building being dedicated or otherwise commemorated. Try to capture the personality of the subject in both the large and small incidents of his life that typify his virtues or outlook on life. Know his outstanding achievements well, but do not lose sight of those characteristics of personality that typify the man.

2. *Be objective and fair to the facts.* Perhaps we should not "speak ill of the dead," but neither should we be totally dishonest. To eulogize a lazy, intemperate, hardheaded old lady as "this kind, generous model of moral simplicity" is apt to incite outright laughter and do a disservice to whatever virtues and respect to which the woman was entitled. No person is perfect in every way. Washington was not a model tactician at Valley Forge; young Lincoln was defeated so many times at the polls that his political future was in real jeopardy. You will want to magnify and concentrate on the person's virtues and achievements, but let him be human.

3. *Utilize a style of language and delivery in keeping with the occasion.* The nature of commemorative occasions is often demanding of a slightly more elevated style than that generally prescribed in this book. The

expectations audiences have of a speaker in a church or cemetery are somehow special. In paying tribute to the tragically lost astronauts, one can hardly escape the connotative effect of voice and measured cadence that helps express the grief, reverence, and solemnity of the occasion. There are many happy anniversaries, dedications, and tributes that will call for different adaptations of style. Probably part of every commemorative speech demands some element of elevated style. The model that follows helps illustrate this point. It was delivered on the floor of the United States Senate by Senator Everett Dirksen in the aftermath of President Kennedy's assassination. A formal resolution was read and Senator Dirksen was then recognized.

MR. DIRKSEN: Mr. President, the memory of John Fitzgerald Kennedy lingers in this forum of the people. Here we knew his vigorous tread, his flashing smile, his ready wit, his keen mind, his zest for adventure. Here with quiet grief we mourn his departure. Here we shall remember him best as a colleague whose star of public service is indelibly inscribed on the roll of the U.S. Senate.

And here the eternal question confronts and confounds us. Why mus⁺ it be? Why must the life of an amiable, friendly, aggressive young man, moved only by high motives, lighted on his way by high hopes, guided by broad plans, impelled by understanding and vision, be brought to an untimely end with his labors unfinished? And why, in a free land, untouched by the heel of dictatorship and oppression, where the humblest citizen may freely utter his grievances, must that life be cut short by an evil instrument, moved by malice, frustration, and hate? This is the incredible thing which leaves us bewildered and perplexed.

One moment there is the ecstasy of living when one can hear the treble cries of scampering children over the White House lawn, the pleasure of receiving a Thanksgiving turkey which I presented to him but three days before the evil deed, the pleasure of conversation over many things, including his hopes for the future, the exciting fact of sunshine and green grass in late November, the endless stream of citizens coming to the President's House, the strident voice of the city rising from the hum of traffic, the animation of saluting crowds, and then the sudden strangling death rattle of dissolution. Who shall say, save that there is a Divinity which shapes our ends and marks our days?

As the tumult and grief subside, as the Nation resumes and moves forward, and his own generation measures his works and achievements, what shall we say who knew him well—we in this forum, where he spent eight years of his life—we who knew him best not as Mr. President but simply as Jack?

We saw him come to this body at age 35. We saw him grow. We saw him rise. We saw him elevated to become the Chief Magistrate of this Nation. And we saw him as the leader of both branches of the Republic assembled to deliberate over common problems.

In this moment when death has triumphed, when hearts are chastened, when the spirit reels in sheer bewilderment, what do we say now that the Book of Life has been closed?

Let me say what we have always said when he was alive, gay, happy, friendly, ambitious, and ready to listen.

He had vision that went beyond our own. His determination to effectuate a test-ban treaty is a living example.

He was his own profile in courage. His unrelenting devotion to equality and civil rights attests that fact.

He was devoted to our system of constitutional government. His attitude toward the separation of church and state looms like a shining example.

He had the great virtue of spiritual grace. If at any moment he may have seemed frustrated over a proposition, it was so transitory. If he showed any sign of petulance, it was so fleeting. There were no souring acids in the spirit of John Kennedy.

If at any moment he may have seemed overeager, it was but the reflection of a zealous crusader and missioner who knew where he was going.

If at any moment he seemed to depart from the covenant which he and his party made with the people, it was only because he believed that accelerated events and circumstances did not always heed the clock and the calendar.

If his course sometimes seemed at variance with his own party leaders or with the opposition, it was only because a deep conviction dictated his course.

On the tables of memory, we who knew him well as a friend and colleague can well inscribe this sentiment:

"Senator John Fitzgerald Kennedy, who became the 35th President of the United States—young, vigorous, aggressive, and scholarly—one who estimated the need of his country and the world and sought to fulfill that need—one who was wedded to peace and vigorously sought this greatest of all goals of mankind—one who sensed how catastrophic nuclear conflict could be and sought a realistic course to avert it—one who sensed the danger that lurked in a continuing inequality in our land and sought a rational and durable solution—one to whom the phrase 'the national interest' was more than a string of words—one who could disagree without vindictiveness—one who believed that the expansion of the enjoyment of living by all people was an achievable goal—one who believed that each generation must contribute its best to the fulfillment of the American dream."

The *te deums* which will be sung this day may be wafted away by the evening breeze which caresses the last resting place of those who served the Republic, but here in this Chamber where he served and prepared for higher responsibility, the memory of John Fitzgerald Kennedy will long linger to nourish the faith of all who serve that same great land.[3]

Perhaps the most eloquent commemorative speech of all time was Lincoln's Gettysburg Address. The speech is shown in Figure 14-1 (on pages 368 and 369) in Lincoln's own handwriting. This is his first draft and therefore slightly different from other versions you may have studied.[4]

---

[3] *Congressional Record*, (1964), pp. 21, 596–97.

[4] The first page was written in ink in Washington shortly before November 18, 1863. It is believed that there was once a second page in ink, which was lost. Lincoln completed the draft in pencil in Gettysburg on the evening or morning of November 19. The words "here to the unfinished work which they have thus far, so nobly carried

That tributes combine the showing of appreciation with eulogy is illustrated by the touching speech that Tom Hughes gave in tribute to his brother, football player Chuck Hughes, who died of a heart attack while playing for the Detroit Lions. All of the Lions were at the funeral in San Antonio. Tom gathered the Lions around him and spoke:

> Words cannot express the gratitude for you that I now hold in my heart. Sunday you were names. Today you are and always will be in my heart and the hearts of all of those that I hold dear. The love we have for Chuck, I now feel, was shown by you, the Detroit Lions.
>
> This to me is the finest tribute you could ever bestow on him. I have on numerous occasions heard that the Lions are a team of class. These past three days you have shown it. Please try to continue this. You strike me, an outsider really, as being a tightly knit family. My personal family is this way too.
>
> Please don't let this tragedy spoil the things that make you stand out so prominently. Chuck died doing the one thing he wanted to do for such a long time. It was his life.
>
> I'd prefer it, and so would he, that he died on the field, rather than in some other tragic way. Forget the tragedy of Sunday and remember him as the man you knew personally. He'd like that. He gave his all and I know that if he had to die he would tell you, losing is the tragedy. Play it to win.[5]

AFTER-DINNER SPEECHES

Today's after-dinner speeches are not what they invariably used to be. In our day a banquet may be the setting for a very serious and profound speech to persuade or inform. All the lessons previously discussed obviously apply to these speeches as they would to any other. There is, however, a tradition of after-dinner speaking that is rather special in our society. This is the good-humored, lighthearted, genial situation with the major purpose being a sociable dinner and relaxed enjoyment. This is the type of speech situation with which we are concerned here. The audience has been made content with good food and is tolerant and benevolent. It is not in a mood for contentiousness, moral reevaluation, or complex, logical stratagems. These speeches are typically brief, light, and generally humorous. They are not easy speeches to deliver; for some they appear to be well-nigh impossible. You need not be a professional jokester; indeed, unless you tell a good, relevant joke especially

on" are omitted or lost. He delivered the speech from this draft, but did not follow the text verbatim. See *Long Remembered*, The Gettysburg Address in Facsimile (Washington, D.C., The Library of Congress, 1963), with notes and comments by David C. Mearns and Lloyd A. Dunlap. Library of Congress Catalog Card No.: 63–65145. (Facsimile #3.)

[5] Quoted by Jerry Green in *The Detroit News*, October 28, 1971, p. 5D.

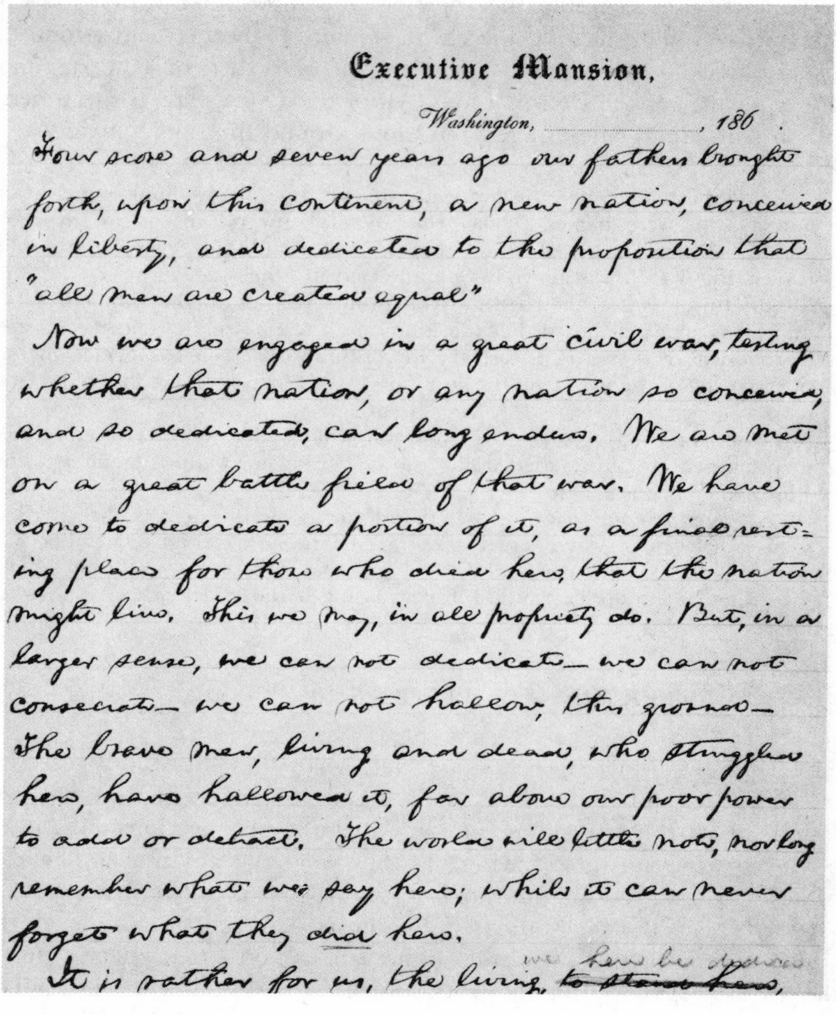

Executive Mansion,

Washington, ..., 186 .

Four score and seven years ago our fathers brought forth, upon this continent, a new nation, conceived in liberty, and dedicated to the proposition that "all men are created equal"

Now we are engaged in a great civil war, testing whether that nation, or any nation so conceived, and so dedicated, can long endure. We are met on a great battle field of that war. We have come to dedicate a portion of it, as a final resting place for those who died here, that the nation might live. This we may, in all propriety do. But, in a larger sense, we can not dedicate—we can not consecrate—we can not hallow, this ground—The brave men, living and dead, who struggled here, have hallowed it, far above our poor power to add or detract. The world will little note, nor long remember what we say here; while it can never forget what they did here.

It is rather for us, the living, ~~to stand here,~~ we here be dedica

FIGURE 14–1.

well, you are better advised to seek your humor in another vein. Some general principles to guide you are as follows:

1. Select suitable topics. "Great Snafus of the Civil War" was a delightful after-dinner speech at a history buff's banquet recently. The group was of course interested in the profound aspects of the war, but not at this particular moment. Look on the lighter side of issues for your subjects. If you are going to talk about teachers, concentrate on their eccentricities, and so on.

ted to the great task remaining before us—
that, from these honored dead we take increased devotion to that cause for which
they here, gave the last full measure of devotion—that we here highly resolve these
dead shall not have died in vain; that
the nation, shall have a new birth of freedom, and that government of the people by
the people for the people, shall not per-
ish from the earth.

2. Be good-humored. The diners are full of food and full of good will. Enhance the fellowship. Avoid bitter argument and contentiousness.

3. Adapt to the audience. A joke or a story is often funny to one group and not to another. More importantly, it may be offensive. Make sure you know the audience, the occasion, and the program format. Capitalize on this information; tie your good humor appropriately and directly to your specific audience. A canned speech for all occasions is seldom successful.

4. Be clear and brief. Avoid complex organization; stick with one or two obvious main points. Do not use elaborate forms of support. Use primarily examples and humorous illustrations, and above all be brief. Attention spans are often short after a long day and a pleasant dinner. Plan several cutoff points in your speech to extricate yourself should the whole program take more time than expected or should the audience seem unusually restless or quiet (asleep).

A good example is a very funny speech by Dorothy Dix (Mrs. E. M. Gilmer, the original advice-to-the-lovelorn columnist), to elementary-school principals after a National Education Association banquet:

EXPERIENCES OF A WOMAN COLUMNIST[6]

> Not very long ago I received a letter telling me about all the harm I was doing. It read: "Dear Miss Dix: I wonder if you know how much harm you are doing in the world. I was in love with a man who did not notice me at all, and I wrote you to ask you how I could attract him, and you told me how to do it, and I did, and married him, and now I wish I had not!"
>
> I am very happy to be able to add my own word to the welcome you have been given in New Orleans. As you know, New Orleans is a convention city, but we rarely have so large a convention as you have brought us today. I suppose the principals of the elementary schools also know that the parents of today have passed the buck, so to speak, and they expect the teacher not only to teach their children learning, but morals and manners as well. The babies have been thrown squarely in your laps, so what happens to the country in the future depends on how you bring these youngsters up.
>
> When I was asked to report at this auspicious assembly, I was proud and pleased, but when I was told I was to talk about myself, my various undertakings seemed to have run out on me.
>
> Our favorite indoor sport in talking about ourselves is in talking about our work. In my occupation of writing a love column, there are many things that are really very funny. I do not know why, because love is a most serious thing in the world—it makes the world go round, and is the cause for most of the trouble made and murders committed. I do not know where my work begins or finishes, of course, but I do my bit toward keeping things going.
>
> I have been writing this column for a long time. When I started, things were not what they are today, and nothing amazes me so much as the different questions people ask me. Forty years ago people asked me whether it was proper to help a boy friend with his overcoat when he called; now it is, "Do you think there is any harm to go over and spend a week-end with him?" I have no end to the number of letters where girls have asked me how to keep their husbands. There is hardly any question in the world that comes up between mothers and fathers, and between them and their children, and between husbands and wives, and sweethearts, that in one way or another does not fall into my collection. One person wrote me that she was thirty-five years old, with a peaches-and-cream complexion, and that she was going to be married to a man of forty; that there was nothing in the way now, except that she had false teeth. "Now," said she, "what must I do about it? Should I tell him before I marry him that I have false teeth and disillusion him, or wait until after we are married and run the risk

[6]*Proceedings*, National Education Association, 1937.

that he might throw them in my face? Shall I break the engagement on some trifling excuse and carry my secret to the grave with me? It is a question. What do you think of it?" I thought long and seriously, and then wrote to her: "Marry your man and keep your mouth shut."

A man not long ago asked me the same question; he also had false teeth. And I told him: "Go on, child, she would not know the difference if she saw you."

You might think, judging by my gray hair, that I was past the marrying age, yet no debutante gets half the proposals that I do, but they always say, "I will not interfere with your career." I spent last summer on a ranch in Colorado, and while there I received a letter from a man who said he had long thought that I would make the kind of wife he wanted. He heard that I was on this ranch, and proceeded to tell me that he was a middle-aged man, owned a huge ranch, and lived ninety miles from a railroad, and then: "I have to come down into your neighborhood anyway, to look over a bunch of beef cattle, so I thought I could come and see how we would like each other." I wrote him that I thought he was better at driving cattle than love on a ranch!

My chores are many, ranging from naming babies to finding ways and means for all sorts of people from all walks of life; but the questions I receive are so unique that I have copied a few from some of the letters I have received:

"My husband tells me to go to hell. Have I a right to take the children?"

"We have been married two weeks, and have not quarreled yet, but are working up to it."

"Shall I tell the boys I stutter?"

"I use Life Buoy soap and still no boy friends."

"I took your advice, Miss Dix, about being a perfect lady, and now I stay at home every night alone."

"I am fifty years old, madly in love with a woman who already has a husband. What is the quickest and most humane way of getting away with same?"

"As soon as I come into the house he yells at me 'you dog' and 'go to hell,' and sometimes he also uses profane language."

"There is nothing you cannot do; thank you in advance for a home, and a husband, and a playmate."

"I have a nice home, a car, a fur coat, jewels—everything a girl marries for."

"I have been a decent girl as far as I can remember."

"My husband beats me until I am black and blue, but my mother advises me to pay no attention and act indifferent."

"Of course we have spats, as all married couples do, and I got one arm broken, but we never have any disagreements of a serious nature."

"There was a great void in my life, so I fell madly in love with a dentist."

"I am married to a bookworm—what is good for worms?"

"A woman depreciates faster than her automobile, and that is going some."

"In high school I was an honor student, with very few friends, and none of them boys."

"Please do not put this in the paper because my girl reads your pieces—she has no sense at all."

"Miss Dix, is my boy friend just a good Catholic, or is he trying to get rid of me; he said he has given me up for Lent?"

"He has bought a license for his dog, and his car—oh, my, why don't he buy a marriage license?"

"My husband and I quarrel like cats and dogs. My birthday is on May 12, and his is on September 15. Are we congenial?"

"My child's father is married, but I am not. What is my relationship to my child's father?"

Some of them are very nice and tell me that I have helped or taught them something. One of the greatest compliments I have ever had in a letter was: "Miss Dix, I usually take my boy friend to dinner, but now I want advice from someone who is really practical, and I am coming to you."

ADAPTING MATERIAL TO RADIO AND TELEVISION

Over 95 percent of our households have television sets today. Seventy million Americans heard and saw the first Kennedy-Nixon debate in 1960. The space shots and the presidential visit to China attracted over 100 million viewers. In 1863 only 20,000 Americans heard Lincoln at Gettysburg. Never before has a speaker had access to such a potentially vast audience. Never before could a speaker be more easily ignored.

Although it is the point of view of this book that the same basic oral speech and communication processes and skills apply in principle whatever the media or situation, some pragmatic differences are obvious when dealing with the mass media, whether in the modern classroom or in your local radio or television station. It is part of the modern speech communication scene.

Despite the practical problems to be discussed shortly, the radio and TV media have marvelous advantages. In addition to potentially giant audiences the speaker is typically free of audience interruptions such as questions, heckling, and rebuttals, as well as the usual distractions of movement, falling chairs, side conversations, and the like. Through the marvel of close-up TV camera work one can show small objects and visual aids that would be impossible to present in regular speech situations. Emphasis and mood can be varied with dramatic effect as the various cameras take close-up shots followed by more distant ones. The viewing screen can be divided so that you can simultaneously and selectively compare or emphasize various objects or concepts pertinent to your message. Audio or video taping for future use gives you the very real advantage of seeing how you appear to the audience, and you also have an opportunity to make changes. The mass media can have an intimacy that is often overlooked—the kind of person-to-person communication that is so very difficult with really large audiences in typical platform speech situations. We are only now learning how to make use of the many instructional and educational advantages of the radio-TV media.

It is not the purpose of this section to explain the engineering, production, and academic intricacies of radio and television performance. We shall instead explain some of the essential differences between platform speaking and the use of microphones and cameras and shall suggest methods of adapting your communication to these differences.

Probably the most difficult problem for a good platform speaker to cope with in radio or television is the lack of feedback from the audience; except for occasional studio audiences, his listeners are unseen and unheard. The truly sensitive platform speaker is constantly checking his audience for signs of fatigue, misunderstanding, confusion, or approval, and he paces his rate, volume, and vocabulary accordingly. A radio studio can be a lonely place. A television studio has a few more technicians and a monitor, which allows you to see yourself, but still no important listener feedback.

The next important difference for a good platform speaker is the great number of mechanical and technical distractions and limitations. This is much more of a problem on television than on radio, because cameras as well as lights and microphones call for more cues, more technicians, and more prearranged signals.

If you are the courageous type who uses a great deal of movement on the platform, you will quickly find yourself in trouble with the producer, the director, and just about everyone else working the show; your movement will cause you to be off camera, off mike, or both. The microphones of today are marvelous and are more adaptable to movement than was so a few years ago, but the camera is still a nemesis for the amateur. Typically, two or more cameras are operating, and you talk to the camera that has its little red tally light on. The TV cameras move quickly and silently, and a momentary glance at your notes or time cues is long enough for the evil eye to appear suddenly right in front of you, so close that you can see yourself reflected in the lens, that is, if the flood lights have not blinded you. Even more frightening is the modern zoom lens that enables a camera to secretly inspect your ear, or whatever, at a distance! The mechanical headaches are mentioned here merely to make sure you inspect the scene and take advantage of any pre-show rehearsals. These actions will help acquaint you with some of these problems and prevent you from being caught flat-footed or open-mouthed while on the air.

If this is not enough to chill the bones of a speaker, there is still one more critical operating difference. Despite the large and diverse broadcast audiences available, they are not assembled in large halls in the manner of a great audience listening to a famed orator. They are individually seated, sometimes within a few feet of your face. They are subject to numerous distractions and are free from the inhibitions of a large hall. A few moments of boredom may cause them to be less attentive.

In addition, sensitive microphones may make "normal" projection, force, and volume adjustments a liability, not to mention oral style. A teacher once had a radio announcer in class who had difficulty adjusting to a regular classroom audience. He spoke in a beautiful, intimate voice as if he were on mike; consequently many in the room could not hear him. He explained that if he projected and used the platform manner suggested while on microphone, he would soon be out of a job. And he was right. What, then, are some guidelines for adapting your speeches and general communications to the special characteristics of the radio-television media?

1. Consider the advantages of microphone and camera. Utilize the variety of camera shots available for presentation of visual aids, for emphasis, or for mood. Let the producer and director help you enhance your presentation. Use the monitor to see how you appear to others.

2. Prepare yourself for a lack of audience feedback. Determine your most likely audience in advance and adapt to them. Try your speech on live audiences of one or two people so that you have a basis for imagining realistic feedback during air time.

3. Accept the differences and limitations of microphone and camera. Limit your movements and bodily action to the range of the equipment. Visualize a small conversational audience rather than a vast multitude assembled in one location. Limit your use of voice and style accordingly. Check your dress and your grooming, particularly for television close-ups.

4. Learn to expect and live with mechanical distractions. Observe a show. Rehearse on the set and learn the cues. Watch the producer, director, or engineer for cues. If you are not sure who's who, ask. In the case of television follow the camera with the red tally light on. Look right into the camera. Check the monitor occasionally for feedback on yourself. Are you inanimate, listing, grinning? Wear cool clothes; the lights are hot.

5. Prepare your speech material carefully. Time is a major concern. Time your material until it is exactly the right length. Write time cues for yourself in the margins of your script. Prepare time fillers in advance; have omission options for timesavers. Keep your organization simple so that time adjustments and adaptations can be exercised without completely baffling the audience. Remember that despite all the headaches and crises discussed in this section, it is what you have to say, the message, that really counts. In the final analysis, it is that way in all communication situations. Don't let the medium become the message!

SUMMARY

All communication is in a sense special, yet many occasions call for surprisingly similar speeches in form and style. Special occasion speaking involves primarily introductions, presentations, tributes and commemorations, after-dinner speeches, and adaptations for radio and television.

The major purpose of a speech of introduction is to create a rapport between the speaker and audience that produces a desire for people to want to hear his subject. Toward this end: (1) make sure that you know something about the speaker and his subject; (2) be brief, but comprehensive; (3) stress the importance and appropriateness of the speaker's subject; (4) speak with sincerity and enthusiasm; and (5) pay attention to the speaker after he starts to speak.

The two general principles for most speeches of presentation are: (1) the speech should sincerely communicate honor, appreciation, and recognition; (2) the speech should be specifically adapted to the occasion and to the award. An acceptance speech should measure up to the total communication situation, including especially the expectations of those making the award.

Tribute and commemorative speeches include such subclassifications as eulogies, anniversary addresses, dedicatory speeches, and some nominating speeches. The purpose of all commemorative speeches is to gain or increase respect, emulation, and appreciation of the people involved and their impact upon society or its institutions. The key topical aspects are personality, achievement, and societal impact. Three general rules are: (1) develop a sensitive understanding about the subject; (2) be objective and fair to the facts; and (3) utilize a style of language and delivery in keeping with the occasion.

After-dinner speaking refers to the good-humored, lighthearted, genial situation, with the major purpose being a sociable dinner and relaxed enjoyment. These speeches are typically brief, light, and generally humorous. Some principles to follow are: (1) select suitable topics; (2) be genuinely good-humored; (3) adapt to the specific audiences; and (4) be clear and brief.

Some guidelines for adapting your speeches and general communications to the special characteristics of the radio and television media are as follows: (1) consider the advantages of microphone and camera; (2) prepare yourself for a lack of audience feedback; (3) accept the differences and limitations of microphone and camera; (4) learn to expect and live with technical distractions; and (5) prepare and carefully time your speech material to facilitate adaptation to the media involved. Remember, the message is still the most important part of any speech.

Speech Communication Principles

1. The successful speech of introduction creates a rapport between the speaker and the audience that in turn creates a desire for people to want to hear about his subject.

2. A good speech of introduction is a form of pragmatic ethical proof that enhances the speaker's credibility.

3. Successful speeches of presentation communicate honor, appreciation, and recognition and are closely adapted to the occasion and the award.

4. Successful commemorative speeches pay tribute to men or institutions, their ideals, and their achievements, for the purpose of increasing respect, emulation, and appreciation of the recipient.

5. The traditional after-dinner speech is by definition brief, light, and generally humorous. It avoids contentiousness, moral reevaluation, and complex, logical stratagems.

6. Except for pragmatic differences, basic oral speech communication processes, skills, and principles apply to radio and television.

7. Successful adaptation to radio and television involves preparing yourself for mechanical distractions, a lack of or different kind of feedback, and rigid time frames.

A. *General Learning Outcomes*

   1. We should learn the basic principles that apply to four standard special occasion speeches.

   2. We should learn the special preparation and speech adaptation techniques necessary when dealing with the mass media.

B. *Specific Learning Outcomes*

   1. We should learn the major purpose, general principles, and specific rules for special speeches of introduction, presentation, tribute or commemoration, and after-dinner occasions.

   2. We should learn the specific guidelines for adapting speeches and general communication to the special characteristics of microphone and camera (especially for television).

   3. We should be able to relate the foregoing general and specific learning outcomes to the speech communication principles above.

C. *Communication Competencies*

   1. We should be able to write and deliver a successful one- to two-minute speech of introduction following explicitly the principles and rules presented in this chapter.

2. We should be able to write and deliver a one- to two-minute successful speech of presentation (or acceptance) that explicitly follows the principles and rules presented in this chapter.

3. We should be able to write and deliver a one- to two-minute successful speech of tribute or commemoration that explicitly follows the principles and rules described in this chapter.

4. We should be able to write and deliver a two- to four-minute after-dinner speech that follows the suggestions in this chapter.

5. We should be able to deliver a one- to three-minute speech or participate in discussion while on microphone and camera without panic or confusion.

D. *Study Projects and Tasks*

1. Prepare a one- to two-minute speech of introduction for a student speaker from your class. Interview the person thoroughly and follow the rules suggested.

2. Prepare a one- to two-minute speech of presentation to a real or hypothetical person of your choice; the gift or award may also be hypothetical (e.g., athlete of the year, dad of the year, most valuable player, recipient of an honorary degree, and so forth).

3. Prepare a one- to two-minute speech of tribute or commemoration to an institution, organization, or person of your choice. Make it sensitive and sincere. See the illustrations in this chapter for ideas and subclassifications.

4. Prepare a two- to four-minute after-dinner speech that is truly good-humored, genial, relaxed, and fun. Try your hand at a joke or two.

5. Prepare to do one of the first three special occasion speech projects on radio or television. Check with your instructor about trying it out in whatever laboratory or studio facilities are available.

6. Prepare for a five- to ten-minute problem-solving discussion (see the topics in study project 2 of Chapter 12) that will be radio- or television-recorded. Prepare as in project 5 above.

7. Watch a live television show and try to second-guess what kind of technical distractions, signals, and cues are going on and what impact they are having upon the message of the sender.

8. If possible, observe a live television show from behind the camera (in the studio) and write a two-page report on the impact the technology has upon the participants and their messages. What advice would you give a person about to go on camera for the first time?

9. Prepare a one- to two-minute speech of introduction (in written form) for the speaker of record in the speech in the appendix. Assume the audience is your class. You may fabricate some of the details for exercise purposes.

10. Review the speech in the appendix and indicate what changes, additions, and/or adaptations you would make if the speech were to be given live on public television. (e.g., Would you use audio-visual aids, different language, fewer words?)

11. Prepare an oral report or essay attempting to prove or disprove any of the speech communication principles listed earlier.

Appendix A

Communication and the Survival of Democracy*

1. As I think back over the year just past, I am tempted
2. to spend these last few minutes with you reviewing the
3. high points of a Presidential term that I shall never
4. forget. But with the adoption of our first long-range
5. goals, this convention represents a beginning, not an
6. end, and so I shall forego the temptation to look back.

7. Instead, in the spirit of the occasion, I offer
8. you a swansong whose refrain is a challenge. It is a
9. challenge, not for the seventies, but for the century.
10. It is a challenge to commitment—not to this Associa-
11. tion, but of it, not to our parochial welfare, but to
12. the well-being of this nation and, perhaps through her
13. example, of western democracy.

14. I believe that the latent expertise of our profession
15. has a special relevance to the needs of our time; that
16. if we fail to meet those needs, someone else will have
17. to do so in our place; and that if no one meets them,
18. the days are numbered to the fall of democratic
19. government.

*Reprinted from *Spectra*, 9, No. 1 (February 1973), 3–4. Delivered by Dr. Theodore Clevenger, Jr., president of the Speech Communication Association at the annual SCA convention, Chicago, Illinois, December 30, 1972.

20. Having heard this, perhaps some of you are ready to
21. leave now and avoid the rush. This refrain is all
22. too familiar, and you may feel that you have heard
23. it all before. But before you reach for your over-
24. coat, let me assure you that I am not going to repeat
25. Chapter 1, Section 0 of the fundamentals textbook. I
26. will not appeal for wider educational programs in de-
27. bate, general semantics, group dynamics, parliamentary
28. procedure, or the exercise of First Amendment freedoms.
29. As important as these disciplines are, my proposal is
30. more radical than that; for I shall ask you, not to do
31. more and better what you are already doing, but to
32. commit some of your time to something altogether different.

33. However, before we come to the proposal, let us examine
34. the problem that gives rise to it.

35. I submit to you that western democracy stands today on
36. the brink of disaster. Moreover, I submit that techno-
37. logical and social developments now in progress push us
38. closer to that brink every day. I further submit that
39. the problems brooding over our society today lie just
40. beyond the horizon for the less-well-developed nations,
41. and that as they move into the communication revolution,
42. identical problems will confront them in equal or
43. greater degree.

44. On the surface, the pervasive symptom of our political
45. failure is disharmony and dissent, a symptom which leads
46. to many secondary complications. Now, I know that there
47. are many who welcome dissent as the harbinger of needed
48. social change; but even they admit that dissent is good,
49. not in itself, but as an impetus to social reform.

50. Incidentally, this is why we see such a close correla-
51. tion between political liberalism and the defense of
52. dissent. People who praise dissent tend to feel that
53. there is much in our society that needs changing. What
54. throws one into confusion nowadays is the increasing
55. amount of dissent arising to the right of political
56. center, and in groups that refuse to ally with any
57. established political philosophy. Once the private
58. property of the political liberal, organized dissent
59. is rapidly becoming a standard operating procedure for
60. any group that perceives itself as outside the political
61. mainstream; and as the mainstream dwindles to a trickle,
62. the tactics of dissent emerge as a dominant political
63. trend.

64. And I believe that the mainstream will continue to
65. dwindle for several reasons. For one thing, the silent
66. majority will, in due course, become a silent minority,
67. because the commercial newscast is locked into a news-
68. gathering and reporting format which rewards the tactics
69. of dissent at the expense of other approaches to polit-
70. ical action. Moreover, once a dissenting group passes

71. a certain point in news coverage, it becomes material
72. for the hour-long documentary and feature articles in
73. the print media. This makes the group even more widely
74. known, which renders it more newsworthy, leading to
75. still more intensive news coverage. The cycle is
76. inevitable, and it must be fueled with a constant
77. supply of "events," the easiest of which to arrange
78. are street actions, confrontations, and other tactics
79. of dissent. Newsmen know this, and in their more
80. candid moments, admit it, yet they are powerless to
81. stop it.

82. But even if we could somehow interrupt this cycle,
83. disharmony and dissent would continue to increase, and
84. for a much more fundamental reason. The simple fact
85. is that during the past fifteen years, the individual
86. citizen has become increasingly aware of government.
87. Because TV newscasts and specials nightly bring govern-
88. ment leaders and programs into our living rooms, and
89. because the wire services have greatly expanded the
90. amount of background and analysis of those leaders and
91. programs available in morning papers, all of us
92. today feel somehow closer to government than we did
93. twenty years ago. With that growing awareness has
94. come a false sense of familiarity; we are inclined to
95. feel that anything we know that well should be subject
96. in some degree to our influence. Yet we know that the
97. media are strictly one-way; there is no readily avail-
98. able channel through which my individual, specific and
99. detailed response can flow back into government.

100. Thus are planted the seeds of frustration. As the
101. media pour upon us a steadily-expanding flow of infor-
102. mation about our society, the urge grows upon us to
103. participate more extensively in the decisions by which
104. that society is molded and shaped. But the increased
105. channel-capacity for input to the voter is not matched
106. by capacity for feedback—with late twentieth century
107. inputs, today's citizen is trapped in a straight-jacket
108. of eighteenth-century outputs.

109. And just what are the channels through which we may
110. communicate to our society's decision-making centers?
111. We may write letters to our representatives, but the
112. influence here is both uncertain and indirect. At
113. infrequent intervals, we may vote for candidates, but
114. here our opportunities for self-expression and individual
115. response are compressed to a single binary choice.

116. To illustrate the difficulties involved in that choice,
117. consider your own U.S. Senator. Assuming that you know
118. who he or she is, and what they stand for, ask yourself
119. whether you agree with your Senator's stand on most
120. issues. Ask further whether your senator has taken a
121. stand on every issue that is important for you, or

122. indeed whether he or she is aware of the existence of
123. some of those issues. Finally, ask whether your Senator
124. might not be forced to compromise a stand on some issues
125. that are vital to you, in order to secure passage of
126. legislation that stands higher on his or her priority
127. ladder. Putting it all together, the sense in which
128. you are "represented" by your Senator is almost meta-
129. phorical. And yet, next time at the polls you may find
130. yourself forced to vote for that very Senator, because
131. the other candidate would represent you even more poorly.

132. This agonizing choice between poor representation and
133. worse representation has driven many voters into
134. a state of despair. Some have dropped out of the
135. political process altogether, others have joined pro-
136. test groups. But many of the latter experience a rude
137. awakening when they discover that the protest movement
138. itself is as thoroughly bureaucratized as the society
139. it was organized to protest. Structured to bring
140. leverage against the establishment, it becomes, almost
141. of necessity, a mirror image of the establishment
142. with many of the structural details carried over intact.
143. It is probably at least as hard for a rank-and-file
144. citizen to influence the peace movement as it is to
145. influence the Pentagon. Both bureaucracies and anti-
146. bureaucracies resist the influence of individuals.

147. Not only is this situation demoralizing, but it
148. represents an increasingly flagrant violation of the
149. fundamental assumption of democratic government—the
150. assumption that truth and wisdom will triumph in a free
151. marketplace of ideas. The truth is that the market-
152. place for ideas in this country today is anything but
153. free. We have not so much an intellectual free trade
154. as an interlocking network of monopolies and cartels.

155. The development of media has in effect conferred our
156. collective intellectual proxy on a relative handful
157. of opinion leaders, and a massive gatekeeping privilege
158. on another handful of communication managers. These
159. are the new Robber Barons of the Seventies, accumulating
160. power not through wealth but through access to communi-
161. cation channels. And the incomparably richer flux of
162. information to which we are not exposed in no way com-
163. pensates for the disparity between their transmission
164. power and our own. Knowledge should be power, but for
165. the average citizen today, knowledge only sharpens
166. awareness of our individual political impotence.

167. It is that awareness of individual helplessness which
168. lies at the core of our problem. What we confront is
169. nothing less than the impending breakdown of represen-
170. tative government. Sometime before the year 2000, it
171. will have become technologically obsolete. By that
172. date, I predict that certain provisions of our Federal

173. Constitution will have been rewritten, or else the
174. Constitution and the Republic will have passed into
175. history. During the last quarter of this century,
176. we will move inexorably toward either dictatorship or
177. participatory democracy.

178. Let's assume for purposes of argument that you agree
179. with me that the latter represents the more palatable
180. alternative. It is, in the view of many, the govern-
181. mental ideal upon which western democracy was formed.

182. (I trust that you will forgive me if I refuse to deal
183. seriously with an ultra-Madisonian viewpoint that
184. enjoys a certain popularity in academic circles today—
185. the argument that representative government is prefer-
186. able to participatory democracy because it somehow
187. invests the wisest and best qualified people with
188. decision-making power. If I believed that the majority
189. of citizens were unqualified to participate directly
190. in democratic decision-making, I would also have to
191. conclude that they lacked the good sense to elect
192. qualified representatives. No, the Madisonian view-
193. point is undisguised elitism, and I think it should
194. be dismissed as inappropriate to the twentieth century.)

195. I think the only reasonable position is that recourse
196. to elected representatives is necessary because it
197. has always been impractical to give every citizen an
198. active voice in the real decision-making processes of
199. the country. After all, the difficulties of trans-
200. porting a hundred million voters to a single locale
201. for democratic decision making are insuperable; even
202. if you could somehow overcome that problem, they could
203. never all meet face-to-face; and even if they could,
204. the ensuing debate would no doubt last for the estimated
205. duration of the universe. Limits of time and space
206. dictated a compromise; if a citizen cannot participate
207. in the debate, then let him vote for a representative
208. to debate for him.

209. Note that this compromise rests on a practicality
210. strictly determined by limits of time and space. But,
211. the technology of 1972 has reduced the natural limits
212. of time and space by several orders of magnitude, par-
213. ticularly where messages are concerned. Great masses
214. of information can be sorted, analyzed and stored in
215. less time than your Senator spends on a coffee break.
216. It can be retrieved, duplicated, processed and trans-
217. mitted thousands of miles while he is asking for the
218. floor. The hardware is now available to vitiate the
219. compromise which eighteenth-century technology forced
220. on democratic governments.

221. If appropriate software can be developed soon enough,
222. we shall be able to overcome the limits of time and
223. space which deprive the individual citizen of the

224. opportunity to participate directly in societal decisions.
225. That citizen will then be able to help decide what we
226. shall do, not merely who will decide what we shall do.

227. The hardware is already with us in the form of two-way
228. interactive cable television augmented by electronic
229. data storage and time-sharing computers. Computers
230. we have in abundance. The interactive cable systems
231. are now under test in a sample of businesses and pri-
232. vate homes in Washington, Orlando and several other
233. major markets, where subscribers are using response
234. systems attached to their TV sets to register opinions,
235. buy products, and request information. It is estimated
236. that by 1980 nearly 90 percent of all homes will be equipped
237. with cable TV, many of these with some interactive
238. capability. Assuming that cable lives up to its
239. commercial promise, most U.S. homes will have inter-
240. active systems within twenty years.

241. It is comforting to hope that when that day comes, the
242. groundwork will have been laid to allow us to incor-
243. porate this new technology into an enriched democratic
244. process. I cannot emphasize too strongly that hardware
245. will not be enough. Unless we begin now to investigate
246. its potential for the democratic process, the hardware
247. may only contribute to the problem, not its solution.

248. Let us then examine what a solution to this problem
249. might look like.

250. The simplest solution, and the least satisfactory,
251. would use multiple-choice feedback in a sort of
252. electronic public opinion poll, with the results
253. counting as a referendum. Such an approach has the
254. merit of directness and technological simplicity,
255. and the hardware to implement it is cheap and avail-
256. able. However, it limits the voter to a narrow choice
257. on issues defined and predigested by someone else.
258. If the interactive capability never goes beyond this
259. level, it cannot deal with an issue in depth, nor
260. will it provide the voter with a fully-satisfactory
261. spectrum of input to the democratic process.

262. A more complicated solution, and a better one, would
263. allow the voter to use a teletypewriter to input
264. problem definitions, request information on specific
265. points of contention, and recommend courses of action.
266. From the engineering point of view, such a system
267. could be implemented in perhaps a decade or so,
268. especially if one did not insist on a console in
269. every home. An alternative would be neighborhood
270. political centers where several consoles could be
271. served by a single cable installation. The feedback
272. channel for each response console would require much
273. less bandwidth than a single telephone line, thus
274. with multiplexing equipment now available, the feed-

275. back needs of an entire neighborhood could be served
276. by the electronic equivalent of a single twisted pair.
277. Moreover, such an arrangement might have other advan-
278. tages as well. With proper attention to the architec-
279. ture and administration of such a center, it could
280. serve as a focus for both formal and informal political
281. dialog. Given immediate access to information in the
282. center, such dialog could be much more informed,
283. meaningful and productive than is most political
284. discussion today. For example, points of controversy
285. over matters of fact could be settled by recourse
286. to the computer's data file.

287. To carry the process a step further, such a system
288. should be interfaced with the mass media. At present,
289. TV documentaries and in-depth press analyses are
290. dictated by what newsmen think it important for us
291. to know. Unquestionably, newsmen should retain the
292. right to print or broadcast whatever they choose;
293. but with a system of the type we are discussing, it
294. would be possible also to monitor information requests
295. and thus determine what significant groups of voters
296. wanted to know. Alternative channels, like those now
297. being set aside as public access channels on TV,
298. could then be created for the broadcast of documen-
299. taries and publication of analyses tailor-made to
300. voter needs.

301. Clearly, whatever hardware problems may be involved
302. in designing such a system are dwarfed by the problems
303. we encounter in software and philosophy of operation.

304. At the very least, software for this kind of system
305. will involve information-retrieval techniques far
306. beyond anything envisioned by either library scientists
307. or industrial decision-makers. First of all, there
308. are tough problems of semantic indexing to be worked
309. out. Perhaps paramount among these is the still-
310. unsolved problem of shifting categories. Everyone
311. who has tried to work with information retrieval in
312. a growing field has discovered that today's categories
313. will not serve tomorrow's information needs. Cer-
314. tainly the shifting sands of political dialog represent
315. the ultimate challenge in information storage and
316. retrieval.

317. Problems of semantic indexing shade by imperceptible
318. degrees into problems in the theory of argument and
319. evidence. As a crude example, if I ask for informa-
320. tion about a guaranteed annual wage, the information
321. I get will depend upon what arguments are identified
322. as relevant to the G.A.W., and what information is
323. held to be relevant to each of those arguments. The
324. question of how to identify relevant arguments and
325. relevant evidence—that is, how to identify it un-

326. equivocally and algorithmically—has never been
327. answered. Ask yourself how you would program a com-
328. puter to recognize either of these crucial components
329. of policy debate, and you can see how much we still
330. have to learn about applied argumentation.

331. In a still more sophisticated version of our system,
332. an advanced and explicit theory of argument would be
333. even more important. Suppose that analysis of voter
334. interests and information-seeking behavior should
335. reveal that few voters are interested in every aspect
336. of any policy question, but that most of them tend
337. to specialize their interest on some aspect or other.
338. In that case, it is possible for the voter to cast a
339. ballot not only on the policy question as whole, but
340. on the acceptability of various contentions supporting
341. it. Thus, one might vote not just on whether or not
342. to adopt a guaranteed annual wage, but on such
343. matters as the level of support, the groups that
344. should receive it, whether the need for such a pro-
345. gram were convincingly demonstrated, whether certain
346. advantages or disadvantages would accrue, and
347. whether the values served or threatened by the pro-
348. gram were important or unimportant. Given a valid,
349. in-depth analysis of the question, plus accumulated
350. voter opinions on individual arguments and evidence,
351. an automatic decision paradigm might be written.
352. This would allow a decision to be made automatically
353. and rationally from voter input on the issues.

354. Of course, this paradigm would represent the heart
355. of a sweeping constitutional revision. But more to
356. the point for us, the paradigm cannot be written
357. without much fuller development of the theory of
358. rational decision-making on general policy questions.

359. Once the basic theoretical work were done, it would
360. be possible to develop a variety of refinements in
361. application. For example, the system could be structured
362. so as to interact with the voter in a simulated debate,
363. giving him an opportunity to confront arguments both
364. supporting and contrary to his point of view. It
365. would even be possible to set up voting "gates" such
366. that the voter would be required to proceed through
367. a certain amount of information and argument before
368. casting a ballot.

369. Here, of course, we move from the theory of argument
370. to the philosophy of self-government; do we have the
371. right to insist that a citizen go through a semblance
372. of rational thought before casting a vote? And if
373. we have such a right, what limits should be set to
374. our exercise of it?

375. I suggest to you that the spectrum of problems posed

376. by the development of such a democratic decision-
377. making system provides grist for the mill of virtually
378. every specialty represented in this Association.
379. There are problems here for the empiricist and the
380. philosopher; for the rhetorician and the communication
381. theorist; for the humanist as well as the social
382. scientist. The challenge encompasses linguistics and
383. speech science, general semantics, interpersonal and
384. group communication, argument, rhetoric, mass communi-
385. cation and general systems theory. It is not the sort
386. of problem that is likely to be solved by RAND or HEW;
387. it will require the committed interest of many
388. scholars, thinkers and researchers working in
389. different fields toward a common goal—the creation
390. of a system whereby the individual citizen can
391. participate directly in the affairs of government,
392. and can make an unfiltered, undiluted, uncompromised
393. personal contribution to the key decisions affecting
394. our society.
395. As you order your personal and our corporate priorities
396. for research and development over the years ahead, I
397. ask only that some of you bear in mind what I have
398. said here today. I believe that our society faces
399. no greater challenge than the need to bring democratic
400. machinery into line with the demands of the twenty-
401. first century. As we approach the year 2000, signs
402. are growing that unless we can radically change course,
403. we may be faced with a choice between autocracy and
404. chaos. That is a choice over which mankind has never
405. had much trouble making up its mind.
406. I believe that you hold the power to create a third
407. alternative—a system for converting our increasingly
408. unsatisfactory system of representative government
409. into a full-scale participatory democracy. I invite
410. you to exercise that power, and thereby to set the
411. stage for a quantum jump in man's struggle toward
412. freedom and self-realization.

Appendix B

Communication Models

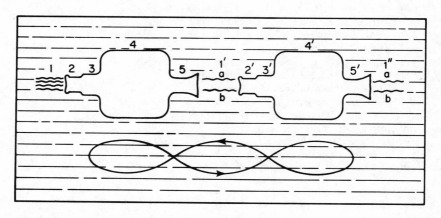

FIGURE A–1. Johnson Model.

Key: Stage 1. Event, or source of stimulation, external to the sensory end
         organs of the speaker.
      Stage 2. Sensory stimulation.
      Stage 3. Pre-verbal neurophysiological state.
      Stage 4. Transformation of pre-verbal into symbolic forms.
      Stage 5. Verbal formulations in "final draft" for overt expression.
      Stage 1'. Transformation of verbal formulations into air waves (*a*)

and light waves (*b*), which serve as sources of stimulation for the listener.
Stage 2', etc.

Stage 2' through 1" (see diagram) correspond in the listener to stages 2 through 1'. The arrowed loops represent the functional interrelationships of the stages in the process as a whole.[1]

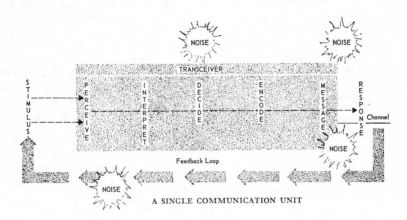

A SINGLE COMMUNICATION UNIT

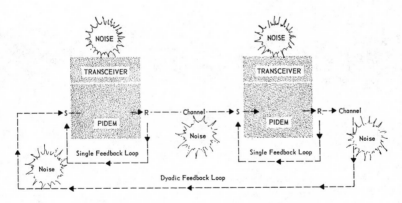

TWO COMMUNICATION UNITS IN DYADIC SYSTEM

FIGURE A–2. Zelko-Dance Model[2]

[1]Wendell Johnson, "The Fateful Process of Mr. A. Talking to Mr. B." *Harvard Business Review*, 31 (January–February 1953), 50. (Rearrangements of quotations and parentheses are this author's).

[2]From *Business and Professional Speech Communication* by Harold P. Zelko and Frank E. X. Dance. Copyright © 1965 by Holt, Rinehart and Winston, Inc. Reprinted by permission of Holt, Rinehart and Winston, Inc. pp. 6–7.

FIGURE A–3.   Goyer Model.[3]

Key: "G" represents a generator, "S" represents a sign/symbol stimulus, "P" represents a perceiver, "R" represents a differential response, ⟶ represents a projection in time. Communication thus occurs with reference to G and P whenever the response of P to the sign/symbol stimulus projected by G is consistent with the response intended by G; that is, when the referent responses of G and P to the sign/symbol stimulus are systematically correlated. The greater the correlation between the response intended by G and the response provided by P, the more effective is the communication.

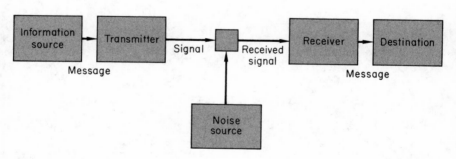

FIGURE A–4.   Shannon-Weaver Model.[4]

[3]Robert S. Goyer, *Communication Process: An Operational Approach*, Center for Communication Studies, Special Report No. 16 (Athens, Ohio: Ohio University, November 1967), pp. 5–6; see also Robert S. Goyer, "Communication, Communicative Process, Meaning: Toward A Unified Theory," *Journal of Communication*, 20: 1 (March 1970), 4–16.

[4]C. E. Shannon and W. Weaver, *The Mathematical Theory of Communication* (Urbana, Ill.: University of Illinois Press, 1949), p. 98.

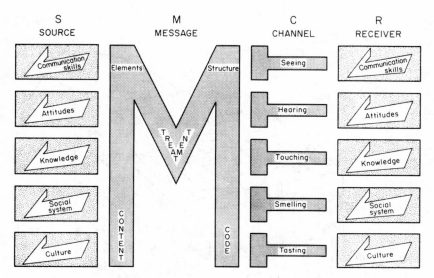

FIGURE A–5. Berlo Model.[5]

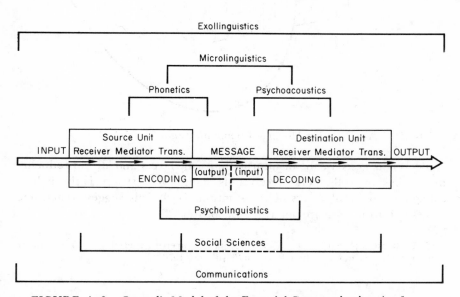

FIGURE A–6. Osgood's Model of the Essential Communication Act.[6]

[5]D. K. Berlo, *The Process of Communication* (New York: Holt, Rinehart & Winston, Inc., 1960), p. 72.

[6]Charles E. Osgood (ed), "Psycholinguistics: A Survey of Theory and Research Problems," *Journal of Abnormal and Social Psychology*, 49 (October, 1954), Morton Prince Memorial Supplement, p. 3. Copyright 1954 by the American Psychological Association. Reprinted by permission.

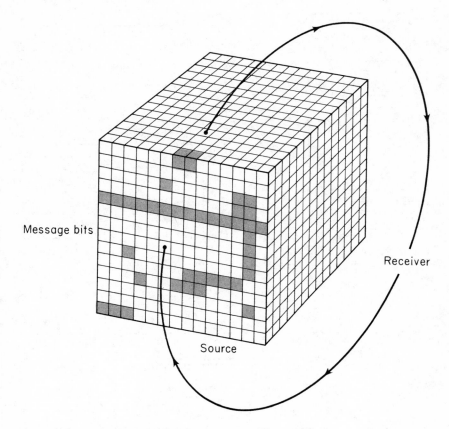

Message bits

Receiver

Source

FIGURE A–7.   Becker Model of Communication.[7]

Becker suggests a cube of information with layers and slices producing mini-cubes or cells. The receiver is figuratively strained through a changing mosaic of layers of information. Dark cells suggest that some pieces of information are not available for use.

[7]S. L. Becker, presented at the Wayne State University special graduate seminar "Potpourri '70: Communication Relations," July 20, 1970.

Appendix C

Outlines

General End: To inform.
Specific Purpose: To explain five basic functions of managing.

Introduction

    I. In a well-run organization confusion pertains 25 percent of the time.
       A. Visual aid with data and another with list of functions.
       B. Studies show that communication breakdowns occur.
   II. Management is getting work done through others.
       A. That makes communication the heart of all management functions.
       B. That takes a knowledge of the other basic functions.
          1. Planning.
          2. Organizing.
          3. Directing.   Human relations and
          4. Coordinating.   communication area
          5. Controlling.

Body

    I. The planning function.
       A. Determine objective.
       B. Consider tools available.

Note: Several outlines contain the same message, but they are repeated to show various outline forms.

    1. Time.ˑ
    2. Space.
    3. Personnel.
    4. Material available.
  C. Consider possible lines of action.
  D. Select the best line of action.
  E. Determine the actual process.
    1. Who?
    2. When?
    3. What?
    4. Where?
    5. How?
 II. The organizing function.
  A. Line of authority.
  B. Span of Control.
    1. Number of personnel.
     a. Nature of job.
     b. Ratios (1–20, 3, 7).
    2. Distance.
    3. Time.
  C. Homogenous assignment.
    1. Like functions grouped together.
    2. Avoid several unrelated responsibilities.
  D. Delegation of authority.
    1. Cannot delegate responsibility.
    2. Clearly define limits of delegated authority.
 III. The directing function.
  A. Communication.
  B. Understanding people.
 IV. The coordinating function.
  A. Relating to lateral organizations.
  B. Relating to the parent organization.
 V. The controlling function.
  A. Reporting.
  B. Inspecting and evaluating.

Conclusion

 I. I have tried to make clear the five basic management functions.
  A. Planning.
  B. Organizing.
  C. Directing.
  D. Coordinating.
  E. Controlling.
 II. Communication is the heart of all management functions! It has to be—management is getting work done *through* people—and that takes communication.

THE ROLE OF THE MANAGER

General End: To inform.
Specific Purpose: To explain five basic functions of managing.

Attention

    I. In a well-run organization confusion pertains 25 percent of the time.
        A. Visual aid with data and another with list of functions.
        B. Studies show that communication breakdowns occur.
    II. Management is getting work done through others.
        A. That makes communication the heart of all management functions.
        B. That takes a knowledge of the other basic functions.

Overview

    I. The planning function.
    II. The organizing function.
    III. The directing function.
    IV. The coordinating function.   Human relations and
    V. The controlling function.   communication area

Information

    I. The planning function.
        A. Determine objective.
        B. Consider tools available.
            1. Time.
            2. Space.
            3. Personnel.
            5. Material available.
        C. Consider possible lines of action.
        D. Select the best line of action.
        E. Determine the actual process.
            1. Who?
            2. When?
            3. What?
            4. Where?
            5. How?
    II. The organizing function.
        A. Line of authority.
        B. Span of control.
            1. Number of personnel.
               a. Nature of job.
               b. Ratios (1–20, 3, 7).
            2. Distance.
            3. Time.
        C. Homogenous assignment.
            1. Like functions grouped together.
            2. Avoid several unrelated responsibilities.
        D. Delegation of authority.
            1. Cannot delegate responsibility.
            2. Clearly define limits of delegated authority.
    III. The directing function.
        A. Communication.
        B. Understanding people.

IV. The coordinating function.
    A. Relating to lateral organizations.
    B. Relating to parent organization.
V. The controlling function.
    A. Reporting.
    B. Inspecting and evaluating.

Review

  I. I have tried to make clear the five basic management functions.
    A. Planning.
    B. Organizing.
    C. Directing.
    D. Coordinating.
    E. Controlling.
 II. Communication is the heart of all management functions! It has to be—management is getting work done through people—and that takes communication.

THE DIETARY LAWS OF THE JEWISH PEOPLE

General End: To inform.
Specific Purpose: To inform the class about the ancient Jewish dietary laws that are practiced even to this day.

Introduction

  I. Jewish culture is interesting to study not only because of its religious aspect but also because of the fact that the laws promulgated by Moses in ancient times are still practiced by observing Jews.
 II. The dietary laws I will discuss are the following:
    A. Consumption of meat.
    B. Consumption of fish.
    C. Consumption of dairy foods.
    D. Consumption of a living animal.
    E. Consumption of blood.
    F. Ritualistic slaughter.

Body

  I. The Bible prohibits the consumption of meat that comes from animals that do not possess cloven (split) hoofs and that do not chew their cud.
    A. Animals that belong to the category that possesses both characteristics are permissible as food.
      1. Cows.
      2. Goats.
      3. Lambs.
    B. Animals that chew their cud but do not have cloven hoofs are prohibited as food.
      1. Rabbits.
      2. Camels.

C. Animals with cloven hoofs that do not chew their cud, especially hogs, are prohibited as food.

D. Animals that possess neither characteristic are prohibited as food.
   1. Dogs.
   2. Cats.
   3. Horses.

II. The Jewish people are prohibited from consuming fish that do not have both scales and fins.
   A. Those with both characteristics are permitted.
      1. Pike.
      2. Bass.
      3. Carp.
   B. Those with only one characteristic are prohibited.
      1. Catfish.
      2. Bullheads.
   C. Those with neither characteristic are prohibited.
      1. Crabs.
      2. Lobsters.
      3. Clams.

III. Another law prohibits the cooking or eating of meat and dairy foods together.
   A. This law is based on Exodus 23:19: "Thou shalt not seethe a kid in the milk of its mother."
   B. Rabbinic legislation provided that two separate sets of dishes be maintained.

IV. The Bible prohibits the eating of any part of a living animal.
   A. This is one of the seven laws of Noah derived by the Talmud from scriptural references.
   B. This prohibition precludes cruelty to animals.

V. The Bible prohibits the eating of blood.
   A. The biblical reason given for this law is that because blood is the symbol of life it must be respected.
   B. From this law stems the practice of koshering meats.
      1. The rabbis prescribed that before the meat could be cooked it had to be soaked in water for one-half hour.
      2. After the meat is soaked, it must be heavily salted in coarse salt for one hour and rinsed with water.
      3. Meat that is broiled need not be salted.
      4. These practices all draw off the blood.

VI. Only meat from an animal that has been ritually slaughtered may be consumed.
   A. Ritual slaughter is the severing of the jugular vein in one stroke.
   B. The animal is killed instantly and painlessly and the blood removed.

Conclusion

I. There were probably also pragmatic reasons for the laws.
   A. Preserving foods was difficult for the nomadic Jews.
   B. Fish without both fins and scales are typically inedible.
   C. Many of the rules prevented cruelty to animals.
   D. These laws helped prevent disease.

II. In review, I have discussed the dietary laws of the Jewish people. An observing Jew may *not:*
   A. Consume meat that comes from animals that do not possess cloven hoofs and that do not chew their cud.
   B. Consume fish that do not have both scales and fins.
   C. Consume or cook meat and dairy foods together.
   D. Eat any part of a living animal.
   E. Consume blood (hence koshering).
   F. Consume meat from an animal that has not been ritually slaughtered.
III. These laws are not merely obsolete observances, but have real meaning to observing Jews to this day.
   A. The dietary laws in the total system of commandments represent submission to a divine discipline.
   B. The acceptance of this discipline has served as a significant instrument of group survival for the Jewish people.

The Dietary Laws of the Jewish People

General End: To inform.
Specific Purpose: To inform the class about the ancient Jewish dietary laws that are practiced even to this day.

Attention

I. The Jewish dietary laws are interesting because of their religious significance.
II. The ancient dietary laws of Moses are still practiced today.

Overview

I. Laws on consumption of meat.
II. Laws on consumption of fish.
III. Laws on consumption of dairy foods.
IV. Laws on consumption of a living animal.
V. Laws on consumption of blood.
VI. Laws on ritualistic slaughter.

Information

I. The Bible prohibits the consumption of meat that comes from animals that do not possess cloven (split) hoofs and that do not chew their cud.
   A. Animals that belong to the category that possesses both characteristics are permissible as food.
      1. Cows.
      2. Goats.
      3. Lambs.
   B. Animals that chew their cud but do not have cloven hoofs are prohibited as food.
      1. Rabbits.
      2. Camels.
   C. Animals with cloven hoofs that do not chew their cud, especially hogs, are prohibited.

  D. Animals that possess neither characteristic are prohibited as food.
  1. Dogs.
  2. Cats.
  3. Horses.
II. The Jewish people are prohibited from consuming fish that do not have both scales and fins.
  A. Those with both characteristics are permitted.
  1. Pike.
  2. Bass.
  3. Carp.
  B. Those with only one characteristic are prohibited.
  1. Catfish.
  2. Bullheads.
  C. Those with neither characteristic are prohibited.
  1. Crabs.
  2. Lobsters.
  3. Clams.
III. Another law prohibits the cooking or eating of meat and dairy foods together.
  A. This law is based on Exodus 23:19: "Thou shalt not seethe a kid in the milk of its mother."
  B. Rabbinic legislation provided that two separate sets of dishes be maintained.
IV. The Bible prohibits the eating of any part of a living animal.
  A. This is one of the seven laws of Noah derived by the Talmud from scriptural references.
  B. This prohibition precludes cruelty to animals.
V. The Bible prohibits the eating of blood.
  A. The biblical reason given for this law is that because blood is the symbol of life it must be respected.
  B. From this law stems the practice of koshering meats.
  1. The rabbis prescribed that before the meat could be cooked it had to be soaked in water for one-half hour.
  2. After the meat is soaked, it must be heavily salted in coarse salt for one hour and rinsed with water.
  3. Meat that is broiled need not be salted.
  4. These practices all draw off the blood.
VI. Only meat from an animal that has been ritually slaughtered may be consumed.
  A. Ritual slaughter is the severing of the jugular vein in one stroke.
  B. The animal is killed instantly and painlessly and the blood is removed.
VII. There were probably also pragmatic reasons for the laws.
  A. Preserving foods was difficult for the nomadic Jews.
  B. Fish without both fins and scales are typically nonedible.
  C. Many of the rules prevented cruelty to animals.
  D. These laws helped prevent disease.

Review

  I. In review, I have discussed the dietary laws of the Jewish people. An observing Jew may *not:*

    A. Consume meat that comes from animals that do not possess cloven hoofs and that do not chew their cud.

    B. Consume fish that do not have both scales and fins.

    C. Consume or cook meat and dairy foods together.

    D. Eat any part of a living animal.

    E. Consume blood (hence koshering).

    F. Consume meat from an animal that has not been ritually slaughtered.

II. These laws are not merely obsolete observances, but have real meaning to observing Jews to this day.

    A. The dietary laws in the total system of commandments represent submission to a divine discipline.

    B. The acceptance of this discipline has served as a significant instrument of group survival for the Jewish people.

ROCK MUSIC[1]

General End: To persuade.
Specific Purpose: To persuade the audience that "rock" music has significant social impact.

Introduction

(Attention)

    I. Rock music blares out of our radios and TVs.
        A. Radio tape demonstration.
        B. TV tape (audio) demonstration.
    II. Thousands pay to see and hear rock stars.
        A. Festivals have been big.
        B. Club bookings are big.
        C. Records are popular.

Body

    I. The history and evolution of rock.
        A. Originally improvisation from the blues.
            1. Chuck Berry.
            2. Little Richard.
        B. Big stars won rock fans.

(Interest)

            1. Elvis Presley.
            2. The Beatles.
        C. New electronics advanced rock.
            1. The San Francisco sound.
            2. Electric instruments.
            3. Super amplification (short demonstration).
    II. Performers had impact by being daring, wild, and weird.
        A. Elvis Presley's gyrations were banned from TV.
        B. Jim Morrison arrested for his act.
        C. Jim Hendrix set rock afire.

[1]From a student speech by Robert Walker, Wayne State University.

(Interest)
    D. The Who open a new dimension of violence.
    E. Iggy Stooge used fear to become popular.
    F. Alice Cooper makes use of sadism.
    G. David Bowie captured the unreal.
   III. Rock performers have changed our fashion codes.
    A. The Beatles caused the long hair thing.
    B. Rock caused more casual dress (pictures).
    C. Rock heroes caused wilder clothes (pictures).
   IV. Rock has had an impact on our moral standards.
    A. The hippie movement is related.
    B. Drug use is related (demonstration of "drug music").

(Vital Factors)
    C. Rock songs aid gay liberationists (demonstration).
    D. Some performers openly instigate bisexuality.

Conclusion

   I. Rock music has gained the attention of millions.
    A. Radio, TV.

(Reinforcement)
    B. Festivals et al.
    C. New electronics.
   II. Rock music has had a significant social impact.
    A. Brings social problems to light.
    B. Affects individuals and group social behavior.

A RAMPANT KILLER

General End: To persuade.
Specific Purpose: To persuade the audience that they should have their chests X-rayed.

Attention

(Possible Procedures)
{ Startling Statement
  Illustration
{ Rhetorical Question
  Reference to the
   Subject

   I. There is a subtle killer loose in the room.
    A. It killed 40,000 people last year.
    B. It likes young people.
   II. No one is immune to tuberculosis.
    A. You may be infected now!
    B. How long has it been since you had a chest X-ray?

Problem

(Development)
{ Statement
  Illustration
{ Ramification
  Pointing

   I. Despite wonder drugs, TB is our number six killer disease in America.
    A. Last year 40,000 Americans died from it.
    B. Nearly 2,000 died in Michigan alone.
   II. No one is immune to TB.
    A. You can get it by contagion.

B. The most susceptible ages are from fifteen to thirty-five.

III. It maims and handicaps as well as kills.

    A. Many of those who recover cannot lead normal lives.

        1. They cannot travel in warm, damp climates.

        2. They cannot exert themselves.

            a. Cannot run to class.

            b. Cannot dance.

            c. Cannot play athletic games.

    B. TB may spread to other parts of the body.

        1. One may lose a limb.

        2. It often attacks the spine.

        3. One can lose a vital organ like an eye or a kidney.

Solution

(Development)

{ Statement
  Explanation
  Demonstration
  Illustration
  Objections

I. A yearly X-ray check-up is the surest way to avoid a serious case of TB.

    A. It can most effectively be stopped if caught in time.

        1. For the most part it is a slow-developing disease.

        2. Its growth depends on the resistance of the victim.

        3. Even if detected in its early stages, a cure would take at least six months.

    B. An X-ray check-up is the most positive means for detecting the disease.

        1. A patch test merely indicates the presence of TB germs, but the disease may not actually be present.

        2. A lesion is the positive sign when it shows on the X-ray.

II. We can benefit from an X-ray easily and quickly.

    A. It is free.

        1. The money from the sale of Christmas Seals pays for the X-rays and other tests you get.

        2. The state is particularly interested in preserving the health of its young, college-age people.

    B. It is convenient to get.

        1. The mobile unit comes to the campus during the first week of the semester.

            a. It is open weekdays from 8 A.M. to 4 P.M.

          b. It parks near the Health Center.
       2. There is also a permanent clinic in town.
         a. It is open five days a week for adults from 8:30 A.M. to 4:30 P.M.
         b. A special appointment may be arranged after 4:30 P.M.
         c. It is located on the corner of Cass Street and Putnam Avenue.
         d. The phone number there is TE1-0100.
     C. It is painless and quick.
       1. If you've ever had an X-ray, you know it doesn't hurt.
       2. You need only remove your outer garments, such as coats and jackets.
       3. You can be in and out in five minutes.
     D. The results are mailed to you immediately.

Visualization

(Project the
Future)
(Methods)
⎧ Summary
⎨ Challenge
⎩ Inducement
 Specificity

   I. A few minutes now can beat this killer.
     A. Avoid pain and suffering.
     B. Avoid years in a tuberculosis sanitorium.
     C. Avoid physical handicaps.
   II. Enjoy a normal life physically and psychologically.

Action

   I. Get a chest X-ray this week.
   II. It is simple and convenient.
     A. The mobile unit is on campus at the library.
     B. It will take just five minutes of your time.
     C. It is absolutely free.
   III. The X-ray examination program is an effective way to fight this disease.

Index

Abelson, R., 263
Abstracting, 84
Abstraction, 74–77
Acceptance and presentation speeches, 362
Ad hominem, 300
Ad ignorantiam, 301
Adler, B., 105
Ad populum, 300
Ad verecundiam, 300
Affections, 251
After-dinner speeches, 367–72
Agendas, 318
Agenda systems, 322–29
Alliteration, 217
Allport, F., 47
Allusion, 217
Altman, I., 315
Amato, P., 102
American Management Association, 2, 256
Anadiplosis, 215
Analogy, 209
Anaphora, 215
Anderson, N. H., 266
Anderson, V. A., 130
Anniversary speech, 364
Anonymity, 47
Antagonistic receivers, 266
Anthropology, 80

Antimetabole, 218
Anxiety (*see* Speech fright)
Apostrophe, 217
Argument, 286
Argumentation, 289 (*see also* Evidence)
  causal relations, 290
    cause to effect, 290
    effect to cause, 290
  enthymeme, 294
  fallacies, 296
  syllogistic reasoning, 291
    categorical, 291
    enthymeme, 294
    hypothetical, 293
  Toulmin system, 295
Aristotle, 189, 248, 259, 261, 264, 265, 273, 286, 294, 296
Aronson, E., 43
Arrangement, 184, 261
  body, 189
  conclusion, 189
  introduction, 185
    models, 186–89
  natural order, 270 (*see also* Order)
  orientation, 186
  persuasive systems, 273
  psychological order, 264
  systems, 185

Arrangement systems, 273
Articulation, 130, 140
  faults, 140
  organs, 140
Artistic proof, 286
Asyndeton, 216
Attention, 185, 270, 271
Attitude, 239, 265
Attitude similarity, 265
Audience, 172
  participation, 348–55 (*see also* Participation, audience)
    principles, 350
    rules, 351–53
    techniques, 353
  questions and interruptions, 348
Audience analysis, 84
Audience configuration, 52
  arrangement, 53
  physical setting, 53
  ritual, 52
  seating, 53
Audience-message analysis, 54–56, 174 (*see also* Audience psychology)
Audience psychology, 48
  analysis, 54
  collective behavior, 42
  communication competencies, 58
  conversional audience, 48
  crowds, 43
  fear, 52
  feedback response, 49
  interstimulation, 49
  learning outcomes, 57, 58
  mass media, 48
  mobs, 43
  polarization, 49
  principles, 57
  proximity, 53
  Ross model, 49, 50
  study projects, 59
  types of audience, 49, 51 (*see also* Audience types)
Audience types, 49–52
  concerted, 51
  configuration, 52 (*see also* Audience configuration)
  discussion-passive, 51
  organized, 51
  pedestrian, 51
  selected, 51
Audio-visual aids, 222–32
  area diagram, 226
  bar graph, 226
  line graph, 227
  organization chart, 227
  pictogram, 224

  preparing, 231
  stream chart, 228
  tabular chart, 230
Auer, J. J., 15, 54, 315
Authority, 287
Autism, 21
Avoidance, 136

Baird, A. C., 7, 91, 97, 188, 259, 265
Baker, E. E., 265
Balance theory, 263
Bales, R. F., 322, 335
Bambridge, Mrs. G., 153
Barker, L., 3, 11, 33, 48
Barnlund, D. C., 310, 316, 323, 330
Barrick, J. E., 94
Barrios, A. A., 266
Bartley, S. H., 20
Barton, B., 307
Bass, B. M., 315
Bateson, G. 8
Batiuk, T., 17
Battelle, P., 93
Bauer, W. W., 74
Becker model, 392
Becker, S. L., 392
Begging the question, 299
Bell Telephone Laboratories, 14
Bentham, J., 248
Bergevin, P., 319
Berlo, D. K., 265, 391
Berlo model, 391
Bernard, L. L., 248
Berne, E., 8
Bevans, M., 229
Binder, F. E., 34
Biological nature of man, 243
Biological needs, 254
Birdwhistell, R. L., 113
Bittle, C. N., 293
Bitzer, L. F., 295
Blake, R. R., 20
Bodily action:
  elements, 119–23
  standards of, 123–25
Bodily expression, 115 (*see also* Bodily action)
  stereotypes, 116
Body action language:
  communication competencies, 128
  learning outcomes, 127
  speech communication principles, 126
  study projects, 128
Body language, 113
Booth, S., 93
Both-sides persuasion, 267
  characteristics, 269

Bowers, J. W., 73
Brainstorming, 317
Brean, H., 21
Breathiness, 139
Brigance, W. N., 78, 316
Brilhart, J. K., 324
Brock, A. J., 245
Brockriede, W., 295
Brooks, P., 307
Brown, Charlie, 28
Brown, R. W., 43, 47, 48
Bruner, J. S., 19
Buehler, E. C., 91
Buzz group, 318

Campbell, D. T., 266
Campbell, J. H., 11, 111
Cannon, W. B., 99
Canons of rhetoric, 259
  arrangement, 261
  delivery, 261
  invention, 259
  memory, 261
  style, 261
Capp, G. R., 361
Carotta, G., 195
Carroll, J. B., 12
Carroll, L., 85
Carroll model, 12
Case conference, 317
Catachresis, 217
Chase, S., 29, 81, 298
Cherry, C., 7
Circulus in probando, 299
Clarity, 208
  analogy, 209
  illustration, 208
  restatement, 211
  statistics, 210
  testimony, 211
Clergyman's throat, 139
Clevenger, T., 49, 93, 379
Closure, 21
Coacting group, 313
Cognitive consistency, 262
  balance theory, 263
  cognitive dissonance, 263
  congruity theory, 262
Cognitive dissonance, 263 (*see also* Cognitive consistency)
Coherence, 182
Cohesion, 313, 332
Collective mind, 46 (*see also* Collective phenomena)
Collective phenomena, 42 (*see also* Audience psychology)
  contagion, 45

hyperinterstimulation, 45
mechanisms, 47
  anonymity, 47
  contagion, 47
  suggestibility, 47
mental unity, law of, 46
panics, 45
social facilitation, 47
taxonomy, 43
Collins, B. E., 321
Commemorative and tribute speeches, 363–67
Committees, 317
Communication, 1–41
  amount, 2
  business, 2
  defined, 6, 7, 10
  learning outcomes, 4
  models, 9–19, 388–92
  nature of, 1
  process, 6–41
  publications, 2
  Ross definition, 10
  subliminal, 20
  transactional, 8
"Communication and the Survival of Democracy" (model speech), 379–87
Communication climate, 332
Communication competencies:
  audience participation, 357
  audience psychology, 58
  body action language, 128
  communication process, 37
  discussion, 340
  emotion and confidence, 108
  language and semantics, 88
  logical supports, 304
  message preparation, 202
  nonverbal communication, 128, 147
  persuasion, 282
  presenting information, 234
  process nature, 37
  purpose and delivery, 168
  special occasion speaking, 376
  speech fright, 108
  voice and articulation, 147
Communication models, 9–19, 388–92
Communication principles, 35 (*see also* Speech communication principles)
Communication process:
  communication competencies, 37
  learning outcomes, 36
  principles, 35
  speech communication principles, 35
  study projects and tasks, 37
Competence, 287 (*see also* Credibility)
Cone of experience, 223

Conferences, 317
Confidence, 91 (see Speech fright)
Conflict, 212
Confucius, 72
Congruity theory, 262
Connectives, 182
Constitution, 249
Contagion, 47
Cooper, L., 184, 261, 286
Corbett, E. P. J., 261
Cortright, R. L., 30
Cortwright, D., 322
Counterargument, 266
Counterattitudinal advocacy, 264
Counterpersuasion, 266
Counterpropaganda, 268
Crabtree, J. W., 363
Credibility, 264
Crocker, L., 291
Crowd taxonomy, 43
Crowell, L., 322
Crutchfield, R. S., 23
Culture, 249
Curiosity, 213
Curry, S. S., 118

Dahle, T. L., 16
Dale, E., 223
Dance, F. E. X., 7, 15, 389
Darley, F. L., 135
Davidson, D., 327
Debate, 312
Deductive reasoning, 289
deLaguna, G. A., 6
Delivery, 160, 261 (see also Purpose and
    delivery; Speech delivery)
    style, 173
Delsarte, 118
Democratic society, 310
Demonstration speech, 225–31
    hazards, 228
Denes, P. B., 14
Denes-Pinson model, 14
Desensitization, 94
Desire, 21
Detroit Lions, 367
Detroit News, The, 69, 70, 93, 230, 367
Detroit riot, 43
Dewey, J., 210, 321
Dewey thought process, 321
Dialect, 140, 142
Dialogue, 317
Dictionary, Webster's Eighth New Colle-
    giate, 142
Dirksen, E., 365
Discussion, 310
    agenda systems, 318, 322–30

cohesion, 313
communication climate, 332
communication competencies, 341
contemporary forms, 316 (see also Dis-
    cussion forms)
definitions, 316
evaluation, 334–37
leadership, 330–34 (see also Discussion
    leadership)
learning outcomes, 340
participant configurations, 319, 320
participant responsibilities, 333
research generalizations, 315
small groups, 313
social facilitation, 313
sociogram, 346
speech communication principles, 339
study projects, 342
Discussion configurations, 319, 320
Discussion forms, 316
    dialogue, 317
    panel, 317
    symposium, 317
Discussion leadership, 330–32
    communication climate, 332
    functions, 330
    goal achievement, 331
    interpersonal relations, 331
    procedural, 331
    sources, 330
    styles, 330, 331
Discussion participation, 333
Discussion types, 316 (see Discussion
    forms)
Dissonance theory, 263 (see also Cognitive
    consistency)
Dix, D., 370
Dollard, J., 271
Dooher, J., 2
Dove Counterbalance General Intelligence
    test, 89
Dubner, F. S., 111
Ducking the issue, 300
Dunlap, L. A., 367
Dusenbury, D., 117
Dynamism, 117

Ebony magazine, 69
Ego needs, 255
Ehninger, D., 271, 295
Ehrensberger, R., 206, 272
Eisenson, J., 15, 54, 315
Either-or, 299
Eliot, G., 29
Emotion, 96 (see also Speech fright)
    communicating, 117
    recognition, 117

Emotion and confidence, 91 (*see also* Speech fright)
Empathy, 118
Emphasis, 183, 206, 207, 272
Engineering, 80
English, A. C., 8
English, H. B., 8
Enthymeme, 261, 294, 295
Epanalepsus, 216
Epanodos, 216
Erickson, E. C., 316
Esteem needs, 255
Ethical proof, 264 (*see also* Credibility)
Ethics, 262, 265
Ethos, 261 (*see also* Source credibility)
Etkin, W., 15
Eulogy, 363, 365
Euphemism, 217
Evans, R. L., 305
Evidence, 286 (*see also* Argumentation)
  authority, 287
  deductive proof, 289
  examples, 288
  expertise, 287
  inductive proof, 289
  statistics, 288
  testimony, 287
Examples, 288
Expectancy, 21
Experiential field, 28
Expertise, 287
Extemporaction, 318
Extemporaneous speaking, 164
Extrapolation, 298
Extrasensory perception, 20
Extrinsic proof, 286
Extrovert, 246

Fabun, D., 26
Facial expression, 116, 122
Fairbanks, G., 135, 149
Fallacies, 296
  begging the question, 299
  ducking the issue, 300
  false cause, 298
  ignoratio elenchi, 300
    ad hominem, 300
    ad ignorantiam, 301
    ad populum, 300
    ad verecundiam, 300
  non sequitur, 298
    consequent, 299
    either-or, 299
    loaded questions, 299
    post hoc ergo propter hoc, 298
    tu quoque, 298
  overgeneralization, 297

petitio principii, 299
  circulus in probando, 299
  direct assumption, 300
  secundum quid, 297
    extrapolation, 298
    sampling, 297
False cause, 298
Fast, J., 113
Fausti, R. P., 7
Fedoravious, A., 94
Feedback, 17, 137, 373
Feedback-response, 49
Feierabend, R. L., 266
Feleky, A., 116
Fest, T. B., 316, 323
Festinger, L., 263
Figures of speech, 215
Fonda, J., 92
Foy, E., 45
Freeley, A. J., 289, 291
Freeman, J. T., 102
French Revolution, 46
Furbay, A. L., 53, 174

Galen, 245
Garrett, H. E., 116
Gellerman, S. W., 256
General purpose, 157 (*see also* Speaking purposes)
General semantics, 79–80 (*see also* Semantics)
  principles, 80–82
Gerbner, G., 7
Gestures, 122
Gibb, J. D., 21, 214
Gilkenson, H., 108
Gilmore, J. B., 94
Glowgower, D., 275
Goble, F., 257
Goetzinger, C. S., 2
Goldstein, K., 256
Goyer model, 390
Goyer, R. S., 7, 30, 390
Grapevine, 1
Gray, C. E., 98
Green, J., 367
Group discussion, 312 (*see also* Discussion)
Group membership, 249
Group mind, 48
Growth needs, 257
Gruner, C., 214
Guetzkow, H., 321
Gulley, H., 312, 316, 323
Gunther, B., 113

Haiman, F. S., 310, 316, 323, 330
Hall, E. T., 111, 113

Hance, K. G., 317
Hare, A. P., 315
Harlow, A. F., 46
Harnack, V., 316, 323
Harrison, R., 111
Harshness, 139
Hart, J., 306
Hayakawa, S. I., 73, 79, 80
Hearing, 29
Hedde, W. G., 316
Hedonism, 248
Heider, F., 263
Henrikson, E., 94
Hepler, H. W., 11, 111
Hinds, G. L., 30
Hippocrates, 245
Hirschfeld, A., 318
Holiday, J., 93
Hollingworth, H. L., 51, 52, 184, 223, 271
Holmes model, 9
Holmes, O. W., 8
Homans, G. C., 316
Homeostasis:
    biological, 244
    psychological, 245
Hostile receivers, 266
Hovland, C., 263, 266, 267, 271
Hughes, C., 367
Hughes, T., 367
Humor, 214, 265
Hunsaker, D. M., 290
Hurst, C., 3
Huskiness, 139
Hutchins, R. M., 245
Hyperbole, 216
Hyperinterstimulation, 42
Hypnosis, 272

Ignoratio elenchi, 300
Illustration, 288
Immediacy, 213
Impromptu speaking, 163
Impromptu speech topics, 169
Inductive reasoning, 289
Informative speech, 204 (see also Present-
    ing information)
    emphasis, 206, 207
    known to unknown, 204
    model outlines, 219–22
    objectives, 208
        clarity, 208 (see also Clarity)
        interest, 212 (see also Interest)
    organization, 218
    rating scale, 236
    reinforcement, 205
    serial learning, 205
Inglehart, J., 38

Inspiration, 190
Instinct theory, 247
Interaction, 313, 332
Interaction process analysis, 335
Interest, 212
    audio-visual aids, 222
    conflict, 212
    curiosity, 213
    figures of speech, 215
    humor, 214
    immediacy, 213
    novelty, 213
    specificity, 212
    vital factors, 215
International Phonetic Alphabet, 142, 143
Interpersonal influence, 42
Interpersonal interaction, 313
Interruptions, audience, 348–55
Interstimulation, 49
Interviewing, 175, 176
Intrinsic proof, 286
Introductions, 173
Introduction speeches, 359
    model, 361
    rules, 360
Introvert, 246
Invention, 259
Irion, A. L., 205, 271
Iroquois Theatre fire, 45
Irwin, J. V., 15, 54, 315

James-Lange theory, 96, 133
James, W. J., 96, 271
Janis, I. L., 264, 266, 268
Johnson, W., 78, 84, 389
Johnson model, 388
Jung, C. G., 246

Kaiser Aluminum and Chemical Corpora-
    tion, 26
Kardiner, A., 249
Katz, E., 48
Kelley, H. H., 315
Keltner, J. W., 114
Kennedy, A. J., 214
Kennedy, J. F., 186, 365
Kent State University, 73
Kerner Commission, 43
Kibler, R. J., 11, 48
Killian, L. M., 47
Kilpela, D., 214
Kimber, D. C., 98
Kinesics, 113
King, B. G., 244, 264
King, M. L., 190
King, T. R., 93
Kipling, R., 152

Kloman, W., 111
Kluckhohn, C., 249
Knapp, M. L., 113, 116
Knower, F. H., 7, 91, 97, 117, 239
Koch, S., 263
Korzybski, A., 76, 80
Krech, D., 23
Kretschmer, E., 246
Kumata, H., 265

LaBarre, W., 118
Lamb, D. H., 92
Landis, C., 116
Lange, C., 96
Language, 61 *(see also* Semantics)
  abstraction, 74
  code, 61
  context, 73
  dates, 72 *(see also* Semantics)
  emotional, 74
  ghetto words, 66
  improvement, 78
  meaning, 74
  models, 75
  obscenity, 53, 73
  overgeneralization, 77
  personality, 77
  presymbolic, 79
  propositional nature, 81
  racial identification, 69, 70
  signal response, 84
  slang, 72
  specificity, 76
  symbols, 61, 62
  syntax, 63
  words, 62
Language and semantics:
  communication competencies, 88
  learning outcomes, 87
  speech communication principles, 87
  study projects, 89
Larynx, 133
Lasswell, H. D., 12
Lasswell model, 12
Law, G. M., 94
Lazarus, R. S., 20
Lazy lips, 141
Leadership, 330–32, 350
Learning, 204
Learning outcomes:
  audience participation, 357
  audience psychology, 57, 58
  body action language, 127
  communication process, 36, 37
  discussion, 340
  language and semantics, 87
  logical supports, 303

message preparation, 156, 201
  nonverbal communication, 114, 127, 147
  persuasion, 241, 280
  presenting information, 233
  purpose and delivery, 167
  small group and special occasion communication, 310
  special occasion speaking, 376
  speech fright, 107
  voice and articulation, 147
Lebon, G., 46
Lee, I. J., 84
Leeper, R. W., 25
Library, 175
Lincoln, A., 209, 366
Lindzey, G., 43
Linguistics, 80
Listening, 29–34
  attributes, 30
  comprehension, 33
  defined, 34
  evaluation, 34
  factors, 30, 33
  habits, 33
  improvement, 34
  inventory, 40
  process, 31
  quiz, 33
  speed, 32
Lloyd, D. J., 63
Loaded questions, 299, 352
Locating materials, 174
Locked jaw, 140
Logic, 80, 286
  principles, 81
Logical supports of persuasion:
  communication competencies, 304
  learning outcomes, 303
  speech communication principles, 302
  study projects, 305
Logos, 261, 286
Loudness, 136
Love needs, 255
Ludlum, T., 269
Lull, P. E., 214
Lumsdaine, A. A., 267, 268

Maddox, G. A., 70
Mann, P. B., 228
Manuscript reading, 160
Manuscript writing, 161
Marquis, V., 2
Martin, E. D., 46
Maslow, A. H., 254, 256
McCleary, R. A., 20
McClelland, D. C., 256
McCroskey, J. C., 92, 94, 265

McDougall, W., 247
McGeoch, J. A., 205, 271
McGlone, E. L., 7, 34
McGrath, J. E., 315
McKee, D. J., 17
McKinsey, J. C. C., 327
Meaning, 74, 80, 118
Mearns, D. C., 367
Meglomania, 47
Mehrabian, A., 113
Meichenbaum, D. H., 94
Memorization, 103, 162
Memory, 102, 261
Menninger, K., 79
Message arrangement (*see* Arrangement)
Message organization, 171 (*see also* Organization)
Message preparation (*see Speech* preparation):
    communication competencies, 202
    learning outcomes, 156, 201
    speech communication principles, 200
    study projects, 202
Metaphor, 216
Metonymy, 216
Meyer, C. J., 39
Michener, J. A., 73
Michigan Chronicle, The, 69
Michigan Speech Association, 317
Microphones, 373
Milgram, S., 43
Miller, F., 219
Miller, G. R., 7
Miller, N. E., 266, 271, 333
Mills, G. E., 182, 218
Mob psychology, 43
Model outlines, 195–99, 219–22, 393–402 (Appendix C)
    persuasion, 273–77
Model speech, 379–87 (Appendix A)
Model speech of introduction, 361
Models, communication, 9–19, 388–92 (Appendix B)
Moe, J. D., 114, 117
Monroe, A. H., 165, 184, 271
Moon, T. J., 228
Morphological types, 246
Morris, D., 319
Morrison, G., 112
Morsell, J. A., 71
Mosley, A., 70
Motivated sequence, 271
Motivation, 243 (*see also* Persuasion)
    biological nature of man, 243
    biological needs, 245, 254
    cognitive consistency, 262
    Maslow system, 254–59

    esteem needs, 255
    love needs, 255
    physiological needs, 254
    safety needs, 254
    self-actualization needs, 256
    personality influence, 245–51 (*see also* Personality)
    social needs, 251–53 (*see also* Needs)
    social-psychological nature of man, 245
    springboards, 243
Motive appeals, 251 (*see also* Needs)
Murphy, G., 21
Murray, E., 3
Murray, H. A., 249, 252, 253
Mushy mouth, 141

NAACP, 71
Nasality, 139
Nathan, E., 30, 31
Native propensities, 247 (*see also* Needs)
Needs (*see also* Native propensities):
    biological, 245, 254
    classification of, 251
    ego, 255
    esteem, 255
    growth, 257
    love, 254
    Maslow hierarchy, 254–59
    motive terms, 254
    native propensities, 247
    Ross diagram, 257
    safety, 254
    self-actualization, 256
    social, 252
Newcomb, T. M., 263, 267
New Jersey theatre experiment, 21
New York Amsterdam News, 68
New York Times, 72
Nichols, R. G., 29, 32, 33
Nixon, R. M., 187
Nonartistic proof, 286
Non sequitur, 298
Nonverbal communication, 111–14
    body language, 113 (*see also* Chapter 5)
    communication competencies, 128, 147
    dress codes, 113
    facial expression, 116
    kinesics, 113
    learning outcomes, 114, 127, 147
    proxemics, 111, 113
    speech communication principles, 126, 146
    study projects, 128, 148
    time codes, 111
    unconscious, 115
    voice, 114, 130 (*see also* Chapter 6)
Note taking, 177

Novelty, 213

Obscenity, 53, 73
Ochs, D. J., 73
Ogden, C. K., 74
Oliver, R. T., 190
Onomatopoeia, 218
Open forum, 349
Order, 264, 266, 270 (*see also* Arrangement)
Organic unity, 181
Organization, 171, 178
    chronological, 179
    difficulty, 180
    information, 218
    logical, 180
    need-plan, 181
    spatial, 181
    topical, 179
Osborn, A. F., 318
Osborne, W. J., 91, 108
Osgood, C. E., 262, 391
Ostermeier, T. H., 102
Otto, J. H., 228
Outlines, model, 393–402 (Appendix C)
Outlining, 190
    form, 194
    models, 195–99
    principles, 191
    study projects, 202
    types, 195
Overgeneralization, 77, 84, 297
Oxymoron, 218

Page, W. T., 92
Panel discussion, 317
Panics, 45
Pantomime, 128
Paradox, 217
Paralipsis, 217
Paranoia, 21
Paromasia, 216
Participation, audience, 348–55 (*see also* Audience)
    communication competencies, 357
    learning outcomes, 357
    speech communication principles, 356
    study projects, 358
Pathos, 261, 286
Paul, G. L., 95
Paulson, S. F., 95, 269
Pauses, 135
Perception, 19–29
    closure, 21
    expectancy, 21
    extrasensory, 20
    selective, 25

set, 21, 29
    subthreshold, 20
Personality, 4, 77, 130, 245
    determinants, 249
        constitution, 249
        group membership, 249
        role, 250
        situation, 251
    hedonism, 248
    instinct theory, 247
    introvert-extrovert, 246
    morphological types, 246
    needs, 251–59 (*see also* Needs)
    psychological types, 246
    typological theories, 245
Personality determinants, 249 (*see also* Personality)
    constitution, 249
    group membership, 249
    role, 250
    situation, 251
Personification, 217
Persuasion, 239 (*see also* Motivation)
    antagonistic receivers, 266
    arrangement, 266–73
    both-sides characteristics, 269
    cognitive consistencies, 262 (*see also* Cognitive consistency)
    communication competencies, 282
    learning outcomes, 280
    logical supports, 286 (*see also* Evidence)
    oral argument, 239
    sex differences, 241
    speech communication principles, 279
    study projects, 282
    theories, 259
Persuasion theories, 259
Petitio principii, 299
Phenomenal field, 28
Phillips, A. E., 251
Phillips, G. M., 92, 95, 316
Phillips, J. D., 318
"Phillips 66", 318
Philology, 80
Phonetic inventory, 149
Physiological needs, 254
Physiology, 243
Piaget, J., 21
Pinson, E. N., 14
Pitch, 137
Plato, 241, 249
Pleasure-pain, 248
Polarization, 49
Polyptoton, 216
Popa, R., 70
Post hoc ergo propter hoc, 298
Postman, L., 19

Posture, 120
Pratt, J. M., 296
Preparation, 171 (see also Speech preparation)
Presentation and acceptance speeches, 362
Presenting information:
  communication competencies, 234
  learning outcomes, 233
  speech communication principles, 233
  study projects, 235
Primacy, 266
Problem solving, 322
Process of communication, 6–41 (see also Communication)
Pro-con order, 266
Prohibition study, 240
Projection, 136, 373
Pronunciation, 141
  errors, 142–45
  systems, 142
Proof, 286
Prosopopoeia, 217
Proxemics, 111
Proximity, 173
Psychology of persuasion:
  learning outcomes, 241
Public-address system, 174
Purdue University, 11
Purpose, 171
Purpose and delivery:
  communication competencies, 168
  learning outcomes, 167
  speech communication principles, 167
  study projects, 168

Quality, voice, 138
Questions, audience, 348–55 (See also Audience)
Quintilian, 262

Radio and television speeches, 372–74
Rahskopf, H., 316
Ralph, D. C., 53, 94
Ramsey, G. V., 20
Rate, 135
Rating scale, 236
Rationalistic persuasion, 269
Ratliffe, S. A., 284
Reading selections, 152
Recency, 265
Reference, 217
Reflective thinking, 270, 321
Reinforcement, 205
Repression, 101, 136
Resonation, 133
Restatement, 211
Reticence, 92, 95 (see also Speech fright)

Rhetoric, classical, 259
Rhetorical principles, 181
  coherence, 182
  unity, 181, 183
Rhythm, 136
Richards, I. A., 74
Ritual, 52, 173
Rogers, C. R., 8, 28, 332
Rohrer, J. H., 19
Role, 250
Role playing, 264, 318
Roosevelt, F. D., 189
Rosenberg, M., 263
Ross, E. A., 46
Ross, R. S., 15, 70, 91, 108, 257
Ross model, 15
Rothwell, J. D., 74
Ruch, F. L., 272
Ruesch, J., 8, 113

Safety needs, 254
Sartain, A. Q., 361
Sattler, W. M., 333
Savage, N., 117
Scheidel, T. M., 322
Schlosbery, H., 117
Schramm, W., 13
Schramm model, 13
Scott, W. D., 48
Secundum quid, 297
Self-actualization, 256
Self-concept, 17
Self-image, 17
Self-percept, 17
Semantics, 79
  defined, 79, 80
  principles, 80
Sensation, 20
Sentiments, 252
Serial learning, 205
Set, 21, 23, 29, 259
Sex differences, 241
Shannon, C. E., 15, 390
Shannon-Weaver model, 390
Shearer, N. A., 92
Sheets, B. V., 94
Sheffield, F. D., 267
Sheldon, W. H., 246
Shepherd, C. R., 332, 334
Sherif, M., 19
Sherwood, J. J., 19
Showers, M. J., 244
Signal response, 84
Simile, 217
Simons, H. W., 332
Situation, 251
Slang, 72

Small group and special occasion communication:
learning outcomes, 310
Small groups, 313
research generalization, 315
Smith, A. G., 7, 113
Smith C. R., 290
Smith, R. L., 11
Smith, R. M., 319
Social facilitation, 47, 313
Social-psychological nature of man, 245
Sociogram, 346
Solley, C. M., 21
Sommer, R., 319
Sound, 144
Source credibility, 264 (*see also* Credibility)
Speaking purposes, 157
entertain, 160
inform, 158
persuade, 159
Special occasion speaking, 359
after-dinner, 367–72
communication competencies, 376
introductions, 359–62
learning outcomes, 374
presentation and acceptance, 362
radio and television, 372–74
speech communication principles, 375
study projects, 377
tribute and commemorative, 363
anniversary, 364
eulogy, 363, 366
rules, 364
Specificity, 212
Specific purpose, 171
Speech:
defined, 3
Speech arrangement (*see* Arrangement)
Speech communication (*see* Communication)
Speech Communication Association, 170, 377
Speech communication principles:
audience participation, 356
audience psychology, 57
body action language, 126
collective behavior, 57
communication process, 35
delivery, 167
discussion, 339
emotion and confidence, 106
informative speech, 233
language and semantics, 87
logical supports, 301
message preparation, 200
nonverbal communication, 126, 128, 146

persuasion, 279
presenting information, 233
process nature, 35
purpose and delivery, 167
special occasion speaking, 374–75
speech fright, 106
voice and articulation, 146
Speech delivery:
characteristics, 164
extemporaneous, 164
impromptu, 163
manuscript reading, 160
memorization, 162
Speech fright, 91-106
bodily reactions, 99
communication competencies, 108
control, 97, 100, 106
desensitization, 94
James-Lange theory, 96
learning outcomes, 107
nature of, 96
personality, 93
prevalence, 91
repression, 101
speech communication principles, 106
study projects, 108
symptoms, 46
therapy, 95
trembling, 98
Speech introduction, 185
Speech organization, 171 (*see also* Organization)
Speech preparation, 171
arrangement, 184
audience analysis, 172
library research, 175
locating materials, 173
note taking, 177–79
orientation, 186
outlining, 190 (*see also* Outlining)
coordination, 192
discreteness, 193
form, 194
models, 195–99
simplicity, 191
subordination, 192
symbolization, 193
types, 195
Speech purposes, 157 (*see also* Speaking purposes)
inspiration, 190
specific purpose, 171
Stackpole, C. E., 98
Staff meetings, 317
Stage fright, 91 (*see also* Speech fright)
Statistics, 210, 288
Steil, L. K., 284

Stevens, L. A., 29, 32
Stevens, S. S., 246
Stevenson, A., 105, 185
Stewart, J., 8
Strodtbeck, F. L., 322
Study groups, 317
Study projects:
   audience participation, 358
   audience psychology, 59
   body action language, 128
   communication process, 37
   discussion, 342
   informative speech, 235
   language and semantics, 89
   logical supports, 305
   message preparation, 202
   nonverbal communication, 148
   persuasion, 282
   presenting information, 235
   purpose and delivery, 168
   special occasion speaking, 377
   speech fright, 108,
   voice and articulation, 148
Style, 173, 261
Subception, 20
Subliminal communication, 20
Suggestibility, 47
Suppes, P., 327
Syllogism, categorical, 291
Syllogism, hypothetical, 292
Syllogistic reasoning, 291
   categorical syllogism, 291
   enthymeme, 294
   hypothetical syllogism, 293
Symposium, 317, 349
Symposium forum, 349
Synecdoche, 216
Syntax, 80

Tannenbaum, P. H., 262
Taxis, 261
Television and radio speeches, 372–74
Television cameras, 373
Testimony, 211, 287
Thayer, L., 3
Thibaut, J. W., 315
Thomas, G. L., 53
Thompson, E. C., 219
Thonssen, L., 259, 265
Timbre, 138
Time, 111
Timebinding, 2
Titchener, E., 99
Toch, H., 43
Tolch, J., 117
Toulmin, S., 295
Toussaint, S. R., 165

Transactional communication, 8
Trent, J. D., 296
Tribute and commemorative speeches, 363–67
Trustworthiness, 287 (see also Credibility)
Tschirhart, D., 45
Tucker, 246
Tu quoque, 298
Turner, R. H., 47

Unity, 181
Uten, D., 273

Valentine, M. A., 2
Vannette, R., 210
Van Riper, C., 131
Verbal emphasis, 206
Visual aids, 174
Vital factors, 215
Vocal process, 132 (see also Voice)
Vocal variety, 137
Voice, 130
   assimilation, 135
   breathiness, 139
   defective, 131
   disorders, 138–40
   energy source, 132
   functional disorders, 131
   harshness, 139
   loudness, 136
   modifiers, 134
   nasality, 139
   pauses, 135
   pitch, 137
   process, 132
   projection, 136
   quality, 133
   rate, 135
   resonators, 133
   rhythm, 136
   stereotypes, 131
   timbre, 138
   vocal cords, 133
   vocal variety, 137
Voice and articulation:
   communication competencies, 147
   learning outcomes, 147
   speech communication principles, 146
   study projects, 148

Walker, R., 400
Walking, 121
Warfel, H. R., 63
Washington, B. T., 188
Watson, J. B., 248
Wayne State University, 25, 66, 91, 117, 256
Weaver, C. H., 34

Weaver, W., 15, 390
White, E. E., 190
Willard, R., 197
Williams, F., 117
Winans, J. A., 165
Winkerbean, Funky, 17
Wiseman, G., 3
Wittman, J. F., 116
Wolpe, J., 94
Words, 62, 66, 77, 84

Workshops, 317

Yeager, W. H., 363
Young, D., 239
Young, K., 48

Zander, A., 322
Zelko-Dance model, 389
Zelko, H. P., 7, 15, 389